ORGANIZATIONS
AND MANAGEMENT
IN CROSS-CULTURAL
CONTEXT

Praise for *Organizations and Management in Cross-cultural Context*

'I am most excited by this forthcoming text for two reasons. First, the integration of major theoretical orientations and research findings with cultural contexts within which they may be applied is most critical as globalization burgeons. Second, the authors are uniquely suited by background and expertise to accomplish the integration in an informative, scholarly fashion. Additionally the notion of including issues and questions for reflection cannot help but foster critical thinking on the part of the reader. The text should soon become a classic in our literature.'

Edward Levine, Fellow of the Society for Industrial and Organizational Psychology, University of South Florida

'This book has been long overdue, filling an acutely felt lacuna in the field of cross cultural human resource management and organizational behavior. Actively provoking thought and reflection, I consider this well structured volume a compulsory, highly suited read for graduate students as well as practitioners who wish to deepen their understanding of their multicultural organizational settings.'

Simcha Ronen, Professor Emeritus of Organizational Psychology and International Management, Tel Aviv University

'Aycan, Kanungo and Mendonca adopt a non-US lens to examine the important topics pertaining to managing in a global context. A useful text for both US and non-US students to understand the dynamics and complexities of managing in the twenty-first century.'

Rosalie L. Tung, The Ming & Stella Wong Professor of International Business, Simon Fraser University

'A much needed text which provides excellent cross cultural application to the study of organisation. Invaluable to students and practitioners alike'

Paul Hill, Senior Lecturer in Human Resource Management, Northumbria University

ORGANIZATIONS AND MANAGEMENT IN CROSS-CULTURAL CONTEXT

Zeynep Aycan • Rabindra N Kanungo • Manuel Mendonça

Los Angeles | London | New Delhi
Singapore | Washington DC

Los Angeles | London | New Delhi
Singapore | Washington DC

SAGE Publications Ltd
1 Oliver's Yard
55 City Road
London EC1Y 1SP

SAGE Publications Inc.
2455 Teller Road
Thousand Oaks, California 91320

SAGE Publications India Pvt Ltd
B 1/I 1 Mohan Cooperative Industrial Area
Mathura Road
New Delhi 110 044

SAGE Publications Asia-Pacific Pte Ltd
3 Church Street
#10-04 Samsung Hub
Singapore 049483

Editor: Kirsty Smy
Development editor: Robin Lupton
Assistant editor: Nina Smith
Production editor: Sarah Cooke
Copyeditor: Rose James
Proofreader: Lynda Watson
Indexer: Silvia Benvenuto
Marketing manager: Alison Borg
Cover design: Francis Kenney
Typeset by: C&M Digitals (P) Ltd, Chennai, India
Printed and bound in Great Britain by Ashford
Colour Press Ltd

© Zeynep Aycan, Rabindra N. Kanungo, and Manuel Mendonça, 2014

First published 2014

Library of Congress Control Number: 2013945235

British Library Cataloguing in Publication data

A catalogue record for this book is available from the British Library

ISBN 978-1-4129-2873-1
ISBN 9781412928748 (pbk)

Dedication

To our teachers and students for nurturing environments of
continuous learning

Contents

About the Authors

Zeynep Aycan is a Professor with dual appointment in the Department of Psychology and Faculty of Management at Koç University, Istanbul, Turkey. She holds the Koç Holding Chair of Management and Strategy. She is the Graduate Dean of Social Sciences and Humanities.

Zeynep received her Doctoral Degree from Queen's University, Canada and conducted post-doctoral studies at McGill University, Faculty of Management. Her research focuses on the impact of culture on various aspects of organizational processes, including leadership, human resource management, women's career development and work–life balance.

She has authored or co-authored four books and more than 50 book chapters and research articles which have appeared in journals including *Annual Review of Psychology, Science, Journal of International Business Studies, Applied Psychology: An International Review, Human Relations, Journal of Cross-cultural Psychology*, and *International Journal of Human Resource Management*.

Zeynep was the co-founder and the co-editor of the *International Journal of Cross-cultural Management* (Sage Publishing). She was the past president of the International Society for the Study of Work and Organizational Values (ISSWOV) and of the Turkish Psychological Association, Istanbul Branch.

She has been invited as a research fellow and guest lecturer to Aston Business School, Bordeaux School of Management, and Renmin University of China.

Zeynep has received several awards and recognitions, including the Outstanding Young Scholar by the World Economic Forum – Inter Academy Panel, Outstanding Young Scientist Award of the Turkish Academy of Sciences, Best Paper Award (Applied Psychology: An International Review), Gordon Allport Intergroup Relations Award (co-recipient), Outstanding Faculty Award (Koc University), and Outstanding Teaching Award (Renmin University of China).

Zeynep is the Elected Fellow of the Society for Industrial and Organizational Psychology (SIOP), Association for Psychological Sciences (APS), and Global Young Academy of Sciences.

Rabindra N. Kanungo is Professor of Organizational Behavior and holds the Faculty of Management Chair at McGill University, Montreal, Canada. His work experience as a university professor, researcher and consultant spans both East (India) and West (Canada and United States). He has published widely in both basic and applied areas of psychology and management. His publications include more than 100 professional articles in top journals in the field, including *Experimental Psychology, Journal of Applied Psychology, Journal of Personal and Social Psychology, Academy of Management Review, California Management Review* and *Psychological Bulletin*. He has written several books, including *Memory and Affect, Biculturalism and Management, Work Alienation, Compensation: Effective Reward Management, Management of Work and Personal Life, Charismatic Leadership, Management in Developing Countries, Work Motivation* (with M. Mendonça), *Ethical Dimensions of Leadership* (with M. Mendonça) and *Charismatic Leadership in Organizations* (with J. Conger).

For his contributions to psychology and management, Rabi is an Elected Fellow of the Canadian Psychological Association and has won Commonwealth and Seagram Senior Faculty Fellowships and Best Paper Awards.

Manuel Mendonça is an Associate Professor at McGill University, Montreal, Canada.

He has taught at McGill University Faculty of Management and the School of Continuing Studies since 1984. Since his retirement in 2008, he has continued as a lecturer at McGill's School of Continuing Studies. His research interests include leadership, employee compensation and cross-cultural management.

Manuel has authored or co-authored five books, four edited volumes, 22 chapters and 14 articles in journals including *Applied Psychology: An International Review, Journal of Management Inquiry, Canadian Journal of Administrative Sciences, International Journal of Manpower, California Management Review* and *Psychology and Developing Societies*.

Manuel has conducted executive development workshops and seminars on leadership and human resource management in Indonesia, India, Kenya, Kazakhstan, Romania and Hungary – with a focus on management practices that fit the societal culture of these countries.

He also served as Guest Co-Editor, *Canadian Journal of Administrative Sciences* for the journal's special issue on Ethical Leadership and Governance in Organizations.

His awards include the Distinguished Teaching Award from McGill's School of Continuing Studies and the Best Paper Award for 2000 from *Applied Psychology: An International Review* for a paper he co-authored.

About the Book

Over the years we have been teaching cross-cultural management, human resource management (HRM) and organizational behaviour (OB) courses, we have always felt the need of a book that would merge these areas. We realized that our colleagues and students were also in need of a book that focuses on cross-cultural issues in managing organizations in the global context, but while doing so presenting the fundamental theories of HRM and OB. The present book essentially combines the key elements in typical OB, HRM and cross-cultural management textbooks.

Chapters in the book discuss the fundamental theoretical approaches in the following content areas, each of which are then discussed in the context of culture and cross-cultural management: leadership, teamwork, motivation, communication, conflict management, employee attitudes, work–life balance, human resource management, performance management, ethics, corporate social responsibility and organizational structure and change. The primary audience of the book is students at undergraduate and MBA levels, but we also hope that the book will be a useful resource for global managers, consultants and researchers.

This book is dedicated to those who dedicate their lives to continuous learning and knowledge-sharing. A critical aspect of learning is 'reflection'. Exercises, assessments and cases in the book allow for learning through self-reflection, while end-of-chapter questions, 'thinking across-cultures' boxes, cartoons and videos allow for critical appraisal and reflection on the theories and research findings presented in each chapter. In this book, we aim to strike the delicate balance between providing answers for complex questions (e.g., the 'Guidelines for cross-cultural managers' section in each chapter) and letting our readers reflect on answers for the questions we pose. By doing both, we hope to give our readers *some fish to eat*, but also teach them *how to fish*.

This book could not be realized without the inspiration and support of institutions and individuals we like to thank. First and foremost, we would like to thank McGill University and Koç University for being such excellent examples of learning organizations in a cross-cultural context. The first author wishes to thank Renmin University of China for providing the environment to finalize the manuscript during her sabbatical. We would like to thank SAGE Publishing team, especially Robin Lupton, Nina Smith, Kirsty Smy, Sarah Cooke and Alison Borg.

We are indebted to our parents who raised us with social consciousness to care and nurture the incredible diversity in the world. We have been fortunate to live our lives with multicultural identities holding multiple citizenships. This book definitely benefited from our multicultural identities as well as our multidisciplinary backgrounds. In all of our life adventures our spouses Servet Aycan, Minati Kanungo and Rita Mendonça have been with us – without them the adventure would not have revealed its true meaning.

Zeynep Aycan, Rabindra N. Kanungo, Manuel Mendonça

About the Companion Website

To better support your studies, *Organizations and Management in Cross-cultural Context* comes with a companion website. Visit the companion website at www.sage pub.co.uk/kanungo to access:

- End of chapter videos
- Web links
- Case Studies
- Flashcards of key terms

Guided Tour

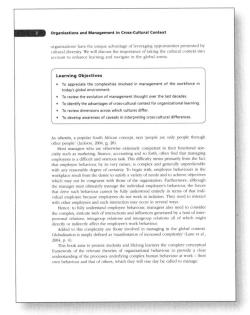

Learning Objectives Highlight at a glance the key content that will be covered in each chapter to focus your learning

Case Studies Taken from around a range of countries and cultures, case studies and examples help link theory to practice

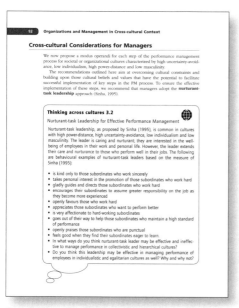

Cross-Cultural Consideration for Managers
These sections will get you thinking like a manager working with an international team
Thinking across Cultures Examples of cross-cultural business scenarios encourage you to think critically about how cross-cultural issues can be resolved

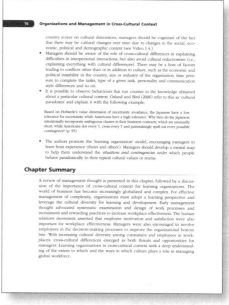

Chapter Summaries Recap key concepts covered in the chapter to aid your revision

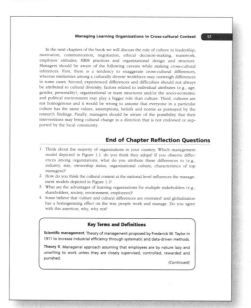

End of Chapter Reflection Questions Test your understanding of the chapter and help you to revise for exams

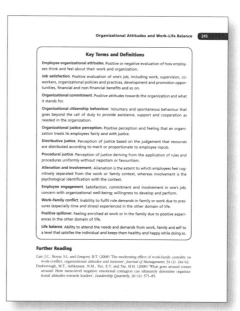

Key Terms and Definitions Key terms are bolded within the text and defined at the end of the chapter for quick reference

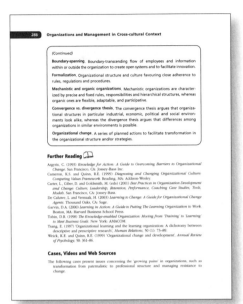

Further Reading Lists of useful readings to deepen your understanding and improve your grade

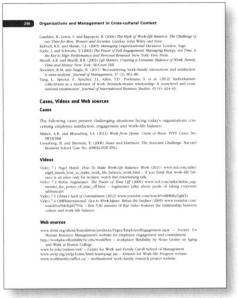

Cases, Videos and Web Sources Links to interesting articles, videos and case studies to further enhance your learning experience

1

Managing Learning Organizations in Cross-cultural Context

Chapter Outline

The following story captures the evolution of management thought (adopted from Eczacibasi, 2000, p. 176).

> At first, organizations believed that 'employees had the *stomach*' to fill; if you provided them with the conditions to satisfy their basic needs, they would work hard.
>
> Then came the realization that 'employees also had a *heart*'. To motivate them to work, you had to appeal to their emotions (e.g., job satisfaction, appreciation).
>
> Later, organizations found out that 'employees had the *brain*' and that their participation in strategic decisions in the organization would improve the organizational bottom line.
>
> In recent years, we know that 'employees have different *cultural values, beliefs and behavioural patterns*' to learn from to enhance the chance of survival in the global competition.

What do you think has changed over the years in the management of workforce? Do you think these changes pose a threat or offer opportunities for organizations? Do you think management has become more challenging over the years? Has it become more rewarding for managers and organizations?

In this chapter we will briefly discuss the changes occurring in management thought and practices over the years. In today's global competition 'learning organizations' have the unique advantage of leveraging opportunities presented by cultural diversity. We will discuss the importance of taking the cultural context into account to enhance learning and navigate in the global arena.

Learning Objectives

- To appreciate the complexities involved in management of the workforce in today's global environment.
- To review the evolution of management thought over the last decades.
- To identify the advantages of cross-cultural context for organizational learning.
- To review dimensions across which cultures differ.
- To develop awareness of caveats in interpreting cross-cultural differences.

As *ubuntu*, a popular South African concept, says 'people are only people through other people' (Jackson, 2004, p. 28).

Most managers who are otherwise extremely competent in their functional specialty such as marketing, finance, accounting and so forth, often find that managing employees is a difficult and onerous task. This difficulty stems primarily from the fact that employee behaviour, by its very nature, is complex and generally unpredictable with any reasonable degree of certainty. To begin with, employee behaviours in the workplace result from the desire to satisfy a variety of needs and to achieve objectives which may not be congruent with those of the organization. Furthermore, although the manager must ultimately manage the individual employee's behaviour, the forces that drive such behaviour cannot be fully understood entirely in terms of that individual employee because employees do not work in isolation. They need to interact with other employees and such interaction may occur in several ways.

Hence, to fully understand employee behaviour, managers also need to consider the complex, intricate web of interactions and influences generated by a host of interpersonal relations, intragroup relations and intergroup relations all of which might directly or indirectly affect the employee's work behaviour.

Added to this complexity are those involved in managing in the global context. Globalization is simply defined as 'manifestation of increased complexity' (Lane et al., 2004, p. 4).

This book aims to present students and lifelong learners the complete conceptual framework of the relevant theories of organizational behaviour to provide a clear understanding of the processes underlying complex human behaviour at work – their own behaviour and that of others, which they will one day be called to manage.

The chapters will discuss the following key content areas in managing people in organizations. In each chapter, the book will focus on one dimension of complexity, namely the cultural context and cross-cultural interactions. Each of the following content areas will be discussed in the context of 'culture', allowing students to evaluate the applicability of the basic OB theories in 'cultural context'.

- Motivation (Chapter 2)
- Performance management (Chapter 3)
- Communication (Chapter 4)
- Conflict management and negotiation (Chapter 4)
- Leadership (Chapter 5)
- Teamwork (Chapter 6)
- Employee attitudes (Chapter 7)
- Work–life balance (Chapter 7)
- Organizational structure and organizational change (Chapter 8)
- Human resource management practices (Chapter 9)
- Ethics and corporate social responsibility (Chapter 10)

In each chapter, major theoretical frameworks introducing key concepts and processes will be presented. This is followed by a discussion of the applicability of these theoretical approaches in various cultural contexts. Why is a relatively in-depth treatment of the theories necessary? The need for a fairly thorough treatment came home to us when we discovered that whenever students had a good grasp of the conceptual framework, they were able to understand its managerial implications much better and utilize it in different contexts. This way, we hope to teach students *how to fish*, rather than *giving them the fish*. Such an understanding also enabled them to make much more sense of their own life and work experiences which, in turn, served to provide them with face validity of the theoretical model.

Management and Learning Organizations: A Developmental Perspective

The history of management thought reveals that scientific interest in behavioural issues in management started with Frederick Taylor and his **scientific management** movement. The implicit concern for these issues is evident in Taylor's (1911) four principles of scientific management, which were stated as follows:

1. Develop a science for each element of an employee's work. This approach replaced the rule-of-thumb method which was quite common at that time.

2. Scientifically select and then train, teach and develop the workers. This was contrary to the prevailing norm that workers should train themselves as best they could.
3. Cooperate with the workers to ensure that work was done in accordance with the scientific management principles.
4. The work and the responsibility was restructured between management and the workers. Management now took over the work for which they were believed to be better qualified than the workers. This was a radical change, because in the past almost all the work and the greater part of the responsibility was borne by the workers.

The research of Taylor and his associate Frank Gilbreth, based on these principles, led to the popularization of time and motion studies and of incentive compensation systems in organizations. The psychologists of the period were also involved with problems of work methods and initiated research on industrial fatigue, accidents, and the development of selection tests and measurements for industrial use. In its theory regarding the nature of employees and organizations, the scientific management approach reflected the temper of the time in which it evolved. It embodied the view of the worker that had developed in the early stages of the Industrial Revolution. Workers were seen as lazy, greedy, selfish and uncooperative people who had a natural tendency to avoid work and responsibility.

Furthermore, such attributes were considered to be fixed and not amenable to change. Therefore, the only way to keep people working was through satisfying their basic needs and promising of financial rewards for good work (i.e., the 'employees have the stomach to satisfy' approach). The managerial implications of this view have been critically reviewed by Douglas McGregor (1960) who described such beliefs about human nature as **Theory X**.

The scientific management approach emphasized production efficiency as the only goal of organizations, and considered workers involved in the production process as little more than adjuncts to the machines they operated. The approach led to the programmed rigour with which work was designed; the worker's job performance instructions being spelt out in minute detail. It also established a clear-cut division of labour between managers and workers – the managers specialized in planning and giving directions and the workers expected to follow these directions to the letter.

The assumption that employees' only motivation was economic, the concept of 'economic man', led to strictly monetary incentive systems, which were contingent upon the actual productivity of the individual. Competition was fostered because the workers knew that to achieve greater financial rewards, they would have to produce more than the others. This system also fostered an individual work orientation to facilitate the measurement of individual productivity. Performance below the established standard was handled with the implicit threat of censure and ultimate dismissal. Thus the motivational system adopted by scientific management became known as the *carrot and stick approach*.

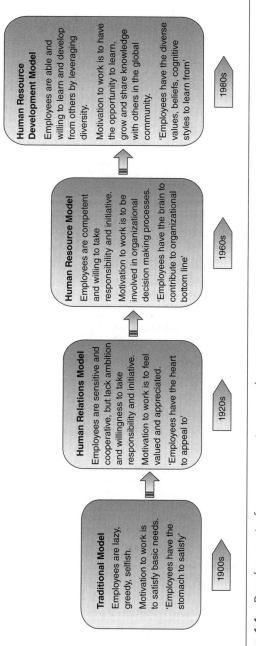

Traditional Model

Employees are lazy, greedy, selfish.

Motivation to work is to satisfy basic needs.

'Employees have the stomach to satisfy'

1900s

Human Relations Model

Employees are sensitive and cooperative, but lack ambition and willingness to take responsibility and initiative.

Motivation to work is to feel valued and appreciated.

'Employees have the heart to appeal to'

1920s

Human Resource Model

Employees are competent and willing to take responsibility and initiative.

Motivation to work is to be involved in organizational decision making processes.

'Employees have the brain to contribute to organizational bottom line'

1960s

Human Resource Development Model

Employees are able and willing to learn and develop from others by leveraging diversity.

Motivation to work is to have the opportunity to learn, grow and share knowledge with others in the global community.

'Employees have the diverse values, beliefs, cognitive styles to learn from'

1980s

Figure 1.1 *Development of management approaches*

The total of thrust of the scientific management approach resulted in very rigid, formal ways of organizing work, with an exclusive emphasis on the physical needs of workers, to the detriment and neglect of other more human needs. The shift away from the Tayloristic thinking began when Elton Mayo and his associates at Harvard University started a series of studies on work behaviour during the 1920s. These studies came to be known as the classic Hawthorne experiments. The Hawthorne studies revealed (a) that work is essentially a group rather than an individual activity and (b) that needs for recognition, security and belonging to groups are more important in determining a worker's productivity and morale than the physical conditions of the work (i.e., the 'employees have the heart to appeal to' approach). These conclusions had such a profound effect on management thinking that they were instrumental in starting a new movement called the *human relations movement*.

The human relations movement emphasized the need for understanding the social environment as a determiner of work behaviour in the same way that the scientific management movement emphasized the need for understanding the physical environment. The popularity of the human relations approach as a solution to behavioural problems in industry came about as a result of the changing environment of that period brought about by the growth in the size of organizations and of the organized labour movement, social security legislation, the Great Depression and the opening of new frontiers in behavioural research. In addition, the scientific management movement, with its individual work orientation, seemed inadequate to the managerial challenges posed by the increasing complexity of organizational growth and economic environment. Neither could it explain and solve the problems which arose due to the changing composition of the labour force and the nature of jobs. For example, there was an enormous increase of white-collar jobs which could not be programmed in the same manner as the blue-collar jobs.

The human relations movement thus became a 'people-oriented' approach to management. The labour union movement joined the growing protest against scientific management because the increased production and efficiency was perceived as nothing more than the unscrupulous exploitation of the worker under scientific management. The labour movement questioned management priorities and sought to change the way the worker was thought of in the production process, arguing that the worker is not a mere adjunct to the machine. The economic devastation of the Great Depression hastened the change of emphasis in the workplace – from the sole emphasis on production to one that also included more human considerations. Perhaps the most important developments contributing to this change were the studies in the area of behavioural research.

The pioneering Hawthorne studies conducted by Elton Mayo questioned for the first time the validity of some of the basic assumptions about human beings underlying the scientific management approach. The most important conclusions of these studies were that 'man did not live by bread alone' and that the rational concept of 'economic man' was not entirely valid. This was replaced by the new concept of 'social man', which placed as much emphasis on the workers' social and psychological needs as on their physical needs. Thus the proponents of the human relations approach recognized the importance of the social atmosphere in the work environment. As a result, informal groups, team spirit and nonfinancial as well as unconditional rewards began to be emphasized. In contrast to the rational coldness of the scientific approach, the human relations movement introduced the warmth of social relations to the workplace.

In the new era permeated by the human relations movement, employers recognized the importance of the social dimensions in the work environment. However, some of the assumptions underlying their attitudes about work and workers did not differ substantially from those of scientific management. At best, their assumptions might be characterized as benevolent Theory X approach, if we were to use McGregor's terminology. The worker was still believed to be passive and indifferent to organizational needs, to lack ambition, to work as little as possible and to dislike responsibility. Whereas scientific management used the carrot and stick approach to gain workers' cooperation, human relations advocated a paternalistic approach to gain workers' cooperation through the unconditional fulfilment of their needs, the manager would improve workers' morale and thus lower their resistance to achieving organizational goals.

The research work that followed the Mayo tradition emphasized the importance of the social environment and marked the beginning of the applied discipline called organizational psychology. Organizational psychology primarily addressed problems arising from personal interaction within the organization. For example, it studied problems of leadership, motivation, communication and interpersonal and intergroup influences. With the maturing of these applied disciplines over the past three decades, **behavioural science** has gained strength and is now in a better position to offer useful knowledge and technology for dealing with the behavioural issues of management.

Behavioural science in the 1960s represented a merger between the early tradition of scientific management and the later tradition of human relations. During the last two decades, it has become obvious that neither scientific management nor the human relations tradition alone can provide an adequate base for our understanding of human behaviour within the organization. The two traditions should be viewed as complementary rather than mutually exclusive. The Taylorian approach focused on the understanding of economic man and paid little attention to the complexities of human motivation. The human relations tradition, on the other hand, focused on the social nature of employees, but ignored the broader organizational issues which go beyond those of the small face-to-face group. Consequently, the behavioural science of the 1960s was forced to develop an eclectic approach, which meant adopting principles and techniques from various sources so long as these helped us to understand and explain behaviour in the workplace. It was concerned with both the complex physical environment of the organization (internal and external) and the complex nature of the people who interact with it.

The philosophy and the underlying assumptions of this eclectic approach represent a departure from both the 'hard' scientific management and the 'soft' human relations approach. Its assumptions about working people in organizations have been best summarized by McGregor (1960) in his discussion of Theory Y. It is not surprising that such an approach should have developed in view of the changes in social norms that have occurred in recent years. These include, for example, the whittling away of formal authoritarian relationships, the growing acceptance of the right of all individuals to pursue their chosen goals irrespective of race or gender and the emphasis on communal effort as opposed to individual accomplishment.

In his statement of **Theory Y,** McGregor suggested that working people are not by nature passive or resistant to organizational needs. Motivation, intelligence, creativity, potential for growth and the capacity to assume responsibility are all present in working people (i.e., the 'employees have the brain to contribute to organizational bottom line' approach). The task of management is to create the right kind of environment in which people can best achieve their own goals by directing their efforts towards organizational objectives. Thus McGregor emphasized the fact that management should recognize the higher needs of individuals, such as achievement, recognition and self-fulfilment, and cater to them by appropriate job designs.

In 1980s there was an increasing awareness that employees had different cultural values, beliefs and cognitive styles. This awareness was raised by the observation that Japanese business was thriving and that this success was achieved thanks to culturally embedded managerial practices. Japan became one of the world's leading economies competing with the US between 1970 and 1990. They created the Japanese miracle (e.g., annual growth of 10 per cent, export rate of 20 per cent, world giants such as Sony, Honda, Nissan, Seiko, Toyota, and Olympus) through managerial practices that were different from those leading to success in the US. Japanese emphasis on lifelong employment, a seniority-based promotion system, strong organizational culture, employee loyalty, concern with employee well-being in the workplace and beyond, and a collective sense of responsibility were the key to managerial success. Japanese managerial principles were described by Ouchi in 1981 in his powerful book **Theory Z**: *How American business can meet the Japanese challenge.* Japan was indeed a challenge to the US. One of the covers of the *Fortune* magazine in 1990 was headlined 'Fear and Loathing of Japan: Why it's growing; why it's dangerous; what to do about it'.

Hence, cross-cultural differences were surfaced and cultural constraints in management theories were widely discussed among scientists and practitioners (e.g., England, 1983; Hofstede, 1993). Hofstede's seminal 1980 work, *Culture's consequences: international differences in work-related values,* has become the earmark of the era witnessing systematic investigations of cross-cultural differences. Values, assumptions, beliefs, cognitive and behavioural patterns varying across cultures were identified, as will be discussed in the next section. Managing cross-cultural differences emerged as one of the key challenges for managers dealing with expatriation and culturally diverse workforces in both the global and local business contexts. In recent years cross-cultural differences are perceived less as a *threat* to positive organizational outcomes and more as an *opportunity* to leverage for organizational growth and learning.

Global competition requires that organizations adopt the learning perspective from employees at all levels and from all cultural backgrounds. Senge (1990) defined the **learning organization** as one 'where people continuously expand their capacity to create the results they truly desire, where new and expansive patterns of thinking are nurtured, where collective aspiration is set free and where people are continually learning how to learn together' (p. 7). The learning organization *learns continuously* and *transforms itself* to adopt to the changing environment (Watkins & Marsick, 1993). Global organizations are especially forced to continually adapt to and survive in the new global environment (Zuboff, 1988), where the learning organization is seen as an ideal organization type (Gheradi, 2006) (see Video 1.1).

Perception of *threat* resulting from cross-cultural differences should be replaced by a perception of *opportunities* to learn from 'to respond to the demands of global economy, to reap the full benefit of cross-border alliances and to enhance organizational learning' (Holden, 2002, p. 45).

This book presents the key managerial theories and practices in the areas of motivation, leadership, teamwork, communication, organizational attitudes, HRM and organizational structure to satisfy employees' 'stomach, heart and mind'. We acknowledge that in the globalized world, employee needs driven from cultural diversity should also be satisfied. In each chapter we will discuss how cross-cultural differences manifest themselves and how these differences should be managed and leveraged to increase organizational learning. Let us first present the major approaches to understanding cross-cultural differences.

The Importance of Cultural Context for Learning Organizations

Managing cross-cultural differences has become an item in the managerial agenda in all types of organizations. Multinational organizations unavoidably deal with the challenges and opportunities of managing culturally diverse workforce. Domestic organizations face similar challenges, because the majority of them have a culturally diverse workforce in the local context or they have to understand cross-cultural issues in dealing with business partners (e.g., suppliers, vendors, outsourced service providers) around the world.

The aim of **cross-cultural management** is to 'describe organizational behaviour within countries and cultures; compare organizational behaviour across cultures and countries and perhaps most importantly seeks to understand and improve the interactions of co-workers, clients, suppliers and alliance partners from different countries or cultures' (Adler, 1991, pp. 10–11). In each chapter, we discuss the topic in the cultural context to help future managers handle possible conflicts or inefficiencies resulting from cross-cultural differences and improve the interactions within the diverse workforce.

What is this mysterious thing called **culture**? Try to list the attributes of people who you perceive to be culturally dissimilar and culturally similar to you. Share your list with your colleagues and discuss what makes a person culturally similar and dissimilar to you – how do they look, talk, behave, think, believe, value in life? Let's get back to your list after we review some of the most common definitions of culture.

Culture has been defined in more than 150 ways by many disciplines. In this book, we refer to culture as a loosely coupled system of values, assumptions, beliefs, norms and behaviours shared among the members of a human group and differentiating it from other groups. When you visit a new country, you may almost immediately realize that you are in a different culture by observing driving behaviour, eating habits, dress code, greeting patterns, conversational styles and so on. However, it takes time to realize that a culture is different from your own also because people hold different assumptions, values, beliefs and norms.

Effective management of global workforce requires understanding and appreciation of cross-cultural differences in the subtle aspects of culture including values, assumptions, beliefs and norms. Consider the following mini-cases.

CASE 1.1

What is wrong with this award?

I just don't understand why we cannot motivate people here by showing appreciation for good work. Selection of the employee-of-the-month is an event widely celebrated back in the US, but it is taken almost like a tragedy here. The *winner* of the award this year feels quite unhappy and wants to return it!!

Why do you think the winner wants to return the award? What would have been the right way to praise the good work in that organization?

Without understanding cultural values, assumptions and beliefs, a manager can mistakenly conclude that rewarding people is demotivating in some cultural contexts. However, the correct interpretation of the above episode would be that people in some cultures may find *public* recognitions discomforting because they fear that it would damage group harmony or attract the so called evil eye and harm them. These cultures are typically collectivistic or fatalistic. In such cultures, reward or praise is indeed motivating but when offered in *private*.

CASE 1.2

Apparently, the sky *has* the limit!

It is so hard to convince top management in this country that training is necessary for seasoned employees to upgrade their skills. In the meeting yesterday I said 'the sky is the limit for those who want to improve themselves; we should spend more on training and development' and people looked at me like I was crazy.

Why do you think there is resistance to training; do you think the resistance is related to budgetary constraints?

The incorrect interpretation of the resistance by top management to training in this case would be that it was due to budgetary constraints. However, knowledge of cultural values, assumptions, beliefs and norms would help us to correctly identify the problem as one that had nothing to do with budget, but one that had to do with the cultural assumption that 'people, by nature, cannot change'. An effective manager, therefore, should not fight for budget but try to change this assumption in the organization in order to offer more training and development opportunities to employees.

Now let us get back to your list of similarities and differences between those culturally similar and dissimilar to you. Does your list include more observable (e.g., dress, language, physical appearance, behaviours) or subtle (e.g., values, beliefs) characteristics of the person you consider to be culturally dissimilar to you? How do you think you can manage your relationship with that person if you know more about the values, assumptions, beliefs and norms underlying their behaviour? Probably much better than the case when you only know that they are different without knowing why!

We can understand each other better, manage our relationships more effectively and learn from each other only when we are aware of the cultural values, assumptions, beliefs and norms underlying differences in our behaviour. For that reason, we focus on these aspects of culture to unveil its mysteries.

Cross-cultural Differences

Cross-cultural differences are captured through surveys assessing values, assumptions, norms and beliefs. Responses to these surveys are grouped into categories generally referred to as 'dimensions'. When cultures are compared the following **cultural**

dimensions are used by researchers, consultants and managers (Table 1.1; see also Video 1.2.). In each chapter, cross-cultural similarities and differences in motivation, leadership, teamwork, HRM practices and so on will be discussed in light of these dimensions.

Table 1.1   Cultural dimensions used in cross-cultural comparisons

Cultural Dimension	Description
Power distance (House, et al., 2004, p.192)	The degree to which members of an organization or society expect and agree that power should be unequally shared and power holders are entitled to have more privileges than those less powerful in the society.
Collectivism (as opposed to individualism) (House, et al., 2004, p.192) (Hofstede, 1980, p.171)	The degree to which organizational and societal institutional norms and practices encourage and reward collective distribution of resources and collective action. The extent to which people place importance to extended families or clans, which protect them in exchange for loyalty. The 'in-group' – 'out-group' difference is salient.
Future orientation (House, et al., 2004, p.192)	The degree to which individuals in organizations or societies engage in future-oriented behaviours such as planning, investing in the future, and delaying gratification.
Performance orientation (House, et al., 2004, p.192)	The extent to which an organization or society encourages and rewards group members for performance improvement and excellence.
Universalism (Trompenaars, 1993, p.46)	The extent to which an organization or society strives for consistency and uniform procedures, institutes formal ways of changing the way business is conducted, seeks fairness by treating all like cases in the same way.
Particularism (Trompenaars, 1993, p.46)	The extent to which an organization or society accepts building informal networks and create private understandings, tries to alter informally accustomed patterns, seeks fairness by treating all cases on their special merit.
Specificity (Trompenaars, 1993, p.90)	The degree to which private and business agendas are kept separated; clear, precise and detailed instructions are seen as assuring better compliance.
Diffuseness (Trompenaars, 1993, p.90)	The degree to which private and business agendas are interpenetrated; ambiguous and vague instructions are seen as allowing subtle and responsive interpretations.
Ascription (orientation towards ascribed status; Trompenaars, 1993, p.105)	The degree to which status is accorded on the basis of social class, family background, educational background, or titles, rather than merit or achievement.
Paternalism (Aycan, Kanungo, et al., 2000, p.197)	The extent to which an organization or society encourages and accepts that people in authority provide care, guidance, and protection to their subordinates, just as they would do to their own children. In return, subordinates are expected to show loyalty and deference to the superiors.
Fatalism (Aycan, Kanungo, et al., 2000, p.198)	The extent to which people in an organization or society believe that it is not possible to control fully the outcomes of one's actions.
Uncertainty avoidance (Hofstede, 1980, p.140)	The extent to which people in an organization or society considered uncertainty inherent in life as a continuous threat that must be fought. There is high avoidance of deviant and different persons and ideas.
Femininity (Hofstede, 1980, p.205)	The degree to which people in an organization or society value interpersonal harmony more than money and achievement; gender roles are fluid.
High and low context (Hall & Hall, 1995, p.87)	The degree to which people in an organization or society present message in an explicit manner. In high context cultures, most of the information is already in the person, while very little is in the coded, explicit, transmitted part of the message. In a low context culture, the mass of information is vested in the explicit code.

Cultural Dimension	Description
Tightness – looseness (Gelfand et al., 2011, p. 1102).	The degree to which social norms are pervasive, clearly defined, and reliably imposed.
Societal Cynicism (Bond, Leung, et al., 2004, p. 559)	Societal Cynicism relates to a lower emphasis on striving for high performance, a sensible outcome if there is a general suspicion of the social system, and a general expectation of negative outcomes.

Source: Adapted from Aycan, 2005.

Country scores based on survey findings are available on these dimensions in the references provided in Table 1.1. For example, according to country scores published by House and colleagues (2004), countries like Morocco, Nigeria and El Salvador are the most hierarchical (i.e., value high power-distance), whereas the Netherlands, South Africa and Denmark are the most egalitarian (i.e., value low power distance).

Thinking across cultures 1.1

The First Cross-cultural Encounter

The following e-mail exchange demonstrates how cross-cultural differences in communication style and its underlying assumptions may be a potential problem.

From: James Pandur

Sent: Friday, June 17, 2012, 14.53 pm

To: Alistair Mayfraud

Subject: Administrative assistant

Dear Alistair,

Warm greetings from our new project office. I hope you and your family are keeping well since our meeting last week. Thank you again for your hospitality extended to me and my family.

Alistair, my friend, I must bring a potential problem to your attention. The new administrative assitant Ms. Gilborne has sent me the following e-mail few days ago. Her e-mail gave me the impression that she had no manners, especially as

(Continued)

(Continued)

a young lady. She was addressing me as if I was a friend. She is talking about having fun together! Does she not know that I am her superior and that she is supposed to work very hard in this project?

Please advise my friend. Do you think we should think about a replacement?

May God's blessings come upon you and your family.

James Pandur

From: Jackline Gilborne

Sent: Friday, June 15, 2012, 11.53 am

To: James Pandur

Subject: Greetings

Dear James,

I am Jackline; your new administrative assistant in the Power Inc. Project! How are you?

I plan to be in the office on Tuesday, will you be in? I look forward to meeting you in person and having fun working on the project.

Take care and see you soon.

Jackline

- Can you guess the cultural background of James and Jackline? To what extent do you think the 'potential problems' would be due to cross-cultural differences versus other personal characteristics of the actors?

Cross-cultural Considerations for Managers

Managers should be aware of cross-cultural differences to successfully manage the global workforce and leverage the learning opportunities presented by diversity. However, they should also be aware of the following caveats in interpreting and managing cross-cultural differences.

- There is a tendency to overlook cross-cultural similarities and exaggerate differences. Cultural groups are indeed different from one another (e.g., 'Culture is the collective programming of mind which distinguishes the members of one human group from another' – Hofstede, 1984, p. 21), but they are also similar in essence (e.g., 'Culture is varieties of common knowledge' – Holden, 2002, p. 99). Managers are advised to look for similarities that unite people, while being cognizant of differences.

- Culture shapes people, but people also shape culture. Therefore, cultural change is possible. Managing cross-cultural differences may imply creating change in the cultural values, assumptions, norms and beliefs. Managers should be aware of the possibility that their interventions (e.g., HRM practices) may bring culture change in the local community in the long run and that the change should be in the direction endorsed by the locals. Otherwise, there is a danger of committing cultural imperialism. One way to check whether or not culture change is in the desired direction by the local community is to consult research findings comparing cultural orientations 'as they are' and 'as they should be' from the local community's perspective (e.g., the GLOBE project's 'should be' scores; House et al., 2004).

- Cultural groups may appear homogeneous (e.g., national culture), but they involve wide variations within them. It would be wrong to assume that everyone in a particular culture would think the same, feel the same and act the same (see Video 1.3.). Country scores on cultural dimensions should not be blindly generalized to everyone in that country (e.g., not everyone in South Africa values low power difference; some may value high power-distance). Managers should be aware of wide variations within each culture across regions, ethnic groups, organizations and individuals. It should also be noted that increasing numbers of people recognize themselves as 'biculturals', for example Japanese-American (e.g., Brannen & Thomas, 2010).

- We can consider culture at multiple levels, although the majority of cross-cultural research we cite in this book are conducted at the national level. At the highest level, we can talk about the 'global culture' referring to shared values transcending national borders imposed by forces of globalization. There may be regional cultures, such as Asian, Middle Eastern, or Latin American. Within regions, there are national-level cultures (e.g., Swedish culture, Indian culture, Israeli culture). Within each nation, there may be wide variations across organizational-level cultures. Within organizations, there may be cultural differences across departments, units, or teams. This 'Russian-doll' model of culture once again reminds us that culture is not a homogeneous entity. Managers should avoid gross generalizations about cultural characteristics and appreciate different cultural characteristics at multiple levels.

- Cultures change, but they also stay the same (as in the famous French saying *plus ça change, plus c'est la même chose*). When interpreting research findings about country scores on cultural dimensions, managers should be cognizant of the fact that there may be cultural changes over time due to changes in the social, economic, political and demographic context (see Video 1.4.).

- Managers should be aware of the role of cross-cultural differences in explaining difficulties in interpersonal interactions, but also avoid cultural reductionism (i.e., explaining everything with cultural differences). There may be a host of factors leading to conflicts other than or in addition to culture, such as the economic and political instability in the country, size or industry of the organization, time pressure to complete the tasks, type of a given task, personality and communication style differences and so on.

- It is possible to observe behaviours that run counter to the knowledge obtained about a particular cultural context. Osland and Bird (2006) refer to this as 'cultural paradoxes' and explain it with the following example:

Based on Hofstede's value dimension of uncertainty avoidance, the Japanese have a low tolerance for uncertainty while Americans have a high tolerance. Why then do the Japanese intentionally incorporate ambiguous clauses in their business contracts, which are unusually short, while Americans dot every 'i', cross every 't' and painstakingly spell out every possible contingency? (p. 95)

- The authors promote the 'learning organization' model, encouraging managers to learn from experience (theirs and others'). Managers should develop a mental map to help them understand the *situations and contingencies* under which people behave paradoxically to their typical cultural values or norms.

Chapter Summary

A review of management thought is presented in this chapter, followed by a discussion of the importance of cross-cultural context for learning organizations. The world of business has become increasingly globalized and complex. For effective management of complexity, organizations must adopt a learning perspective and leverage the cultural diversity for learning and development. Early management thought advocated systematic examination and design of work processes and recruitment and rewarding practices to increase workplace effectiveness. The human relations movement asserted that employee motivation and satisfaction were also important for workplace effectiveness. Managers were also encouraged to involve employees in the decision-making processes to improve the organizational bottom line. With increasing cultural diversity among consumers and employees in workplaces, cross-cultural differences emerged as both threats and opportunities for managers. Learning organizations in cross-cultural context seek a deep understanding of the extent to which and the ways in which culture plays a role in managing global workforce.

In the next chapters of the book we will discuss the role of culture in leadership, motivation, communication, negotiation, ethical decision-making, teamwork, employee attitudes, HRM practices and organizational design and structure. Managers should be aware of the following caveats while making cross-cultural inferences. First, there is a tendency to exaggerate cross-cultural differences, whereas similarities among a culturally diverse workforce may outweigh differences in some cases. Second, experienced differences and difficulties should not always be attributed to cultural diversity; factors related to individual attributes (e.g., age, gender, personality), organizational or team structures and/or the socio-economic and political environment may play a bigger role than culture. Third, cultures are not homogenous and it would be wrong to assume that everyone in a particular culture has the same values, assumptions, beliefs and norms as portrayed by the research findings. Finally, managers should be aware of the possibility that their interventions may bring cultural change in a direction that is not endorsed or supported by the local community.

End of Chapter Reflection Questions

1. Think about the majority of organizations in your country. Which management model depicted in Figure 1.1. do you think they adopt? If you observe differences among organizations, what do you attribute these differences to (e.g., industry, size, ownership status, organizational culture, characteristics of top managers)?
2. How do you think the cultural context at the national level influences the management models depicted in Figure 1.1?
3. What are the advantages of learning organizations for multiple stakeholders (e.g., shareholders, society, environment, employees)?
4. Some believe that 'culture and cultural differences are overrated' and globalization has a homogenizing effect on the way people work and manage. Do you agree with this assertion; why, why not?

Key Terms and Definitions

Scientific management. Theory of management proposed by Frederick W. Taylor in 1911 to increase industrial efficiency through systematic and data-driven methods.

Theory X. Managerial approach assuming that employees are by nature lazy and unwilling to work unless they are closely supervised, controlled, rewarded and punished.

(Continued)

(Continued)

Theory Y. Managerial approach assuming that employees are willing to work, learn, seek out responsibility and grow in their careers if given the opportunity.

Theory Z. Managerial approach promoting loyalty and well-being of the employee through long-term employment, sense of cohesion and sense of moral obligation to serve the organization.

Behavioural science. Scientific disciplines including psychology, sociology, cognitive sciences and anthropology exploring the principles of human behaviour and its interaction with its complex environment.

Learning organization. An organization that facilitates learning and knowledge transfer at all levels to continuously transform itself to meet challenges.

Culture. Values, assumptions, beliefs, norms, and behavioural patterns shared by a group of individuals that differentiate them from others.

Cross-cultural management. Managerial approach aiming at understanding the extent to which and the ways in which cultural context influences behaviour at multiple levels thus improving the effectiveness of cross-cultural encounters.

Cultural dimensions. Values, assumptions, beliefs and norms along which cultures (national or organizational level) are shown to differ in scientific research.

Further Reading

Adler, N.J. (2008) *International Dimensions of Organizational Behavior* (5th edition with Alison Gundersen). Mason, OH: Thomson-South-Western.

Chen, M. and Miller, D. (2011) 'The relational perspective as a business mindset: Managerial implications for East and West', *Academy of Management Perspectives*, 25 (3): 6–19.

Lane, H.W., Maznevski, M.L., Dietz, J. and DiStefano, J. (2009) *International Management Behavior: Text, Readings, Cases*. Chichester, West Sussex: Wiley.

Leung, K. and Bond, M.H. (eds) (2009) *Psychological Aspects of Social Axioms: Understanding Global Belief Systems*. New York: Springer.

Molinsky, A. (2013) Global Dexterity: How To Adapt Your Behavior Across Cultures Without Losing Yourself in the Process. Boston, MA: Harvard University Press.

Ronen, S. and Shenkar, O. (2013) 'Mapping world cultures: Cluster formation, sources and implications', *Journal of International Business Studies*, 44 (6).

Smith, P.B., Peterson, M.F. and Thomas, D.C. (2008) *Handbook of Cross-cultural Management Research*. London: Sage.

Taras, V., Kirkman, B.L. and Steel, P. (2010) 'Examining the impact of culture's consequences: A three-decade, multilevel, meta-analytic review of Hofstede's cultural value dimensions', *Journal of Applied Psychology*, 95 (3): 405–39.

Thomas, D.C. (2002) *Essentials of International Management: A Cross-cultural Perspective.* London: Sage.

Cases, Videos, Web Sources

Cases

The following cases illustrate the importance and difficulty of handling sensitive issues in the local context (especially in emerging economies). The cases also illustrate that difficulties experienced are not only result of cross-cultural differences, but also of political, economic and legal context.

Butler, C. and de Bettignies, H.C. (2007) *Changmai Corporation Case.* France: INSEAD-EAC.

Blake, W.R. (1999) Footwear international case. In H.W. Lane, J.J. DiStefano and M.L. Maznevski (Eds.). *International Management Behavior*, 3rd edn, pp. 173–80. Malden, MA: Blackwell Publishers, Inc.

Videos

Video 1.1 Peter Senge: *The Learning organization* (2013): www.youtube.com/watch?v=ONttCcOq944

Video 1.2 Geert Hofstede: *Recent Discoveries about Cultural Differences* (2013): www.youtube.com/watch?v=LBv1wLuY3Ko

One of the most influential scholars in cross-cultural management – Geert Hofstede – updates us about the recent developments in the understanding of culture.

Video 1.3 Liu Bolin: *The Invisible Man* (2013): www.ted.com/talks/lang/en/liu_bolin_the_invisible_man.html

Bolin is a Beijing-based artist who reminds us that 'context' should not mask the uniqueness of the the individual.

Video 1.4 Hyeonseo Lee: *My Escape from North Korea* (2013): www.ted.com/talks/hyeonseo_lee_my_escape_from_north_korea.html

Lee's story makes us wonder how one nation grows so much apart in their culture in just 60 years after an artificial border splits it into half.

You may also watch the concert video featuring 'Gangnam Style' to appreciate the sharp contrast between the cultures of North and South Korea: www.youtube.com/watch?v=rX372ZwXOEM

Web sources

www.geerthofstede.nl/ – all you want to know about Hofstede's work including value scores of cultures.

www.worldvaluessurvey.org – Inglehart's World Values Project.

http://business.nmsu.edu/programs-centers/globe/ – introduction to the GLOBE project.

www.grovewell.com/pub-GLOBE-intro.html – introduction to the GLOBE project.

www.solonline.org – Society for Learning Organization founded by Peter Senge.

www.dhl.com/en/about_us/logistics_insights/studies_research/global_connectedness_index/global_connectedness_index_2012.html - Global Connectedness Index.

References

Adler, N.J. (1991) *International Dimensions of Organizational Behavior*. Boston, MA: PWS Publishing Company.

Aycan, Z. (2005) 'The interface between cultural and institutional/structural contingencies in human resource management', *International Journal of Human Resource Management*, 16 (7): 1083–20.

Aycan, Z., Kanungo, R.N., Mendonça, M., Yu, K., Deller, J., Stahl, G. and Kurshid, A. (2000) 'Impact of culture on human resource management practices: a 10-country comparison', *Applied Psychology: An International Review*, 49 (1): 192–222.

Bond, M.H., Leung, K., et al. (2004) 'Culture-level dimensions of social axioms and their correlates across 41 cultures', *Journal of Cross-cultural Psychology*, 35 (5): 548–70.

Brannen, M.Y. and Thomas, D. (2010) 'Bicultural individuals in organizations: implications and opportunity', *International Journal of Cross-cultural Management*, 10 (1): 5–16.

Eczacibasi, B. (2000) 'New perspectives to HRM practices', in Z. Aycan (ed.), *Management, Leadership and HRM Practices in Turkey*, pp. 23–40. Istanbul: Turkish Psychological Association Press.

England, G.W. (1983) 'Japanese and American management: theory Z and beyond', *Journal of International Business Studies*, 13 (2): 131–42.

Gelfand, M.J., Raver, J.L., Nishii, L., Leslie, L.M., Lun, J., Lim, B.C., Duan, L., Almaliach, A., Ang, S., Arnadottir, J., Aycan, Z., Boehnke, K., Boski, P., Cabecinhas, R., Chan, D., Chhokar, J., D'Amato, A., Ferrer, M., Fischlmayr, I., Fischer, R., Fulop, M., Georgas, J., Kashima, E.S., Kashima, Y., Kim, K., Lempereur, A., Marquez, P., Othman, R., Overlaet, B., Panagiotopoulou, P., Peltzer, K., Perez-Florizno, L.R., Petrovna, L., Realo, A., Schei, V., Schmitt, M., Smith, P.B., Soomro, N., Szabo, E., Taveesin, E., Toyama, M., Van de Vliert, E., Vohra, N., Ward, C., Yamaguchi, S. (2011). Differences between tight and loose cultures: A 33-Nation Study. Science, May, 332, 1100–1104.

Gheradi, S. (2006) *Organizational Knowledge: The Texture of Workplace Learning*. Malden, MA: Blackwell Publishing.

Hall, E.T. and Hall, M.R. (1995) *Understanding Cultural Differences*. Yarmouth, ME: Intercultural Press.

Hofstede, G. (1980) *Culture's Consequences: International Differences in Work-Related Values*. Beverly Hills, CA: Sage Publications.

Hofstede, G. (1984) *Culture's consequences: International differences in work-related values*, Abridged Edition. Beverly Hills: Sage Publications.

Hofstede, G. (1993) 'Cultural constraints in management theories', in J.T. Wren (ed.), *The Leader's Companion*, pp. 253–70. New York: Free Press.

Holden, N. (2002) *Cross-cultural Management: A Knowledge Management Perspective*. Harlow: Prentice Hall.

House, R.J., Hanges, P.J., Javidan, M., Dorfman, P.W. and Gupta, V. (2004) *Culture, Leadership and Organizations: The GLOBE Study of 62 Societies*. Thousand Oaks, CA: Sage Publishing.

Jackson, T. (2004) *Management and Change in Africa: A Cross-cultural Perspective*. London: Routledge.

Lane, H.W., Maznevski, M.L. and Mendenthall, M.E. (2004) 'Globalization: Hercules meets Buddha', in H.W. Lane, M.L. Maznevski, M.E. Mendenhall and J. McNett (eds), *The Blackwell Handbook of Global Management: A Guide to Managing Complexity*, pp. 3–26. Malden, MA: Blackwell Publishers, Inc.

McGregor, D. (1960) *The Human Side of the Enterprise*. New York: McGraw-Hill, Inc.

Osland, J.S. and Bird, A. (2006) 'Beyond sophisticated stereotypes: cultural sensemaking in context', in H.W. Lane, J. DiStefano and M.L. Maznevski (eds), *International Management Behavior*, pp. 95–111. Malden, MA: Blackwell Publishers, Inc.

Ouchi, W. (1981) *Theory Z: How American business can meet the Japanese Challenge*. New York: Avon Books.

Senge, P. (1990) *The Fifth Discipline: The Art and Practice of the Learning Organization*. New York: Doubleday.

Taylor, F.W. (1911) *The Principles of Scientific Management*. New York: Harper and Brothers.

Trompenaars, F. (1993) *Riding the Waves of Culture*. London: The Economist Books.

Watkins, K. and Marsick, V. (1993) *Sculpting the Learning Organization: The Art and Science of Systemic Change*. San Francisco, CA: Jossey-Bass.

Zuboff, S. (1988) *In the Age of the Smart Machine: The Future of Work and Power*. New York: Basic Books.

Want to learn more? Visit the companion website at www.sagepub.co.uk/kanungo to gain access to videos from the end of each chapter, weblinks and flash cards of key terms.

2

Work Motivation in Cross-cultural Context

Chapter Outline

A rich businessman from a rich country decided to spend his vacation in a small fishing village in the Indian Ocean. He enjoyed observing locals and chatting with them. There was one fisherman who attracted the attention of the rich man; he seemed very intelligent and hard working. The rich man approached him one day. 'Hello' he said. 'I have been watching you with admiration; you are a smart and hard-working man. Why don't you enhance your business? You can go to the big city and open up a restaurant.' The fisherman looked at him in bafflement and said 'Thank you for your kind words, sir. But why should I do it?' The rich man thought that the fisherman had higher goals in life and admired him more. He tried to increase fisherman's appetite by saying 'Well, in time, you can have your own chain of restaurants. Wouldn't it be nice?' The fisherman asked calmly 'Yes, but why?' The rich man did not quite understand why the fisherman asked this question but answered anyway 'To be rich, of course!' The fisherman asked again 'Why?' The rich man was beginning to lose his patience; he thought maybe fisherman was not that smart after all. He raised his voice slightly and talked slowly so that the fisherman could understand 'When you are rich, you will retire and live peacefully in a fisherman's village for the rest of your life.' The fisherman looked directly in the eyes of the rich man and said 'That's exactly what I am doing, sir and I desire nothing beyond that.' (Anonymous tale)

What motivates this fisherman in life? If he is not interested in money or career advancement, does this mean that he is a 'loser' or an uneducated person with a simple mind? If some people are not motivated by awards, promotions or bonuses, is there anything wrong with them?

The rich man in this story may certainly think this way and so may a lot of managers working with culturally diverse workforces in the world. However, this would only confirm the apt observation of the famous author Anaïs Nin: 'we don't see things as they are, we see things as *we are.*'

Just because getting rich and famous are the motivating forces for some does not mean that they should be the motivating forces for all. In this chapter we will examine motivation through cross-cultural lenses and argue that cultural values, beliefs and norms have an important impact on what motivates employees and how employees are motivated. We will present a review of cross-cultural studies testing the applicability of 'content' (examining *what* motivates employees) and 'process' (examining *how* employees are motivated) theories across cultures.

Learning Objectives

- To understand the extent to which and how US-based motivation theories are applicable in different cultural contexts.

- To identify the cultural characteristics underlying variations in motivational approaches.

- To discover similarities and differences across cultures in the approaches to employee motivation.

- To provide guidelines for culturally appropriate methods of motivating employees in diverse work environments.

What is Employee Motivation?

Money was never a big motivation for me, except as a way to keep score. The real excitement is playing the game. Donald Trump

The greater the loyalty of a group toward the group, the greater is the motivation among the members to achieve the goals of the group and the greater the probability that the group will achieve its goals. Rensis Likert

Most management literature on motivation is psychologically oriented and is based on psychological models developed and tested almost exclusively in the United States. (Fatehi, 1996, p. 231)

The classical definition of **work motivation** is that 'it is a set of energetic forces that originate both within as well as beyond an individual's being, to initiate work-related behaviour and to determine its form, direction, intensity and duration' (Pinder, 1998, p. 11). Traditionally work motivation theories have been categorized as content and process theories. The content theories included in this chapter (i.e., Maslow's hierarchy of needs, Herzberg's motivation-hygiene theory, McClelland's typology of needs) explain work behaviour as the individual's attempt to satisfy a need. The content theories postulate that when an individual's need is not met or satisfied then that individual experiences tension which motivates the individual towards a behaviour to satisfy that need. The content theories can be said to answer the '*what*' of motivation processes, i.e., what needs and in what order do these needs vary in their strength to initiate, energize and sustain the individual's work behaviour? The process theories, on the other hand, explain work behaviour in terms of the cognitive process which the individual goes through before and during the behaviour. It thus seeeks to identify the process, i.e., '*how*' does an individual start, direct and stop a behaviour? In so doing the process theories examine the individual's needs, as well as their perceptions of ability to perform the requisite behaviour and also the individual expectations relative to the outcomes of behaviour. The process theories included in this chapter are equity theory, expectancy theory, goal-setting theory and job characteristics theory.

Maslow's Hierarchy of Needs

Maslow's theory of motivation suggests that humans are motivated to satisfy their needs, which are structured in a hierarchical order. At the lowest level there are physiological and safety needs to be satisfied for our survival, whereas at the top there are self-esteem and self-actualization needs to be satisfied for our growth. Does this theory have cross-cultural applicability? Two questions will be tackled in this chapter. First, is the hierarchy similar in countries other than the US and is '**self-actualization**' indeed the most important need to satisfy? Second, is the effect of organizational practices to satisfy higher- and lower-order needs the same across cultures?

Is the order and importance of needs the same across cultures?

Hofstede (1984) stated that 'the ordering of needs in Maslow's hierarchy represents a value choice – Maslow's value choice. This choice was based on his mid-twentieth century U.S. middle class values' (p. 396). Maslow's theory was developed in the context of Cold War when the essence of American culture emphasized individualism and individual achievement (Cooke et al., 2005). The theory would have limited generalizability when taken out of this context and there is enough research evidence to suggest that.

Indeed, as early as 1970s and 1980s studies showed that the importance of needs was not similar across cultures (e.g., Haire, Ghiselli and Porter, 1966) and that the ordering of needs, especially in economically developing countries (e.g., India, Peru), was similar but not the same as proposed by the original theory (e.g., Jaggi, 1979; Badawy, 1980). Social needs (e.g., a sense of belonging and sense of contribution to society) tend to be more important for employees in collectivistic and feminine cultures than esteem needs (e.g., a sense of personal accomplishment). An African manager in Cameroon observed that 'most of our managers are motivated by the objective to build a country' (Jackson, 2004, p. 116). This confirms Adler's (1991) assertion that social needs take precedence over ego enhancing self-actualization needs in collectivistic cultures.

Maslow's hierarchy also reflects low uncertainty avoidance and high masculinity values (Hofstede, 1984). In cultures characterized by low uncertainty avoidance and low masculinity (e.g., Northern European countries) one can expect a predominance of belongingness over self-actualization. In those characterized by high uncertainty avoidance one can expect predominance of safety than self-actualization needs (Adler, 1991). In such cultures, having job security (i.e., continuation of employment and income) is more important than having autonomy, challenge or interesting work in one's job. It appears that employees in economically developing regions are primarily motivated to satisfy lower-order needs compared to those in economically developed countries motivated to satisfy higher-order needs (e.g., Adigun & Stephenson, 1992).

Nevis (1983) compared managerial assumptions in individualistic and collectivistic cultural contexts prior to proposing a framework for a Chinese hierarchy of needs. The assumptions underlying the mainly Chinese collectivistic management concepts include priority of and loyalty to the nation; consideration for the family; due respect for age, wisdom, traditional norms and communal property relative to private possessions. Hence, at the bottom of the hierarchy are the belonging needs followed by physiological and safety needs; at the top is self-actualization in the service of society need. As stated by Punnett (2004): 'For some, self-actualization is being a CEO in a large organization, whereas for others it is leading an exemplary spiritual life' (p. 140).

Are there other needs that motivate people in different cultural contexts? Murray (1938; cited in Markus & Kitayama, 1991) proposed a list of dominant needs in collectivistic cultures, including deference (the need to admire and willingly follow a superior), similance (the need to imitate and emulate others), affiliation (the need to form friendships and associations), nurturance (the need to nourish, aid and protect) and avoidance of blame (the need to avoid blame and punishment).

It is worth mentioning that Schwartz's typology of motivational domains of values (Schwartz & Bilsky, 1987) resembles Maslow's classification of needs – as follows:

the security domain of values (e.g., safety, stability, harmony) corresponds to Maslow's physiological and safety needs; the achievement domain of values (e.g., competence, achievement) is similar to Maslow's esteem need; the prosocial value domain (e.g., altruism, benevolence, kindness) is similar to Maslow's need for affiliation; and the maturity domain (e.g., learning, growth, attainment of goals) is similar to Maslow's self-actualization need category (Gambrel and Cianci, 2003). Schwartz's framework demonstrated vast cross-cultural variations in these value dimensions (see Schwartz, 1994 for value scores of countries).

Does satisfying higher- and lower-order needs lead to the same outcomes across cultures?

The second question we posed at the beginning of this section was whether or not satisfying higher- and lower-order needs yielded similar results across cultures. In a study based on surveys of employees in 49 nations, Huang and Van de Vliert (2003) found that satisfying higher-order needs does not have the similar effect across cultures. Job characteristics that would satisfy higher-order needs (e.g., autonomy, challenge) are associated with high job satisfaction in economically developed countries with a strong social security system and low power distance. The authors arrived at the following conclusion:

> Workers in nations with high social security are more likely to take survival for granted and, therefore, may attach more value to higher-order needs, such as self-actualization and self-esteem ... Moreover, if the low social security nations have a low power distance national culture, there might still be a strong relationship between intrinsic job characteristics and job satisfaction because people in low power distance national cultures are socialized to have higher-order needs and do value intrinsically motivating and challenging jobs. (Huang & Van de Vliert, 2003, p. 84)

Thinking across cultures 2.1

Mapping Cultural Characteristics onto Maslow's Hierarchy of Needs

Examine the 'motivating factors' listed on the right-hand side. Try to map them onto the Maslow's need classification. For example, what need or needs does 'praise from the supervisor' *primarily* satisfy?

Next, try to map the 'cultural characteristics' on the left onto the needs. For example, if 'praise from the supervisor' satisfies esteem needs, then in which cultural context should we expect this need to be strong and require satisfaction to be motivating?

(Continued)

Cultural Characteristics

- Individualism / collectivism
- Power distance
- Uncertainty avoidance
- Performance orientation
- Future orientation
- Humane orientation
- Assertiveness
- Gender egalitarianism
- High-low context culture
- Particularism – universalism
- Fatalism

Maslow's Hierarchy of Needs

Self Actual ization

Esteem Needs
Self-esteem
Recognition
Status

Social Needs
Sense of belonging
Love

Safety Needs
Security
Protection

Physiological Needs
Hunger
Thirst

- Having power and authority
- Autonomy in my Job
- Awards for Superior Performance (e.g., medals of achievement)
- Benefits (health insurance, pension fund, option of company shares etc)
- Feedback on my performance
- Good interpersonal relations
- Close supervision/guidance
- Peaceful work environment
- Interesting work
- Job security (long-term employment in the company)
- Challenging job
- Meaningful work
- Opportunity for creativity
- Opportunity to make friends
- Opportunity to use various skills
- Participation in decision making
- Pay

Motivating Factors

- Opportunity for personal growth and development
- Praise from co-workers
- Praise from supervisor
- Work in a prestigious company
- Sense of pride in work
- Opportunity for career advancement
- Recognition
- Responsibility in my job
- Sense of achievement
- Sense of belonging
- Use of company car
- Sense of contribution to society
- Work safety
- Financial stability
- Probability of getting rewards based on my performance
- Existence of goals
- Knowledge of what is expected from me

Other studies also showed that **empowerment** of employees to satisfy high-order needs was not successful to increase job satisfaction and work performance in high power-distance cultures such as China (Eylon and Au, 1999) and India (Robert et al., 2000). In such cultural contexts, satisfaction comes from close guidance and supervision.

It is found that satisfying lower-level needs also did not have the similar effect on employees in different countries. Russians were found to be motivated more than Swedish when their salary increased (Fey, 2005). This is expected in a country like Russia, where the social security system functions poorly and earnings are shared with ageing parents who receive very little pension: increased salary is the key to satisfy survival and safety needs for most Russians and their families. On the other hand, because they live in an affluent country, Swedish employees' motivation increased not as a function of salary increase, but as they were able to satisfy their higher-order needs, such as a pleasant work environment and an interesting job.

Herzberg's Motivation-Hygiene Theory

Herzberg suggested that factors that lead to job satisfaction and job dissatisfaction are different. According to the theory, factors related to the job content (e.g., autonomy, challenge, opportunity to learn and grow) are generally referred to as '**intrinsic factors**' or **motivators** which produce job satisfaction and, therefore, the motivation to perform. Factors related to the job context (e.g., safe work environment, pay, compensation package, supervision), are generally referred to as '**extrinsic factors**' or hygiene factors which do not produce job satisfaction and, therefore, do not motivate performance; but their absence is dissatisfying (see Video 2.1).

For example, working in a safe office environment is something that every employee should expect and feel entitled to. Therefore, it is not necessarily motivating. However, absence of safety would be highly demotivating, leading to employee dissatisfaction. Take another example of an office practice; one which enhances learning and growth, such as allowance of a day off at the end of each month to participate in a corporate social responsibility programme. When this new practice is introduced it is likely to have a motivational effect on employees, not only because it is associated with employee learning and growth, but also because it is something that employees would not take for granted as part of their contract with the organization. Presence of this programme would lead to employee satisfaction, but the absence of it would not necessarily lead to employee dissatisfaction. Herzberg's theory suggests that 'motivators' may become 'hygiene factors' after a while.

From a cross-cultural perspective, what is considered to be a hygiene factor in a particular cultural context may be a motivator in another, or vice versa. Can you think of a practice that is considered as hygiene, say, in low power distant cultural context, but a motivator in a high power distant cultural context? How about top managers' willingness to share strategic organizational goals and plans with supervisory-level employees? Information-sharing seems to be a standard managerial practice in egalitarian and participative cultures, which may not necessarily increase motivation. However, in a hierarchical culture where decision-making is centralized, sharing information with employees may demonstrate managers' trust and respect to employees, which may increase motivation.

In this section we will present research evidence to examine whether or not the two-factor model holds across cultures and whether or not factors that lead to job satisfaction and job dissatisfaction are the same in different cultural contexts.

There is a close correspondence between Herzberg's approach and Maslow's Hierarchy of Needs. The hygiene factors (i.e., extrinsic factors) correspond to Maslow's lower-order needs; whereas the motivators (i.e., intrinsic factors) correspond to Maslow's higher-order needs. Using this analogy, we can predict that Herzberg's theory has similar limitations in cross-cultural settings as Maslow's theory. Whereas the theory suggests that intrinsic factors are more motivating and satisfying than extrinsic ones, research in different cultural contexts does not support this assertion. Because satisfaction of lower-level needs is more critical to employees in economically less developed countries than satisfaction of higher-order needs, the presence of extrinsic factors does not decrease job dissatisfaction, as predicted by the theory, but increases job satisfaction. Similarly in collectivistic cultures, strong social ties with supervisors and colleagues (i.e., hygiene/extrinsic factors) would enhance job satisfaction (Hines, 1973).

Thinking across cultures 2.2

'Doing the Work with Little Thought and in a Clean Environment'

> I worked on a project in a small, developing island country. The project took place at a factory where electronic parts were assembled. Part of the project looked at ways to increase motivation. When asked why they continued to work for the firm, long-time employees said that it was because they could do their particular task with little thought while conversing with their coworker friends, that their supervisor helped them to do their jobs and that the factory was clean. When asked if rotating jobs would make the work more interesting, the answer was that they preferred to do the job they already knew well. When it was suggested that each person should check their own quality, the response was that the quality people knew that aspect and should continue to do their specialized job. Job variety, autonomy and feedback were essentially seen as being ineffective and would likely have been demotivating. Job significance did seem to provide a potential motivating tool; employees were most interested to know and see physical evidence, that the electronic parts they made were used in computers. (Punnett, 2004, pp. 144–5)
>
> *(Continued)*

(Continued)

- What do you think is the cultural context this consultant's report comes from?
- Do you think that worker characteristics and the industry also matter in the ways in which employees are motivated; and if yes, how?
- What other institutional or individual differences play a role in what motivates employees?

Brislin and colleagues (2005) found that Herzberg's distinction between hygiene factors and motivators held in Japan and that three of the top five motivating factors were intrinsic whereas four of the bottom five were extrinsic. Authors suggested that the similarity between the US and Japanese findings was mainly due to the level of economic development that was enjoyed by both countries. Authors also attribute the similarity to the changing values and organizational practices in Japan.

Huang and Van de Vliert (2003) also demonstrated that intrinsic factors were associated with job satisfaction in economically advanced countries with strong welfare systems. The authors suggests that overall, in poorer countries, in less individualistic countries and in countries with larger power distance, intrinsic job characteristics (e.g., challenge, recognition, autonomy, feedback) are less closely related to job satisfaction than extrinsic job characteristics (e.g., pay, job security and working conditions). However, not only culture but also the level of economic development influences the relationship between motivators and job satisfaction (see also research of Furnham et al., 1994 in 41 countries arriving at a similar conclusion).

Moneta (2004) found that Chinese employees reported the highest level of intrinsic motivation in conditions requiring low challenge and high skill level. The author attributes this to the influence of Taoism in the Chinese cultural system which emphasizes prudence, interconnectedness and emotional moderation based on trust and mutual respect.

An interesting study conducted by De Voe and Iyengar (2004) showed that North American managers perceived their employees to be motivated more extrinsically than intrinsically, whereas Asian managers perceived their employees to be motivated equally by both intrinsic and extrinsic factors and Latin American managers perceived their employees to be motivated more intrinsically than extrinsically. Furthermore, North American managers assigned high performance evaluation scores to those employees whom they believed to be intrinsically motivated, whereas Asian managers assigned high scores to those who are both intrinsically and extrinsically motivated. The authors claim that the cultural value of individualism played a role in explaining North American managers' positive evaluations of those who are unique and stand out in the crowd. Asian culture values conformity to the norm and does not necessarily punish those who are like others (i.e., employees extrinsically motivated). Hofstede (1983) explains this through the uncertainty avoidance dimension of culture. Accordingly in low uncertainty-avoiding cultures like North American culture, deviance is not treated as a threat, whereas in high uncertainty-avoiding cultures like the ones in Asia, deviant persons and ideas are not tolerated. Asian culture also values a holistic approach to life and considers personal as well as situational demands (e.g., financial needs) in evaluating employees.

British and Nigerian employees reported different factors leading to high and low job satisfaction (Adigun and Stephenson, 1992). Nigerians included more extrinsic factors in their accounts of positive job experiences (e.g., feeling good and working hard), compared to their British counterparts who included mostly intrinsic factors. For example, promotion in the job was stated to be important by only 6 per cent of British employees, as opposed to 44 per cent of Nigerian employees. Among intrinsic factors, 90 per cent of British employees reported sense of achievement to be a factor underlying positive job attitude, whereas only 40 per cent of Nigerian workers did so. The work itself was associated with positive job attitudes by 77 per cent British and 30 per cent of Nigerian employees.

In a study with Zambian workers, both intrinsic and extrinsic factors were cited as impacting motivation and demotivation (Machungwa and Schmitt, 1983). For example, the most frequently cited motivating factors were as follows: work that was not too much (i.e., having too much work to do) or not too difficult, work that was interesting and important, recognition, promotion and pay. The most frequently cited demotivating factors were discrimination and favouritism, bad interpersonal relationships, low pay, supervisors not caring about employee well-being and lack of promotion opportunities.

Aycan and Fikret-Pasa (2003) found that both intrinsic and extrinsic factors were associated with motivation in Turkey. The top ranking motivating factors were having power and authority, a peaceful work environment, opportunity for career development, and pay and autonomy, whereas the lowest in the ranking factors were close supervision and guidance, feedback on performance and sense of belonging.

One of the most important managerial implications of Herzberg's theory is the need for job enrichment and empowerment (i.e., intrinsic factors) to enhance motivation. There is research evidence demonstrating the influence of cultural context on the extent to which job enrichment and empowerment are provided. For example, Aycan et al. (2000) compared human resource management practices in ten countries including Canada, US, Germany, Israel, Romania, Russia, China, Turkey, Pakistan and India and found that in cultures high on fatalism managers assume that human nature is not malleable and did not provide job enrichment and empowerment. In other words, managers who were socialized by the cultural value of fatalism (i.e., importance of believing in fate and control by higher-order forces) assumed that people were born with certain characteristics that could not be easily changed. Based on this assumption managers felt that providing job enrichment

'And this one is for my greatest achievement —
raising a family and staying married for 40 years!'

**Cartoon 2.1   Different approaches to achievement in life. Copyright © Randy
Glasbergen.**

and empowerment would be pointless. It was also found that in collectivistic cultures, managers assumed that they had obligations to fulfil towards their employees and engaged in empowering supervision. The importance of these two values can be seen in the writings of Confucius: 'In the world there are two great decrees: one is fate and the other is duty' (Confucius, the Analects: Book III, cited in Els, 2012).

McClelland's Typology of Needs

McClelland (1961) suggested that individuals can be grouped into three categories according to their dominant needs: achievement, affiliation and power. Those with a high **achievement motive** derive satisfaction from achievement as well as from the relentless effort in pursuit of it. Those with a high affiliation motive, on the other hand, derive satisfaction from warm and friendly relationships: they make considerable effort to be sensitive to others' feelings and to conform to their wishes. Power motivation refers to the individuals' desire to influence and control others or to have a strong impact on others.

McClelland suggested that of the three motives, achievement motivation was the most important associated with high performance. In this section we will review research evidence and discuss whether the triadic model of needs is applicable in non-US cultures and whether achievement motivation is considered to be the key for high performance across cultures.

An early study (Hines, 1973) provided supporting evidence for McClelland's typology of needs, in particular the achievement motive, in New Zealand, an English-speaking Anglo-Saxon country with a culture of low uncertainty avoidance and masculinity. Implicit in these cultural dimensions are willingness to take risk and a desire to achieve a visible success – factors most conducive to the achievement motive (Hofstede, 1983).

Masculinity cultural orientation is characterized by an achievement ideal, sympathy for the successful achiever, excelling and trying to be the best, whereas femininity orientation (i.e., low masculinity) is characterized by a service ideal, sympathy for the unfortunate and levelling with others, rather than trying to be better than them. Given the wide range of countries on the masculinity–femininity continuum, it is hard to imagine that achievement motivation is a dominant motivation in all cultural contexts.

The term 'achievement' may have different connotations in different cultures (see Video 2.2): 'The word *achievement* is hardly translatable into any other language (than English)' (Hofstede, 1983, p. 67) – as we can see in the following examples: The Thais closely relate success to respect for others and tradition (Yu and Yang, 1994); continuity in family tradition is more highly praised in Japan than the attainment of individual achievements (DeVos, 1973); for the Chinese, achievement motivation is in essence the contribution to the social group and the fulfilment of the expectations of the family and the social group (Pusey, 1977). Chinese businessmen reported the factors that motivate them to be 'glorifying the family and ancestors', 'heightening family reputation', 'fulfilling filial piety' (Chen, 1989). Yu and Yang (1994) argued that the 'individual-oriented achievement motivation' scale, developed in North America contains items such as 'I prefer to follow my own will to do the right thing rather than take my parents' opinions into account' is inappropriate and misleading in collectivistic cultures: they developed a scale which focused on the 'social-oriented achievement motivation' with items such as: 'The major goal in my life is to work hard to achieve something which will make my parents proud of me' (see 'Thinking across cultures 2.3.').

Achievement orientation was investigated in five countries: US, Netherlands, Israel, Hungary and Japan by Sagie et al. (1996). Similarities were found in regards to the structure of achievement motivation but differences were found in regards to the strength of it. The more individualistic orientation a person adopted in a given culture, the higher the achievement motivation they tended to have. The findings of the study suggested two types of achievement motivation: personal – the need for personal success, and collective – the need for group success which cannot be achieved without teamwork: 'nothing of consequence occurs as a result of individual effort; everything important in life happens as a result of teamwork and collective effort' (Ouchi, 1981, p. 50).

Thinking across cultures 2.3

What is your Primary Orientation Towards Achievement?

Put the appropriate number from the following scale in the spaces at the beginning of each statement.

1	2	3	4	5
Strongly Disagree	Disagree	Neutral	Agree	Strongly Agree

Socially Oriented Achievement Motivation (SOAM)

1. _____ In order not to disappoint my parents, I always try to do what they expect.
2. _____ I study hard because teachers usually praise the students who study hard.
3. _____ I often wonder whether my current performance has reached my parents' standards.
4. _____ If I cannot do better than others I would feel that I couldn't face my elders.
5. _____ Before I do anything, I would first consider whether my own goal fits my parent's expectations.
6. _____ When teachers praise other classmates, I feel that I should work harder.
7. _____ I wish to know how others evaluate my performance.
8. _____ I want to try to achieve what the general public values.
9. _____ I often try to do something to show to others that I am constantly improving.
10. _____ I would not feel a sense of achievement if I finished a job and no one knew about it.

Individually Oriented Achievement Motivation (IOAM)

1. _____ I usually wonder whether my present performance has reached my own standards.
2. _____ After finishing a job I like to evaluate it according to my own standards.
3. _____ The goals I pursue in life are determined by me.
4. _____ The reason I like studying is because of the knowledge I gain from learning.
5. _____ I am willing to constantly work hard in order to reach personal success.
6. _____ I feel a sense of achievement when I complete a job, even if no one else knows about it.
7. _____ No matter what other people might think, I will try my best to do what I consider valuable.

(Continued)

(Continued)

8. _____ I have a very clear standard on how to evaluate my own performance when I finish a task.
9. _____ Attaining a high level of education is not for glorification of my ancestors but for my own knowledge and interests.
10. _____ Whether a person has high or low achievement should be judged by themselves.

Source: selected items from Yang and Yu (1988, cited in Chang, Wong and Teo, 2000, pp. 60–63)

Calculate your scores on both scales by adding up the numbers you assign to each item. Then reflect on your 'achievement orientation': is it socially- or individually-oriented?

• To what extent does your cultural background play a role in your scores vis-à-vis your age, gender, personality, upbringing, work experiences and so on?

Equity Theory

In its most fundamental sense, **equity** means fairness or being treated fairly. According to the Equity Theory (Adams, 1965) an employee brings to the job what they perceive are their set of inputs and expects for them a set of outcomes. The employee will determine the equity or fairness of the outcomes by comparing the ratio of their outcomes to inputs to the ratio of a 'relevant other person'. What motivates employees is to restore equity when it is distorted and to maintain the balance among input:outcome ratios of employees.

As the perception of the concept of 'fairness' is most critical to motivation, equity theory is one of the few theories of motivation that has been subjected to extensive cross-cultural replications. The cumulative findings from cross-cultural research have been summarized in several meta-analyses. In this section, we will discuss the applicability of the basic principles of the equity theory across cultures by addressing the following questions:

1. Is equity the primary motivating principle of reward allocation across different cultural contexts?
2. How do cultures differ in their perception of what constitutes inputs, outcomes and referent groups?
3. What do people do in different cultural contexts to restore equity when it is distorted?

Reward allocation: Equity, equality, need?

The first question has received the most research attention. Early studies asserted that equity principle in distributing rewards had limited motivating utility in non-US contexts (e.g., Gergen et al., 1980) and that employees had a tendency to prefer **equality** and need principles more than they did the equity principle (e.g., Chen, 1995). However, later studies yielded mixed results, as follows:

1. Equity was preferred by employees in individualistic cultures, whereas equality was preferred by employees in collectivistic cultures, especially towards in-group members – family, close friends and relatives (Sama and Papamarcos, 2000);
2. Reward allocation preference was not related to individualism–collectivism (Fischer and Smith, 2003).

The role of the contextual factors in these preferences may explain the contradictory findings. For example, Leung (1997) found that if the reward allocator was also the reward receipient (e.g., they are a member in the team), then there is a preference for equality in collectivistic cultures; whereas if the reward allocator is not a recipient of rewards (e.g., an external agent), then equity would be preferred in both cultures – individualistic and collectivistic. Chen et al. (1998) showed equity was preferred by both Americans and Hong Kong Chinese when employees did not work interdependently and the goal was to increase productivity, whereas equality was preferred when employees worked interdependently and the goal was to increase solidarity.

Fischer and Smith (2003) showed that cultural dimension of power distance was more important than individualism–collectivism to predict individuals' preferences of equity over equality. Equity is preferred in high power-distance cultures, whereas equality is preferred in low power distance cultures. They also found that Hofstede's masculinity dimension was correlated strongly with the preference of equity, while femininity correlated strongly with the preference for equality. Fey (2005) compared Russian and Swedish employees and found that Russians are less motivated by equitable environments, compared to Swedish employees, mainly because they feel uncomfortable with the possibility of losing power enjoyed by the middle management cadres. Only a few studies focused on need as a reward distribution criterion. Fischer (2004) reported cross-cultural differences in the need-based allocation of rewards and resources. People had a preference for need-based distribution in conditions of high unemployment and high collectivism.

In an interesting study comparing American and Russian employees' preferences to use need, equity and equality in reward allocation Giacobbe-Miller and Miller (1995) prepared scenarios describing a situation in which a work unit was successful in generating a surplus and the manager decided to distribute money to five employees in the unit as a bonus. Employee 1 produced more than others on average; he was married with two young children and his wife was also working in the same factory. Employee 2 was a single woman with three small children; she was an average performer. Employee 3 was a single 20-year-old man living with his parents. He was also an average performer. Employee 4 was a young single woman living with her parents; she was an exceptional performer. Employee 5 was a 60-year-old man with a disabled wife. He had two children, both of whom were married with families of their own. He was an average performer. *What would you think should be the criterion to distribute the surplus among these 5 employees?* The study found that 59 per cent of the American subjects reported that the bonus should be distributed on the basis of equity, followed by equality (31 per cent) and need (10 per cent). On the other hand, only 8 per cent of the Russian subjects preferred equity, 36 per cent equality and 55 per cent need. All but 3 Russian subjects stated that need should be the sole criterion, whereas only 3 American subjects held the same opinion. The following excerpts from participants of the study reveal the rationale for differential preferences (Giacobbe-Miller and Miller, 1995, p. 180).

> I grew up in the socialist system and it was a slogan that 'children are the flowers of life'. But I know how much these flowers cost to their mothers. (Russian subject)

> The productivity and relations in the work unit depend on the family conditions. If you improve the family condition, productivity will increase. (Russian subject)

> I allocated the dollars according to the keyboards assembled because the original purpose of the bonus was to award exceptional work. It would be unfair to those who did an exceptional work if we award the bonus because of need. (American subject)

> The three top performers deserve the money because they worked hard and do a better than average job. If the other employees see that you get awarded for good work, they will be motivated to do better. I would not give the money out by need because it is a company not a welfare program. (American subject)

What is considered to be the input, outcome and referent group?

There are important cross-cultural differences in the ways people consider what constitutes inputs, outcomes and referent groups. Inputs are employees' perception of contributions in the exchange relationship and outcomes are their receipts from the exchange in the work context. In the original theory inputs typically include effort, education, skills, seniority, experience, intelligence and outcomes include pay, promotion, benefits and status symbols. What about other criteria counted as input, say, in high power distant cultures that would warrant promotion for example? Consider two employees with similar performance scores and training records over the years. Who is more likely to be promoted to the next level: one with 'family ties' with the president of the organization or the other without such ties? How about seniority, age, social class, good character and loyalty as inputs? What can be valued as outcomes other than pay, promotion and benefits in other cultural contexts? How about praise from the supervisor as an outcome in the equity equation; what would be the cultural context that considers it as a valued outcome?

Thinking across cultures 2.4

Valued Inputs and Outcomes in Cultural Context

Inputs	Cultural Context	Outcomes

Inputs

Age
Gender
Job performance
Tenure
Effort
Ethnicity or religion
Loyalty
Good character
Trustworthiness
Close ties with the authorities
Socio-economic status
Knowledge, skills, abilities
Family background
Reputation of the college graduated from

Cultural Context

▲ Individualism / collectivism
▲ Power distance
▲ Uncertainty avoidance
▲ Performance orientation
▲ Future orientation
▲ Humane orientation
▲ Assertiveness
▲ Gender egalitarianism
▲ High-low context culture
▲ Particularism – universalism
▲ Fatalism

Outcomes

Power and authority
Autonomy
Awards for superior performance
Peaceful work environment
Interesting work
Job security
Challenging job
Opportunity for creativity
Participation in decision making
Salary increase
Praise from supervisor
Sense of pride in work
Recognition
Promotion in the job
Childcare benefits
Flexible work hours

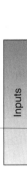

(Continued)

(Continued)

- What do you think would be the valued inputs and valued outcomes in various cultural contexts? Please try to add more inputs and outcomes to the list, considering a wide range of diverse cultural and organizational contexts.
- Do you think there are individual differences in the ways inputs and outcomes are valued? If yes, how?
- Do you think differences among individuals are wider or narrower than differences across cultures (i.e., whether within-cultural differences are larger than between-cultural differences)?

Seniority and education are emphasized more than performance as important inputs in Korea (Hundley and Kim, 1997). Gómez and colleagues (2000) found that in collectivistic cultures, employee's behaviours that contribute to the maintenance of harmony and enhancement of team environment are valued more than in individual-istic cultures. Hence in collectivistic cultures these behaviours – i.e., helping others and maintaining good interpersonal relationships in work environment – are regarded as more important than job performance (see also Bolino and Turnley, 2008). In high power-distance cultures, seniority, age and social class are regarded as inputs that deserve to be rewarded by outcomes such as promotion. In the exchange relationship, loyalty, respect and adherence to social norms are also considered to be inputs which need to be suitably rewarded (Fadil et al., 2005).

What is perceived to be a valued outcome may also differ across cultures. In col-lectivistic cultures, valued outcomes may include good interpersonal relationships, long-term employment and respect and recognition from the supervisor (Fadil et al., 2005). In high power-distance cultures, people expect to earn status symbols (e.g., a bigger office, company car, job title) in exchange for inputs (e.g., hard work or loyalty).

Who is considered to the referent group depends on the cultural context to a certain extent. According to Bolino and Turnley (2008), cross-cultural differences occur in three ways. First, in high power distant cultures, employees are unlikely to consider their high-level managers as their referent group, because they accept and expect their managers, by virtue of their status, to have more privileges. Second, in individualistic cultures, employees consider those with the most similar jobs as their referent group. In collectivistic cultures employees are also concerned with the fair treatment of their group members (e.g., the team members in the work unit); and thereby may also be involved in comparisons between their groups and other groups inside or outside of the organization. Accordingly, when they are evaluating the fairness of their own input:outcome ratio, they also consider the same for the in-groups. Their satisfaction not only depends on how *they* fare, but also how their colleagues in the in-group fare in the comparison. Third, employees in past-oriented cultures (value the past experiences, take past precedents as guide) use the past referents for comparison, while those focused on the present use the current referents.

How to restore equity?

What happens when the equity is distorted and employees feel unfairness in the input:outcome ratio comparisons in the organization? Let us first discuss reactions towards inequity. Some people have a strong preference for equitable situations; they are called 'equity sensitives', whereas others prefer slightly inequitable situations. Those referred to as 'benevolents' prefer a higher ratio of inputs to outcomes in relation to the comparison person. They can be considered to have an altruistic attitude – they feel content in knowing that they have made a valuable contribution even though they have not been rewarded equitably for this (Wheeler, 2002). On the other hand, 'entitleds' prefer to have higher outcome to input ratio than the referent. They are concerned more with receiving than giving (Wheeler, 2002). There are few cross-cultural studies guided by the general assumption that collectivistics are benevolents and individualistics are entitleds. There are mixed results reported in the literature. In line with the expectations, Chinese employees were found to be benevolents, whereas the British and French respondents were found to be entitleds (Fok et al., 1996). In another study (Allen et al., 2005), Japanese workers were found to be more entitlement-oriented than the Americans. However, Americans in the same study were more willing than Japanese to ask for a salary rise to restore inequity in the under-payment situation.

In reaction to inequity, both Americans and Koreans were found to feel anger in response to an under-reward situation (i.e., distortion of equity to the *disadvantage* of the person) (Westerman et al., 2007). However, in response to an overreward situation (i.e., distortion of equity to the *advantage* of the person), Americans were less angry, compared to Koreans. When there is an inequitable situation, Koreans were more concerned to restore equity compared to Americans, either by changing their own behaviour or asking their partners to change their behaviour. Americans took a passive stand with regard to equity restoration, rather than doing something to correct the situation. They reported losing interest in the relationship and decreasing their liking of the partner. Koreans, on the other hand, did not decrease their liking of the partner despite their feeling of anger. The findings overall indicate that compared to individualistic cultures, people in collectivistic cultures are more concerned about restoring the equity to save the relationship. Towards this end, people in collectivistic cultures tend to resort to cognitive restoration of equity (i.e., restoring the equity in one's mind by thinking that the situation must have been deserved for reasons that are not apparent to the individual). The underlying rationale for this approach is a concern that taking any action to correct the situation would harm the relationship (Bolino and Turnley, 2008). The other rationale could be that the fatalistic beliefs in a culture would lead to accepting the inequities as they are (Bolino and Turnley, 2008), in the hope that equity will be established one day, if not in the short term, then in the distant future (Weick et al., 1976).

Thinking across cultures 2.5

Reacting to Inequity and Restoring Equity

You work for a large financial institution as a financial analyst and have been there for six years. In terms of background, you have a degree from a large state university and have done a little graduate work in the financial area. You have an acquaintance, Pat, who has a similar background and years of experience and who also works for the institution. You are able to learn some additional background information about Pat and the situation in general. Please indicate your satisfaction level for each situation described below.

	Very satisfied	Satisfied	Indifferent	Dissatisfied	Very dissatisfied
1. You and Pat work harder than most financial analysts. However, Pat is paid significantly more than you and the industry average.					
2. You and Pat are paid about the same and less than the industry average, but Pat works fewer hours than you.					
3. You and Pat are working significantly harder than the average but Pat is being paid a lower salary than you and the average analyst.					
4. You and Pat are working significantly less than the average analyst. You are being paid significantly less than the average and Pat is being paid significantly more.					
5. You and Pat are working a lot less than the average analyst and are being paid a lot more than the average analyst makes.					

(Continued)

(Continued)

Source: Chhokar, Zhuplev, Fok and Hartman (2001, pp. 94–6).

- How do you think your satisfaction level would have changed if your acquaintance was Sanjay, Xiaoyun, or Ari? Do you think the cultural background and the gender of the acquaintance would make a difference in your satisfaction level?
- What would you do to restore equity in these situations?
- Pick two situations and discuss the similarities and differences in the strategies you prefer with one of your colleagues/classmates.

Expectancy Theory

Expectancy theory (Vroom, 1964) holds that employees are motivated when they believe that their behaviour will enhance the probability of desired outcomes. Magnitude of motivation is determined by the product of the three critical elements in the theory: (1) expectancy: the perception of the probability to meet the performance standards if enough effort is exerted, (2) instrumentality: the perception of the probability to receive the outcomes as a result of achieving the performance standards, and (3) valence: the desirability of the outcomes associated with high performance. An early test of the theory showed that the motivational force score predicted by the theory was associated with effort and performance outcomes of sales personnel in both the US and Japan (Matsui and Terai, 1975). However, more recent research shed doubt to the cross-cultural validity of the original theory and its three elements.

Let us start with the first element in the theory: expectancy. Do people everywhere have a similar propensity to believe that if they put in enough effort they will perform at the desired level? It seems not. There are a number of assumptions underlying the belief that 'I will perform well if I put in enough effort'. These are that: (1) it is the *individual* whose effort is important for performance, (2) the individual has the control of events in life – therefore it is *up to* them to meet high performance standards and (3) the individual *rationally* evaluates the likelihood of achieving performance goals and *chooses* the ones which will be worth expending effort on.

As Punnett (2004) aptly puts it:

In many parts of the world the context is essentially reverse: the *group* is more important than the individual for performance outcomes, the world is *controlled* by those in position of power and by the spirit realm and people's thinking is *circular* (rather than linear and rational). (p. 152).

Jackson (2004) also challenges the individual-centric assumption in the expectancy theory:

> Individualists perceive performance as a personal quality. Therefore, if a person does not expend any effort and if he or she does not have the ability, they will not see performance. However, the collectivists see performance as a group quality. It is therefore possible to show performance if one member of the group has the ability and other members expend a lot of effort. (p. 131)

People also vary in their belief in how much control they have in their life. Adler (1991) states that

> Most American managers believe that 'where there is a will, there is a way'... But for example, Moslem managers believe that things will happen only if God wills them to happen; Latin American managers believe that it is important to be from the right family and social class; Hong Kong Chinese executives believe that there is an element of *joss*, or luck, involved in all transactions. (p. 164)

Geiger and colleagues (1998) tested the expectancy theory in ten cultures: Australia, Canada, Hong Kong, India, Indonesia, Malaysia, Mexico, Oman, Singapore and the US. They found that individualism and long-term orientation (i.e., importance of planning) were positively associated with the expectancy belief, whereas power distance and uncertainty avoidance were negatively associated with it. More specifically, people were found to believe that effort would lead to performance if they also believed in the importance of planning and individual control and accountability. Whereas, people's belief in the effort–performance association was less strong if they lived in cultures where decision-making power is invested in those in authority rather than themselves, and where there are uncertainties in the environment that prevent people from feeling confident about the usefulness of spending effort to achieve the targeted performance levels.

Emery and Oertel (2006) found that there was a strong correlation between German employees' belief that it is possible to perform well when high effort is exerted and their belief that working closely with their supervisor is an important factor to successfully accomplish a task. In other words, German employees (coming from a power distance culture) believe that effort would lead to high performance when employees had close working relationships with their supervisors.

Cultural context plays a role also on the instrumentality component of the theory (i.e., the expectation to receive the outcomes based on high performance). Research showed that performance–reward contingency is low in cultures that are high on power distance and fatalism (Aycan et al., 2000). Furthermore, rewards are based on criteria other than performance in some cultural contexts. For example, in high power-distance cultures reward allocation is based on criteria, such as seniority or good relationships with top management (e.g., Hui and Luk, 1997; Leung, 1997). In countries with high level of uncertainty avoidance, seniority-based compensation is preferred because it is based on specific criteria such as length of service, which being objectively determined does not cause uncertainty. On the other hand, considerable uncertainty is inherent in performance and skill-based compensation, which is more preferred in countries with low uncertainty avoidance (Schuler and Rogovsky, 1998). Performance-based pay is used widely in individualistic cultures, whereas group-based rewards are preferred in collectivistic cultures (Gluskinos, 1988). The characteristics of collectivistic culture are more conducive to the equality principle; hence, the compensation/reward systems in these cultures reflect the equality principle. For this reason, the wage differential is narrow even among the lowest- and highest-ranking officials in collectivistic cultures, whereas it is very high in individualistic and performance-oriented cultures (Easterby-Smith, et al., 1995; Huo and von Glinow, 1995).

CASE 2.1

Does the performance-based incentive system motivate employees?

A medium-sized organization in Indonesia has recently introduced an incentive system and announced that employees' monthly income will comprise the base salary plus the commission. The top management was hoping that employees' motivation would increase by the newly introduced 'pay for performance' system. After all, they had the opportunity to earn more. However, the reverse has happened; and here is why from the perspectives of the employees.

> I have been a loyal and dedicated employee of this organization for six years. Imagine a new comer earning more than me, just because his so-called numbers exceed mine. This is not fair!

> I have two children in school. With this new system I can potentially make enough money to send one or both to a private school. But given the uncertainties in our economic and political situation in the country, no one can guarantee the continuity of my income. In the new pay-for-performance system I can earn a lot one month and I can earn half of it the next month. I don't like to live with this kind of uncertainty.

Equality principle also applies to bonus schemes (Björkman and Lu, 1999; Easterby-Smith et al., 1995). Quinn and Rivoli (1991) argue that bonuses based on organizational performance coupled with employment guarantee and amicable labour relations yield a high propensity to innovation in Japanese firms. In addition to salary and bonuses, employee ownership plans are popular in North American firms. Schuler and Rogovsky (1998) found that employee share options and stock ownership plans are more prevalent in cultures that are low on power distance. Profit-sharing and saving plans were associated with intention to stay in the organization of Mexican employees in American-owned plants in Mexico, while other pay forms (e.g., productivity bonus, overtime pay) were not associated with turnover intention (Miller et al., 2001).

Promotion is usually considered to be an important outcome of good performance. However, promotion of an individual to a higher position may mean separating the individual from their work team, increasing the jealousies of others who did not get the promotion, having extra responsibilities and therefore working longer hours and taking risks in one's job. This is what 'promotion' may represent for some employees in collectivistic, high power-distance or uncertainty-avoidant cultures (Adler, 1991).

Let us move on to the last component in the model, valence of outcomes. We have already discussed the influence of cultural context on what are perceived as valued outcomes. Cultural context determines what is regarded as a reward, based on salient needs and values. For example, reward programmes to high-performing employees may not be effective in collectivistic cultures where gratification of an *individual* employee induces resentment among the peers in the work team. The discussion on reward allocations in the cross-cultural literature mostly focuses on economic rewards. However, non-economic rewards that satisfy needs for affiliation and recognition may be more satisfying in collectivist and high power-distance cultures (Mendonça and Kanungo, 1994). Kim et al. (1990) posit that 'social rewards' such as friendship outside the working group are more salient in Korea and Japan than in the US.

> The Linux and Toyota Production System (TPS) communities dissociate money from key transactions. Yet despite weak financial incentives, they command a level of motivation higher than that found in conventional environments … Compared with their counterparts in the rest of the auto industry, TPS workers enjoy fewer controls, greater encouragement of individual initiative, fewer metrics attached to individual performance and louder peer applause. Professional and corporate pride, not Toyota's honorarium, was the payoff for the team at Kyoritsu Sangyo when it delivered the first batch of P-valves. The same pride is felt by a junior assembly-line worker when he is trusted by his peers to experiment with process improvements and stop the line if something goes wrong. (Evans and Wolf, 2005, p. 42)

The above quotation provides an excellent example of what motivates employees in a specific cultural and industrial context. As illustrated in this example, in Japan and in high-tech industries the key motivators include autonomy on the job, encouragement of initiative and risk-taking and pride in the work, rather than attachment of incentives to individual performance outcomes.

CASE 2.2

Expectancy theory applied in China

'The change and development of organizational management in China, along with increasing exposure to alternative management models, worker preferences for empowerment, as well as for procedural and distributive justice, have the potential to increase, enhancing the applicability of Western theories such as the expectancy theory.

It is possible that expectancy theory concepts may be relevant in certain regions and economic sectors. For example, companies located in the coastal regions may be more ready for these concepts relative to those in inland cities, because of the more rapid rate of development in the coastal regions and the greater presence of Western firms, facilitating a more rapid diffusion of practices and values. With regard to economic sectors, in industries where innovative thinking, creativity and quick response times among employees are desirable performance management built on the expectancy theory may well be effective. Haier Limited Corporation is an example (Yi and Ye, 2003) of a hybrid performance management system that includes individualized output-based incentives alongside evaluations of teamwork and obedience.

Some China-based companies may employ practices that send mixed messages to employees from an expectancy perspective. For example, many firms are reforming their evaluation system to incorporate more merit pay or contingent rewards (Satow and Wang, 1994). Some enterprises have two parallel evaluation systems – one for employees who joined the company prior to the reform and another for the new employees. The old system emphasizes privileges associated with seniority, applied uniformly and not tied to performance. The new system provides for enriched tasks, results-oriented challenges and higher compensation. While such a dual system may be less acceptable in a Western context where uniform application of practices is paramount, Chinese employees may tolerate it because of high power-distance, deference to authority, holistic and communal perspective, long-term orientation and a lower degree of uncertainty avoidance (Hofstede, 2001). Chinese employees have the expectation that fairness will prevail in the long term.'

Source: Zhang et al. (2006, pp. 289–90).

Goal-setting Theory

The core of the goal-setting theory (Locke, 1978) is that employees are motivated when they have clearly set goals that are *specific, challenging* and *acceptable*. We will review cross-cultural research evidence under two headings: the characteristics of goals to motivate people and the method of goal-setting. The theory of goal-setting is based on the assumptions of individualistic cultures. As such, the basic recommendation of the theory for *goal characteristics* is that goals should be specific and challenging, and for *goal-setting methodology* is that goals should be set participatively, so that employees accept the goals and feel committed to them.

Are there cross-cultural variations in the attributes of goals that motivate people? Although few studies have directly examined this question, based on what we know from cross-cultural research on values and needs, the answer seems to be yes. In a variety of countries such as those in the Caribbean, Australia, Israel, Sri Lanka and so on, specific and challenging goals are found to be more effective in increasing performance compared with statements such as 'do your best' (Punnett, 2004). However, it has been suggested that specific and challenging goals may not be welcome in collectivistic and feminine cultures, because such goals have the potential to increase competition in the workplace (Punnett, 2004). Furthermore, people in high collectivistic cultures may resist challenging goals, fearing that they may not reach the goals and, thereby, lose face to their in-group, including people outside of the work context such as family, relatives, friends and neighbours. Indeed, Kurman (2001) found that in the collectivistic and high power-distance cultures, setting goals with moderate difficulty levels was more motivating than setting goals that are challenging.

People who have a strong achievement need (e.g., individualistic cultures) are more likely to be motivated by specific and challenging goals. For those with strong affiliation needs (e.g., collectivistic cultures) this goal attribute is likely to be less motivating. People in a collectivistic culture may also resent the individually set goals because it may bring individual differences to the surface and give people individual accountabilities. Finally, in fatalistic cultures goals may have limited motivational value: 'Where people feel that they have little control over their environment, the idea of setting a specific target may seem foolish at best and possibly thought of as going against God's will' (Punnett, 2004, p. 150).

Grouzet and colleagues (2005) compared the preferred goal type of employees in 15 different countries. The goals are classified in four categories that are derived from the combination of two dimensions: the intrinsic vs. extrinsic dimension and the self-transcendence vs. physical self-dimension as primary goals in life. For example, in the category of self-transcendent and intrinsic goals there are spirituality and service to community, whereas in the category of physical self and extrinsic goals, there is financial success. The structure of goal categorization was similar across cultures, however the placement of goals was different. For instance, financial success as a goal in life was further from hedonism and closer to safety–physical health goals in poorer cultures than in the wealthier cultures. That is, financial success was the goal that served as the basis for survival in poorer cultures, self-actualization was the goal in wealthier ones. Another cross-cultural study which compared the work goals of employees from Singapore, Malaysia, India, Thailand, Brunei and Mongolia found that there were wide variations among Asian employees in their work goals (e.g., autonomy, variety, promotion, learning, salary). For example, 'opportunity to learn new things' was the most important goal for employees across the cultural, gender and job position categories. However, there were cross-cultural variations in some of the goals such as 'interesting work', where it was most important for India and Singapore and least important for Malaysia (Chatterjee and Pearson, 2002).

Does **participative goal-setting** motivate employees the most and do assigned goals (goals that are usually assigned by the management without participation from employees) motivate people the least? Again, this depends on the cultural context. Participative goal-setting increases the motivation of people in egalitarian cultural contexts. On the other hand, people do not have difficulty accepting and committing to assigned goals in hierarchical (Sue-Chan and Ong, 2002) and in paternalistic cultures, because in such cultures those in a position of power are assumed to know what is best for the employee (Aycan, 2006). The role of the cultural characteristics in determining whether participative goal-setting is more effective than assigned goals is illustrated by Erez and Earley (1987) in a comparative study between employees in Israel and the US. The study found that the Israelis performed lower than the Americans when the goals were under the assigned rather than the participative goal-setting condition. The authors replicated this study with different samples and found that lack of participation in goal-setting led to a lower level of commitment among the Israelis than among the Americans (Latham et al., 1988). In both studies, the Americans were found to be committed to goals that are either assigned or participatively set; whereas the Israelis were committed to goals only in the participative goal-setting condition. The authors concluded that the difference between US and Israel was due to the power distance experienced in these cultures. According to Hofstede's and GLOBE's data, the US is more hierarchical than Israel and therefore Americans find it easier than Israelis to commit to goals assigned by their supervisors. Participative leadership and decision-making in different cultural contexts are discussed in more detail in Chapter 5.

Job Characteristics Theory

According to the job characteristics theory (Hackman and Oldham, 1976), employees are motivated when their jobs are enriched. **Job enrichment** involves increasing autonomy, feedback, **skill variety, task significance and task identity**. Are these job characteristics equally effective in different cultural contexts for enhancing motivation and job satisfaction? (see Thinking across cultures 2.2, p. 29). Research suggests this is doubtful.

Job enrichment did not yield the same positive effect on motivation proposed by the original theory in all cultural contexts; more specifically, the characteristics of enriched jobs have been found to have differential impacts on psychological states and organizational attitudes of employees:

- Autonomy, feedback and skill variety had positive impacts on psychological and work outcomes in Netherlands, but had no or marginal impact in Bulgaria and Hungary (Roe and colleagues, 2000);
- Feedback had a marginally positive impact on employees' performance in Russia but not in Sweden (Fey, 2005);
- According to Aycan and colleagues (2000), managers in fatalistic cultures did not provide enriched jobs because they assumed that employee nature could not be changed; but, in collectivistic cultures, managers implemented job enrichment because they believed that doing so was their obligation to employees.

In the North American literature, having freedom and autonomy in one's job are considered to be critical factors motivating employees. However, there are important debates about the value of choice and its implications for intrinsic motivation. Iyengar and Lepper (1999) conducted a series of experiments with Anglo-American and Asian American subjects and found that Asian Americans' intrinsic motivation and performance were highest when trusted in-group members made choices for them. In contrast, Anglo-Americans had the highest intrinsic motivation when they had the autonomy to make choices for themselves. Schwartz (1994) reported a vast difference across cultures on their value of intellectual autonomy (i.e., self-direction) and affective autonomy (i.e., stimulation and hedonism). The top-ranking countries in his ranking of autonomy as a value included Anglo-Saxon countries with a high level of economic development (e.g., France, Switzerland, Germany, New Zealand) and the bottom of the ranking included those from the cluster of countries referred to as 'emerging economies' (e.g., Slovakia, Singapore, Estonia, Bulgaria).

Compared to other job characteristics, feedback on the job attracted the most attention from cross-cultural researchers. Culture has a bearing on the way in which feedback is given and received. Although feedback is very important in motivating employees, there are significant cross-cultural differences in the prevalence and method of giving and receiving feedback. For example, in collectivistic and high power-distance cultures, there is reluctance to seek feedback. The process is usually initiated by the superior who is trusted for their expertise and wisdom (Huo and Von Glinow, 1995). In collectivistic cultures, feedback is indirect, nonconfrontational, subtle and private (Fletcher and Perry, 2001); face-to-face performance interviews are extremely rare (Elenkov, 1998).

Cross-cultural research also sheds light on negative and positive feedback – on the way it is given and received. In diffuse cultures where the distinction between life and work space is blurred (Trompenaars, 1993), negative feedback on job performance is perceived as an attack on the person. For this reason, it is avoided to spare the employee from losing face (Seddon, 1987). In some organizations in the Philippines, two feedback forms are submitted; one to the HR department and the other to the employee: the employee version has a more positive tone. In collectivistic cultures, positive feedback on individual performance is not well received because it could disturb group harmony, especially when it is offered in public; and it may create jealousy and resentment among those who did not receive such feedback. Also, in collectivist cultures, when a manager praises their own employees it is perceived as self-serving; for this reason, positive feedback is generally expected to originate from the outside (Triandis, 1994). According to Bailey et al. (1997, p. 611), Japanese and Chinese employees did not take any initiative to seek feedback on individual performance because it was perceived as 'vulgar self-centeredness'. Clearly, in collectivistic cultures, feedback on *group* performance is more acceptable than that on individual performance. Moreover, high-context communication patterns prevail in collectivistic cultures (Gibson, 1997). In high-context communication patterns, feedback on performance can be embedded in contextual cues which provide indirect, implicit and subtle messages about performance and thereby prevent tension and conflicts that may arise as a result of direct and confrontational communication.

Finally, as illustrated by the following quotation, job enrichment for the group, rather than individual employee, enhances motivation in collectivistic cultures. Erez (2000) discusses why sociotechnical systems or autonomous work groups involving job enrichment at the group level by enhancing team autonomy, team responsibility, feedback on team performance and task meaningfulness should continue its existence in performance-driven organizations:

'The most famous sociotechnical project is that implemented in the Volvo auto plants in Kalmar and Uddevalla during the eighties. Although these plants were shut down in 1993–1994 due to poor markets and low capacity usage, they still serve as excellent examples of the benefits and limitations of autonomous work groups … The work was organized for teams. Each team was responsible for a particular portion of the car. The members had the opportunity to develop task identity by assuming responsibility for a specific portion of the work. In addition, all team members developed multiple skills that allowed them to rotate jobs and substitute for each other. A sense of responsibility was developed by self-inspections of product quality. This inspection also provided immediate feedback on quality performance and enhanced the work motivation and performance.' (Erez, 2000, p. 224)

Cross-cultural Considerations for Managers

The review of research on culture and motivation suggests that applicability of American theories may be limited, because they are based on the assumption that employees are primarily motivated by practices that would satisfy their personal needs and enhances their individual self-concept (Erez, 1997). As such, satisfaction and enhancement of the individual 'self' (as opposed to collective 'self') is at the core of these theories. The questions posed by the content and process theories, namely 'what motivates employees and how employees are motivated?' are therefore answered as 'whatever satisfies and enhances the individual's "self"'.

One source of cross-cultural differences is the way that 'self' is defined. In individualistic cultures, the *independent self* pervades and represents a person's view of what makes them unique. In collectivistic cultures the self is represented as the *interdependent self* and guided by the desire to achieve goals of the social group (e.g., family, organization) and fulfil obligations to the social group one feels one belongs to. For the interdependent self, achievement in one's job means getting the approval and recognition of esteemed and beloved people in one's life (e.g., family, supervisor or employer), fulfilling their expectations and not losing face to them. Some of our students in collectivistic cultures who did well in class tell us how relieved they felt because they did not lose face to us – their 'esteemed professors'. In the work context, 'personal attachment to the leader and ensuing obligation to him or her are the strongest motivators' (Markus and Kitayama, 1991, p. 240).

Another cross-cultural difference lies in the way **self-enhancement** is perceived. Self-enhancement and self-promotion are perceived negatively in collectivistic cultures (e.g., Yoshida et al., 1982). For example in job interviews, applicants find it difficult to talk about their competencies. Therefore work conditions (e.g., rewards, job enrichment) that would *primarily* enhance the individual's own self are not approved by the social group and do not act as a motivator. Let's consider a case in which the organization is in a financial crisis, the boss expects some compromise from employees, decides to appeal to the employees and ask for their hard work and support in difficult times. Which statement would be more motivating to employees in collectivistic countries: 'I ask you to work harder because we will all benefit from it at the end' or 'I ask you to work harder because those who work hard will be rewarded'? Most probably the former statement is more motivating than the latter.

A Korean expatriate in the US reported one of his culture shocks.

> The first morning in the office, I greeted a colleague by saying 'how are you?' He said 'I am great!' I thought I did not hear him well or maybe I asked a wrong question. But when others were saying the same thing in different times, I thought perhaps I was among people who were either really great or snobbish. Finally, I realized that it was just their style of communication. I am still annoyed with this statement. Whenever I hear it I feel like saying 'how can you be great all the time and even if you think you are great, how can you say it aloud in a shameless way?'

The reaction of the Korean expatriate shows how inappropriate self-enhancement and self-promotion appear in collectivistic cultures. Being better than others (i.e., being the nail that stands out) is not desirable and therefore not motivating. That is why employee of the month failed as a motivation tool in many collectivistic countries. Standing out in the social group for personal achievements may harm interpersonal

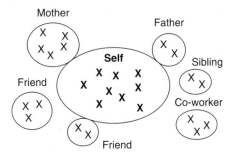

A. Independent View of Self

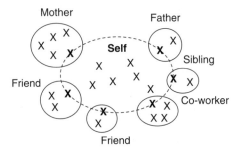

B. Interdependent View of Self

Figure 2.1 *Independent and Interdependent selves (Markus & Kitayama, 1991, p. 226)*

relationships and harmony in the group. That is why some employees who are nominated for this award turned it down! (See Case 1.1. in Chapter 1.)

Self-improvement (awareness of weakness and a desire to improve oneself) is a stronger motivator for employees in collectivistic cultures than self-enhancement. Heine and his colleagues (2001) conducted a series of studies to compare North American and Japanese students and employees. The findings were consistent and showed that Japanese worked harder after failure than after success. In contrast, Canadian and American subjects persisted more on tasks they succeeded in than the ones that they failed. Similar findings were obtained by other researchers (e.g., Kitayama et al., 1997). Incidences of success improve the self-esteem of Americans more strongly than incidences of failures decrease their self-esteem. In other words, success was associated to their self-esteem more strongly than was failure. On the other hand, for Japanese self-esteem decreased more in the failure situations than it would increase in the success situations. Failures lead to the desire to self-improve and motivate Japanese workers, whereas successes lead to self-enhancement and motivate Americans.

Let us offer some recommendations on how to motivate culturally diverse workforces.

- Always keep in mind that employees may have needs, values, preferences and goal priorities that may go against your assumptions of them. Remember, your assumptions about what employees want to be motivated are to a large extent based on your own cultural lenses. Keep an open mind and revisit your assumptions.
- If people's needs, values, preferences and goal priorities do not match with yours, don't misjudge them as lazy and lacking ambition or achievement motivation. Remember that they are also motivated to succeed but perhaps for different reasons (e.g., saving face, fulfilling obligations towards others, avoiding punishment).
- Make sure that there is a good fit between employees' values and that of the organization before making a hiring decision.
- Even though we offer generalizations about cross-cultural differences in this chapter, be aware that there are individual differences within each culture, especially when it comes to factors that motivate people. Avoid overgeneralizations based on cultural assumptions (e.g., all Mexicans are motivated by teamwork).
- Always 'take the pulse' of the workforce and tailor-make your motivational approach to fit the needs, values, preferences and goal priorities of culturally diverse employees. You can conduct anonymous surveys or arrange meetings to get a sense of their needs and expectations. However, while tailoring your motivational approach, be very careful to maintain *fairness* among employees.
- Don't just assume that certain motivational approaches (e.g., goal-setting) can never be applied in certain cultural contexts. Take the basic principle of the approach to heart (e.g., setting goals is important) and adopt it to the cultural context (e.g., what kind of goals, how to set goals).
- Don't forget that money is not always the best motivator (*see Video 2.3*). In some cultural contexts there are other factors that motivate employees more than money – even for the sales force!

The results of this study are quite consistent with prescriptions offered during our recent interviews of more than 20 American executives managing sales forces in Japan. That is, they consistently agreed that compensation systems used in the U.S. will not work in Japan. They confirmed that other than customary winter and summer bonuses, the variable portion of Japanese salesperson's pay is small, usually less than 5 percent. More than one manager advised that large commission portion of compensation would probably confuse and frustrate most Japanese sales representatives. Also, U.S. recognition practices such as 'salesperson of the month' tend to embarrass, not motivate the group oriented Japanese. One manager reported that treating the entire sales force to a special occasion such as a dinner works much better than individual recognition. Indeed, such advice from U.S. managers working in Japan, combined with the findings of systematic studies such as reported herein, strongly support the notion that sales management, perhaps more than other aspects of the marketing mix, must be localized. (Money and Graham, 1999, p. 169) (pp. 149–72)

- Share the responsibility of motivation with your employees! Remember that employees have the responsibility to motivate themselves or inform you about their needs, values, expectations, preferences and goal priorities, especially when there is high level of diversity in the workforce. We believe that the following advice on 'problem employees' is valid for all employees:

> After 30 years of studying business organizations and advising executives, I have concluded that ... you can't motivate these problem people: Only they themselves can. Your job is to create the circumstances in which their inherent motivation – the natural commitment and drive that most people have – is freed and channeled toward achievable goals. (Nicholson, 2003, p. 57) (pp. 57–65)

Chapter Summary

Motivating employees to engage in goal-directed behaviour and persist in that pursuit may be a challenge. The challenge is amplified when dealing with culturally diverse workforces. In this chapter we discuss the factors and processes leading to work motivation across different cultural contexts. Although need satisfaction is a key for motivating employees at work, cultural and socio-economic contexts determine the type and strength of needs. Satisfying social/belonging needs and safety needs (e.g., job security) are more important than satisfying esteem or self-actualization needs for employees in economically developing countries and those in collectivistic cultures. What is considered a 'hygiene' factor (e.g., training and development at all levels in the organization), say, in a performance-oriented culture may be a 'motivator' in hierarchical culture. Research shows that job enrichment and empowerment practices do not increase motivation and satisfaction in all cultural contexts to the same extent as they do in individualistic and performance-oriented contexts. 'Achievement motivation' is important in collectivistic cultures to the extent that achievements serve the society or meet the expectations of significant others (e.g., family, supervisor, colleagues). There are also cross-cultural differences in the perception of fairness of the ways resources are distributed (e.g., rewards, benefits, bonus). In individualistic cultures employees are motivated to the extent that valued outcomes are distributed according to the inputs (e.g., job performance), whereas in collectivistic cultures equal or need-based distribution are also perceived fair and motivating depending on the context (e.g., whether or not receipients are in-group members). Volatile socio-economic context or fatalistic cultural values limit the motivational potential of the expectation that 'efforts lead to desired outcomes'. In such contexts employees tend to believe that they do not have the full control of the work outcomes and are not strongly motivated to initiate goal-directed behaviour. Due to uncertainty and fatalism, challenging goals would also not motivate employees to the same extent as they motivate employees in economically developed and individualistic contexts. Finally, designing enriched jobs through increasing feedback, autonomy, skill variety, task significance and task identity does not have a uniformly positive effect on employee motivation in different cultural contexts. The chapter reviews the findings of the cross-cultural research literature on motivation and concludes with suggestions for managers dealing with employee motivation in culturally diverse work contexts.

End of Chapter Reflection Questions

1. Multinational corporations (MNCs) have to develop strategies to increase employee motivation in different regions of the world while maintaining fairness among employees across the offices. What would be some examples of specific motivational strategies (e.g., rewards, incentives, employee development programs) to satisfy culturally diverse employees as well as to maintain fairness across MNC offices?
2. Based on the information in this chapter, what do you think are the 'universal' motivational techniques that lead to heightened performance and satisfaction among employees, regardless of the cultural context?
3. According to research findings presented in this chapter, employees in some cultures do not experience high levels of job enrichment and empowerment. Does that mean that job enrichment and empowerment should not be used as motivational techniques in such cultures? Why and why not?

Key Terms and Definitions

Work motivation. Forces that energize employees to initiate goal-directed behaviours and persist in these behaviours.

Self-actualization. Being all one can be and one wants to be; actualizing one's full potential and fulfilling one's wishes.

Empowerment. Managerial practice to instil the feeling of control, competence and goal internalization in employees.

Intrinsic vs. extrinsic motivation. Energetic force originating from the wish to enhance one's learning and growth (intrinsic) vs. one's financial gains, benefits or reputation (extrinsic).

Achievement motivation. Energetic force originating from one's wish to achieve and succeed in a challenging task or situation.

Equity vs. equality. Norm of distributing resources on the basis of merit (equity) vs. membership irrespective of merit (equality).

Participative goal-setting. Goals set via discussion, information exchange and eventually consensus between subordinates and superiors.

(Continued)

(Continued)

Skill variety. Jobs that require employees to use multiple skills; jobs that are not repetitive or monotonous.

Task significance. Jobs that contribute to the lives of others in positive and significant ways.

Task identity. Jobs that allow employees to identify with the work as a whole and complete and to feel proud of contributing to the outcome.

Job enrichment. Designing jobs to enhance meaningfulness, responsibility and knowledge of work results through increased autonomy, feedback, skill variety, task significance and task identity.

Self-enhancement. Type of motivation to make people feel good about themselves and maintain high self-esteem, especially in conditions perceived to be threat to one's positive self-image.

Further Reading

Erez, M., Kleinbeck, U. and Thierry, H. (eds) (2001) *Work Motivation in the Context of a Globalized Economy*. Mahwah, NJ: Lawrence Erlbaum.

Justine D.C. and Sadri, G. (2003) 'Do all carrots look the same? Examining the impact of culture on employee motivation', *Management Research News*, 26 (1): 29–40.

Kanungo, R.N. and Mendonça, M. (eds) (1994) *Work Motivation: Models for Developing Countries*. London: Sage.

Latham, G.P. and Pinder, C.C. (2005) 'Work motivation theory and research at the dawn of the twenty-first century', *Annual Review of Psychology*, 56: 485–516.

Minbaeva, D. (2008) 'HRM practices affecting extrinsic and intrinsic motivation of knowledge receivers and their effect on intra-MNC knowledge transfer', *International Business Review*, 17 (6): 703–13.

Sachau, D.A. (2007) 'Resurrecting the motivation-hygiene theory: Herzberg and the positive psychology movement', *Human Resource Development Review*, 6 (4): 377–93.

Terry, J. (2007) 'Motivating a multicultural workforce', *Industrial and Commercial Training*, 39 (1): 59–64.

Cases, Videos, Web sources

Cases

The following cases illustrate the issues concerning management of motivation in profit and non-profit organizations, with specific focus on goal setting and incentives.

Edelman, R. and Hiltabiddle, T. (2006) The nice guy. *Harvard Business Review*, February: 21–31.

Grasby, E. and Tattersall, T. (2001) St. Matthew's Human Resource Center. IVEY cases no: 9B01C012.

Videos

Video 2.1. Dan Pink: *The puzzle of motivation* (2009) www.ted.com/talks/dan_pink_on_motivation.html – Pink talks about how intrinsic and extrinsic motivators work and whether or not there are cross-cultural differences.

Video 2.2. Jessica Hamilton: *What is success?* (2013) www.youtube.com/watch?v=MOhVy_9fWdE – we need motivation to be successful in life. This video discusses what 'success' is from different points of view.

Video 2.3. *The most motivating video of success.* www.youtube.com/watch?v=NAeha727ZWI. This is a motivational video featuring inspiring words of celebrities, including Steve Jobs, Richard Branson, Donald Trump and Will Smith. Try to identify the 'universal' as well as 'culture-bound' lessons to take from this video (i.e., how would cultural context influence what motivates people in life).

Web sources

www.shrm.org/ – *Society for Human Resource Management.*
www.associationforcoaching.com/ – *Association for Coaching.*
www.recognition.org/ – Recognition Professionals International (the art and science of employee recognition and motivation).

References

Adams, J.S. (1965) 'Inequity in social exchange', *Advanced Experimental Social Psychology*, 62: 335–343.

Adigun, I.O. and Stephenson, G.M. (1992) 'Sources of job motivation and satisfaction among British and Nigerian employees', *Journal of Social Psychology*, 132: 369–76.

Adler, N.J. (1991) *International Dimensions of Organizational Behavior*, 2nd edn. Boston, MA: PWS-Kent.

Allen, R.S., Takeda, M. and White, C.S. (2005) 'Cross-cultural equity sensitivity: A test of differences between the United States and Japan', *Journal of Managerial Psychology*, 20 (8): 641–62.

Aycan, Z. (2006) 'Paternalism: Towards conceptual refinement and operationalization', in K.S. Yang, K.K. Hwang and U. Kim (eds), *Scientific Advances in Indigenous Psychologies: Empirical, Philosophical and Cultural Contributions*, pp. 445–66). Cambridge: Cambridge University Press.

Aycan, Z. and Fikret-Pasa, S. (2003) 'Career choices, job selection criteria and leadership preferences in a transitional nation: The case of Turkey', *Journal of Career Development*, 30: 129–44.

Aycan, Z., Kanungo, R.N., Mendonça, M., Yu, K., Deller, J., Stahl, G. and Kurshid, A. (2000) 'Impact of culture on human resource management practices: A 10-country comparison', *Applied Psychology*, 49: 192–222.

Badawy, M.K. (1980) 'Styles of mid-eastern managers', *California Management Review*, 22: 51–8.

Bailey, J.R., Chen, C.C. and Dou, S.G. (1997) 'Conceptions of self and performance-related feedback in the U.S., Japan and China', *Journal of International Business Studies*, 28: 605–25.

Björkman, I. and Lu, Y. (1999) 'The management of human resources in Chinese Western joint ventures', *Journal of World Business*, 34 (3): 306–24.

Bolino, M.C. and Turnley, W.H. (2008) 'Old faces, new places: Equity theory in cross-cultural contexts', *Journal of Organizational Behavior*, 29: 29–50.

Brislin, R.W., MacNab, B., Worthley, R., Kabigting, F. and Zukis, B. (2005) 'Evolving perceptions of Japanese workplace motivation: An employee-manager comparison', *International Journal of Cross-cultural Management*, 5: 87–104.

Chang, W.C., Wong, W.K. and Teo, G. (2000) The socially oriented and individually oriented achievement motivation of Singaporean Chinese students. *Journal of Psychology in Chinese Society*, 1 (2): 39–63.

Chatterjee, S.R. and Pearson, C.A.L. (2002) 'Work goals of Asian managers: Field evidence from Singapore, Malaysia, India, Thailand, Brunei and Mongolia', *International Journal of Cross-cultural Management*, 2: 251–68.

Chen, C.C. (1995) 'New trends in rewards allocation preferences: A Sino-US comparison', *Academy of Management Journal*, 38: 408–28.

Chen, C.C., Meindl, J.R. and Hui, H. (1998) 'Deciding on equity or parity: A test of situational, cultural and individual factors', *Journal of Organizational Behavior*, 19: 115–29.

Chen, C.N. (1989). Family ideology and economic ethics of enterprise. *Contemporary*, 34, 57–65.

Chhokar, J.S., Zhuplev, A., Fok, L.Y. and Hartman, S.J. (2001) 'The impact of culture on equity sensitivity perceptions and organizational citizenship behavior: A five-country study', *International Journal of Value-Based Management*, 14 (1): 79–98.

Cooke, B., Mills, A.J. and Kelley, E.S. (2005) 'Situating Maslow in cold war America: A recontextualization of management theory', *Group and Organization Management*, 30: 129–52.

De Voe, S.E. and Iyengar, S.S. (2004) 'Managers' theories of subordinates: A cross-cultural examination of manager perceptions of motivation and appraisal of performance', *Organizational Behavior and Human Decision Processes*, 93: 47–61.

De Vos, G. (1973) *Socialization for Achievement*. Berkeley, CA: University of California.

Easterby-Smith, M., Malina, D. and Lu, Y. (1995) 'How culture sensitive is HRM? A comparative analysis of practice in Chinese and UK companies', *The International Journal of Human Resource Management*, 6 (1), 31–59.

Elenkov, D.S. (1998) 'Can American management concepts work in Russia?', *California Management Review*, 40: 133–57.

Els, P. van (2012) Confucius' sayings entombed: On Two Han Dynasty *Analects* Manuscripts. *Analects Studies*. Leiden: Brill.

Emery, C.R. and Oertel, S. (2006) 'An examination of employees' culture-based perceptions as a predictor of motivation', *Journal of Organizational Culture, Communications and Conflict*, 10: 13–30.

Erez, M. (1997) A culture-based model of work motivation. In P.C. Earley and M. Erez (eds), *New Perspectives on International Industrial / Organizational Psychology*, pp. 193–243. San Francisco: New Lexington Press.

Erez, M. (2000) 'Make management practice fit the national culture', in E.A. Locke (ed.), *Basic Principles of Organizational Behavior: A Handbook*, pp. 418–34. New York: Blackwell.

Erez, M. and Earley, P.C. (1987) 'Comparative analysis of goal-setting strategies across cultures', *Journal of Applied Psychology*, 72: 658–65.

Evans, P. and Wolf, B. (2005) Collaboration rules. *Harvard Business Review*, 83 (7), 96–104.

Eylon, D. and Au, K.Y. (1999) 'Exploring empowerment cross-cultural differences along the power distance dimension', *International Journal of Intercultural Relations*, 23: 373–85.

Fadil, P.A., Williams, R.J., Limpaphayom, W.T. and Smatt, C. (2005) 'Equity or equality? A conceptual examination of the influence of individualism/collectivism on the cross-cultural application of equity theory', *Cross-cultural Management: An International Journal*, 12: 17–35.

Fatehi, K. (1996) *International Management*. New Jersey: Prentice Hall.

Fey, C.F. (2005) 'Opening the black box of motivation: A cross-cultural comparison of Sweden and Russia', *International Business Review*, 14: 345–67.

Fischer, R. (2004) 'Organizational justice and cultural values in Europe: Justice is in the eye of the beholder', in S. Schmidt and A. Thomas (eds), *Impact of Values and Norms on Intercultural Training and Education*, pp. 83–92. Vienna: IDM.

Fischer, R. and Smith, P.B. (2003) 'Reward allocation and culture: A meta-analysis', *Journal of Cross-cultural Psychology*, 34: 251–68.

Fletcher, C. and Perry, E.L. (2001) 'Performance appraisal and feedback: A consideration of national culture and a review of contemporary research and future trends', in N. Anderson, D.S. Ones, K. Sinangil and C. Viswesvaran (eds), *Handbook of Industrial, Work and Organizational Psychology*, pp. 127–44. Thousand Oaks: CA: Sage.

Fok, L.Y., Hartman, S.J., Villere, M.F. and Freibert, R.C. III. (1996) 'A study of the impact of cross cultural differences on perceptions of equity and organizational citizenship behavior', *International Journal of Management*, 13: 3–14.

Furnham, A., Kirkcaldi, B.D. and Lynn, R. (1994) 'National attitudes to competitiveness, money and work among young people: First, second and third world differences', *Human Relations*, 47: 119–132.

Gambrel, P.A. and Cianci, R. (2003) 'Maslow's hierarchy of needs: Does it apply in collectivist culture?', *Journal of Applied Management and Entrepreneurship*, 8: 143–62.

Geiger, M.A., Cooper, E.A., Hussain, I., O'Connell, B.T., Power, J., Raghunandan, K. and Sanchez, G. (1998) 'Using expectancy theory to assess student motivation: An international replication', *Issues in Accounting Education*, 13: 139–56.

Gergen, K.J., Morse, S.J. and Gergen, M. (1980), Behavior exchange in cross-cultural perspective, in H. Triandis and R.W. Brislin (eds), *Handbook of Cross-cultural Psychology, Vol.5*, pp. 121–153. Boston, MA: Allyn & Bacon.

Giacobbe-Miller, J.K. and Miller, D.J. (1995) 'A comparison of U.S. and Russian pay allocation decisions and distributive justice judgments', *Academy of Management Best Papers Proceedings*, 177–81.

Gibson, C.B. (1997) 'Do you hear what I hear? A framework for reconciling intercultural communication difficulties arising from cognitive styles and cultural values', in P.C. Earley and M. Erez (eds), *New Perspectives on International Industrial and Organizational Psychology*, pp. 335–62. San Francisco, CA: The New Lexington Press.

Gluskinos, U.M. (1988) 'Cultural and political considerations in the introduction of Western technologies: The Mekorot project', *Journal of Management Development*, 6: 34–46.

Gómez, C., Kirkman, B.L. and Shapiro, D.L. (2000) 'The impact of collectivism and ingroup/outgroup membership on evaluation generosity', *Academy of Management Journal*, 43: 1097–2007.

Grouzet, F.M.E., Kasser, T., Ahuvia, A., Fernandez-Dois, J.M., Kim, Y., Lau, S. and Sheldon, K.M. (2005) 'The structure of goal contents across five cultures', *Journal of Personality and Social Psychology*, 89: 800–816.

Hackman, J.R. and Oldham, G.R. (1976) 'Motivation through the design of work: Test of a theory', *Organizational Behavior and Human Performance*, 16: 250–79.

Haire, M., Ghiselli, E.E. and Porter, L.W. (1966) *Managerial Thinking: An International Study*. Chichester: Wiley.

Heine, S.J., Kitayama, S., Lehman, D.R., Takata, T., Ide, E., Lueng, C. and Matsumoto, H. (2001) 'Divergent consequences of success and failure in Japan and North America: An investigation of self-improving motivations and malleable selves', *Journal of Personality and Social Psychology*, 81: 599–615.

Hines, G.H. (1973) 'The image of industrial psychologists in cross-cultural perspective', *Professional Psychology: Research and Practice*, 4: 64–71.

Hofstede, G. (1983) 'Dimensions of national cultures in fifty countries and three regions', in J.B. Deregowski, S. Dziurawiec and R.C. Annis (eds), *Explorations in Cross-cultural Psychology*, pp. 335–55. Lisse: Swets and Zeitlinger.

Hofstede, G. (1984) *Culture's Consequences: International Differences in Work-related Values*. Newbury Park, CA: Sage.

Hofstede, G. (2001) *Culture's consequences: Comparing values, behaviors, institutions, and organizations across nations* (2nd edn). Thousand Oaks, CA: Sage Publications, Inc.

Huang, X. and Van De Vliert, E. (2003) 'Where intrinsic job satisfaction fails to work: National moderators of intrinsic motivation', *Journal of Organizational Behavior*, 24: 159–79.

Hui, C.H. and Luk, C.L. (1997) 'Industrial/organizational psychology', in J.W. Berry, Y.H. Poortinga and J. Randey (eds), *Handbook of Cross-cultural Psychology*. Boston, MA: Allyn and Bacon.

Hundley, G. and Kim, J. (1997) 'National culture and the factors affecting perceptions of pay fairness in Korea and the United States', *International Journal of Organizational Analysis*, 5: 325–41.

Huo, Y.P. and Von Glinow, M.A. (1995) 'On transplanting human resource practices to China: A culture-driven approach', *International Journal of Manpower*, 16: 3–11.

Iyengar, S.S. and Lepper, M.R. (1999) 'Rethinking the value of choice: A cultural perspective on intrinsic motivation', *Journal of Personality and Social Psychology*, 76: 349–66.

Jackson, T. (2004) *Management and Change in Africa: A Cross-cultural Perspective*. London: Routledge.

Jaggi, B. (1979) 'Need importance of Indian managers', *Management International Review*, 19: 107–13.

Kim, K.I., Park, H.J. and Suzuki, N. (1990) 'Reward allocations in the United States, Japan and Korea', *Academy of Management Journal*, 33: 188–99.

Kitayama, S., Markus, H.R., Matsumoto, H. and Norasakkunkit, V. (1997) 'Individual and collective processes in the construction of the self: Self-enhancement in the United States and self-criticism in Japan', *Journal of Personality and Social Psychology*, 72: 1245–67.

Kurman, J. (2001) 'Self-regulation strategies in achievement settings: Culture and gender differences', *Journal of Cross-cultural Psychology*, 32: 491–503.

Latham, G.P., Erez, M. and Locke, E.A. (1988) 'Resolving scientific disputes by the joint design of crucial experiments: Application to the Erez-Latham dispute regarding participation in goal setting', *Journal of Applied Psychology (monograph)*, 73: 753–77.

Leung, K. (1997) 'Negotiation and reward allocations across cultures', in P.C. Earley and M. Erez (eds), *New Perspectives on International Industrial/organizational Psychology*, pp. 640–75. San Francisco, CA: The New Lexington Press.

Locke, E.A. (1978) 'The ubiquity of the technique of goal setting in theories of and approaches to employee motivation', *Academy of Management Review*, 3: 594–601.

Machungwa, P.E. and Schmitt, N. (1983) 'Work motivation in a developing country', *Journal of Applied Psychology*, 68: 31–42.

Markus, H.R. and Kitayama, S. (1991) 'Culture and the self: Implications for cognition, emotion and motivation', *Psychological Review*, 98: 224–53.

Maslow, A.H. (1954) *Motivation and Personality*. New York: Harper.

Matsui, T. and Terai, T. (1975) 'A cross-cultural study of the validity of the expectancy theory of work motivation', *Journal of Applied Psychology*, 60: 263–5.

McClelland, D.C. (1961) *The Achieving Society*. Princeton, NJ: D. Van Nostrand.

Mendonça, M. and Kanungo, R.N. (1994) 'Managing human resources: The issue of cultural fit', *Journal of Management Inquiry*, 3; 189–205.

Miller, J.S., Hom, P.W. and Gomez-Mejia, L.R. (2001) 'The high cost of low wages: Does Maquiladora compensation reduce turnover?', *Journal of International Business Studies*, 32: 585–95.

Moneta, G.B. (2004) 'The flow experience across cultures', *Journal of Happiness Studies*, 5: 115–21.

Money, R.B. and Graham, J.L. (1999) 'Salesperson performance, pay and job satisfaction: Tests of a model using data collected in the United States and Japan', *Journal of International Business Studies*, 30 (1): 149–72.

Nevis, B.C. (1983) 'Using an American perspective in understanding another culture: Toward a hierarchy of needs for the People's Republic of China', *Journal of Applied Behavioral Science*, 19: 249–64.

Nicholson, N. (2003) 'How to motivate your problem employees', *Harvard Business Review*, 81 (1): 57–65.

Ouchi, W.G. (1981) *Theory Z: How American Business can Meet the Japanese Challenge.* Reading, MA: Addison-Wesley.

Pinder, C.C. (1998) *Work Motivation in Organizational Behavior.* Upper Saddle River, NJ: Prentice Hall.

Punnett, B.J. (2004) *International Perspectives on Organizational Behavior and Human Resource Management.* London: M. E. Sharpe.

Pusey, A.W. (1977) *A comparative study on achievement motivation between Chinese and Americans.* (Unpublished Masters thesis.) Bucknell University.

Quinn, D.P. and Rivoli, P. (1991) 'The effects of American- and Japanese-style employment and compensation practices on innovation', *Organization Science*, 2 (4): 323–41.

Robert, C., Probst, T.M., Martocchio, J.J., Drasgow, F. and Lawler, J.J. (2000) 'Empowerment and continuous improvement in the United States, Mexico, Poland and India: Predicting fit on the basis of the dimensions of power distance and individualism', *Journal of Applied Psychology*: 85: 643–58.

Roe, R.A., Zinovieva, I.L., Dienes, E. and Ten Horn, L. (2000) 'A comparison of work motivation in Bulgaria, Hungary and the Netherlands: Test of a model', *Applied Psychology: An International Review*, 49 (4): 658–87.

Sagie, A., Elizur, D. and Yamauchi, H. (1996) 'The structure and strength of achievement motivation: A cross-cultural comparison', *Journal of Organizational Behavior*, 17: 431–44.

Sama, L.M. and Papamarcos, S.D. (2000) 'Hofstede's I-C dimension as predictive of allocative behaviors: A meta-analysis', *International Journal of Value-Based Management*, 13: 173–88.

Schuler, R.S. and Rogovsky, N. (1998) 'Understanding compensation practice variations across firms: The impact of national culture', *Journal of International Business Studies*, 29: 159–77.

Schwartz, S. (1994) 'Are there universal aspects in the structure and contents of human values?', *Journal of Social Issues*, 50: 19–45.

Schwartz, S.H. and Bilsky, W. (1987) 'Toward a psychological structure of human values', *Journal of Personality and Social Psychology*, 53: 550–62.

Seddon, J. (1987) 'Assumptions, culture and performance appraisal', *Journal of Management Development*, 6: 47–54.

Stephens, D., Kedia, B. and Ezell, D. (1979) 'Managerial need structures in US and Peruvian industries', *Management International Review*, 19: 27–39.

Sue-Chan, C. and Ong, M. (2002) 'Goal assignment and performance: Assessing the mediating roles of goal commitment and self-efficacy and the moderating role of power distance', *Organizational Behavior and Human Decision Processes*, 89: 1140–61.

Triandis, H.C. (1994) 'Cross-cultural industrial and organizational psychology', in H. C. Triandis, M.D. Dunnette and L.M. Hough (eds), *Handbook of Industrial Organizational Psychology, Vol. 4*, pp. 103–72. Mountain View, CA: Consulting Psychologists Press.

Trompenaars, F. (1993) *Riding the Waves of Culture.* London: The Economist Books.

Vroom, V.H. (1964) *Work and Motivation.* New York: Wiley.

Weick, K.E., Bougan, M.G. and Maruyama, G. (1976) 'The equity context', *Organizational Behavior and Human Performance*, 15: 32–65.

Westerman, K.C.Y., Park, H.S. and Lee, H.E. (2007) 'A test of equity theory in multidimensional friendships: A comparison of the United States and Korea', *Journal of Communication*, 57: 576–98.

Wheeler, K.G. (2002) 'Cultural values in relation to equity sensitivity within and across cultures', *Journal of Managerial Psychology*, 17 (7): 612–27.

Yoshida, T., Kojo, K. and Kaku, H. (1982) 'A study on the development of self-presentation in children', *Japanese Journal of Educational Psychology*, 30: 120–27.

Yu, A. and Yang, K. (1994) 'The nature of achievement motivation in collectivist societies', in U. Kim, H. Triandis, C. Kagitcibasi, S. Choi and G. Yoon (eds), *Individualism and Collectivism: Theory, Method and Applications*, pp. 239–50. London: Sage.

Zhang, K., Song, L.J., Hackett, R.D. and Bycio, P. (2006) 'Cultural boundary of expectancy theory based performance management: A commentary on DeNisi and Pritchard's performance improvement model', *Management and Organization Review*, 2: 279–94.

Want to learn more? Visit the companion website at www.sagepub.co.uk/kanungo to gain access to videos from the end of each chapter, weblinks and flash cards of key terms.

3

Behavioural Modification and Performance Management

Chapter Outline

John works for Honest Ed Enterprises as a retail salesperson. To ensure that John generates sales, he receives a sales commission every time he makes a sale.

A critical job task of Charena – a technician in a continuous-process chemical plant, is to monitor the temperature and pressure gauges to maintain the correct temperature and pressure levels. Whenever the temperature or pressure rises beyond the acceptable level, a loud buzzer and a flashing red light is activated and continues until Charena operates the appropriate switch to reduce the temperature or pressure. Charena now finds herself paying more attention to her task of monitoring the gauges in order to maintain the temperature and pressure at the right level.

Professor Ang insists that students maintain the specified word limit in the term paper. Every time a student exceeds the word limit the professor reduces the student's grade on that paper by 5 per cent.

Susan is an administrative assistant in the controller's office and one of her major duties is to prepare and mail the budget variance reports of the month before the seventh of the following month. Whenever Susan mails the report after the scheduled date, she receives a written reprimand from the controller, a copy of which is placed in her personal dossier.

The overdue accounts receivable of Honest Ed Enterprises have reached an alarmingly high level. Closer examination revealed that the salespersons were paid their commissions on credit sales even though they did not submit the required credit report on such sales. To eliminate the violation of this procedure, salespersons receive their commissions on credit sales only after the credit report is submitted.

These scenarios vary widely in respect of the nature, content and context of the job tasks. However, an underlying common thread is clearly noticeable. In each scenario the individual's performance is managed by the supervisor's actions, which are designed to bring about in the individual those behaviours that are appropriate and contribute to achieving the job and organizational objectives.

Like the motivational theories discussed in Chapter 2, the behaviour modification approach provides an effective managerial tool that explains and predicts work performance. Its objective is to maintain the desired employee behaviour or to bring about changes in employee behaviour in order that the established task of the work unit is efficiently and effectively accomplished.

However, unlike other motivational theories, the behaviour modification approach uses operant conditioning, whose fundamental processes are unconcerned with or are outside the sphere of cognition. The overriding principle involved in operant conditioning is the *future occurrence of a behaviour is a function of the environmental consequences that it brings about or generates.*

Our discussion explores the principles of operant conditioning and its use in the major behaviour modification techniques, including positive reinforcement, negative reinforcement, punishment by application, punishment by removal and extinction or omission. We discuss the implications of the behaviour modification approach for managing performance which takes the form of a step-by-step action plan that managers can adopt to maintain or modify employee behaviour in order to attain the job and organizational objectives.

We then discuss the **performance management** process – consistent with the behaviour modification approach. We first present the current knowledge of performance management process and its essential preconditions which have been found to be effective in organizations. We outline the challenges facing organizations in different countries in performance management and propose solutions to overcome these challenges.

Learning Objectives

- To learn the principles of operant conditioning and understand the process of behaviour modification and its critical elements.

- To identify and explain types of reinforcement contingencies and the operative principles governing each contingency.

- To understand how the performance management process is an illustration of the action plan to maintain or modify performance behaviours.

- To review the challenges facing organizations in various countries in the performance management process.

- To learn what actions organizational managers in cultures characterized by high power-distance, high uncertainty avoidance, low individualism and low masculinity can take to overcome the cultural constraints to the performance management process.

One of the principal sources of competitive advantage for an organization is the efficient and productive use of its human resources. In fact, the proper utilization of human resources is often considered to be the primary task of management. It is for this reason that the term 'management' has been utilized as the process of getting things done through controlling, changing and predicting the *behaviour of employees*. The effective management of employees primarily involves two sets of managerial actions: (1) to identify and maintain the appropriate work behaviours that are conducive to accomplishing organizational objectives; and (2) to modify or extinguish inappropriate work behaviours that hinder or impede the attainment of organizational objectives. The scenarios at the beginning of the chapter illustrate these two sets of managerial actions.

In this section, we describe the principles of operant conditioning as advocated by B.F. Skinner (1974) and his followers. The application of these principles first led to the development of various behaviour modification techniques in educational and clinical settings to modify the specific job behaviour of its employees in the desired direction.

The scenarios described earlier illustrate each of the major **behaviour modification** techniques. These are positive reinforcement, negative reinforcement, punishment by application, punishment by removal, and omission or extinction. We discuss each of these at length with a specific focus on how a manager can use these to maintain employee behaviour or bring about behavioural changes in employees to attain the clearly defined organizational and task objectives.

Shaping Behaviour through its Consequences

The process of behavioural modification

We constantly respond to and cope with the demands of our physical and social environment. While interacting with the environment, we learn to emit (i.e., use) specific patterns of behaviour that are beneficial to us and learn to drop those patterns of behaviour that either have harmful effects or no consequence for us. Operant conditioning deals with the process of learning voluntary behaviour, as opposed to the reflexive or non-voluntary behaviour in our day-to-day lives.

The environmental consequences associated with our voluntary behaviours lead to our learning – that is, to repeat or modify the voluntary behaviours in the future. The learning of behaviour in this manner is called *operant*, because the voluntary behaviour becomes the operant: the instrument that leads to an environmental consequence.

The overriding principle that explains the operant conditioning process is that the present and future occurrence of a behaviour is a function of the consequences that it brings about or generates. The analysis of behaviour under operant conditioning should be based on three observable elements:

- A (the *antecedent* environmental event),
- B (the *behaviour* or operant), and
- C (the *consequence* of the behaviour).

Thus, behaviour results from the contingency of A→B→C: behaviour (i.e., B) results from a *prior* event (i.e., A) and a *subsequent* event (i.e., C). Let's consider the following example:

> Jyoti, the supervisor, sets Harry, the maintenance mechanic, a goal of cleaning and repairing five machines every week. This goal, set by Jyoti, is the *antecedent event* that precedes and triggers Harry's behaviour. Harry performs *the behaviour* of maintaining the five machines in one week. As a *consequence* of that task behaviour, Harry receives compliments from Jyoti. According to operant conditioning, Harry's present task behaviour follows the antecedent event and his task behaviour in future is determined by the consequence associated with the present behaviour. Since this consequence is pleasant to Harry, he will repeat the behaviour next week. If, instead of the compliment, Jyoti expressed disapproval of Harry's behaviour, then this disapproval – an aversive consequence which Harry associates with the task behaviour, may cause Harry not to repeat that behaviour. Thus both *antecedents* and *consequences* are the environmental determinants of behaviour.

The antecedent environmental event acts only as a stimulus cue that triggers a given behaviour. However, it is the consequence that results from the behaviour that controls the future occurrence of the behaviour. In other words, the frequency of occurrence of a behaviour in the future depends upon the results associated with that behaviour in the past.

This implies that in order to understand employee behaviour in response to the work environment we must consider three questions: (1) what triggers the behaviour? (2) what is the behaviour? (3) what are the consequences of the behaviour?

As stated above, the process of behaviour modification involves controlling two types of contingencies: A→B and B→C. To control the A→B contingency it is necessary to know what stimulus cue triggers the behaviour. For instance, when a manager sets the task goal and notifies employees of it, the notice can act as the antecedent that triggers the task behaviour. However, it is the B→C contingency, also known as the 'contingencies of reinforcement', that is more critical in determining whether employees will engage in the task behaviour on future occasions.

To understand how the contingencies of reinforcement work, we shall first examine the various types or arrangements of **reinforcement contingencies**. We will then discuss the various schedules of reinforcement contingencies – that is whether the reinforcement contingencies should be applied on a continuous or on a partial (i.e., intermittent) basis.

Reinforcement Contingencies

A manager has the choice of five types of reinforcement contingencies to manage employee behaviour. These are positive reinforcement, negative reinforcement, punishment by application, punishment by removal and omission or extinction (Figure 3.1). Before we examine each reinforcement contingency in detail, we provide an overview of their similarities and differences.

In the case of both **positive reinforcement** and **punishment by application**, an event is presented following the behaviour. But the two contingencies are different because in positive reinforcement the event is pleasant, whereas in punishment by application it is unpleasant. Consequently positive reinforcement, a behaviour associated with a pleasant event, increases the future occurrence of that behaviour, whereas punishment by application, a behaviour associated with an unpleasant event, decreases the future occurrence of that behaviour.

	Consequence Presented	Consequence Removed
Positive Consequence	Positive Reinforcement (Increase behaviour occurrence)	Punishment by removal (Decrease behaviour occurrence)
Aversive Consequence	Punishment by application (Decrease behaviour occurrence)	Negative reinforcement (Increase behaviour occurence)
No Consequence	Extinction or Omission (Decrease behaviour occurrence)	

Figure 3.1 *Five Reinforcement Contingencies*

The remaining three contingencies – negative reinforcement, punishment by removal and extinction – are similar in that in each contingency a certain event is removed. But they are different in other ways. In the case of **negative reinforcement** an unpleasant event is removed as a consequence of the behaviour. This *removal of the unpleasant* event following the behaviour in effect becomes a pleasant consequence and, thereby, increases the future occurrence of the behaviour. In the case of **punishment by removal**, a pleasant event is removed as a consequence of behaviour. The *removal of the pleasant* event following the behaviour in effect becomes an unpleasant consequence, and thereby decreases the future occurrence of the behaviour. Finally, in the case of **omission or extinction**, the pleasant events which followed the behaviour in the past are simply withdrawn. The effect is that the behaviour now does not have the pleasant consequence with which it was associated in the past. This suggests a decrease in the future occurrence of the behaviour. The distinction between punishment by removal and extinction contingencies will be made clear later in the section on punishment.

Positive Reinforcement

Knowing that employees tend to repeat those behaviours that lead to positive consequences for them, a manager will use positive reinforcers whenever the employee performs the desirable behaviour. A positive reinforcer is, therefore, defined as a pleasant stimulus event which is given as a consequence of a behaviour and increases the probability of the future occurrence of that behaviour. Thus, the two critical characteristics of a positive reinforcer in the work context are: (1) the employee finds it to be a pleasant event; and (2) it increases the probability of the future occurrence of a desirable behaviour when it is presented as a consequence of that behaviour. In the first scenario at the beginning of the chapter, the commission John receives every time he makes a sale operates as a positive reinforcer to repeat the desired behaviour of making a sale.

The term positive reinforcer should not be confused with the term reward. A **reward** is an event which is conventionally considered as pleasant, but an employee may not find it to be a pleasant event. When a manager praises an employee following desirable behaviour, the praise may be considered as a reward by the manager, but it may not act as a positive reinforcer *unless* the employee finds it rewarding. Furthermore, even if the employee finds the reward to be a pleasant event, it is not a positive reinforcer if it is not given in consequence of a specific behaviour to increase the probability of the future occurrence of that behaviour. For example, merit pay – designed to increase the future probability of outstanding performance, is given to Harry when his present performance is below average. Although Harry will find merit pay to be a pleasant event, it will not operate as a positive reinforcer for outstanding performance as was intended. On the contrary, its effect will be to make Harry continue with his below-average performance. In other words, the timing is wrong and it is not given as a consequence of the behaviour that is intended to be increased. Therefore, we can say that *all positive reinforcers are rewards, but all rewards may not be positive reinforcers.*

Reinforcers, positive or negative, are classified as either primary reinforcers or secondary reinforcers. Examples of primary reinforcers are food, water, sex and so on. These reinforcers are termed primary not because these are considered to be more important than the secondary reinforcers, but because the effects of these reinforcers are not derived from past experience or learning. Instead, the effects of these reinforcers are physiologically or biologically determined. The secondary reinforcers such as job advancement, praise, recognition and money derive their effects from a consistent pairing with other reinforcers in the past. Secondary reinforcement, therefore, depends on the individual employee and their past reinforcement history. Furthermore, a secondary reinforcer (e.g., praise from supervisor) that is rewarding to one person may not be rewarding to another.

Principles of positive reinforcement

The successful application of positive reinforcement depends on four guidelines or principles:

- *Principle of contingent reinforcement.* The manager must design the contingencies in such a way that the reinforcing events are made contingent upon the performance of the desired behaviour. This is the rule of reinforcement which is most often violated in the work context. For example, the weekly wages may have reward value for employees, but when these wages are given to all employees, regardless of their performance levels, the weekly wages are not contingent on employee performance. Hence, these do not act as a reinforcer of performance.
- *Principle of reinforcement size or importance.* Generally, the larger the size of the reinforcers or the more important they are for employees, the more effective they would be. Large rewards should follow higher performance if they have to act as reinforcers. However, the size or importance of the reinforcer depends on the past experience of the individual employee with the reinforcer. Thus in determining the size or importance, a manager must consider both the performance level and the past experience of the employee.
- *Principle of reinforcement deprivation.* The manager must make sure that the employee is not satiated with the reinforcer that follows as a consequence of the desirable behaviour of employee. The effectiveness of a reinforcer is greatly enhanced when an employee has been deprived of it, at least in the recent past. The frequent use of

the same reinforcer may lead to the satiation effect. For example, when praise is used all the time for any and every behaviour, its overuse may lead to the loss of its reward value.

- *Principle of immediate reinforcement.* This is critical to the effectiveness of the reinforcer. A reinforcer strengthens the probability of the future occurrence of a behaviour when it is available immediately after the performance of that behaviour. Reinforcement is said to be delayed when the reinforcer is given after a time delay that weakens the association between the behaviour and the reinforcer. Such delayed reinforcement makes the reinforcer less effective in controlling the future occurrence of the desired behaviour.

Schedules of positive reinforcement

Effectiveness of the reinforcement contingency in modifying behaviour depends on the frequency and scheduling of reinforcement. For this purpose, we now consider the schedules of reinforcement contingencies – that is, whether the reinforcement contingencies should be applied on a continuous or a partial (i.e., intermittent) basis.

Continuous reinforcement schedule

Under this schedule, every time the desired behaviour is emitted by the employee, it is followed by a reinforcer. With a continuous reinforcement schedule, behaviour occurrence increases very rapidly. However, when the reinforcer does not follow the behaviour the future occurrence of the behaviour decreases equally rapidly. In practical terms, despite the best intentions of the manager, it may not be feasible for them to reinforce every occurrence of the behaviour.

However, the continuous reinforcement schedule is absolutely critical when the employee is learning a new behaviour response, or during the shaping of complex behaviour patterns. Once the behaviour is learnt, then maintaining it is better achieved by using one or more of the partial reinforcement schedules. Of course, the content of the rewards (pleasant events) could be a mix of economic and non-economic rewards. Economic rewards include items such as pay, bonus, time off; non-economic rewards include items such as praise, status symbols, and participation in decision-making.

Partial reinforcement schedules

In a partial reinforcement schedule, reinforcement does not occur after each performance of the desired behaviour. Instead, the reinforcement is provided in an intermittent manner because intermittent or partial reinforcement has been found to lead to a stronger retention of the learned behaviour. In other words, learning is more permanent or enduring when the manager reinforces behaviour only partially or intermittently. There are four basic types of partial reinforcement schedules for behaviour modification.

Fixed interval schedule   The basis of this schedule is a time interval that is fixed. Under this schedule, a reinforcer is administered only when the desired behaviour response occurs after the passage of a specific period of time following the previous reinforcement. Thus a worker paid on a weekly basis would receive a full pay cheque every Friday, assuming that the worker was performing the minimally acceptable behaviour during the week. This method initiates *the least motivation* for hard work among employees. To illustrate the behaviour pattern under a fixed interval schedule, suppose the plant manager of a company visits the shipping department for inspection each day at approximately 10:00 a.m. This fixed schedule of supervisory inspection will probably cause performance to be at its peak just prior to the plant manager's visit and then performance will probably steadily decline thereafter and not reach its peak again until the next morning's visit.

Variable interval schedule   The basis of this schedule is also a time interval, but the interval varies. Under this schedule, reinforcement is administered at some variable interval of time. This schedule is not recommended for use with a pay plan (e.g., distributing wages to employees in variable time intervals), but it is an ideal method for administering praise, promotions and supervisory visits to monitor performance. Since the timing of dispensing the reinforcers cannot be easily predicted, variable schedules generate higher rates of behaviour response, and more stable and consistent performance. Suppose the same plant manager visits the shipping department on an average of once a day but at randomly selected time intervals, i.e., twice on Monday, once on Tuesday, no visit on Wednesday and Thursday and twice on Friday, all at different times during the day. With such a variable interval schedule, performance will be higher and fluctuate less than under the fixed interval schedule.

Fixed ratio schedule   Here a reinforcer is administered only when a fixed number of desired responses take place. The fixed ratio schedule is essentially the basis of the piece-work schedule for pay – for example, for every five sales made the salesperson receives a commission. The response level here is significantly higher than that obtained under any of the interval schedules.

Variable ratio schedule   Under this schedule, a reinforcer is administered only after a certain number of desired responses, but the exact number of desired responses varies from the occurrence of one reinforcer to the next. The non-economic reinforcers such as praise or recognition are generally used on a variable ratio schedule. Let us suppose that the supervisor uses this schedule to administer praise to the salesperson who meets the daily quota of customer contacts. Such a supervisor might offer praise on the average of once every five days when quotas are met. Sometimes the supervisor praises after three days and at other times after seven days. Research evidence reveals that of all the variations in scheduling procedures available, this is the most powerful in sustaining learned behaviour.

In many cases, it may be necessary to use a combination of the various schedules for administering rewards: for example, base pay cheque on a fixed interval schedule; promotions and raises on a variable interval schedule; recognition of above average performance with a fixed-ratio schedule such as in a piece-rate plan; and supplementary bonuses or prizes for good performance on a variable ratio schedule.

Negative Reinforcement

The second type of contingency arrangement available to the manager is negative reinforcement. Just as is the case with positive reinforcement, this is a method of increasing the future probability of the desired behaviour. In negative reinforcement, an aversive consequence is used and it leads to increasing the probability of the desired behaviour in one of two ways: by escape, and by avoidance.

In the escape response, the aversive consequence is initiated in the environment when the desirable behaviour is not performed and stopped only when the desirable behaviour is performed. The individual performs the desired behaviour in order to escape the aversive consequence, which will continue to be present in the environment until the desired behaviour is performed. An example of learning by escape is found in the second scenario at the beginning of the chapter. In that scenario, the unpleasant loud buzzer and flashing red light stop when Charena operates the switch to reduce the temperature and pressure to the right level. Charena 'escapes' the aversive consequence of the buzzer and light by performing the required behaviour of adjusting the switches.

The second way of learning through the negative reinforcement contingency is by avoidance. In this case, the desired behaviour is performed to avoid the threat of aversive consequence from being actualized when the desired behaviour is not performed. Returning to the example of Charena, her past experience with the threat of the aversive consequence of loud buzzer and flashing red light leads her to attend more closely to the gauges to maintain the right temperature and pressure levels in order to avoid the threat of the aversive consequences being actualized. In negative reinforcement, the behaviour leads to the prevention of or escape from an aversive or punishing consequence which is seen as reinforcing; hence the increase in the future occurrence of that behaviour.

Negative reinforcement is used quite frequently as a control strategy in the work environment. For example, employee punctuality is often maintained by avoidance learning. The aversive event is the criticism by the office manager for being late. In order to avoid the criticism before it occurs, employees make a special effort to come to work on time. In avoidance learning, through their behaviour employees prevent an aversive event from occurring. In the case of escape learning, the employees' behaviour terminates an ongoing aversive event. For example, a supervisor who would begin criticizing a worker for goofing off may have the effect of the worker returning to work and intensifying their work efforts to escape the criticism.

Before we conclude this section, it is important to point out the distinction between: (a) negative reinforcement and positive reinforcement; and (b) negative reinforcement and punishment. In both positive and negative reinforcement, the objective is to increase the future occurrence of the desired behaviour. In the case of positive reinforcement, the individual performs the desired behaviour (e.g., on-time reporting) to gain the pleasant consequences following the performance of the desired behaviour. In the case of negative reinforcement, the individual performs the desired behaviour (e.g., on-time reporting) to avoid or escape the noxious or aversive consequences.

Negative reinforcement is often confused with punishment because aversive events are used in both cases to influence behaviour. However, it must be emphasized that in negative reinforcement, the aversive consequence is used to *increase* the future occurrence of a *desired* behaviour. In punishment, as discussed below, the aversive consequence is used to *decrease* the future occurrence of an *undesired* behaviour.

Punishment

Another strategy for reducing the frequency of the future occurrence of undesired behaviour is through the use of punishing events. It is not uncommon for managers to maintain control over employee behaviour through penalties for violation of rules and directives. The punishment contingency can be deployed in two forms: punishment by application and punishment by removal.

In punishment by application an aversive consequence is presented or applied following employees' undesirable behaviour. The fourth scenario in the introduction of the chapter – Susan receiving a reprimand for mailing the report after the scheduled date – is an illustration of punishment by application. Another similar example would be the supervisor reprimanding the salesperson whenever they are found to be rude or impolite to customers.

In punishment by removal, a positive consequence or reward is removed contingent on the employee's undesirable behaviour. The third scenario in the introduction, Professor Ang reducing students' grades by 5 per cent every time the prescribed word limit on the term paper is exceeded, is an example of punishment by removal. Another example of punishment by removal is the docking of an employee's salary every time they are absent from work or a training.

The successful administration of the punishment contingency depends on the similar principles of *contingent reinforcement, immediate reinforcement and the size of reinforcement* discussed under positive reinforcement. Thus, a punishing event is most effective if it is a direct consequence of the undesirable behaviour; if it is administered immediately after the undesirable behaviour; and if its effects are felt and considered as strongly negative by the employee (e.g., reprimand is not considered to be a negative event for some employees, while it is devastating for others).

In general, compared to the other contingencies, the punishment contingency is considered to be less effective as a means of behaviour modification. The effectiveness of punishment is questioned on several grounds. First, punishment is considered the most controversial method of behaviour modification and the technique raises several ethical questions. One of the principal objections to punishment stems from the widespread belief that it has harmful effects on employees and that it suppresses the undesirable behaviours only temporarily. In the absence of the punisher, the employees soon revert to the same undesirable behaviour. Second, there are other side effects of punishment that reduce its effectiveness. Out of fear, the punished employee may avoid the manager who is the punishing agent and thereby impair the interpersonal relationship that is so vital to effective supervision. An employee who is punished may get angry or emotionally distressed. The emotional states of anger and fear may interfere with the normal task behaviour, and in fact may result in destructive work behaviour such as vandalism and sabotage that is detrimental to the interest of the organization.

Such emotional states can also lead the employee to inflict physical harm on the supervisor and co-workers, which can sometimes prove to be fatal as is often reported in the media. The state of depression brought on by punishment can cause the employee to be apathetic, which is not conducive to employee initiative and resourcefulness at work. Finally, the punished employees may withdraw or avoid the work environment altogether, causing increased absenteeism and turnover. For all these reasons, summarized in Figure 3.2, it is recommended that the punishment contingency be used with some caution.

Extinction/Omission

While positive reinforcement and negative reinforcement can be used by managers to increase the future occurrence of a desired behaviour, omission (or extinction) and punishment are methods available to managers to reduce the future occurrence of the undesired behaviour of employees.

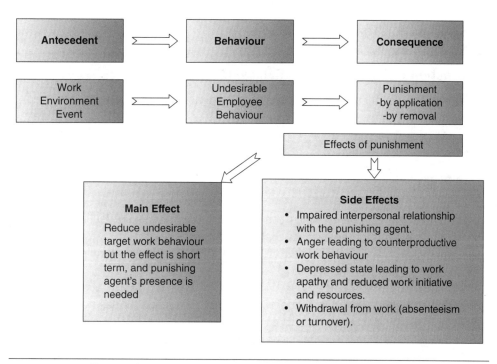

Figure 3.2 *Effects of punishment*

When positive reinforcement for a previously learned behaviour is withheld, employees will continue to exhibit that behaviour for some period of time. However, if the positive reinforcement continues to be withheld, the occurrence of the behaviour will eventually disappear. This decline in the response rate as a result of the discontinued reinforcement of the behaviour is defined as extinction; another term for extinction is omission because the positive reinforcer associated with the behaviour which the manager wishes to see eliminated or reduced is omitted every time that behaviour occurs.

In both the punishment by removal contingency and in the extinction contingency, we see that a reward or pleasant event is withheld. Nevertheless, there is an important difference in the reason why the reward or pleasant event is withheld. In the extinction contingency the aim is to eliminate or reduce the occurrence of a behaviour which was previously reinforced with appropriate rewards. In the past these behaviours were regarded as desirable, but now they are found to be undesirable. For this reason, the rewards that are withheld in the extinction contingency are those which were formerly reinforcers of this behaviour. On the other hand, in punishment by removal a reward is withheld because the behaviour has always been regarded as undesirable and it has never been reinforced by a reward.

CASE 3.1

Extinction or Punishment by Removal?

Bill, a young electrician, repaired electrical appliances with the power switched on, which is a safety hazard. He has followed this practice ever since he joined the company two years ago. The manager decides to change this undesirable behaviour.

Applying the principles of reinforcement contingencies, the manager can adopt one of three strategies:

- Withhold the comments which conveyed to the employee the feeling that he was a risk-taker and enjoyed its challenges.
- Give the employee an oral or written reprimand for violation of safety procedures.
- Reduce his merit pay increase.

The first strategy uses the extinction contingency. The manager has now realized that his sarcastic comments that the young man was a 'macho, risk-taker' had, in fact, operated as a positive reinforcer of the undesirable behaviour. Therefore, he now pays no attention to him, thereby withholding the former reinforcer. The second strategy involves punishment by application. The employee's undesirable behaviour is followed by a reprimand – an aversive consequence. The third strategy is punishment by removal. The employee's undesirable behaviour is followed by a reduction in merit pay. This is a withholding of a positive consequence, but it must be noted that this positive consequence (i.e., merit pay) was never functioning as a positive reinforcer of the undesirable behaviour. For this reason, the third strategy is not categorized as an extinction contingency.

- Do you think the type of strategy used should differ depending on certain employee characteristics? If yes, what are the characteristics (e.g., age, gender, cultural background) that should influence managers' choice of strategy?

When managers desire to employ the contingency of extinction they should follow a three-step procedure. First, identify the specific employee behaviour that is not desired. Second, identify the reinforcer that maintains the behaviour. Finally, eliminate the reinforcer so that the behaviour now no longer results in any pleasant consequence for the employee. This procedure is illustrated in the fifth scenario in the introduction of this chapter where Honest Ed Enterprises finds that its accounts receivables have reached an unacceptably high level. What is the undesirable behaviour?

The salespersons are lax in conducting the required credit check on credit sales. What is the positive reinforcer? The salespersons earned commission on the credit sales even when the credit report was not submitted by the salesperson. Having identified the reinforcer, the final step in extinction is to withhold the commission on credit sales for which the credit reports have not been submitted. Managers need to exercise caution in the use of extinction, because in the process of extinguishing an undesirable behaviour the desirable behaviours could also be eliminated. This is illustrated in the next case (Case 3.2).

C A S E   3 . 2

'Stop joking but not thinking!'

This is a work group whose productivity is jeopardized by the disruptive behaviour of one of its members, Andrei. Andrei is a talented comedian in addition to being a creative worker. The group members responded to his jokes with much laughter and also praised his problem-solving suggestions.

However, when working in teams Andrei's joking behaviour is having a disruptive effect on the group's performance. The supervisor decided to use the extinction contingency and during Andrei's absence the supervisor advised the group to refrain from laughing and withhold similar responses that reinforce Andrei's undesirable behaviour in the group.

At the next few meetings this strategy was followed with effective results. Andrei no longer disrupted the meeting with his jokes. However, he also stopped taking the initiatives in problem-solving and his participation was reduced to the barest essentials. Clearly, the extinction contingency unintentionally extinguished Andrei's desirable behaviours.

- What would have been the best way to eliminate Andrei's undesirable behaviours while keeping the desirable ones?

Often, managers fail to reinforce the desirable behaviour of employees and thereby may unintentionally extinguish such behaviour. It is very important that managers be vigilant about both desirable and undesirable behaviour in employees to provide positive reinforcements for the former and withhold reinforcements for the latter. In the work context the removal of an undesirable behaviour must also be accompanied by the substitution of a desirable behaviour in its place. To achieve this objective the extinction method for undesirable behaviour should be combined with positive reinforcement for desirable behaviour.

Shaping Behaviour

If the behaviour that a manager wishes to strengthen is already present and occurs with some frequency, then the contingent applications of reinforcers can increase and maintain the desired performance patterns at a high level. However, when new and complex behaviour patterns have to be established, the manager has to use behaviour modification techniques to gradually bring about the desired behaviours in the employee. This process of training employees to engage in new pattern of responses or behaviours by reinforcing a series of successive steps which lead to the desired new behaviours is called the shaping of behaviour. Using the principles of behaviour modification in a well-designed training programme allows the manager to accomplish the shaping of the employee's behaviour to meet performance standards and levels set by the organization. Shaping behaviour is necessary when the behavioural response to be learned is not currently in the individual's repertoire of behaviours and when it is a fairly complex behaviour.

In shaping, a desired pattern of behaviour is learned by reinforcing the series of successive steps which lead to the final set of responses or behaviour. This method is essentially the one driving instructors use to teach individuals to drive a car. The student is first taught how to adjust the seat and mirror, then to fasten the seatbelt, turn on the lights and windshield wipers and then to start the engine. Each time the student successfully completes a set of activities, they are positively reinforced by verbal praise. After reasonable proficiency in manipulating the internal control devices, the student is allowed to practice driving on empty lots and back roads and finally on the main streets and highways. By focusing on these critical aspects one at a time and appropriately reinforcing the proper behavioural responses, the driving instructor is able to shape a student's driving behaviour until the final stage of passing the driving licence test.

Action Plan to Maintain or Modify Performance Behaviours

The preceding outline of the behaviour modification approach provides a framework to manage the performance patterns in an organization to attain the job objectives and, eventually, the organization's objectives. This framework and related procedural steps, illustrated in Figure 3.3, considers four aspects: (1) the employee; (2) the behaviour; (3) the consequence of that behaviour; and (4) the work environment. These aspects provide the manager with the essential information for developing appropriate strategies for behaviour change. The framework assumes that the employee is capable of performing the behaviours that lead to accomplishing the job tasks.

The first step is to specify the desired performance level in specific, measurable terms, such as 'the telephone operator must answer 90 per cent of the calls within the first three rings of the telephone'. The second step is to identify the baseline

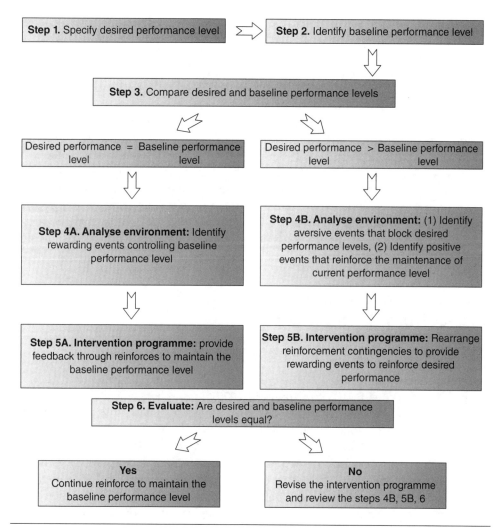

Step 1. Specify desired performance level ⟹ **Step 2.** Identify baseline performance level

Step 3. Compare desired and baseline performance levels

Desired performance = Baseline performance level level

Desired performance > Baseline performance level level

Step 4A. Analyse environment: Identify rewarding events controlling baseline performance level

Step 4B. Analyse environment: (1) Identify aversive events that block desired performance levels, (2) Identify positive events that reinforce the maintenance of current performance level

Step 5A. Intervention programme: provide feedback through reinforces to maintain the baseline performance level

Step 5B. Intervention programme: Rearrange reinforcement contingencies to provide rewarding events to reinforce desired performance

Step 6. Evaluate: Are desired and baseline performance levels equal?

Yes Continue reinforce to maintain the baseline performance level

No Revise the intervention programme and review the steps 4B, 5B, 6

Figure 3.3 *Action plan to maintain or modify baseline performance level*

behaviour in terms of the unit of measure used in step 1. Thus, the baseline behaviour might be identified as 75 per cent of the calls are currently answered within the first three rings. In step 3 compare the data of steps 1 and 2. If identical, then proceed to steps 4a and 5a. Step 4a enables the manager to analyse and identify the reinforcers (i.e., the rewarding events). In step 5a, the manager provides feedback by administering the reinforcers that are identified in 4a to maintain the baseline behaviour. If different, then plan intervention strategies as indicated in steps 4b, 5b and 6.

In step 4b, analyse and identify the environmental conditions that maintain the present performance level; these are the rewarding events such as peer approval. Also analyse and identify the environmental conditions that block or prevent performance behaviour at the desired level. These are the aversive events such as lack of incentives to perform better, a stressful job, or work overload. Step 5b is the development of an intervention programme. It involves managerial actions to rearrange the reinforcement contingencies such as providing incentives for higher performance levels.

Step 6 is an equally, if not more, critical step. In this step, the manager evaluates the intervention programme. If the desired performance level is reached, then the manager will maintain this level continuing the rearranged reinforcement contingencies initiated in step 5b. If the desired performance level is not reached, the manager will revise the intervention programme. For this purpose, the manager will need to repeat steps 4b, 5b and 6, as appropriate. Sometimes, if the job content changes necessitating a new set of desired behaviours, it might even be necessary to go back to step 1 and repeat the entire process.

Performance Management: Universal Trends and Cross-cultural Differences

Studies confirm that the application of behaviour modification has improved employee performance in different areas (Luthans, 2005), such as reduction of absenteeism and tardiness (Luthans and Maris, 1979), prevention of accidents and the promotion of safety (Zohar and Fussfeld, 1981; Atkinson, 2000), and enhancement of sales performance (Peterson and Luthans, 2003; Luthans, Paul and Taylor, 1985). Behavioural modification has been found to have had a positive impact on performance behaviours not only in the United States, but also in the Middle East (Elizur, 1987), Russia (Welsh, Luthans and Sommer, 1993) and South Korea (Luthans et al., 2008). Although the fundamental processes of operant conditioning are unconcerned with cognitive processes, later developments in the behaviour modification approach have incorporated certain cognitive and group processes in managing human behaviour. We now discuss the behaviour modification approach for managing performance, which takes the form of a step-by-step action plan managers can adopt to maintain or modify employee behaviour. This discussion also explores the culture fit of the action plans in the context of the different cultural characteristics.

Performance Management Process

Performance management is a process of planned activities to improve employee performance in organizations. Performance *management* should not be confused with performance *evaluation*, as the former includes the latter. Performance management entails an ongoing cyclical process with four steps:

1. Identify and clarify critical aspects of employees' jobs.
2. Setting goals and expectations.
3. Monitoring performance.
4. End-of-period formal review and preparation of the action plan for the following period.

In the first step, the manager *identifies* all the important aspects of the job and *clarifies* how it is related to the goals of the organization. It is a joint effort by the manager and the employees which leads to an agreed upon understanding of and commitment to the appropriate job behaviours. One way of identifying job objectives that are concrete and appropriate to organizational goals is to view the recipient of the job's products or outputs as the 'customer' of that job. The customer approach enables the employees to experience the significance of their tasks and promotes their identification with the organization's goals.

The second step of the cycle is the *setting of goals and expectations*. It specifies how well the tasks must be done, the time period by which these have to be done and the rewards such as bonus, promotion, etc., that will follow on completion of the tasks within the specified time period. As discussed in Chapter 2, the standards or goals ought to be difficult but attainable; specific, but appropriate to the objectives of the organization. By setting expectations, the employee is informed of the specific standards by which their job performance will be appraised and the specified rewards to be given.

The process of performance appraisal, despite the most sophisticated attempts to introduce objective procedures, will always remain a subjective process and, as such, highly vulnerable to fallible judgements. Therefore, employee participation in the goal-setting process is crucial. The knowledge and expertise of both the supervisor and the employees contribute to setting performance standards that are reasonable, realistic and appropriate. Furthermore, the joint goal-setting process promotes manager–subordinate agreement and gives the subordinate 'ownership and control', which generates trust, acceptance and commitment (Locke and Latham, 1984).

To illustrate these two steps let us consider the job of a salesman. Based on his own knowledge and experience and that of his salesmen, the sales manager lists all the job behaviours that are critical to successful sales performance, such as developing a prospects list, setting up appointments with customers, demonstrating products, customer follow-up, responding to customer complaints/enquiries, communications with the sales manager, developing budgets, sales reports, training juniors and initiating new sales approaches. These behaviours are then arranged in the order of how critical they are to increasing sales. Specific measures such as five customer demonstrations per week, ten new appointments every month, sales report by the first day of each month, etc., are assigned to each of the required behaviours, which then becomes the standards and measures of performance for which the employee will receive the specified rewards. Contemporary organizations refer to these performance standards as **Key Performance Indicators** (KPIs).

In setting the goals or standards, the manager and employees need to recognize the fundamental difference between **performance** and **productivity** (Kanungo, 1986). 'Performance' refers to an employee's actual manifest behaviour at work. 'Productivity', on the other hand, is the result, in terms of output, of that behaviour (i.e., performance). However, this behaviour involves the employee's interaction with the other inputs of the social system (co-workers, supervisors, subordinates), the technical system (materials, tools, machines, transforming process used) and the environment (market, economy, regulations). Thus, while performance depends upon the employee's knowledge, skills, ability and motivation, productivity depends not only on the employee's performance but also on the sociotechnical system and the environment.

The salesman in our earlier example, despite an excellent performance, could lose to a competitor if the plant is unable to guarantee delivery as per the customer's schedule. For this reason, the manager's role in this stage of the performance management cycle is also to (a) work at identifying and removing the environmental or organizational constraints; and (b) provide an adjustment mechanism that recognizes performance which meets the predetermined standards but fails to achieve the desired level of productivity owing to factors beyond the control of the employee.

The third step of the performance management cycle is *monitoring the performance*. During this phase, the manager provides informal or formal ongoing feedback, which is to be viewed not in terms of performance evaluation, but rather as on-the-job coaching. When managers function as coach, they seek to help employees grow and reach desired performance levels. Coaching involves knowing how well the employees are performing relative to performance standards in terms of specific measurable behaviours and discussing areas for improvement. The coach gives praise for work well done and offers constructive criticism when appropriate, including specific suggestions on how to correct the performance problems. Performance standards can never be written in stone; their validity always assumes a relatively stable environment. The manager who functions like a coach will be sensitive to changing environmental factors and will make suitable adjustments to the performance standards. Perhaps the shortfall in performance is because the employee is deficient in certain skills. The coaching approach enables the manager to become immediately aware of such deficiencies and provide remedial measures, e.g. training. In their coaching stance, managers are careful to create an open relaxed atmosphere which encourages employees to seek guidance in sorting out priorities or in resolving problems.

The fourth step is the *formal appraisal review* at the end of the predetermined performance period and *development of an action plan* to maintain high performance or increase poor performance. The nature of the activities in this step suggests that the manager plays the role of a judge. However, considering the possibility that the employee's performance might not be up to par, or needs some improvement it is recommended that the manager adopts a problem-solving approach.

Such an approach enables the manager to focus on the identification and removal of obstacles to good performance such as inappropriate or obsolete work procedures, lack of resources and certain skills and lack of a clear understanding of the job role and requirements. A joint discussion between the manager and the subordinate increases subordinates' trust in the fairness of the assessment process, because it is now certain that the manager has all the information needed for a fair evaluation. Furthermore, it provides an opportunity to discuss the short- and long-term career objectives of the subordinates, as well as their training and development needs. The problem-solving approach creates a climate of mutual trust, is non-threatening and therefore makes the appraisal review the ideal event to discuss and set goals for the next performance period. In this approach, managers function as both coach and judge, but the obvious emphasis is on their mentoring role as they seek to nurture the subordinates' strengths and minimize the negative effects of their weaknesses, if they cannot be completely eliminated.

In an effective performance management process, performance evaluation results should be linked to some consequences, rather than filed and stored in vain. This is indeed the basic principle of behavioural modification: desirable work behaviours should be rewarded and undesirable ones should be modified or eliminated. Rewards of good performance may include allocation of direct monetary resources, such as salary increase, bonus, merit pay, gain sharing or stock option schemes. Non-monetary rewards are also of importance, such as praise from top management or supervisors, awards and recognitions. Interventions to prevent poor performance from reoccurring may include training and development, elimination of certain rewards or benefits, withholding salary increase until there is proof of heightened performance, warning from the supervisor or top manager, changing the job processes, or transfer to a different job or department.

Effective Performance Management Across Cultures: Challenges and Recommendations

Cultural context may constrain the effective implementation of performance management practices. For example, high uncertainty avoidance may cause employees to be reluctant to exercise autonomy and accept responsibility. As a result, employees grow dependency on managers for detailed instructions and directions. Such an attitude is an obstacle to effective performance management, which requires employee willingness to act proactively in solving problems and finding resources to achieve predetermined goals.

In cultures of low individualism achievement of group goals is more important than achievement of individual goals. Employees may be resistant to meeting individual goals, especially if goal achievement depends on competition with others in the work group for resources or rewards.

High power-distance leads employees to accept their manager's directions and decisions without questioning. Employees do not view their manager as a partner. Hence, it is difficult for them to develop the relationship of joint problem-solving or joint goal-setting that is essential to successful performance management.

In cultures of low masculinity maintaining good relationships in the work team would be more important than meeting the agreed-upon goals. Work relationships are personalized, rather than contractual. As such, performance feedback may be misconstrued as an attack to the person, rather than an intervention to improve performance. The predominance of interpersonal considerations over goal achievement is incompatible with the performance management processes, requiring an objective and rational focus on goals and action plans to meet them.

Thinking across cultures 3.1 presents key challenges facing effective performance management (PM) in different countries and proposed recommendations for each challenge (cf. Varma et al., 2008).

Thinking across cultures 3.1

Performance Management Across Cultures: Challenges and Recommendations

The United States (Pulakos et al., 2008)

- **Challenge 1.** PM is perceived as an administrative burden, rather than a strategic tool for superior business results.

Recommendations:

(a) Consistently use strategy-driven competencies (SDCs) in all stages of PM: set *goals* to improve SDCs; use SDCs as criteria in *performance appraisal*; provide *training and development activities* to improve SDCs; give *incentives, rewards* and recognitions to employees who demonstrate SDCs.
(b) Demonstrate improvements in business results when PM is used as a strategic tool.

- **Challenge 2.** Managers and employees refrain from engaging in candid performance appraisal and discussions.

Recommendations:

(a) The problem arises partly because of the fear that performance appraisal results have a direct impact on critical HR decisions such as pay, promotion and discharge. Make sure that employees receive ample and timely feedback about their performance throughout the year. Also provide them with opportunities (training or developmental activities) to improve poor performance.

(b) Convey messages (verbal and non-verbal) throughout the year that performance appraisal should not be perceived as a threat to the work relationships between rater and ratee.

- **Challenge 3.** Time pressure and judgemental nature of evaluations impede accurate assessment of employee performance.

Recommendations:

(a) Set up systems (preferably web-based) to encourage managers to record critical incidences demonstrating poor and outstanding performance of employees. Such records taken throughout the year not only increase the accuracy of evaluations but also reduce the evaluation time.
(b) Provide managers with clear guidelines to judge employees' behaviours. For example, prepare behavioural-based performance evaluation systems and guidelines to indicate which behaviours should be judged in what ways.

Mexico (Davila and Elvira, 2008)

- **Challenge 1.** It is difficult to relate a PM system to organizational performance and therefore individual incentive plans in Mexico's unstable economic and political environment.

Recommendations:

(a) Organizations should carefully plan the consequences of performance appraisal and offer employees incentives other than financial rewards, such as training and promotion opportunities in exchange for high performance.
(b) Organizational practices (e.g., activities that involve employee families) should be used to promote loyalty, commitment and performance in the collectivistic culture of Mexico.

(Continued)

(Continued)

- **Challenge 2.** Methods and tools that emphasize individual accountability and individual performance conflict with the cultural values of collectivism.

Recommendations:

(a) Performance goals should be set both at the individual and group levels. Employees' individual performance should be appraised in relation to their contribution to the overall performance of the team, department or the organization.
(b) Performance objectives and evaluations should include desired cross-hierarchical or subgroup performance.

- **Challenge 3.** Employees experience a tension between satisfying their superiors' demands on the one hand and meeting the performance standards set by the organization on the other.

Recommendations:

(a) Mexican organizations should speed up the institutionalization process so that high-performing employees do not fear losing their jobs when they do not satisfy the demands of their superiors.
(b) Performance standards or objectives should be set jointly with participation of top-level management as well as line managers and superiors.

The United Kingdom (Sparrow, 2008)

- **Challenge 1.** There is cynicism about the contribution of PM systems to organizational bottom line:

UK managers believe that this is an outdated model of strategy ... many HR strategies are 'illusions in the boardroom' ... the realities of people and performance HR strategies are dry, over-engineered plans that have been developed by a small coterie of 'experts' in the rarefied atmosphere of the boardroom. (2008, pp. 140–41)

Recommendations:

(a) To regain the credibility of PM system, it should be carefully designed and implemented *especially* in times of downsizing, outsourcing, acquisition or cost-cutting.
(b) The focus should shift from PM to talent management involving strong leadership, coaching and communication programmes.
(c) The focus should also shift from the bureaucratic technicalities of PM by e-enabling it to capability development and strategic support required for superior organizational outcomes.

- **Challenge 2.** While US organizations mainly focus on issues of accuracy and fairness in performance appraisals, UK organizations focus on motivational issues of dissatisfactions with using such systems, especially in the public sector: the 'PM system is either loved or hated on ideological grounds' (Sparrow, 2008, p. 142).

Recommendations:

(a) PM in a public sector context should be framed in such a way that it is perceived as a process associated with good governance to meet the expectations of multiple constituencies and stakeholders, rather than a process of control over civil servants.
(b) Organizations (especially the public sector) should clearly relate PM with total quality management (TQM).

- **Challenge 3.** There is an increasing concern that performance appraisal outcomes are biased by the length of hours spent at work which makes work–life balance difficult to maintain.

Recommendations:

(a) The performance evaluation system should protect employees from being penalized for spending time with their families during off-hours and weekends.
(b) Organizational culture should promote work–life balance for all employees, not just those who have family-related responsibilities.
(c) Performance ratings should only reflect performance outcomes and competencies demonstrated at work, rather than number of hours worked.

(Continued)

(Continued)

India (Sharma, Budhwar and Varma, 2008)

- **Challenge 1.** PM is reduced to a form-filling exercise conducted once a year. This is partly because no real consequences are attached to performance appraisal results.

Recommendations:

(a) Employees and managers should understand that PM is a process that includes numerous activities to enhance performance throughout the year. The champions of the system in the organizations (especially the top management team) should clearly articulate the purpose of the process and its integrated phases including planning, monitoring, motivating, appraising, providing timely feedback and improving.
(b) Managers should be coached, evaluated and rewarded for successfully implementing the integrated phases of the PM.
(c) Organizations should establish transparent systems to show the link between performance and outcomes (e.g., rewards, promotion decisions, discharges).

- **Challenge 2.** Performance ratings may be highly subjective and biased, reflecting the nature of the relationship between the rater and ratee.

Recommendations:

(a) Performance appraisal systems should be based on assessing objective work outcomes in numerical terms as well as assessing competencies using scales based on behavioural observations (e.g., behaviourally anchored rating scales). This way bias is minimized.
(b) The performance appraisal process should involve multiple raters, rather than relying only on supervisor ratings.
(c) Raters should be encouraged to monitor and record performance throughout the year so that they can present evidence (e.g., records of critical incidents) to justify their high or low performance.

- **Challenge 3.** Performance management in team environment is an unknown territory for organizations.

Recommendations:

(a) An effective system should be developed to ensure fairness in evaluating individual performance in teams.
(b) Reward allocation to individuals in teams should be based on both team performance as well as each individual's contribution to performance in teams.
(c) In the planning phase of PM, roles and responsibilities of team members should be emphasized but flexibility should also be given to allow shift in roles whenever necessary.

China (Cooke, 2008)

• **Challenge 1.** PM is not perceived as a strategic management tool.

Recommendations:

(a) Because such strategic management systems are new for Chinese culture, top-level management should be the champion of these systems.
(b) There must be a clear articulation of *why* and *how* PM is associated with the strategies and outcomes (e.g., financial success, growth, adaptability, learning) of Chinese organizations competing in the global context. Employees should be presented with the best practices from the domestic and international markets.
(c) Training for PM should be widespread in organizations.

• **Challenge 2.** Performance appraisal is seen as a formality.

Recommendations:

(a) As indicated above, top management has a key role and responsibility to demonstrate that performance appraisal is critical for workforce management. The motto 'you can't manage what you don't measure' should be understood and appreciated by employees at all levels.
(b) Performance appraisal results *must* be linked with employee outcomes, such as pay, promotion, discharge, reward allocation, training and development, transfer and so on. If performance appraisal has no consequences, it is bound to be seen as a useless exercise.

(Continued)

(Continued)

- **Challenge 3.** There is bias and subjectivity in the performance appraisal process.

Recommendations:

(a) 'Performance criteria in Chinese organizations tend to be generic, broad and focus on effort and behaviour instead of/as much as outcome' (Cooke, 2008, p. 205). It is strongly recommended that performance criteria are set jointly by senior and middle management so that there are agreed-upon, specific and observable performance indicators. If mid-level managers (or other raters) participate in the determination of performance criteria, they will be more likely to stick to them in the appraisal process.
(b) Multiple raters, measurable criteria, ratings based on behavioural observations and evidence-based judgements, when used in combination, are most likely to minimize bias.

Australia (De Cieri and Sheehan, 2008)

- **Challenge 1.** Diversity of workforce and shift from manufacturing to service industry require new perspectives to performance management.

Recommendations:

(a) The PM system should ensure that women and employees with diverse ethnic backgrounds have an equal chance to receive developmental opportunities and promotion possibilities.
(b) Organizations should pay special attention to the training of new entrants to service sector lacking the necessary knowledge and skills to perform in the service industry.
(c) PM systems should be developed to minimize bias and subjectivity: 'Australian employers need to ensure that PM system is free of bias to capitalize on the perspectives and values that a diverse workforce can contribute to improving product quality, customer service, product development and market share' (2008, p. 245).

- **Challenge 2.** PM should be designed to manage the rising contingent workforce (e.g., part-time workers, temporary/seasonal workers, telecommuters).

Recommendations:

(a) Contingent workforces tend to receive low share in employee development programmes. Organizations should allocate more resources to develop their contingent workers, whose performance contributes substantially to that of organizations.
(b) Contingent workers should be trained to use technology to give and receive timely feedback and information about their performance.
(c) Organizations should closely monitor the PM system to minimize biases in evaluating and rewarding the contingent workforce.
(d) Organizations should develop special programmes to increase the motivation and commitment of the contingent workforce.

- **Challenge 3.** Australian organizations may face serious legal charges if their PM system fails to comply with anti-discrimination and Equal Employment Opportunity EEO legislations.

Recommendations:

(a) Employers must ensure that there is a transparent performance appraisal system that is applied consistently; performance reviews are made against clearly specified criteria; results of previous appraisal assessment are taken into account; there is timely counselling and warning to employees with low performance; reasons for action (especially dismissal) are clearly documented and shared with the employee.
(b) Those who are involved in performance review and evaluation should be trained to effectively use the PM and to minimize bias in the evaluation process.
(c) Employers should not force an employee to resign or make work conditions unpleasant enough that they will resign – these actions would also be interpreted as dismissal and taken to court.

According to this review of PM in different countries, what do you think are the similarities in key challenges facing organizations in the majority of countries?

What are the differences across countries and what are the factors (e.g., cultural context, workforce characteristics, level of country's industrialization) leading to these differences?

Cross-cultural Considerations for Managers

We now propose a modus operandi for each step of the performance management process for societal or organizational cultures characterized by high uncertainty-avoidance, low individualism, high power-distance and low masculinity.

The recommendations outlined here aim at overcoming cultural constraints and building upon those cultural beliefs and values that have the potential to facilitate successful implementation of key steps in the PM process. To ensure the effective implementation of these steps, we recommend that managers adopt the **nurturant-task leadership** approach (Sinha, 1995).

Thinking across cultures 3.2

Nurturant-task Leadership for Effective Performance Management

Nurturant-task leadership, as proposed by Sinha (1995), is common in cultures with high power-distance, high uncertainty-avoidance, low individualism and low masculinity. The leader is caring and nurturant; they are interested in the well-being of employees in their work and personal life. However, the leader extends their care and nurturance to those who perform well in their jobs. The following are behavioural examples of nurturant-task leaders based on the measure of Sinha (1995):

- is kind only to those subordinates who work sincerely
- takes personal interest in the promotion of those subordinates who work hard
- gladly guides and directs those subordinates who work hard
- encourages their subordinates to assume greater responsibility on the job as they become more experienced
- openly favours those who work hard
- appreciates those subordinates who want to perform better
- is very affectionate to hard-working subordinates
- goes out of their way to help those subordinates who maintain a high standard of performance
- openly praises those subordinates who are punctual
- feels good when they find their subordinates eager to learn.
- In what ways do you think nurturant-task leader may be effective and ineffective to manage performance in collectivistic and hierarchical cultures?
- Do you think this leadership may be effective in managing performance of employees in individualistic and egalitarian cultures as well? Why and why not?

The nurturant-task leader sets performance goals and standards which are clear, specific, *within the employees' control* and expressed as *service to others* inside and outside the organization. This is consistent with the high power-distance, high uncertainty-avoidance and low masculinity characteristics of the work culture.

The leader then provides nurturance through training, support and recognition which builds on the characteristics of low individualism and low masculinity. As employees meet the performance goals and receive the appropriate rewards, these managerial actions will increase employees' self-efficacy belief that they can perform as required. However, the employees would continue to be dependent on the manager. Hence the manager must repeat the first and second set of actions, but gradually decreases the directions related to the task, while continuing with the nurturance. The gradual decrease in task directions and the employees' experience of successful attainment of job goals reduces their dependence on the manager and, at the same time, empowers them to function autonomously.

Let us discuss the set of managerial actions to ensure the cultural fit of each step of the performance management process.

In step 1, the manager:

- establishes departmental and job objectives which constitute the directions employees expect in *a high power-distance* culture;
- states these objectives in specific measurable terms which serve to overcome the effects of *high uncertainty-avoidance*;
- expresses these objectives as meeting the needs of the recipient of the job's product/service, as well as contributing to organizational goals which ultimately impact the larger external community (neighborhood, region, country); this action is consistent with *low masculinity*.

In Step 2, the manager:

- sets performance goals and standards for each job that are within the employee's control which reduces the debilitating effects of *high uncertainty-avoidance*;
- provides directions consistent with *high power-distance* and also provides support and encouragement. The manager's empowering actions enable employees, as they complete the tasks, to experience a personal sense of task accomplishment which reduces the constraining effects of *low individualism*; as the employees experience success in the assigned tasks, they begin to feel more capable which makes them less dependent on the manager;

In Step 3, the manager provides employees, on an ongoing basis, feedback:

- as their coach and mentor which reduces the constraining effect of *high power-distance*;

- geared to employees' performance improvement and their development which enables them to see work concerns and accomplishment of job objectives as meaningful; as a result, they are not inhibited by the cultural characteristic of *low individualism.*
- relating to performance standards within their control which reduces the effects of *high uncertainty-avoidance*;
- that highlights the impact of employee performance – positive and negative, on people – inside and outside the organization, which builds on *low masculinity.*

In Step 4, the manager, at the end of the performance period:

- continues the role of coach and mentor which reduces the constraining effects of *high power-distance*;
- recognizes and rewards successful performance at organization's community events which builds on the *low masculinity* characteristic of the work culture;
- recognizes factors beyond the employee's control which impeded performance which serves to reduce the effects of *high uncertainty-avoidance*;
- formulates a specific action plan for employee development and removal of contextual obstacles to good performance, as needed; and thereby overcomes the constraining effects of *low individualism.*

Chapter Summary

This chapter explores the principles of operant conditioning and examined its application in the workplace through the major behaviour modification techniques: positive reinforcement, negative reinforcement, punishment by application, punishment by removal and extinction or omission. The process of behaviour modification and the operative principles of the reinforcement contingencies are discussed. The overriding principle involved is that the present and future occurrence of a behaviour is a function of the environmental consequences that it brings about or generates (see Video 3.1). Finally, we discuss the implications of the behaviour modification approach for performance management and present a step-by-step action plan which managers can adopt to maintain or modify the current baseline behaviour.

The effectiveness of the performance management process is largely dependent on certain preconditions without which it becomes a meaningless exercise in futility with the potential to harm the employees and the organization. The first precondition is that managers recognize that an organization is not composed of automatons whose successful functioning depends upon endless elaborate rules and control systems. An organization is a dynamic social system of living human beings with specific aptitudes, abilities, motives and aspirations. The tremendous potential of this social system cannot be tapped by developing hierarchical power structures with a bewildering array of committees, subcommittees, position titles and sycophantic relationships. Rather, it can only be done by a clear articulation of the vision for the organization – its mission and purpose, that will excite and challenge its employees to use their talents and abilities for the mutual benefit of themselves and the organization (see Video 3.2).

The second precondition is closely related to the first. Because employees are a vital resource, expenditure relating to employees such as recruitment, compensation, training and development can only be looked upon as an investment much like, if not more critical than, expenditure on capital assets. When managers regard their employees as an investment, logically there follows an implicit obligation to get an adequate return from this investment, which leads to a conscious deliberate action plan to manage employee performance, to establish specific job objectives and to set in motion the process, described in this chapter, of evaluating employee performance and coaching and developing employees towards the attainment of the job objectives (see Video 3.3).

Rewarding managers for employee development is the third precondition for successful management of employee performance. Implicit in this condition are the concomitant conditions that managers are trained with the necessary skills in using the system of performance management. In an extensive study of performance appraisal practices, Lawler et al. (1984) found that when the organizational climate was one of high trust, support and openness it had a significant positive impact on the performance appraisal process. In a supportive and trusting climate, senior managers, through personal examples, can transmit the appropriate appraisal behaviour which can then be emulated by managers at all levels in the organization.

We outlined the difficulties organizations face with performance management in different countries: the US, UK, Australia, Mexico, India and China. There are culture-general challenges facing organizations, such as the difficulty of linking performance management systems with organizational strategy. There are also culture-specific challenges resulting from the nature of superior–subordinate relationships. We explored performance management in the context of the non-Western cultures (characterized by high power-distance, high uncertainty-avoidance, low individualism and low masculinity) and provided a step-by-step approach to guide practitioners functioning in such contexts.

End of Chapter Reflection Questions

1. Some scholars and managers believe that rewards and punishment kill intrinsic motivation and joy of work. Do you agree or disagree with this assertion? Under what circumstances do you think this assertion may be true?

2. 'Punishment is the evil sister of reward – they are the two faces of the same coin.' What do you think about this statement? Should we do away with rewards and punishment in organizations? If yes, what should we replace reward and punishment with to increase performance?

3. In recent years, some management consultants have recommended that organizations should stop worrying about overcoming *weaknesses* in employees and start focusing on how to make best use of their *strengths*. Would this approach put an end to behavioural modification, if adopted? Why and why not?

Key Terms and Definitions

Behaviour modification. The process in which desirable work behaviours are reinforced and undesirable ones are modified or eliminated.

Reinforcement contingencies. Consequence associated with a particular behaviour that will either increase or decrease the occurrence of the same behaviour.

Reinforcement vs. reward. Reinforcement is an event (positive or negative) following a behaviour to increase the occurrence of that behaviour, whereas reward is an event conventionally considered as positive or pleasant that follows a desirable behaviour.

Positive reinforcement. Increasing the occurrence of behaviour by presenting a pleasant event following that behaviour (e.g., presenting a letter of appreciation followed by a desirable work behaviour).

Negative reinforcement. Increasing the occurrence of behaviour by removing an unpleasant event following that behaviour (e.g., removing the budgetary constraint followed by a successful project completion).

Punishment by application. Decreasing the occurrence of behaviour by presenting an unpleasant event followed by that behaviour (e.g., presenting a letter of warning followed by an undesirable work behaviour).

Punishment by removal. Decreasing the occurrence of behaviour by removing a pleasant event following that behaviour (e.g., reducing the bonus pay followed by an undesirable work behaviour).

Omission or extinction. Decreasing the occurrence of behaviour once desirable by withdrawing the pleasant events followed by that behaviour in the past.

Performance management. Planned activities to improve employee performance in organizations, including four critical steps: (1) identifying key job duties, (2) setting goals, (3) monitoring performance and providing feedback, (4) evaluating performance and designing an action plan for future.

Key performance indicators. Performance standards expected from employees for outstanding work outcomes.

Performance vs. productivity. Performance refers to employees' actual manifest behaviour at work, whereas 'productivity' is the result of that behaviour (i.e. performance).

Nurturant task leadership. Caring and nurturant leadership behaviour to those who perform well on the job.

Further Reading

Aguinis, H. (2013) *Performance Management*, 3rd edn. Upper Saddle River, NJ: Pearson Prentice Hall.

Armstrong, M. (2007) *Employee Reward Management and Practice*. London: Kogan Page.

Den Hartog, D.N., Boselie, P. and Paauwe, J. (2004) 'Performance management: A model and research agenda', *Applied Psychology: An International Review*, 53 (4): 556–69.

Kanungo, R.N. and Mendonça, M. (1997) *Compensation: Effective Reward Management*. Toronto, Canada: John Wiley and Sons.

London, M. and Smither, J.W. (2002) 'Feedback orientation, feedback culture and the longitudinal performance management process', *Human Resource Management Review*, 12 (1): 81–100.

Podsakoff, N.P., Podsakoff, P.M. and Kuskova, V.V. (2010) 'Dispelling misconceptions and providing guidelines for leader reward and punishment behavior', *Business Horizons*, 53 (3): 291–303.

Smith, N., Smith, V. and Verner, M. (2006) 'Do women in top management affect firm performance? A panel study of 2,500 Danish firms', *International Journal of Productivity and Performance Management*, 55 (7): 569–93.

Stephen, J.P. and White, G. (2011) *Reward management: Alternatives, consequences and contexts*. London: Chartered Institute of Personnel and Development.

White, M., Hill, S., McGovern, P., Mills, C. and Smeaton, D. (2003) 'High performance management practices, working hours and work-life balance', *British Journal of Industrial Relations*, 41 (2): 175–95.

Cases, Videos, Web sources

Cases

The following cases focus on management of low performance and utility of incentive plans as a behavioural modification technique.

Kerr, S. (2003) 'The best-laid incentive plans', *Harvard Business Review*, January, 27–37.
Gandz, J. and Spracklin, E. (2010) *Sara Tsien*. IVEY cases no: 9B10C007.

Videos

Video 3.1 Shawn Achor: *The Happy Secret to Better Work* (2012) www.ted.com/talks/shawn_achor_the_happy_secret_to_better_work.html – Achor 'reverses the causality' and argues that *happiness* is the key for high performance.

Video 3.2 Michael Voltaire: *Behavior Modification Toward a Sustainable World* (2013) www. youtube.com/watch?v=4FTeIHoONjQ – Voltaire advocates behavioural modification not only to improve employee behaviour, but also to increase our chances of creating a sustainable future for generations to come.

Video 3.3 Phillip Zimbardo: *The Pygmalion Effect and the Power of Positive Expectations* (2011) www.youtube.com/watch?v=hTghEXKNj7g – Zimbardo presents a compelling case showing that higher expectations lead to higher performance.

Web sources

http://performanceportal.org/ – *Performance Management Association.*
www.som.cranfield.ac.uk/som/cbp – *Center for Business Performance.*
www.kpimegalibrary.com/ – *1000s Key Performance Indicators.*

References

Atkinson, W. (2000) 'Behavior-based safety', *Management Review*, 45 (3): 41–6.

Cooke, F.L. (2008) *Competition, Strategy and Management in China.* New York: Palgrave Macmillan.

Davila, A. and Elvira, M.M. (2008) Performance management in Mexico, in A. Varma, P.S. Budhwar and A. DeNisi (eds) *Performance Management Systems: A Global Perspective,* pp. 115–130. London: Routledge.

De Cieri, H. and Sheehan, C. (2008) 'Performance management in Australia', in A. Varma, P.S. Budhwar and A. De Nisi (eds), *Performance Management Systems: A Global Perspective,* pp. 239–54. London: Routledge.

Elizur, D. (1987) 'Work and nonwork relations: A facet analysis', *Journal of General Psychology,* 114: 47–55.

Kanungo, R.N. (1986) 'Productivity, satisfaction and involvement: A brief note on some conceptual issues', *International Journal of Management,* 7: 8–12.

Lawler, E.E., III, Mohrman, A.M., Jr. and Resnick, S.M. (1984) Performance appraisal revisited. *Organizational Dynamics,* 13 (1), 20–35.

Locke, E.A. and Latham, G.P. (1984) *Goal Setting: A Motivational Technique that Works!* Englewood Cliffs, NJ: Prentice Hall.

Luthans, F. (2005) *Organization Behavior.* New York: McGraw Hill International.

Luthans, F. and Maris, T.L. (1979) 'Evaluating personnel programs through the reversal technique', *Personnel Journal,* 58: 692–7.

Luthans, F., Paul, R. and Taylor, L. (1985) 'The impact of contingent reinforcement on retail salespersons' performance behaviors: A replicated field experiment', *Journal of Organizational Behavior Management,* 7: 25–35.

Luthans, F., Rhee, S., Luthans, B.C. and Avey, J.B. (2008) Impact of behavioral performance management in a Korean application. *Leadership & Organization Development Journal,* 29 (5), 427–43.

Peterson, S. and Luthans, F. (2003) The positive impact of development of hopeful leaders. *Leadership and Organization Development Journal,* 24, 26–31.

Pulakos, E.D., Mueller-Hanson, R.A. and O'Leary, R.S. (2008) 'Performance management in the United States', in A. Varma, P.S. Budhwar and A. De Nisi (eds), *Performance Management Systems: A Global Perspective*, pp. 97–114. New York: Routledge.

Sharma, T., Budhwar, P. and Varma, A. (2008) Performance management in India, in A. Varma, P.S. Budhwar and A. DeNisi (eds), *Performance Management Systems: A Global Perspective*, pp. 180–92. New York: Routledge.

Sinha, J.B.P. (1995) *The Cultural Context of Leadership and Power*. New Delhi: Sage Publications.

Skinner, B.F. (1974) *About Behaviorism*. New York: Alfred A. Knopf.

Sparrow, P.R. (2008) *International Mobility in the Financial Services Sector: The Challenge of Emerging Markets. GMAC Global Relocation Trends Report*. London: GMAC.

Varma, A., Budhwar, P.S. and De Nisi, A. (2008) *Performance Management Systems*. London: Routledge.

Welsh, D.H.B., Luthans, F. and Sommer, S.M. (1993) 'Managing Russian factory workers: The impact of U.S.-based behavioral and participative techniques', *Academy of Management Journal*, 36: 58–79.

Zohar, D. and Fussfeld, N. (1981) 'Modifying earplug-wearing behavior by behavior modification techniques: An empirical evaluation', *Journal of Organizational Behavior Management*, 3: 41–52.

Want to learn more? Visit the companion website at www.sagepub.co.uk/kanungo to gain access to videos from the end of each chapter, weblinks and flash cards of key terms.

4

Communication and Conflict Management

Chapter Outline

> Whenever you're in conflict with someone, there is one factor that can make the difference between damaging your relationship and deepening it. That factor is attitude.

William James

When a family, whose members have different preferences, has to decide on a restaurant for dinner, or on where to go for their summer vacation ... when parents determine little Susie's weekly allowance ... when individuals make an expensive purchase ... when department managers meet to justify their budget demands in the context of cost-cutting pressures from the finance department ... when managers set job goals for their subordinates and enforce operating procedures ... when teachers assign grades ...

In every one of these situations from personal and work life, there is a potential for conflict and negotiation. In fact, it would not be an exaggeration to say that the potential for conflict is inherent in human relationships and we should not necessarily try to avoid it. The potential for conflict arises especially in cross-cultural interactions. Although it may be difficult to handle conflict, oftentimes it presents itself as an opportunity to deepen our understanding of cross-cultural differences and to motivate us to reconcile them through negotiation. That is why we need to have a positive attitude towards conflict, and see it not as a threat but as an opportunity to build better work relationships.

In this chapter, we first explore the nature and characteristics of social or interpersonal conflict and some of the antecedent conditions that are likely to give rise to conflict. We then discuss various behaviours exhibited by parties in the conflict process, with a particular emphasis on negotiation strategies and their effectiveness in conflict resolution in general and in cross-cultural settings. In addition, we discuss the interpersonal communication skills and the behaviour mode of the conflicting parties that enhance the effectiveness of the conflict resolution strategies. In the last section, we explore cross-cultural differences in the way conflict is handled and negotiation is carried out.

Learning Objectives

- To examine the nature and characteristics of interpersonal conflict.
- To identify and minimize the conditions leading to conflict.
- To describe the steps and strategies in the negotiation process and examine its effectiveness in resolving conflict.
- To understand the nature and purpose of the interpersonal communication skills of active listening and assertive behaviour.
- To learn cross-cultural difference in conflict management and negotiation.
- To review strategies to handle conflict and negotiate effectively in cross-cultural settings.

The Nature and Characteristics of Interpersonal Conflict

Conflict, in the generic sense, is essentially an experience of some form of disagreement or a situation of opposing choices. Conflicts can be broadly classified into intrapersonal and interpersonal. Intrapersonal conflict involves a single person. Such conflict can relate to decisions which involve choices from among equally desirable or equally undesirable outcomes or from a mix of both desirable and undesirable outcomes. Intrapersonal conflict can also result from tension when a person's behaviours are inconsistent with their values.

Interpersonal conflicts, which will be the focus of this chapter, can be described as social conflict. These conflicts involve at least two parties – each can be either an individual or a group – who perceive themselves to have separate but conflicting interests. Such interests could relate to goals and/or values. In the organizational context, interpersonal or social conflict can arise when organizational members differ in their understanding of their job role expectations or when there are role ambiguities. Social conflict can also arise between groups, as would be the case in union–management relations or among department managers competing for limited organizational resources.

A conflict situation then gives rise to certain behaviours which may or may not result in the resolution of the conflict. These behavioural responses depend upon each party's attitude to the conflict situation, which is largely determined by their objectives and goals. The objectives and goals can, and in most cases do, include both tangibles and intangibles. The tangibles are the substantive elements involved in the conflict. For example, in the situations cited at the beginning of this chapter, the tangibles are the specific restaurant, vacation location, weekly allowance, course grades, budget amount, operating procedures, price and terms and conditions of the contract. The intangibles are the psychological factors involved in the conflict situation, such as winning rather than losing; maintaining a reputation of being fair and principled, or of being tough and one who will never capitulate; establishing and preserving a long-term relationship; saving face.

Conditions (Potentially) Leading to Conflict

The conflict process can be said to begin or originate with the **antecedent conditions** potentially leading to conflict. These are real, objective conditions which are present in the environment or context in which the exchange or interaction between the parties is taking place. The fact of their existence in the environment, per se, does not lead to a conflict between the parties. We therefore do not refer to these conditions as antecedents of conflict. If we did, then we would be asserting that these conditions will *necessarily* lead to conflict. However, the nature of the social relationships amidst these conditions is such that a conflict is *likely* (although not certain) to arise when these conditions exist. There are nine such conditions (e.g., Filley, 1975): ambiguous jurisdictions, conflicting interests, communication barriers, dependence of one party, differentiation in organization, association of the parties, need for consensus, behaviour regulations and unresolved prior conflicts.

It is important to recognize that this list does not exhaust the countless number of conditions or characteristics of social relationships which have the potential for conflict. We focus on the nine conditions because these are some of the conditions most likely to be the source of conflict in organizations. Let us elaborate on them.

Ambiguous jurisdictions

Ambiguous jurisdictions exist in an organization when the task and authority structures are not clearly established. At the individual level, it occurs when job descriptions do not clearly define the job roles, which leads to overlapping responsibilities for some job tasks. At the work unit level, it occurs when the boundaries between work units have been established with overlapping responsibilities.

Conflicting interests

Mary and John are the managers of departments 'A' and 'B' respectively. They are the only managers in the company who have asked for increases to their budgets. John has requested €75,000 and Mary has requested €80,000; the available resources are only €100,000. In this scenario, we see a conflict of interest between Mary and John because both are in competition for those limited resources. Both cannot achieve their *entire* goals or objectives at the same time. In a conflict of interest, the goals of one party can only be met at the expense of the other.

Communication barriers

When barriers to communication exist there is a potential for inaccurate and incomplete information and even the total disruption of communication. These situations can lead parties in an exchange situation to misunderstand the goals and interests of each other. Such misunderstanding contains the seeds of a conflict. Barriers to communication can take many forms: the most common are the physical barriers of time and space. However, equally significant as a potential source of conflict are psychological barriers. For example, when groups are in competition, pressure tends to be exerted on group members to refrain from contact and discussion with members of the opponent group. We cannot ignore the communication barriers that result from language differences as well as from the differences in the communication mode imposed by cultural norms.

Dependence of one party

It is easy to see that when Mary is unable to perform her task until John has completed his task, we have a potential for a conflict situation between Mary and John. In such a situation Mary, because of her dependence on John, might experience frustration and anger. Furthermore, she is also vulnerable to possible exploitation by John. It needs to be recognized that *dependence of one party* is significantly different from *interdependence*. In the latter case, both parties are dependent upon each other, which generally gives rise to the mutuality of interests and, as a result, a greater likelihood of contributing to a reduction in conflict.

Differentiation in organization

This condition of conflict also relates to the design of the task and authority structures. Consider a company in which the tasks are grouped on a highly specialized basis, the span of control is narrow and there is a high degree of centralization (see Chapter 8). Such a design will create a tall structure with many hierarchical levels. As a result the potential for conflict discussed under ambiguous jurisdictions, conflicting interests, communication barriers and dependence of one party are also likely to exist here.

Another potential for conflict is the way the organization approaches its staff functions. If the staff function is assigned more of a monitoring rather than an advisory role, such differentiation is more likely to create conflict. For example, consider the role of the human resource management function. Suppose the organization assigns to it the exclusive role of hiring employees, instead of the advisory role of assisting line managers in hiring the employees they need. This differentiation has the potential for conflict between the human resources department and the line managers.

Association of the parties

Association here is interpreted to mean both the formal and informal relations that exist in the organization. The more the employees have to work with others in task performance, as happens in situations of joint decision-making or in participative management programmes, the greater the possibility that conflict will occur. Organizations with high employee involvement programmes, such as autonomous work teams, prepare their employees with training in interpersonal skills and team-building in order to reduce the occurrence of conflict that is inherent in such approaches.

Need for consensus

A consensual decision by its very nature requires that those who do not agree are required to go along with the decision. Thus the potential for conflict is already present, because those who disagree need to satisfy themselves that their view or opinion contributes less to the attainment of the work unit or organizational goals than the view or opinion with which they are required to agree. Perhaps the need for consensus might not contribute to conflict as much as it often does if the parties understood the real meaning of consensus. *Consensus* does not require that the decision be unanimously accepted, therefore it does not require the few who dissent to give up their firmly held views or convictions. All that consensus requires is that the dissenters consider two questions: (1) will the acceptance of the decision compromise a basic value or belief? and (2) will the execution of the decision pose unbearable hardships? If the answer to both is negative, then consensus will not be a cause of conflict.

Behaviour regulations

In general behaviour regulations, particularly those which deal with interdepartmental relationships, provide for orderly and predictable ways of managing and coordinating different functions and activities. Ultimately, behaviour regulations are designed to serve the attainment of the organization's objectives, and therefore reflect the organization's mission. They are analogous to the traffic rules and road signs which are not intended to restrict our movement, but to assist us in better achieving our travel objectives. Designed and implemented in this way, behaviour regulations should contribute to reducing the possibility of conflict.

Potential for conflict increases when the behaviour regulations are perceived as arbitrary and not reflecting the organization's mission, and when these regulations needlessly encroach upon the legitimate autonomy and freedom which employees need to function efficiently and effectively. This is particularly the case in organizations where employees have high growth needs and greatly value the opportunity for self-direction.

Unresolved prior conflicts

Just as trust and cooperation breed greater trust and cooperation, so too does conflict. A conflict is said to be unresolved when parties do not perceive mutual satisfaction with the final outcomes. Mutual satisfaction with the final outcomes does not imply that both parties receive the identical set of outcomes, but that the received outcomes – tangible or intangible – satisfy their interests, needs and aspirations. *Resolving* the conflict is not the same as *ending or terminating* the conflict. A conflict can be terminated with outcomes that are mutually satisfactory to the parties. Such termination of the conflict is said to be a resolution of the conflict. On the other hand, when the conflict is terminated and the parties (or, at least, one of the parties) do not experience satisfaction of the outcomes, then the termination of the conflict does not resolve the conflict. This situation then becomes the *unresolved prior conflict* and the unsatisfactory experience of one of the parties will be carried over and impact the exchange relationship in the future. For example, when the manager uses means – physical (control over resources) or psychological (influence inherent in their job) – to get their subordinate to unwillingly yield to their demands, then the subordinate's experience with this conflict situation becomes an unresolved prior conflict and an antecedent condition for future conflict.

The antecedent conditions discussed above, or any others, set the stage for individuals to perceive the conflict. Until and unless the parties perceive the conflict, the antecedent condition remains just as an antecedent condition. When parties perceive a conflict, it is based on their perception or the mental picture which they form of the objective situation. Now, it can happen that in a given situation resources exist which are adequate to satisfy the needs of both parties but the parties' perceptions of that situation do not correspond to the objective facts in that situation: the parties conclude that the available resources are inadequate and, as a consequence, they perceive themselves to be in conflict.

Managerial Actions to Minimize Effects of Conditions Potentially Leading to Conflict

Managers can ensure that jobs are described with sufficient clarity and do not include overlapping responsibilities. The same attention should be paid to definition of the boundaries of work units and conditions under which boundary-spanning is required: these actions contribute to eliminating or reducing ambiguous jurisdictions. Another approach would be to review the organization's structure with a view to eliminating needless differentiation. Some organizations emphasizing high employee involvement have incorporated semi-autonomous work teams that operate in a flat organization structure, a reward system that promotes multi-skilling, and intensive training in interpersonal and problem-solving skills. Such an organization design reduces differentiation and communication barriers and builds into its structure and relationships a capacity for an integrative approach to conflict management. For example, the reward system and other managerial policies and practices in such organizations encourage dissemination of information to those who need it, rather than withholding information and use it as a leverage of power.

Situations of resource shortages are a fertile breeding ground for interpersonal conflicts in organizations. An effective set of actions that promote integrative conflict resolution in these situations would be (1) to clearly and unequivocally state the organization's mission and purpose and (2) to ensure that *all* policies, practices and decisions relating to resource allocations and behaviour regulations stem from and are governed by the values and objectives of the stated mission and purpose. In other words, the organization's mission and objectives become the **superordinate goals** comprising the criteria and principles for resolving conflict. The faithful adherence to the organization's mission and its frequent communication help to make it salient to the employees and to create a climate in which disagreements are an opportunity to develop creative approaches to achieve the organization's objectives more effectively.

Conflict Resolution Strategies

There are many ways in which parties deal with or react to a perceived conflict and the feelings and emotions which may be associated with it. We refer to these manifest behaviours in a conflict situation. Most of these behaviours can be discussed in terms of four strategies used in a conflict: avoidance, defusion, power, and negotiation. The objective of these strategies is to end or **terminate** the conflict. As mentioned previously, to end or terminate a conflict is not the same as resolving the conflict and behaviours that end the conflict do not necessarily resolve the conflict.

The discussion of the four strategies or categories of manifest behaviours which follows will also examine whether the resulting termination of the conflict leads to a resolution or the suppression of the conflict. By **resolution**, we mean that parties experience mutual satisfaction with the final outcomes. The final outcomes do not have to be identical for both parties, but these have to be sufficiently adequate to meet their aspirations and needs. By suppression, we mean that the final outcomes fail to satisfy one or both parties. With suppression there is no resolution of the conflict, which then constitutes an unresolved prior conflict – one of the major antecedent conditions of conflict.

Avoidance

Behaviours in the **avoidance** category are the variety of delaying or stalling actions designed to put off confronting the conflict situation, in the hope that the conflict will eventually cease to exist. Examples of avoidance behaviours include postponing the meeting set up to discuss the conflict issues; when you do meet, you deliberately keep the issues vague or focus on irrelevant issues; you do not return phone calls because you do not wish to confront the party or the issue.

Avoidance behaviours can never lead to a resolution because the issues have not been dealt with and, as a result, the antecedent conditions of the conflict continue to exist. At best, there is suppression: there might be satisfactory outcomes for the party engaging in the avoidance behaviour, but clearly the other party will not experience satisfaction.

Defusion

The **defusion** category of behaviours also consists of delaying or stalling actions such as those of the avoidance category. However, there is a significant difference in the objective. The party resorting to defusion does so in order to reduce the tension in the situation in the firm belief that dealing with the issues in such a state is not conducive to the resolution of the conflict. For example, in a meeting to deal with the conflict, one party might ask for a coffee break or a postponement if they sense that this will help to reduce tensions or provide some relief from the tense atmosphere that has developed. This is a temporary break and, unlike in the avoidance behaviour approach, the party certainly intends to return to the conflict issues and work towards a resolution.

Defusion, by itself, does not lead to a resolution of the conflict. However, it is a useful device to send a message to the other party that addressing the issues in as calm and rational a manner as possible is more likely to get them closer to resolution. Therefore, defusion can be a useful step in the conflict resolution process. Since the conflict still continues to exist, we can say that defusion suppresses the conflict.

Power

The category of behaviours that use power is also referred to as contending behaviours. It consists of the use of physical and psychological force with the intention of intimidating the opponent into accepting one's demands and thereby achieve one's interests. Examples of power are use of physical violence; bribery; flattery; fear of punishment; control of resources; or use of knowledge and expertise in a situation in which the opponent does not have access to such capability in order to respond appropriately and so on.

In general, the use of power does not resolve the conflict because the losing party is forced to submit and usually does so, unwillingly. It also creates considerable hostility, anger and bitterness and certainly does not contribute to establishing and preserving long-term relationships. Because the loser has yielded unwillingly, they do not experience satisfaction with the outcomes. In the loser's eyes, it is a case of suppression of the conflict which thus remains unresolved.

On the other hand, it is possible that the party who submits to the power tactics does so willingly. Now, even though the losing party does not achieve the intended goals, it can happen that they might experience other outcomes, such as developing a relationship with the opponent which is perceived to be beneficial for the future. Should this be the case, then there is a resolution of the conflict.

Negotiation

Negotiation is a more effective strategy than avoidance, defusion and power use to handle conflict. When parties choose negotiation as a means of ending the conflict, there is an implicit recognition of their dependence on each other and that the outcomes of each can be influenced by the other. They therefore prefer to explore the possibility of an agreement. Does negotiation always lead to the resolution of the conflict? It depends upon the nature of negotiation strategies adopted by the parties. When one or both parties adopt the distributive or win–lose strategy in bargaining, it is less likely that there will be mutual satisfaction with the final outcomes. On the other hand, when both parties adopt the integrative or win–win strategy in bargaining, it more likely to lead to a settlement with which both parties are satisfied and, as a result, a resolution of the conflict. The next section explores the negotiation planning process and examines the distributive and the integrative negotiation strategies and the bargaining tactics used in these strategies.

Negotiation planning process

The following six points must be considered when planning for negotiation (Lewicki and Litterer, 1985):

- *Determine the nature of the conflict relationship.* For example, do the perceptions of the conflict correspond to the facts of the objective situation? Also the impact of one's past relationship with the opponent must be assessed. For example, past relationship with the opponent based on trust and fair dealings can be expected to impact positively on forthcoming negotiations.
- *Consider the goals, tangible and intangible, involved in the negotiations.* In addition to being clear on one's own goals, it is important to use all the available knowledge about the opponent in order to understand what the goals of the opponent might be.
- *Develop a negotiating position.* The available information is analysed in order to determine one's bottom line, i.e., the point below which a settlement will not be acceptable. An important consideration here is one's 'BATNA' – that is, the **B**est **A**lternative **T**o **N**egotiated **A**greement (Fisher et al., 1993). The criticality of BATNA lies in the obvious fact that if one can do better than a settlement that violates one's bottom line, then clearly that settlement will not produce mutually satisfactory outcomes. If several issues are involved in the negotiations, they must be prioritized in terms of their importance and the trade-offs one might be willing to make in order to achieve a settlement.
- *Develop information about the opponent's reputation and negotiating style.* This is especially important if one has not negotiated with this person before.
- *Prepare arguments for your position and anticipate the opponent's arguments.* It is also useful to identify the strengths and weakness of these arguments because it helps to modify one's goals to more realistic levels.
- *Decide on the strategy and related tactics you wish to adopt in the negotiations.* The available strategy and tactics choices – distributive or integrative – are now discussed.

Negotiation strategies

Distributive strategy

The **distributive strategy** in negotiations is also known as win–lose or competitive bargaining. Parties who adopt this strategy perceive that their goals are irreconcilable and that they are in a 'fixed pie' or 'zero-sum' situation in which when one party wins the other loses. No attempt is made to explore the possibilities of either increasing the pie or considering other issues which might allow for trade-offs leading to mutually satisfactory outcomes. Instead, each party takes a position that leads each to strive to maximize their outcomes at the expense of the other party.

Before and during negotiations, the parties will minimize the disclosure of their resistance points (that is, the bottom line) and critical information such as the pressure of deadlines, or overstocking of inventory which might reveal the weakness of their position. The bargaining process essentially consists of both parties attempting to influence each other's resistance point through a series of offers and counter-offers which may involve small or large concessions. Each party is unconcerned about the other and seeks their own advantage. In doing so, it is not uncommon for parties to engage in unscrupulous tactics such as concealing information, outright deception, stonewalling, threats and other manipulative actions.

The distributive strategy might seem appropriate under certain conditions. These are: (1) the parties believe that it is fair to want and get more than they can justify as their fair share; (2) long-term relationships and one's reputation is not considered to be important; and (3) the issues involved are not too complex (Fisher et al., 1993). For these reasons, the distributive strategy and its related tactics are not conducive to a resolution of the conflict. The loser, unless they yield willingly, will see it as an unresolved prior conflict.

Integrative strategy

The **integrative strategy** in negotiations is also known as the win–win or cooperative bargaining. Parties who adopt this strategy believe that although the stated positions of the parties might be irreconcilable, it is the interests and aspirations that lie behind these positions that are more important and critical to the parties than the stated positions. Both parties recognize that the stated positions are only one set of means to satisfy their interests and aspirations, and they would be willing to give up completely or modify these positions if alternative means are available to satisfy these needs and interests. Therefore, there is a greater willingness of the parties to focus on each other's needs and interests with a view to searching for solutions to satisfy them. To illustrate the difference between *position* and *interest*, consider Case 4.1.

CASE 4.1

Let's Forget about our *Positions* and Reveal our *Interests*

Arman, the manager of the shipping department, has just been told by Sharon, the plant manager, that his budget must be reduced by 10 per cent. Arman does not know that Sharon's cost-cutting strategy is primarily intended to demonstrate to her superiors that she is an efficient manager. Sharon does not know that Arman's budget request would actually result in increased productivity which, in turn, will considerably improve the bottom line results for the plant. With the budget cut she expects to improve the plant's profitability. The following table shows their respective positions and interests:

Parties	Position	Interest
Sharon	I must cut Arman's budget by 10 per cent	I need to improve the plant's profitability
Arman	I cannot accept the 10 per cent	Replacing some equipment will increase department efficiency by 30 per cent

Now, if Sharon and Arman dig in their heels and hold on to their positions, not much progress is likely in resolving the conflict. On the other hand, when they share the interest underlying their positions, they will be able to see that they do have a common objective which will motivate them to invent and explore options to satisfy their interests. For example, Sharon might agree to let Arman lease the equipment to the extent feasible and utilize the cash generated by the cost savings to buy the equipment in the next budget period. When they focus on their positions (the distributive strategy) they see themselves in an irreconcilable, win–lose, competitive situation. By shifting the focus to their interests (integrative strategy), the situation is transformed which allows for a win–win, cooperative approach.

How would you unveil the 'interest' in a situation like this? Demonstrate in a role play with a colleague.

As in any problem-solving process, integrative strategy also involves the three major steps of identifying the problem, generating alternative courses of actions or solutions to the problem and choosing the alternative solutions which is judged to be most effective in achieving a mutually satisfactory settlement.

In the problem identification stage, the definition and statement of the problem must be a joint effort of both parties and acceptable to both parties. In other words, the problem must be stated in 'neutral terms' and not in a way that 'favours the preferences or priorities of one side over the other' (Lewicki and Litterer, 1985, p. 115).

In generating alternative courses of actions or solutions, the objective is not merely to identify a list of possible alternatives. Rather, the parties should attempt to be creative in developing solutions that accommodate to the maximum the interests and needs of both sides. The creativity and resourcefulness of the parties is often triggered when they refuse to be bound by the situation as it exists and work instead at reframing the problem in a manner that allows them to invent new options and varied choices. When both parties compete for limited resources, the focus of the discussion generally tends towards how to allocate these resources. Such a focus takes for granted that the conflict of interest is irreconcilable. A more creative approach might be to explore ways of expanding the pie so that the shortage is eliminated.

The third step – choice of the solution – is equally important. The concern for mutually satisfactory outcomes (which satisfy the needs and interests of each party) ought to be the principal criterion. When such outcomes are not possible, then the choice of the solution will be the criteria of fairness and equity. This implies that the parties agree on the standards by which the solutions are evaluated.

The critical role of trust in integrative negotiations is obvious. Without it, the free and open flow of information will be impeded. Trust, however, cannot be a one-way street because the party who is trusting can be taken advantage of by the other. Hence the approach in the Russian saying, 'trust, but verify', is prudent. It should also be remembered that trust is the 'rarest commodity' in some cultural contexts, as will be discussed later in the chapter.

The effectiveness of the conflict resolution strategies we have discussed depends on effective communication between the parties, which is considerably enhanced by their interpersonal communication skills and the mode in which these skills are exercised. For this reason, the next section examines the critical interpersonal communication skill of active listening, and the behaviour mode of practicing the interpersonal communication skills of assertiveness.

Active Listening and Assertive Behaviour

Key communication skills in conflict management

Active listening

The purpose of **active listening** is to help people recognize their own feelings, be more open to their experiences and help them change their attitudes and behaviour. Through active listening an atmosphere of support is created, which considerably weakens the need for self-defence. In such an atmosphere, the open and uninhibited communication is characterized by empathy, understanding and acceptance. People see each other as valuable resources of information and assistance, rather than as threat.

CASE 4.2

Active listening

Scenario No.1:

Foreman: Hey, Al, I am shocked to see the revised production order – with an increase of 15 per cent from the beginning of next month. Do they think we are just production robots?

Supervisor: The Management Committee has decided that we need the increased output to survive in today's market.

Foreman: Don't they know that our current production has declined due to equipment breakdown and the resignation of our two qualified employees. And yet, nothing has been done to address these factors.

Supervisor: Look, Kelly, I am not on the Management Committee. My job is not to review the Management Committee's decision but to see that it is implemented; and that is what I'll do.

Foreman: The guys aren't gonna like this.

Supervisor: It is for you to work it out with your group.

Scenario No.2:

Foreman: Hey, John, I don't understand this production order. We can't handle this run today. What do they think we are?

Supervisor: But that is a big order and the company cannot afford to default on it. So you need to get it out as soon as you can.

Foreman: Don't they know we're behind schedule already because of that press breakdown?

Supervisor: Yes, that's true. Have you considered reviewing your current orders? Perhaps you could rearrange the priorities which will then help you to focus on this order. Also, why don't you consider overtime work for your group?

Foreman: The guys aren't gonna like this.

Supervisor: I can give you a hand in this situation. If you see me later today, I can show you exactly how to resolve it. So, don't worry, I'll take care of it for you.

Foreman: Gee, thanks John. You're a swell guy, always so helpful.

(Continued)

(Continued)

Scenario No.3:

Foreman: Hey, Ross, I don't understand this revised production order – an increase of 15 per cent. Do they think we are just production robots?

Supervisor: Sounds like you're pretty sore about it Kelly.

Foreman: I sure am. We worked hard to cope with the production decline due to factors beyond our control – such as: equipment breakdown and lack of budget to replace these resources; and the loss of two of our qualified employees. And, now, we are confronted with a 15% increase in production!!!

Supervisor: As if you didn't have enough work to do, huh?

Foreman: Yeah, this revised production order is, indeed, a nightmare; I don't know how I'm gonna tell the guys about this.

Supervisor: Hate to face 'em with it now, is that it?

Foreman: I really do. They're under a real strain today; given our present circumstances, everything we do around here seems to be a rush, rush towards unrealistic objectives.

Supervisor: I guess you feel like it's unfair to load anything more on them.

Foreman: Well, yeah, I do recognize that there probably is considerable pressure on everybody. If that's the way it is, I shall share it with them.

- In which scenario does the supervisor display 'active listening'? Why?
- Which type of supervisory response would you personally prefer? How does this preferred response make you feel?
- Do you think there are cross-cultural differences in the preference of the supervisory response in these scenarios?

When we analyse these scenarios, we see that the supervisor is listening to the foreman in all cases. However, the effect on the foreman in the third scenario is definitely more positive and, as a result, motivates him to be more creative and constructive in coping with the situation. What did the supervisor do differently in the third scenario? He engaged in active listening. Before we discuss active listening, it is useful to briefly distinguish between *listening* and *active listening*.

The difference consists primarily in the purpose or reason why we engage in these activities. The person engaged in active listening does so because they want to listen in a manner which will help the speaker to better understand their feelings, better appreciate the facts being presented and finally, as a result, assist the speaker to better cope with their problem or to change their behaviour in order to adapt to the demands of the situation.

We can explore the nature of active listening by examining the scenarios in Case 4.2. From the dialogue in the first scenario, we can gather that the supervisor's basic approach reflects his attitude towards the foreman, which is: I listen to you, you have a problem, but that's not my concern; you sort it out. It's a cold indifference that is completely oblivious to his subordinate's feelings and concerns. This approach is neither helpful for the accomplishment of the immediate task at hand, nor is it conducive to building a positive interpersonal relationship. In the absence of such a relationship, the supervisor cannot expect to be effective in managing his subordinates.

In the second scenario, the supervisor is very helpful but, as we can see, he takes control of the situation from Kelly and proceeds to resolve the problem himself. This can be referred to as the directive response or approach. It may solve the problem at hand, but it does not encourage, much less develop, Kelly to solve it himself. If the supervisor habitually responds in such a directive manner, before long the subordinate will develop a dependency on him. The effects of such dependence relationship are obvious: the supervisor will clearly be overwhelmed doing his subordinate's work; the subordinates will not have the opportunity to grow and develop. In addition to the issue of dependence, the directive approach might produce other undesirable effects such as: mistaken belief that the speaker is seeking advice; and implying that the speaker is not competent! (Whetten and Cameron, 1991)

The only circumstance when advice is the appropriate response is when there is clear evidence that the speaker does not have the capability, specific expertise, or willingness to meet the demands of the situation. Even in this circumstance, the listener should first adopt the active listening approach – more fully discussed later – because it enables the listener to properly assess the situation and, based on such assessment, to conclude whether the directive response is, in fact, the appropriate response and then to offer the appropriate advice.

In the third scenario, the supervisor listens for total meaning and responds to the foreman's feelings, concerns and problems along with the facts of the problem situation – as seen in the following analysis:

Supervisor's response	Message to the foreman
'Sounds like you're pretty sore about it, Kelly.'	Acknowledges feelings and emotions.
'As if you didn't have enough work to do, huh?'	Recognizes work situations.
'Hate to face 'em with it now, is that it?'	Recognizes difficulty created by the work situation.
'I guess you feel like it's unfair to load anything more on them.'	Empathizes with foreman.

The supervisor in the third scenario is engaged in active listening which made the foreman realize that the supervisor understood his concerns, feelings and problems and that he was willing to support them in any way he could. The supportive climate, understanding and empathy demonstrated by active listening afforded the foreman an opportunity to vent his feelings and to realize that his situation, however serious and problematic, was not unique. It also encouraged him to draw on his own resources to cope with the situation.

Guidelines for Active Listening

Our discussion of the guidelines will include a set of 'do's' and 'don'ts' of active listening based mainly on the classical work of Rogers and Farson (1957).

'Do's' of active listening

- *Think with, instead of for or about the speaker.* This guideline requires that the listener focuses on the speaker in order to see, feel and understand the situation from the speaker's point of view. Unlike the supervisors in the first and second scenarios, the supervisor in the third scenario observed this guideline. His responses demonstrated that he attempted to view the situation from the foreman's point of view. Statements and questions that help implement this guideline are: 'Can you tell me more about that?'; 'What do you mean by that?'

- *Listen for total meaning.* It means that we focus on the *content* of the message and its underlying feelings because the meaning of the message is conveyed by both the content and feelings. The content of the message is generally apparent from the words, phrases and sentences that are used by the speaker. The feelings come through the tone and voice inflexion with which the message is communicated. For example, in the scenario, Kelly said: 'Hey, Ross, I don't understand this production order. We can't handle this run today. What do they think we are?' To get the full import of Kelly's statements, one needs to recognize the feelings (in our case, frustration), which is usually a difficult task and needs special skills such as 'responding to feelings' discussed next.

- *Respond to feelings.* As we have just suggested, the message communicated by the words often cannot be taken literally. The listener's response should then be to get a sense of the feelings through open-ended questions about the feelings about things, people and events involved in the situation. A good illustration is the supervisor's response in the third scenario: 'Sounds like you're pretty sore about it, Kelly.' The supervisor's response is categorized as a reflective response which communicates to Kelly that the supervisor has listened to and understood his message. It also encourages Kelly to explore the issue further should he choose to do so. The listener can also respond to feelings with statements and questions such as: 'How did you feel when. . .?' 'You say you are discouraged?' When feelings are the key to the meaning of the message, the listener should respond to the feelings first and only later to the content of the message. In addition to words and feelings, the listener should also observe the non-verbal cues provided by posture, facial expressions, eye movements and so on.

- *Test for understanding.* To test for understanding means that the listener paraphrases in their own words what they have understood to be the message of the speaker. Such paraphrasing has two functions. One, it allows the speaker to correct or clarify the listener's understanding of the message. The other function is that the paraphrasing reflects the situation which then can give the speaker a better understanding of it. Statements and questions that can be used for this purpose are: 'Let me see if I understand what you are saying'; 'Are you saying that...?'; 'What I heard you say was...?'

- *Assume an active listening posture.* Several suggestions can be useful in this regard. A relaxed, open, square posture, leaning forward and maintaining eye contact are the body language through which the listener demonstrates their readiness and willingness to give the speaker the required attentiveness and concentration.

'Don'ts' of active listening

- *Don't give advice; don't evaluate or pass judgement.* A very common tendency when one listens to a problem situation is to offer advice. This is an ineffective listener response for reasons discussed earlier. The second tendency is to evaluate or pass judgement either on the speaker or on the message communicated by the speaker. This too is an ineffective listener response because it is certain to trigger the speaker's defensive reactions.

- *Don't cross-examine the speaker.* When the listener cross-examines the speaker, the latter is made to feel that they are an accused whose statements cannot be trusted and therefore need to be rigorously scrutinized. This listener response is undesirable because it also triggers the speaker's defensiveness and creates a distrustful environment which does not make the speaker feel that they are understood, accepted and free to explore the problem situation as they might choose to do.

- *Don't tell about your own experience in a similar situation.* The listener should not give in to the almost irresistible urge to narrate one's own experience in a similar situation. This is often done with the good intention of wanting to reassure the speaker that things are not so bad or that the crisis will soon pass away. However, this response hinders rather than helps the speaker. For one thing, the listener's experience can never be the same as that of the speaker. More importantly, such narration of the listener's experiences defeats the primary purpose of active listening and that is understanding and recognizing the *speaker's* perspective.

Assertive, Non-assertive and Aggressive Behaviour

Assertive behaviour

In **assertive** behaviour, one expresses one's self in a manner that is consistent with one's perception of one's legitimate rights. However, the critical feature of assertiveness is that such expression is done in a way that neither violates the rights of another person nor prevents that person from exercising their rights. Assertive behaviour can take a variety of forms: expression of one's opinions, preferences, needs, or feelings. It also includes non-verbal behaviour such as eye contact, facial expressions, gestures, voice inflexion and so on.

The effects of assertive behaviour is that it allows both parties – the sender and the receiver of the communication – to improve their self-esteem, honestly express their ideas and feelings, to freely choose for themselves and to generally feel good about themselves (Alberti and Emmons, 1990). When one reads this list of favourable effects, one asks: Does assertive behaviour enable the parties to achieve their desired goals? In one sense, the answer is that it might not; in another sense, it does enable the parties to achieve their goals. When we say it might not, we recognize that assertive behaviour may place the parties in a conflictual situation in which their best response might be to agree to disagree. Even in such a situation, they feel good about themselves because the mutual respect inherent in assertive behaviour prevents them from imposing their views on each other. When we say that assertive behaviour does enable the parties to achieve their goals, what we suggest is that the same mutual respect combined with open and honest exchange of views and feelings place the parties in a much better position to generate creative solutions that are mutually satisfactory.

Non-assertive behaviour

In the non-assertive mode of communication individuals do not express their ideas, opinions, preferences, needs, or feelings in a direct manner consistent with their perceptions of their legitimate rights. Instead, they tend to communicate them in an indirect manner and with much hesitation. Also, they are more inclined to express agreement with the views and preferences of others although, in fact, they hold diametrically opposite views and detest the other's preferences. Furthermore, the non-verbal behaviour of the non-assertive individual is generally inconsistent with the message communicated by the verbal behaviour.

The effect of non-assertive behaviour is that the receiver is generally at a loss to understand the exact wishes and feelings of the sender. Often, because the communication is indirect and incomplete, the receiver experiences much frustration and anger and sometimes even guilt because of the responsibility the sender imposes on the receiver to decipher the real meaning in the message. The other effect of non-assertive behaviour is that the sender indirectly, or by default, lets others make the decisions. The result is unsatisfactory to both the sender and the receiver.

Non-assertive behaviour might enable the parties to achieve their desired goals. However, such achievement may be accompanied by feelings of guilt because the receiver might experience a nagging suspicion that perhaps their decisions may have violated the rights of the sender or that the sender may not be satisfied with the consequences of the decisions which the receiver was compelled to make.

CASE 4.3

Which would Be your Typical Response?

1. You bought a shirt. When you took it home you found a misweave in it. You don't want the item as it is. You return the faulty item to the department store. The clerk has just said no one will ever notice. You say:

   (a) Well. I'd still like to return it or change it. I don't want this one.
   (b) Look, give me my money. I don't have all day for you to waste my time.
   (c) Well, are you sure no one will notice it?

2. A co-worker keeps giving you all of her work to do. You've decided to put an end to this. Your co-worker has just asked you to do some more of her work. You say:

   (a) I'm kind of busy. But if you can't get it done, I guess I can help you.
   (b) Forget it. It is about time you do it. You treat me like your slave.
   (c) No, Sue, I don't want to keep doing the extra work coming from you. From now on, let's each focus on our own work.

3. You'd like your roommate to go down the block and pick up a package at your friend's house. You say:

   (a) Nath, I'd like it if you could go over to Mrs. Smith's and pick up a package for me. I'd appreciate it if you could do it by 3 o'clock.
   (b) If you aren't too busy, well ... will you be going to Mrs. Smith's today?
   (c) Hey, it's about time you did something worthwhile. Go down to Mrs. Smith's and pick up a package for me. No back talk. Stop being so lazy.

   (Continued)

(Continued)

In each scenario, identify the assertive, non-assertive and aggressive response.

- Do you think that cultural or other situational factors would influence the preferred response? How? Please elaborate.

Aggressive behaviour

In the **aggressive** mode or style of communication, the sender of the communication expresses themself with full knowledge and intent to deny the legitimate rights of the receiver. Individuals who adopt this communication mode express their views, opinions, preferences, feelings, or needs in a manner that demands of the receiver complete acquiescence, acceptance and compliance. The sender totally and unscrupulously disregards the receiver's views, feelings, or needs in the matter.

The aggressive behaviour and its consequences are inevitable when one adopts the aggressive mode in interpersonal communication. The sender enhances themself, but does so by attacking the self-worth and self-esteem of the receiver. The sender expresses freely their views and feelings, but deprives the receiver of the same freedom of expression. The sender makes decisions unilaterally and, in so doing, deprives the receiver of choosing for themself. Finally, the sender achieves their goals and takes deliberate actions to prevent the receiver from achieving theirs. Of course, it must be recognized that the successes of the aggressive mode experienced by the sender tend to be short-lived. The receiver eventually reacts either by reciprocal aggressive behaviour or leaves the field. The sender too might give up the aggressive mode either because of subsequent feelings of guilt or by the realization that such behaviour seriously jeopardizes the development and maintenance of long-term relationships which are absolutely critical to workplace effectiveness.

Managerial Actions to Foster Assertive Behaviour

A closer analysis of assertive behaviour will reveal that an individual whose belief in self-determination or personal self-efficacy is high is more likely to engage in assertive behaviour. Therefore, the appropriate managerial strategies should be those which empower employees – that is, enable them to increase their self-determination or personal self-efficacy beliefs. We explore examples of such strategies at two levels – individual and group level.

At the individual level, the measures proposed in the goal-setting process would be useful first steps. For example, functioning as coach and mentor, managers can use goal-setting to help individuals develop an internal locus of control which, in turn, can contribute to enhance their personal self-efficacy belief. At the group level, managers can effectively engage in social role behaviours which can help group members to freely express their views and feelings. For example, the social role behaviour of gate-keeper can help to reduce domination by some group members and draw out the quieter members. Likewise, the standards monitor role behaviour (i.e., making sure that high standards are maintained) can ensure that a member with the better proposal is encouraged not to withdraw it. In other words, through the proper performance of the social role behaviours, managers can create a climate which discourages self-oriented behaviours (such as dominator and aggressor) and fosters assertive behaviours in the group.

Conflict Management in Cross-cultural Context

There are cross-cultural differences in the way conflict is construed. For example conflict, when experienced, is perceived as a threat in the US, but as an opportunity for development in China (Yang et al., 2000). It is perceived as inevitable in India, but preventable in the UK (e.g., Aycan, 2008).

> In an interview conducted in Canada, an elderly Chinese man indicated he had experienced no conflict at all for the previous 40 years. Among the possible reasons for his denial was a cultural preference to see the world through lenses of harmony rather than conflict, as encouraged by his Confucian upbringing. Labeling some of our interactions as conflicts and analyzing them into smaller component parts is a distinctly Western approach that may obscure other aspects of relationships. (Hammer and Rogan, 2002, p. 87)

Numerous studies show that in face of conflict collectivistic cultures prefer avoidance and accommodation, while individualistic cultures prefer confrontation (e.g., Kozan, 1997; Leung, 1988). One reason for this difference is that conflict is perceived as an opportunity for personal development and maturation and patience exercised in times of conflict is perceived as a virtue in collectivistic cultures. Dialectic thinking in Confusianism advocates tolerance for contradictions (Peng and Nisbett, 1999). The conflict arising from contradictions is believed to be an opportunity for personal development and maturation and, therefore, must be accepted. 'The concept of paradox is gaining an increasing attention in organization research (e.g., Clegg 2002) ... Yin Yang suggests that human beings, organizations and cultures intrinsically embrace paradoxes for their sheer existence and healthy development' (Fang, 2006, p.77). Collectivistic cultures emphasize interpersonal harmony as a value and protect harmony by avoiding conflict, accommodating others' wishes, or involving a third party to resolve the conflict. Indeed, in collectivistic societies people are more concerned with others' well-being (i.e., helping the other party to save face) than their own self-interest in resolving conflict (e.g., Holt and DeVore, 2005).

Table 4.1   Culture and conflict management approaches

	Harmony Model	Confrontation Model	Regulative Model
Cultural characteristics	Collectivistic	High individualism & low uncertainty avoidance	High individualism & high uncertainty avoidance
Country types	e.g., Asian, Middle Eastern, Latin American	e.g., English-speaking Anglo-Saxon	e.g., Eastern Europe, Iberic
Emotions	Suppression of negative emotions	Expression of negative emotions	Expression of negative emotions
Conflict management behaviour	Avoidance and accommodation	Confrontation and compromise	Avoidance or forcing the universalistic rules
Concerns for outcome	Facesaving concerns	Due process concerns	Due process concerns
Involvement of third parties	Frequent, intrusive, informal	Infrequent, planned, and non-intrusive	Formal appeal system, adjucative
Emphasis of third parties	Harmony, shame	Reason, fairness (equity)	Reason, application of general principles (equality)

Source: Adapted from Kozan (1997), Tables 1 and 2.

How is conflict managed in different cultures? Kozan (1997) proposed a framework to link the cultural dimensions with three distinct conflict management models. In the harmony model, conflict is managed in such a way that in-group harmony is protected and confrontations are avoided; in the confrontational model, conflict is openly acknowledged and resolved through cooperation and, if necessary, confrontation; in the regulative model, conflict resolution is guided by universalistic principles and rules. Table 4.1. presents cultural values associated with each approach and core characteristics of each model.

Note that 'avoidance' may imply a concern for others (e.g., help them to save face) and preferred by collectivistic cultures especially when the dispute is of high intensity and occurring with in-group members or with superiors (Brew and Cairns, 2004; Leung, 1997): 'In all, *avoidance* is … more nuanced in Asia than is typically understood in the West' (Gelfand et al., 2007, p. 490).

Cross-cultural differences in negotiation are well-documented. Let us outline these differences in three phases: preparation, negotiation, agreement.

Preparation for Negotiation

Relationship-building

In collectivistic cultures, relationship-building prior to the negotiation is an integral part of the negotiation process that cannot be skipped or rushed. However, typical American negotiators find this process unnecessary and are eager to 'get down to business' as soon as possible. Relationship-building is essentially trust-building. In cultures where the legal system is not sufficient to enforce agreements, trust is a critical mechanism to ensure that parties will not violate agreements (e.g., Punnett, 2004).

Negotiators from individualistic cultures who do not wish to spend time on relationship-building are perceived to be cold, distant, business-minded and calculative and cannot be trusted. Trust-building is especially critical in cultures where interpersonal trust is very low (see, country scores on trust based on the World Values survey – http://www.jdsurvey.net/jds/jdsurvey.jsp). 'I join a negotiation in order to negotiate the relationship. When we feel that we can trust each other, agreeing on the business takes no time'. (Interview with a Chinese businessman, Mead, 2005, p. 162)

Heavy users of business entertainment, the Japanese spend almost 2 percent of their GNP on entertainment of clients – even more than they spend on national defense (1.5 percent). Americans generally consider this high business entertainment cost absurd, but perhaps Americans' extraordinary high legal expenses reflect the cost of insufficient relationship building. (Adler, 1991, p. 198)

The telephone conversation featured in Thinking across cultures 4.1 makes Dr Thompson feel nervous. He has little time to spend in China and he is eager to get down to business rather than 'keep the business waiting'. What he does not realize is that *business has already started*. Negotiators in collectivistic cultures believe that building good relationships prior to the negotiation will make it easier to force their terms during the negotiation or renegotiate the terms after the contract is signed. Mr Chang tries to please Dr Thompson by being a good host during his visit, not only because hospitality is an important virtue in Chinese cultures, but also because he thinks that Dr Thompson will reciprocate 'the favour' by accepting Mr Chang's terms in the negotiation or by approving extra demands after the negotiation.

Thinking across cultures 4.1

Let's Keep the Business Waiting!

'Welcome to Beijing Dr Thompson; I hope you had a good flight. Why don't we meet for dinner tonight? We will pick you up from your hotel tomorrow morning for a nice city tour and lunch. We will take you to our office in the afternoon and introduce you to our business associates. Some of them know you from previous visits. It would be nice to spend time with common friends, play golf, wine and dine, so to speak. After all, business can wait!'

'Thank you Mr Chang. Yeah, the flight was OK – I am glad that it is over though. You know I have only two days in China and I would hate to go back empty-handed. So, I suggest that we start the business right away. Let's wine and dine after the meetings are over to hopefully celebrate our agreement. What do you say?'

- How do you think Mr Chang will respond to Dr Thompson's request?
- How could these conflicting expectations be reconciled?

'Setting the stage' – time, location, team composition

When, where and who? These are important decisions to make prior to the negotiation as they carry symbolic meanings that can influence the negotiation process. For example, the Chinese prefer a large negotiation team, whereas Americans prefer a small team (e.g., Francesco and Gold, 2005). For Chinese, selection of the team members is based on rank and age, whereas for Americans, selection of the team members is based on knowledge and competence in the negotiated topic. Chinese negotiators (coming from a high power-distance culture) do not trust a team that is small and comprised of young and junior members representing the organization.

Choice of location is another critical decision. Conducting the meeting at the home country has obvious advantages such as low cost, easy access to information and low time pressure to close the deal (Francesco and Gold, 2005). However, in some cultures (e.g., high power-distance) inviting the other team to one's home country may be offensive. 'How dare they call us into their presence? Don't they know who we are!' A neutral place may be preferable to alleviate such concerns.

'Time is money'… But not for everyone. Imagine a negotiation situation where the team, requiring time to build the relationship or to consult with high-level officials, is rushed into a decision. In such a situation, the team that puts time pressure and rushes a decision is most likely to arrive at an agreement that would be to their disadvantage. In preparing for cross-cultural negotiations, both parties' tolerance for time pressures should be taken into consideration.

> A Brazilian company invited a group of Americans to Brazil to negotiate a contract the week before Christmas. The Brazilians, knowing that the Americans would want to return to the United States by Christmas with a signed contract, knew that they could push hard for concession and an early agreement. The final agreement definitely favoured the Brazilians. (Adler, 1991, p. 200)

Negotiation Process

During the negotiation process, cultural differences influence the communication and negotiation tactics. Katz (2007) developed negotiation profiles for 50 countries. Table 4.2 compares the communication styles of UK, Australian, Chinese and Russia negotiators based on Katz's research.

The differences summarized in Table 4.2 can be traced back to an important cultural dimension associated with variations in communication style in negotiations: **high vs. low context** (Hall, 1976). In high-context cultures such as China, communication during the negotiation is not direct (see also Chapter 6). Negotiators have to read the contextual cues or in-between the lines for the meaning. In contrast, in low-context cultures like Australia, what you hear is what is meant. As stated by Ting-Toomey (1985): 'In the high context cultural system the predominant mode of conflict attitude can best be described

Table 4.2 Cross-national differences in the communication style during negotiations

	UK	Australia	China	Russia
Space	British people generally converse standing around three feet apart.	Australians generally converse standing around two to three feet apart.	Chinese generally converse while standing around three feet apart.	Russians generally converse while standing around two to three feet apart.
Tone of voice	– Businesspeople usually speak in a controlled fashion, only occasionally raising their voices to make a point. – At restaurants, especially those used for business lunches and dinners, keep conversations at a quiet level. Being loud may be regarded as bad manners.		– They use quiet, gentle tones, and conversations may include periods of silence. – Carry conversations at a quiet level. Loud and boisterous behaviour is perceived as a lack of self-control.	– While celebrations and social events can get very noisy, being loud may reflect poorly on you in most business settings. However, emotions are often shown openly.
Gestures	– Gestures are usually subtle in the U.K. It is advisable to restrict your body language. – Facial expressions can be very hard to read, making it difficult to figure out what your counterparts may be thinking. – Physical contact is rare and best avoided. It will not be taken as a friendly gesture if you touch other people. – Do not use your fingers to point at others. Instead, point with your head. – Eye contact should be somewhat infrequent. While looking the other in the eye may convey sincerity, do not stare at people.	– Gestures and body language can be lively, but not overly so. – Australians may make some physical contact, such as a backslap as a sign of friendship, but there is usually not a lot of it. – The thumbs-up sign can be taken as a rude gesture in Australia if combined with an upward movement of the arm. – Eye contact should be somewhat infrequent. While looking the other in the eye may convey sincerity, do not stare at people as this will likely make them uncomfortable.	– Gestures are usually very subtle in China. – It is advisable to restrict your body language. – Non-verbal communication is important and you should carefully watch for others' small hints, just as they will be watching you. – Avoid touching other people. – Do not cross your legs if possible since this may be viewed as a lack of self-control. – Also, do not use your hands when speaking since the Chinese will likely get distracted. – Lightly tapping on the table using all fingers of one hand means 'thank you.' – It is considered improper to put your hand in your mouth or to cross your legs while seated. – Eye contact should be infrequent. While it is beneficial to make some eye contact when meeting a person for the first time, It is generally considered respectful to look down when speaking with senior or elder people.	– Russians keep physical contact infrequent. While several gestures may be used, be careful to control your own. – The American OK (thumb and index finger forming a circle) and 'V' signs are obscene gestures in Russia. – Standing with your hands in your pockets may be considered rude. – The thumbs-up gesture is positive as it signals approval. – Eye contact should be frequent, almost to the point of staring. This conveys sincerity and helps build trust.

(Continued)

Table 4.2 (Continued)

	UK	Australia	China	Russia
Show of emotions	–Emotions are not shown openly as the British prefer keeping the proverbial stiff upper lip, so do not assume that something is not deeply felt because it is understated.	–Some people may show both positive and negative emotions openly, while others may believe that they have no place in business. –When someone is teasing you, this may be a sign that the relationship is going well, so try not to be offended. If you feel compelled to tease back, do so in an affable manner.	–Chinese people talking among themselves may appear emotional, but this would be misleading.	
Saying 'yes' and 'no'	–While you may occasionally get a direct 'no,' evasive responses like "I'll get back to you" could indicate a lack of interest in what you have to offer.	–Australians do not find it difficult to say 'no.'	–When responding to a direct question, the Chinese may answer 'yes' only to signal that they heard what you said, not that they agree with it. –People rarely respond to a question or request with a direct 'no.' Instead, they may give seemingly ambiguous answers such as 'I am not sure,' 'we will think about it,' or 'this will require further investigation.' Each of these could mean 'no.'	–They may say nyet (no) frequently and you will have to figure out ways to get past that. –In contrast, people may say things they think you want to hear as a way to lure you into a business deal.
Directness of communication and use of silence	–Levels of directness may vary greatly. This depends primarily on the strength of relationships but is also influenced by education, status, and other factors. –The British tend to make vague statements that may be hard to read. Rather than responding to a direct question, they may instead tell a story, the meaning of which is left to your interpretation.	–Communication may be extremely direct. –Though conversations are usually animated, they may include moments of silence, which may not mean much. –Without any bad intentions, they may be frank to the point of bluntness, which sometimes feels rude to people from other cultures.	–Open disagreement should be avoided and any kind of direct confrontation is discouraged. –It is beneficial to use a similarly indirect approach when dealing with the Chinese, as they may perceive you as rude and pushy if you are too direct.	–Communicating with Russians can be anything from very direct to rather indirect.

UK	Australia	China	Russia
–The British are masters of understatement and often use subtle irony. It is important to listen carefully both to the tone of voice and the message that is being conveyed. In addition, pay attention to what is not being said. –Once they have decided that they want to do business with you, the British can become much more direct, even blunt, and may openly speak their minds as long as there is no risk of direct confrontation. –Silence is often a way to communicate a negative message.	–At the same time, Australians respect people who have strong opinions, no matter whether they agree with them or not. However, be careful not to appear condescending when expressing such opinions. –Australians rarely communicate 'between the lines,' so it is usually best to take what they say quite literally. Try to be equally clear in your own communication. –Keep in mind that in spite of their preference for directness, most Australians are also trying to be polite and friendly. For that reason, a clear expectation may sometimes come disguised as a nice request.	–Because the concept of 'saving face' is so important in this culture, communication is generally very indirect. –Open disagreement should be avoided and any kind of direct confrontation is discouraged. –If you have to convey bad news to the Chinese side, a face-saving way is to use a third party instead of communicating it yourself.	

Source: Katz (2007). www.leadershipcrossroads.com/nib_dld.asp. Used with permission of the author.

as evasive and non-confrontational. A calculated degree of vagueness and circumlocution are typically employed when tensions and anxieties mount' (p. 80).

As discussed earlier in this chapter, assertive communication helps resolve conflicts. However, we need to recognize that assertive behaviour is typically a phenomenon of North American and European cultures which are characterized by relatively high individualism and low power-distance. In the context of non-Western cultures which are high on collectivism and power-distance, individuals experience difficulty behaving assertively. High collectivism implies that loyalty to group takes precedence over individual achievement. Therefore, if behaving assertively is seen as independence and separateness from the group, individuals will not engage in assertive behaviour. Likewise, high power-distance will also discourage assertive behaviour. In high power-distance situations, employees treat supervisors with much respect and deference. Assertive behaviour might be perceived as lack of respect and deference. Therefore, individuals are less likely to engage in direct expression of their views and feelings. Instead, the demands of politeness and the acceptance of the need to **save face** make it more likely that individuals engage in communication that is less direct and confrontational. Hence in these cultures, communication tends to be indirect with a large measure of understatement.

Information exchange is key in the negotiation and should be done tactfully. There are cross-cultural differences in the amount of time and care invested in collecting and sharing information with the negotiation partner. For example, Americans give limited information on a 'need-to-know-basis', whereas the Japanese collect information from multiple sources to arrive at a holistic view before sharing it with the partner.

> Americans provide information in what they see as a straightforward manner, focusing on substantive issue of immediate concern, such as quality, price, delivery and 'telling it like it is'. The Japanese are more interested in a holistic picture and want to see how the current issues will fit into their wider, long-term, overall relationship. (Punnett, 2004, p. 194)

Cross-cultural differences are also observed in other tactics used in the negotiation. Graham and colleagues (e.g., Graham, 1985; Graham et al., 1988) observed Japanese, American and Brazilian teams during negotiations and found that Americans use 'promise' (promising something in exchange of condition) more than Brazilians; Japanese and Americans use 'threats' slightly more than Brazilians; Japanese provide 'recommendations' more than Americans and Brazilians; Americans and Brazilians use 'punishment' more than Japanese; Brazilians use 'command' (ordering someone to do something) more than Japanese and Americans.

Reaching an Agreement

In **monochronic** cultures (e.g., the US) negotiation occurs sequentially; when one issues is agreed upon, the negotiators move on to the next. In **polychronic** cultures (e.g., Mexican), issues raised in the negotiation are discussed in parallel; people go back and forth between topics and agreement cannot be reached unless all important topics are discussed. While monochronic negotiators make concessions for each topic and reach an agreement on one topic before moving to the next, polychronic negotiators make concessions only after all topics are discussed (Adler, 1991). Indeed, making a concession to reach agreement is sometimes perceived as a sign of weakness, rather than goodwill and flexibility (Adler, 1991).

In Western cultures, reaching an agreement is the final stage in the negotiation, but in non-Western cultures, *implementation* of the agreement is the final stage. For non-Western cultures the terms of an agreement can change many times after the negotiation is over. 'When the Chinese negotiate a contract, they never argue at the beginning, they argue when they implement it. In an American negotiation, you argue at the beginning and keep quiet when the contract is signed' (Mead, 2005, p. 163).

Cross-cultural Consideration for Managers

Global managers spend half of their time managing conflicts (Adler, 1991, p. 191). Effective conflict management requires that cultural nuances are carefully observed and integrated into the process. Managers with high cultural intelligence (see Chapter 9, Thinking across cultures 9.3.) are better able to identify the root of conflict as cultural differences, situational demands (e.g., subordinate–superior relationship, limited resources, high or low accountability), individual characteristics (e.g., differences in personality, communication style), or a combination of them. Accordingly, they decide on a strategy that is aligned with the root of the conflict.

In this chapter we argue that cultural context influences conflict management approaches, namely harmony, confrontation, or a regulative models (Kozan, 1997). Global managers will benefit from knowing that individuals from collectivistic cultures prefer the harmony model and, therefore, resolve the conflict in such a way that it will not harm the good interpersonal relationships by, say, suppressing negative emotions, involving third parties, accommodating the demands of the other party and helping the other party to save face. Those from individualistic cultures prefer the confrontation model; they acknowledge and discuss the conflict openly and resolve it on their own by negotiating and compromising. Individuals from uncertainty-avoiding cultures adopt the regulative model. They rely on rules and regulations to resolve the conflict (see Video 4.1. and think about the model featured in it).

Negotiating is more than resolving a conflict. It involves getting the 'yes' from the other party. We discuss cross-cultural differences in conflict management and negotiation processes. What do you think the global managers should do to get *yes* – adopt their style to the style of their partner or impose their style on the partner? In other words should they do as Romans do? In managing a conflict, yes; but in negotiating for a deal, it depends. Weiss (1996) argues that it depends on the level of familiarity of both parties with the cultural characteristics of each other (see Video 4.2).

If neither party is familiar with each others' cultural characteristics, the negotiation should be carried with the employment of an agent or advisor (e.g., attorney, financial adviser, technical expert, translator, or mediator), who has high familiarity with the culture of both parties.

If both parties are knowledgeable and familiar with each others' cultures, an improvisation strategy should be sought. In this approach, both parties attend to situational demands and transcend their own cultural scripts into creating a synergistic third culture approach.

When the negotiator is familiar with the counterpart's culture but the counterpart is not familiar with the negotiator's culture, the negotiator should opt for embracing the cultural ways of the counterpart (i.e., going along with the cultural style of the counterpart). When the reverse is the case, the negotiator should opt for inducing their cultural style on the counterpart in a manner that would not be seen as arrogant (i.e., persuading the counterpart to come along with the negotiator's cultural style).

Both the negotiator and the counterparty may be moderately familiar with each others' cultures. In this situation, the adaptation strategy should be employed, in which the negotiator modifies their typical cultural style by omitting some actions and following the lead of the counterpart. The counterpart is expected to do the same. Thinking across cultures 4.2 presents an example of the five strategies described here.

Thinking Across Cultures 4.2

Five Strategies in Cross-cultural Negotiations (Illustrative Case of the US-Japan)

- **Employ an agent** (neither negotiation nor counterpart are familiar with each others' culture):
  - Use an 'introducer' for initial contracts (e.g., general trading company).
  - Employ an agent the counterpart knows and respects.
  - Ensure that the agent or advisor speaks fluent Japanese.
- **Improvise** (both negotiation and counterpart are familiar with each others' culture):
  - Do homework on the individual counterpart and their circumstances.
  - Be attentive and nimble (pay attention to individual differences).
  - Invite the counterpart to participate in mutually enjoyed activities or interests (e.g., golf).
- **Embrace** (negotiator is familiar with counterpart's culture and counterpart is not familiar with negotiator's culture):
  - Proceed according to an information-gathering, nemawashi (Japanese term indicating 'laying the groundwork'), not information-exchange model.

- o 'Know your stuff'.
- o Assemble a team (group) for negotiations.
- o Speak in Japanese, if possible.
- o Develop personal relationships; respond to obligations within them.

- **Induce** (negotiator is not familiar with counterpart's culture and counterpart is familiar with negotiator's culture):

  - o Be open to social interaction and communicate directly.
  - o Make an extreme initial proposal, expecting to make concessions later.
  - o Work efficiently to 'get the job done'.

- **Adapt** (negotiator and counterpart are moderately familiar with each others' culture):

  - o Follow some Japanese protocol (reserved behaviour, name cards, gifts).
  - o Provide a lot of information (by American standards) up front to influence the counterpart's decision-making early in the process.
  - o Slow down your usual timetable.
  - o Make informed interpretations (e.g., the meaning of 'it is difficult').
  - o Present positions later in the process, more firmly and more consistently.

Source: Weiss (1996, p. 401)

Chapter Summary

No strategies exist that managers can use to make their work units or organizations entirely immune to conflict. However, there are actions managers can take to manage conflict in a positive manner. Specifically, what are some of the actions which either diminish the occurrence of some conflicts, or promote a climate in which organizational members adopt the integrative or win–win approach to conflict management? In this chapter we start out by acknowledging that conflict may be a source of tension as well as an opportunity to learn and build stronger interpersonal relationships. The more positive the attitude towards conflict, the more it would be perceived as an opportunity rather than a threat. Therefore, one should not resort to avoidance and defusion to handle conflict. Next, we present the conditions under which conflict was likely to occur, including ambiguities in roles and responsibilities, conflicting interests, communication barriers, lack of behavioural regulations, and unresolved prior conflicts. To minimize these conditions, we recommend an increase in job role clarity, flexibility in the organizational structure, incentives to promote cooperative behaviour, available resources in the organization and salience of superordinate goals. We discuss that avoidance, defusion and use of power were strategies not fully effective to cope with conflict, whereas negotiation was the strategy having the potential to satisfy the needs of conflicting parties. Cross-cultural differences in communication is another source of unintended interpersonal conflict in work relationships (see Video 4.3.). Negotiation is a process that requires careful planning, such as developing goals, positions, arguments and strategies prior to starting the negotiation. We recommended seeking integrative (win–win), rather than distributive (win–lose) strategies in negotiation. We identify active listening and assertiveness as key communication skills to enhance the effectiveness of negations. Empowering managerial practices are recommended to foster effective listening and assertiveness. In the final section of the chapter cross-cultural similarities and differences are discussed in the negotiation process involving three phases: preparation, negotiation and reaching agreement. Collectivism, power distance, uncertainty avoidance and high- vs. low-context communication were identified as key cultural dimensions influencing the negotiation process. Managerial implications included paying attention to trust building in the negotiation process, familiarizing oneself with the conflict management model in different cultures (i.e., harmony, confrontation, regulation), using cultural intelligence to determine the appropriate negotiation strategy (i.e., using an agent, improvising, embracing, inducing, or adapting).

End of Chapter Reflection Questions

1. According to the findings of the GLOBE Project (House et al., 2004), US respondents' 'should be' score for the assertiveness dimension was lower than their 'as is' score. In other words, US respondents wanted to have less assertiveness in their society in future. The pattern was the reverse in majority of the developing economies. How do you make sense out of this?
2. 'Getting to yes' is the key to negotiation, but is it 'at all costs'? Discuss the advantages and disadvantages of winning in cross-cultural negotiation contexts (e.g., consider the possibility that the other party loses face when you win – how will this influence the long-term relationships?).
3. We examined the role of culture in communication and negotiation. How about the role of gender? To what extent do you think cross-gender communication and negotiation patterns differ across cultures? (See Video 4.4.)

Key Terms and Definitions

Conflict. Experience of disagreement or a situation with opposing choices.

Antecedent conditions of conflict. Conditions under which conflict is likely to arise.

Superordinate goals. Organizational goals agreed upon and important to achieve in spite of individual differences in the ability or willingness to achieve them.

Termination vs. resolution of conflict. Termination ends the conflict with or without a satisfactory solution; resolution arrives at an outcome that satisfies both parties.

Negotiation. The process aimed at ending the conflict by recognizing interdependencies and the possibility of agreement.

Avoidance. Withdrawal from the conflictual situation and unwillingness to resolve it.

Defusion. Delaying or stalling actions to resolve the conflict.

Distributive vs. integrative negotiation strategy. In distributive negotiation one party wins and the other party loses. In integrative negotiation the aim is to satisfy both parties with the distribution of resources.

Active listening. Attentive listening with the aim of acknowledging the problem, understanding its causes and helping the person to find a solution.

Assertive vs. aggressive communication. Assertive communication means expressing one's opinions and feelings freely and in a neutral way, while aggressive communication is to do the same in a way that may be hurtful or offensive.

High vs. low context culture. In high-context cultures the message is hidden in the context and words are not sufficient to express the opinions or feelings; in low-context cultures there is heavy reliance on overt expression of opinions or feelings.

Face-saving. Avoiding embarrassment especially in the presence of esteemed individuals.

Monochronic vs. polychronic cultural orientation. In monochronic cultures, there is preference to address issues sequentially (one at a time), whereas in polychronic cultures they are addressed concurrently (multiple activities at the same time).

Further Reading

Deutsch, M., Coleman, P.T. and Marcus, E.C. (eds) (2011) *The Handbook of Conflict Resolution: Theory and Practice.* San Francisco, CA: Wiley.

Gelfand, M.J. and Brett, J.M. (eds) (2004) *The Handbook of Negotiation and Culture.* Stanford, CA: Stanford Business Books.

Gelfand, M.J., Major, V.S., Raver, J.L., Nishii, L.H. and O'Brien, K. (2006) 'Negotiation relationally: The dynamics of relational self in negotiation', *Academy of Management Review*, 31 (2): 427–51.

Lax, D.A. (2006) *3-D negotiation: Powerful Tools to Change the Game in your most Important Deals.* Boston, MA: Harvard Business School Press.

Schmid, S.M. (ed.) (2001) *Power and Negotiation in Organizations: Readings, Cases and Exercises*. Dubuque, IA: Kendall/Hunt Pub. Co.

Sebenius, J.K. (2001) 'Six habits of merely effective negotiators', *Harvard Business Review*, 79 (4), 87-95.

Cases, Videos and Web-sources

Cases

The following cases focus on the importance of communication in getting the message across especially in the negotiation context.

Dalal, S. and Agarwal, R. (2012) *The Cinnamon Case* (A and B). IVEY cases no. 9B12C046A.

DiStefano, J. (2000) *Johannes van den Bosch Sends an E-mail*. IMD case no. 3-0963.

Zhigang, T., Wei, S. and Chan, P. (2012) *Negotiation in China: How Universal?* IVEY case no. HKU956.

Videos

Video 4.1 *Negotiation, Picard style* (2010) www.youtube.com/watch?v=iYCjqmbsmYA – Captain Picard of the USS Enterprise at his best in negotiating 'across cultures'!

Video 4.2 William Ury: *The Walk from 'No' to 'Yes'* (2010) www.ted.com/talks/william_ury.html – As the mastermind of negotiation, Ury reveals the secrets of 'getting to yes'.

Video 4.3 *10 Surprising Ways to Offend People in Other Countries* (2012) www.youtube.com/watch?v=UTE0G9amZNk – This funny video reveals some of the communication mistakes; don't forget to check the accuracy of advice with the locals!

Video 4.4 *Cross-cultural Communication: a British engineer in Mexico* (2009) www.youtube.com/watch?v=BrJTf97Ev8o – This video focuses on how cultural stereotyping is part of the cross-cultural communication mishaps.

Web sources

www.iacm-conflict.org – International Association for Conflict Management.

http://iaics.dvfu.ru/ – International Association for Intercultural Communication Studies.

http://www.jdsurvey.net/jds/jdsurvey.jsp – *world maps of interpersonal trust and happiness (based on World Values project results)*.

References

Adler, N.J. (1991) *International Dimensions of Organizational Behavior*, 2nd edn. Boston, MA: PWS-KENT Publishing Company.

Alberti, R.E. and Emmons, M.L. (1990) *Your Perfect Right: A Guide to Assertive Living*, 6th edn. San Luis Opispo, CA: Impact Publishers.

Aycan, Z. (2008) Cross-cultural perspectives to work-family conflict, in K. Korabik and D. Lero (eds), *Handbook of Work-family Conflict*, pp. 359–71. Cambridge: Cambridge University Press.

Brew, F.P. and Cairns, D.R. (2004). 'Do culture or situational constraints determine choice of direct or indirect styles in intercultural workplace conflicts', *International Journal of Intercultural Relations*, 28: 331–52.

Clegg, S.R. (2002) Lives in the balance: a comment on Hinings and Greenwoods disconnects and consequences in organization theory, *Administrative Science Theory*, 47 (3): 428–41.

Fang, T. (2006) Negotiation: The Chinese style. *Journal of Business and Industrial Marketing*, 21 (1): 50–60.

Filley, A.C. (1975) *Interpersonal Conflict Resolution*. Glenview, IL: Scott, Foresman and Company.

Fisher, R., Ury, W. and Patton, B. (1993) 'Negotiation power: Ingredients in our ability to influence the other side', in L. Hall (ed.), *Negotiation: Strategies for mutual gain*, pp. 3–13. Newbury Park, CA: Sage.

Francesco, A.M. and Gold, B.A. (2005) *International Organizational Behavior*, 2nd edn. Upper Saddle River, NJ: Prentice Hall.

Gelfand, M.J., Erez, M. and Aycan, Z. (2007) 'Cross-cultural organizational behavior', *Annual Review of Psychology*, 58: 479–514.

Graham, J.L. (1985) 'The influence of culture on the process of business negotiations: an exploratory study', *Journal of International Business*, 16 (1): 81–96.

Graham, J.L., Kim, D.K., Lin, C. and Robinson, M. (1988) 'Buyer–seller negotiations around the Pacific Rim: Differences in fundamental exchange processes', *Journal of Consumer Research*, 15: 48–54.

Hall, E.T. (1976) *Beyond culture*. New York: Anchor Books/Doubleday.

Hammer, M.R. and Rogan, R.G. (2002) 'Latino and Indochinese interpretive frames in negotiating conflict with law enforcement: A focus group analysis', *International Journal of Intercultural Relations*, 26: 551–76.

Holt, J.L. and DeVore, C.J. (2005) 'Culture, gender, organizational role and styles of conflict resolution: A meta-analysis', *International Journal of Intercultural Relations*, 29 (2): 165–96.

House, R.J., Hanges, P.J., Javidan, M., Dorfman, P.W. and Gupta, V. (eds) (2004) *Culture, Leadership, and Organizations: The GLOBE study of 62 societies*. Thousand Oaks, CA: Sage Publications.

Katz, L. (2007) *Negotiating international business: The negotiator's reference guide to 50 countries around the world* (2nd edn). Charleston, SC: BookSurge Publishing.

Kozan, K. (1997) 'Culture and conflict management: A theoretical framework', *International Journal of Conflict Management*, 8 (4): 338–60.

Leung, K. (1988) 'Some determinants of conflict avoidance', *Journal of Cross-cultural Psychology*, 19 (1): 125–36.

Leung, K. (1997) 'Negotiation and reward allocation across cultures', in P.C. Earley and M. Erez (eds), *New Perspectives on International Industrial/organizational Psychology*, pp. 640–75. San Francisco, CA: New Lexington.

Lewicki, R.J. and Litterer, J.A. (1985) *Negotiation*. New York: Irwin.

Mead, R. (2005) *International management: Cross-cultural dimensions* (3rd edn). Oxford: Blackwell Publishing.

Peng, K. and Nisbett, R.E. (1999) 'Culture dialectics and reasoning about contradiction', *American Psychologists*, 54: 741–54.

Punnett, B.J. (2004) *International Perspectives on Organizational Behavior and Human Resource Management*. Armonk, NY: M. E. Sharpe Inc.

Rogers, C.R. and Farson, R.E. (1957) 'Active listening', in R.G. Newman, M.A. Danziger and M. Cohen (eds), *Communication in Business today*, Washington, DC: Heath and Company.

Ting-Toomey, S. (1985) 'Toward a theory of conflict and culture', in W. Gudykunst, L. Steward and S. Ting-Toomey (eds), *Communication, Cultural and Organizational Processes*, pp. 71–87. New York: Sage.

Weiss, S.E. (1996) 'International negotiations: Bricks, mortar and prospects', in B. Punnet and O. Shenkar (eds), *Handbook for International Management Research*, pp. 208–65. Cambridge, MA: Blackwell Publishers.

Whetten, D.A. and Cameron, K.S. (1991) *Developing Management Skills*, 2nd edn. New York: HarperCollins Publishers, Inc.

Yang, N., Chen, C., Choi, J. and Zou, Y. (2000) 'Sources of work–family conflict: A Sino–US comparison of the effects of work and family demands', *Academy of Management Journal*, 43 (1): 113–23.

Want to learn more? Visit the companion website at www.sagepub.co.uk/kanungo to gain access to videos from the end of each chapter, weblinks and flash cards of key terms.

5

Leadership: Role Behaviours and Cross-cultural Perspectives

Chapter Outline

Leadership is influence.

John C. Maxwell

When the effective leader is finished with his work, the people say it happened naturally.

Lao Tzu

Leadership is the capacity to translate vision into reality.

Warren Bennis

Before you are a leader, success is all about growing yourself. When you become a leader, success is all about growing others.

Jack Welch

Become the kind of leader that people would follow voluntarily; even if you had no title or position.

Brian Tracy

The challenge of leadership is to be strong, but not rude; be kind, but not weak; be bold, but not bully; be thoughtful, but not lazy; be humble, but not timid; be proud, but not arrogant; have humor, but without folly.

Jim Rohn

Do what you feel in your heart to be right – for you'll be criticized anyway.

Eleanor Roosevelt

Which of the above quotes compiled by J.D. Meier (http://sourcesofinsight.com/leadership-quotes/) are your favourites? Which ones best describe 'leadership' in your mind – after all, leadership *is* in the eye of the beholder?

According to decades of research and the wisdom of legendary leaders, the first quote tells the defining characteristic of leadership: it is an influence process. Leadership is also about empowering others and developing other leaders; developing vision and realizing it successfully; taking risks and being ethical; and striking the right balance between strength and kindness.

This chapter focuses on roles and behaviours characterizing effective leadership as well as leadership challenges in cross-cultural contexts. We first define what leadership is and how it is different from management. Leadership roles and behaviours are discussed under three headings: decision-making role behaviour, task and social role behaviour, and charismatic role behaviour.

The decision-making role behaviour centres around the question should the leader use the autocratic or participative style in decision-making? To respond to this question adequately we consider the conditions which determine the effectiveness of the participative approach in decision-making: (1) the followers' motivational state; (2) the leader–followers interaction; and (3) the characteristics of the decision-making or problem situation. We then examine the task and social leadership roles. Through the performance of task roles, the leader facilitates the accomplishment of the group's task; the performance of social roles enables the leader to maintain the group – that is, to help group members to work together as they go about accomplishing the group task. We explore the charismatic role behaviour of the leader through the discussion of the three-stage charismatic leadership influence process model proposed by Conger and Kanungo (1998).

In the second part of the chapter we examine the impact of cultural context (i.e., cultural values, norms, assumptions and expectations) on the ways in which leadership roles are enacted and perceived by followers. We also discuss the impact of culture on the relationship of leaders' roles with employees' attitudes and performance.

Learning Objectives

- To examine the key differences between leaders and managers.
- To explore four leadership roles: decision-making, task and social roles and the charismatic role.

- To understand the notion of participative leadership and identify the conditions which facilitate its effectiveness.

- To identify the characteristics of the behaviours that can be performed in the task and social roles and the effect of such behaviours on group effectiveness.

- To define the phenomenon of 'charismatic leadership' and the three stages of the charismatic leadership influence process.

- To review cross-cultural differences in the ways in which effective leadership is defined.

- To determine the role of culture in enactment of participative, task, social and charismatic roles of leadership.

- To discuss a specific type of leadership prevalent in high power distant and collectivistic cultures: paternalistic (or *parentalistic*) leadership.

Leadership

From time immemorial, whenever human beings have come together in pursuit of some goals or objectives, they have felt the need of a leader. So much so that in most cultures and societies the leader role has been institutionalized as, for example, the tribal chief, the head of the household or family, the head of the village, the mayor of the town, the president, prime minister, or monarch of a country. It is true that modern democracies have put in place institutional structures of checks and balances to prevent the abuse of power that results when it is concentrated in one person. Even so, the effectiveness of these structures has been found to be dependent upon the quality of leadership among the people in these institutions. For example, the executive, legislative and judicial branches of government can be successful in attaining its objectives only to the extent of the leadership, formal or informal, that exists or emerges in these organizations.

Leadership is indeed an ubiquitous phenomenon. The exciting, adventurous and the romantic exploits of leaders, together with their foibles and ruthlessness have been the subject of much folklore, myth and literature. However, it is only relatively recently, over the last fifty or more years, that leadership in organizations has been the focus of both theoretical and empirical analysis.

Leadership has been defined in many ways by different scholars. One of the most recent and comprehensive definitions is based on a large-scale cross-national study initiated by Robert House and his colleagues. Global Leadership and Organizational Behavior Effectiveness (GLOBE) project has proposed a 'universal' definition of leadership agreed upon by 54 researchers from 38 different countries: 'the ability of an individual to influence, motivate and enable others to contribute toward the effectiveness and success of the organizations of which they are members' (House et al., 2001, p. 494).

As stated earlier, leadership is essentially an influence process. Effective leaders are those who have a profound influence on followers. This is a potentially dangerous phenomenon, considering some of the most effective and yet destructive leaders of the world (e.g., Hitler or cult leaders). One should also remember that leadership is not reserved to a certain gender, age or ethnic group. Effective leaders may be of any age, gender, ethnic group or position in the organization (see Video 5.1. and 5.2.).

When organizations strive to 'develop leaders at all levels', do they really mean leaders or effective managers? Oftentimes it is the latter (or the combination of both). Let us examine the differences between leaders and managers presented in Table 5.1. Although there are important differences between leaders and managers, these terms are often used interchangeably. For convenience purpose, we will also use them interchangeably in this chapter. Do you think the majority of organizations aim (and should aim) to develop leadership at all levels? Why and why not?

Approaches to understanding leadership

Some of the early studies explored leadership as a cluster of stable personality traits of individual leaders. Such studies (Cowley, 1928) looked at leaders in isolation from their context, and therefore did not take into account the factors

Table 5.1   The distinctions between typical roles and behaviours of managers and leaders

Manager	Leader
Engages in day-to day activities: maintains and allocates resources.	Formulates long-term objectives for reforming the system: plans strategy and tactics.
Exhibits supervisory behaviour: acts to make others maintain standard job behaviour.	Exhibits leading behaviour: acts to bring about change in others congruent with long-term objectives.
Administers subsystems within organizations.	Innovates for the entire organization.
Asks how and when to engage in standard practice.	Asks when and why to change standard practice.
Acts within the established culture of the organization.	Creates vision and meaning for the organization and strives to transform culture.
Uses transactional influence: induces compliance in manifest behaviour using rewards, sanctions, and formal authority.	Uses transformational influence: induces change in values, attitudes, and behaviour using personal examples and expertise.
Relies on control strategies to get things done by subordinates.	Uses empowering strategies to make followers internalize values.
Supports the status quo and stabilizes the organization.	Challenges the status quo and creates change.

Source: Conger & Kanungo, 1998, p. 9.

involved in leader–follower and leader–context interaction which might enhance our understanding of leader behaviours. Later studies took the leaders' context into account, but this context was, in most cases, the relatively small group settings in which the leaders functioned. We can see two major thrusts or directions in these studies.

One set of studies focused on the leader's **decision-making role** in group contexts (see Figure 5.1). The basic question these studies addressed was: Which decision-making behaviour or style, autocratic or **participative**, enables the leader to be more effective in the group? As a result, the leader's autocratic or participatory style of decision-making came to be considered as an important dimension of leadership role behaviour.

The other set of studies sought to identify two other leadership role behaviours that are necessary to attain the group's objectives (e.g., Yukl, 1989):

1. Task roles with a focus on problem identification and solution, including resources allocation and monitoring of the behaviour of organizational members that is necessary to accomplish the task at hand; and
2. Social roles with a focus on people orientation, including interpersonal relationships, which are conducive to building group cohesion and developing the quality of working life of its members.

These two leadership roles seem to reasonably describe leadership role behaviours of managers or supervisors who perceive that their responsibility is to merely maintain the day-to-day, routine functioning of the group. However, these roles do not capture the transformational and charismatic nature of leadership one observes in large corporations or in social and political organizations. In such organizations, successful or effective leaders have been found to engage in behaviours such as

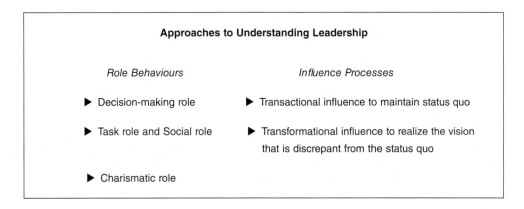

Figure 5.1 *Leadership role behaviours and influences processes*

identifying the deficiencies in the status quo and potential opportunities, formulating and articulating a vision that expresses these opportunities and is shared by the followers and adopting the means, even at personal sacrifice, to achieve the vision. These behavioural dimensions are typically characteristic of the **charismatic role** (Conger and Kanungo, 1998).

The preceding discussion has focused on four types of role behaviours: decision-making, task, social, and charismatic roles, which essentially characterize 'what' leaders do. In this chapter our focus will be on leadership role behaviours. Another approach to understand leadership phenomenon is to examine it through the social influence process. The latter approach allows us to explore the psychological underpinnings or explanations of the influence process involved in leadership. The leader's role behaviours would constitute the content, or what leaders do, whereas the influence process adopted by the leader would constitute the process, the explanation of how and why the leader behaviour becomes effective in influencing followers.

To further elaborate on the 'process' explanation of leadership, we see that basically two influence processes or ways of influencing followers are available to leaders. These are the transactional influence process and the transformational influence process (e.g., Bass, 1985; Bryman, 1992; Conger and Kanungo, 1998).

In the transactional influence process, the leader ensures that the followers perform the required behaviours through the use of rewards and sanctions or control strategies. The effectiveness of the transactional influence mode is obviously limited to the effectiveness 'lifespan' of the commodities offered in exchange. In other words, in the transactional influence mode, the followers' compliance is governed by the value in exchange of the rewards and sanctions that are used. Therefore, when the major concerns of the supervisors and managers are to attend to the day-to-day caretaker activities of their work organization – that is, to maintain the status quo, they are more likely to use control strategies to induce compliance in their subordinates.

On the other hand, in the transformational influence process, the leader works to bring about a change in the followers' attitudes and values, as they move the organization towards its future goals. The leader brings about the change in followers' attitudes and values essentially through empowering techniques which increase the self-efficacy beliefs of the followers that they are capable of working towards established goals. The followers' compliance is the result of two important factors: (a) their internalization of the leader's vision; and (b) the increase in their self-efficacy belief. Therefore, the effect of the transformational influence mode on the followers is more enduring and permanent. When managers do not accept the status quo in their work organization and formulate an idealized vision that is discrepant from the status quo and is shared by the followers, they move away from being caretakers or administrators and function as transformational leaders. Figure 5.1. brings together the role behaviour and the social influence process approaches of understanding leadership.

Leadership Role Behaviours

Decision-making role

One of the key ingredients for a successful organization operating in a turbulent and competitive environment is to be innovative in all aspects of its operation. However, in order to be innovative, employees must think and behave in new and creative ways as they perform their jobs. It means that employees use their knowledge, abilities and experience to respond creatively to the constantly changing demands of the environment. It includes 'ideas for reorganizing, cutting costs, putting in new budgeting systems, improving communication, or assembling products in teams' (Kanter, 1983, p. 20). Employees at all levels have the potential to be innovative. However, in order to realize this potential organizations need to create conditions which foster in employees the willingness to take risks and to innovate.

One of the critical conditions which stifle employee creativity and innovation is the mode of conducting the supervision process inherent in the management function (Kanter, 1983). More specifically, it is the directive or autocratic decision-making style of supervisors which has the effect of depriving employees of autonomy in matters relating to their work, except for rudimentary and insignificant decisions. A shift from the autocratic to the participative style of decision-making is effective under certain appropriate conditions that relate to subordinates' motivational state, supervisors' managerial practices and the problem characteristics. Let us now examine thee conditions under which participative decision-making yields positive results.

Effectiveness of leader's participative decision-making role behaviours is contingent upon subordinate and supervisory characteristics. Despite the enormous potential of participative leadership for employee satisfaction and organizational effectiveness, research suggests that the expected benefits have not always been realized (e.g., Lawler, 1986). The reasons for the 'failure' of participative leadership are partly due to a failure to recognize contingency factors such as the characteristics of the subordinates and the nature of superior–subordinate relations.

The desirability of participative leadership depends upon the subordinate's motivation or need for participation in the decision-making process. Individuals have a need to control and cope with life events and feel empowered when they believe that they can cope with events, situations and people they confront, but feel powerless when they believe that they cannot cope with them. This belief of the individual is referred to as a belief in self-determination (Deci, 1975), or a belief in personal self-efficacy (Bandura, 1986) which has direct implications for participative leadership.

When the subordinate's belief in self-determination or personal self-efficacy is high, participative leadership will be effective. However, when the subordinate's self-determination or self-efficacy belief is low, the effectiveness of participative leadership is only assured if it is accompanied by other **empowering** supervision practices such as:

- supervisory actions to remove organizational obstacles to good performance (Kanter, 1979; House, 1988),
- gradual increments in subordinate's task complexity and responsibility, accompanied by appropriate training and development, and
- setting high performance expectations for subordinates and, at the same time, expressing confidence in their ability to meet these expectations (e.g., Burke, 1986; House, 1988). The mentoring and coaching efforts implicit in these practices are intended to focus on the developmental and positive remedial measures which make employees feel more capable and, as a result, better prepared to be fully involved in participative decision-making process.

Effectiveness of the leader's participative decision-making role behaviours is contingent upon task or problem characteristics. In addition to the employees' motivational state and the supervisory practices discussed above, the characteristics of the decision problem or situation are equally important considerations influencing the manager's choice of participative leadership role. Vroom and his associates (e.g., Vroom and Jago, 1988) have researched this issue and, based on their empirical findings, developed a decision-making model which enables managers to conduct a systematic analysis of the problem or decision situation. The decision tree incorporated into the model *prescribes* the decision-making style for a leader – from a range of most autocratic to most participative – that is appropriate for that particular problem situation.

The objective of the model is to prescribe for the manager in a leadership role to one of the following five alternative decision-making styles:

- AI In this highly autocratic approach, you as the leader make the decision by yourself based only on the information you have or can obtain from sources other than your subordinates.
- AII In this relatively less autocratic approach, you avail yourself of the information which is with your subordinates in order to make the decision, but you do not share the problem with your subordinates when you ask them for specific information. This clearly implies that you do not want or expect your subordinates to be involved in developing solutions for the problem situation. You merely want them to give you the information you ask for.
- CI This approach is a move away from the autocratic to a consultative mode. As in AII, you make your decision after you obtain information from the subordinates. It differs from AII, however, in that you now share the problem with your subordinates. But you do so with each subordinate, *individually* and *not as a*

group. Further, although you have shared the problem with your subordinates and obtained information from them, you may or may not be influenced by their input.

- CII This approach is a further move towards the consultative mode. As in CI, you make your decision after you obtain information from the subordinates. Unlike in CI, you bring the subordinates together *as a group*, you share the problem situation with them and ask them for input which they believe will solve the problem. However, you make the decision on your own without *necessarily* being influenced by the group's input.

- GII This decision making style is the most participative. You bring the subordinates together as a group, share the problem with them and clearly communicate to them that you would like them to: consider the problem, generate and evaluate alternative courses of action and arrive at a decision consensually. You will also make it clear that (a) your role will be that of a 'chairperson' with the sole objective of facilitating their task, (b) although you may have a preferred solution, you will not influence the group to accept it, much less impose it on them, and (c) you will accept and implement the decision which the group supports.

The five types can be viewed as on a continuum from the most autocratic (AI) to the most participative (GII) decision-making style. In order to show what the relative overall effectiveness of each decision-making style will be for the particular problem situation, the decision tree presented in Figure 5.2 (Vroom and Jago, 1988) can be used. The contingencies to be considered in making a decision are presented in Table 5.2.

Participative leadership becomes critical when:

- subordinates' commitment is high;
- the leader does not have sufficient information;
- the problem is not well structured;
- subordinates' commitment probability is low if they are not involved in the decision;
- goal congruence is high;
- conflict among subordinates is likely; and
- the subordinates, as a group, have sufficient information for a high-quality decision.

An autocratic approach is more appropriate when:

- the quality requirement is high;
- subordinates' commitment is low;
- the leader's information is high.

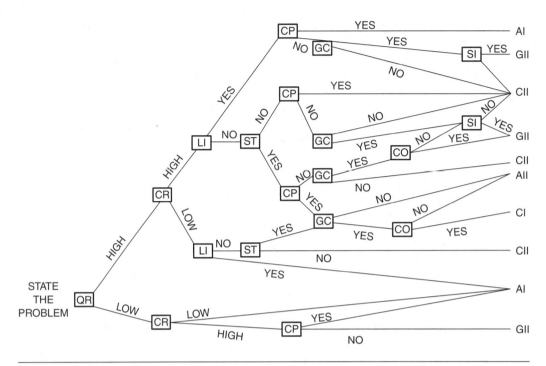

Figure 5.2 *The decision tree to guide leaders on the level of participation required in decision making*

Source: Reprinted with permission from *The New Leadership: Managing Participation in Organizations* by Victor H. Vroom and Arthur G. Jago, 1988, Englewood Cliffs, NJ: Prentice-Hall

Table 5.2   Diagnostic questions to guide leaders in the decision-making process

Problem Attribute	Diagnostic Question	Legend in the Decision Tree (Figure 5.2)
1. Quality Requirement	How important is the technical quality of this decision? (i.e., how big would be the harm if the wrong decision is made?)	QR
2. Commitment Requirement	How important is subordinate commitment to the decision for its successful implementation?	CR
3. Leader's Information	Does the leader himself or herself have sufficient information to make a high quality decision?	LI
4. Problem Structure	Is the problem well-structured? (i.e., is 'what needs to be done and how it should be done' clear?)	ST
5. Commitment Probability	If the leader were to make the decision by himself or herself alone, is it reasonably certain that the subordinates would be committed to the decision?	CP
6. Goal Congruence	Do subordinates share the organization's goals to be attained in solving this problem?	GC
7. Subordinate Conflict	If a decision is made, is conflict among subordinates over preferred solutions likely?	CO
8. Subordinate Information	Do subordinates have sufficient information to make a high-quality decision?	SI

CASE 5.1

Should Tracy be Participative or Autocratic in her Decision-making Role?

Tracy Beauchemin, VP-Operations in charge of a plastics manufacturing company, is concerned that the experiments and related activities in one of the two research laboratories that is, lab # 1 can pose a serious health hazard because of the toxic fumes and the disposal of its toxic waste material. The lab # 1 researchers and technicians are provided with protective clothing and related gear. Tracy is considering the decision to provide similar protective clothing for the maintenance and janitorial employees assigned to lab # 1. Although the cost of such clothing and gear is prohibitively high, Tracy believes that her budget could accommodate the cost for the maintenance and janitorial employees only.

She is uncertain whether these are the only employees who are at risk because other employees such as accounting clerks and some process operators might also be visiting that lab. Besides, she is also not sure if similar health hazards exist in the other laboratory or in other sections of the plant. She recalls that at one of the management committee meetings, the human resource manager had mentioned that the issue of protective clothing for plant employees was a sensitive issue and would likely be raised by the union at the next contract negotiations. The management committee is made up of the managers of the research laboratories and the functional departments and is chaired by the Vice President Operations. The managers are sympathetic to employee welfare programmes but would be reluctant to accept budget cuts to accommodate unnecessary employee welfare expenses. They would also resist any decisions that might be seen by the union as precedents for further demands relating to employee welfare programmes.

How participative should Tracy be in her decision-making role? Please answer the following diagnostic questions and find the right decision approach from the decision tree in Figure 5.2.

- Quality requirement (QR):   _____ High   _____ Low
- Commitment requirement (CR):   _____ High   _____ Low
- Leader's information (LI):   _____ Yes   _____ No
- Problem structure (ST):   _____ Yes   _____ No
- Commitment probability (CP):   _____ Yes   _____ No
- Goal congruence (GC):   _____ Yes   _____ No

(Continued)

(Continued)

- Subordinate conflict (CO):   _____ Yes   _____ No
- Subordinate information (SI):   _____ Yes   _____ No

Proposed solution:

QR: High; CR: High; LI: No; ST: Yes; CP: No; GC: Yes; CO: No; SI: Yes - Decision: GII

Note that it is possible to arrive at a different solution under a different set of assumptions about the case.

Task and social roles

What is it that makes a group effective to the extent that one would like to continue working in it, whereas another group is not only ineffective but its functioning is such that it makes one want to disassociate from it at the earliest opportunity?

This section seeks to address this question. Specifically, it explores the set of task and social role behaviours of a leader which allow the group members to work together in achieving the group's objective. It also discusses the leader's self-oriented role behaviours which impede the group members from achieving the group's objective. The discussion will include the content of the **task, social** and self-oriented role behaviours (Bales, 1970) as well as their impact on effectiveness of the work group.

The task role behaviours

The performance by the leader of one or more of the role behaviours described below enables the group to accomplish its task. This implies that if the needed role behaviours are not performed, the group's effectiveness is impaired.

Idea initiator

Leaders performing this role behaviour offer or propose ideas of how the task is to be done. These ideas could include new approaches, procedures or structures to solve the problems which confront the group.

- *Information-seeker*. This behaviour involves asking group members for information or opinions about a matter that is critical to the group task or about the ideas that have been proposed. The questions that are raised might also seek information on what precisely are the values that are important to the group. The objective is to bring to the group discussion on all relevant information which enables the group to make an informed decision.

- *Information provider.* The leaders who perform this role behaviour offer the kind of information (facts, opinions, beliefs and so on) that would respond to the information-seeker's questions. Such information might be provided either in response to the questions raised, or proactively in the belief that such contribution is relevant and ought to be considered by the group for effective task accomplishment.

- *Problem clarifier.* The objective of this behaviour is essentially to help keep the group focused on the issues relevant to the group task. For this purpose, the ideas, views, or proposals that are being considered are interpreted and analysed. Contradictions or confusion relative to definitions, issues, or proposed courses of action which might adversely affect the group's goal attainment, are identified and clarifications offered to the group.

- *Summarizer.* This role behaviour tends to be more of a coordinator role. In this role, the various ideas and action proposals which have been expressed are brought together into a synthesis. Such a synthesis is offered to the group as a decision to be considered, or as a nucleus upon which to develop alternative proposals.

- *Consensus tester.* A leader as a consensus tester assesses the direction of the discussion in a group on different proposals. When they develop a sense that one of the proposals might be acceptable to the group, they test it out on the group. This is done not as a specific proposal, but rather in the form of a question such as: 'Of the many proposals we have discussed and analysed, I wonder if proposal "X" might be the one we are looking for?' Without a consensus tester in the group, the group discussion might go on forever and not come to a specific conclusion that is necessary to accomplish the group task.

The social role behaviours

The social role behaviours, described below, are also known as the maintenance role behaviours because they help to develop good relationships among members and a congenial climate which facilitates their working together, as a group and not as disparate individuals, to achieve the group task. When these role behaviours are not performed the group risks losing the full participation of its members and, as a consequence, the benefits of their knowledge, expertise and experience.

- *Harmonizer.* This role behaviour is essentially a mediation role and very essential in order to reconcile the differences that inevitably arise in a group. The leader performing this role works at getting members to explore the difference not in terms of the stated positions but more in terms of the interests and aspirations underlying the positions. Such exploration, it is hoped, will lead to a better understanding of members' positions which, in addition to reconciling differences, can also contribute to reducing tensions. Sometimes what the group needs might simply be a reduction of tension. In such a situation, the harmonizer might help with a joke or a remark which permits members to recognize that a more congenial atmosphere is more conducive to problem-solving.

- *Gatekeeper*. When work groups are set up, the implicit notion is that individuals working collectively can accomplish the task more effectively than individuals working separately. The rationale for this is that group members can bring to bear on the task a richer and more varied set of ideas, approaches, knowledge, expertise, experience and so on. Therefore, it is only logical that the communication pattern and procedures in the group be such that it facilitates the participation of every member of the group. The gatekeeper role behaviour works towards this objective. For this purpose, it ensures that the communication procedures allow members to share information and express their views. When necessary, the leader performing this role might intervene to reduce the domination of the discussion by some members and to draw out the quieter members whose contribution might be equally valuable.

- *Supporter*. Also known as the 'encourager', this role behaviour also operates to facilitate contributions by group members. It does this by providing positive reinforcement of the valuable ideas and suggestions made by members. The positive reinforcers are a friendly and warm response and praise. However, the more effective reinforcer is acknowledging the members' contribution in such a way that members genuinely believe that they have been listened to and that their views receive serious consideration.

- *Compromiser*. The basic objective of this role behaviour is to maintain the cohesiveness of the group. For this purpose, a leader might, in a spirit of compromise, offer to withdraw their proposal if it conflicts with other proposals. Another behaviour in this category is the leader's willingness to accept responsibility for their errors – particularly when such errors have become a major bone of contention that threatens to divide the group. In some situations, the compromise can be made by not insisting on one's status vis-à-vis the other members of the group. This is critical in groups whose members do not have equal status, which might be the case in committees in organizations composed of members from different hierarchical levels. It is important to sound a note of caution here. Although compromising might promote group cohesiveness, it needs to be recognized that if the leader is the one with the better idea or proposal such compromising behaviour will jeopardize the group's effectiveness. The best safeguards against the compromise role becoming a group liability are to ensure that the task roles, described earlier and the social role of 'standards monitor', described next, are performed effectively.

- *Standards monitor*. An effective group needs to ensure that its operating norms, which reflect its values, are adhered to. For example, suppose the group has an implicit or explicit norm that its decisions will be by consensus. If the decision seems to be moving in the direction of taking a vote, the performance of this role requires that a question be raised to draw attention to the group norm of decision by consensus. Of course the group can change its norms, but the standards monitor's position is that such changes should not be the result of the expediency of the moment that is accepted by default because no one has questioned it. Rather, a deliberate discussion of the reasons which necessitate the change must precede such changes. Another example of the behaviour of the standards monitor relates to the behaviour as a compromiser to ensure group cohesiveness. As mentioned previously, compromising can be a group liability. In such a situation, the leader might raise the question of whether members are satisfied with seeing the achievement of the group's objective jeopardized when it allows the leader to withdraw a better proposal.

The self-oriented role behaviours

These are the role behaviours that might meet the leader's needs and goals but which are totally irrelevant to the group's task and, often, are obstacles to the effective functioning of the group.

- *Aggressor.* In this role behaviour, we see the leader questioning ideas, views, and proposals in a tone and manner that is not perceived by the group as constructive criticism or as a further development of the discussion. The behaviour is characterized by sarcastic comments and the target of the negative attacks is the group members' capabilities rather than the ideas or proposals that are put forward.
- *Blocker.* This role behaviour is an obstacle to the group's progress because when the leader disagrees with a proposal that has the support of the group, they attempt to slow down its passage by persistently restating objections and arguments which have been rejected by the group after extensive consideration.
- *Recognition seeker.* The principal objective of this behaviour is to draw attention to the leader's own competence and accomplishments, even though such references are entirely irrelevant to the group's task. Such 'bragging' hinders and detracts from group effectiveness because it is annoying as well as a needless waste of time.
- *Dominator.* In this role behaviour, the leader seeks to assert their authority over the group even to the point of interrupting or interfering with the legitimate right of other members to participate in the group deliberations. Some examples of specific behaviours in this role are: 'pulling one's rank' that is, asserting one's status; using flattery and related manipulative actions to influence members to support one's position. The insidious effect of this role is that it prevents full participation by all members in the group's deliberations. The consequences are

that either some members withdraw, or the group's decision does not fully reflect the ideas and competencies of the entire group.

- *Avoider.* When leaders exhibit this role behaviour, they become 'passive' resisters. They are reluctant to take a decisive position on important but controversial issues. By their silence and calculated indifference, they also create an atmosphere of doubt and uncertainty which does not provide the group with the solidarity and support it needs to confront controversial issues in a rational and effective manner.

CASE 5.2

Identify Leadership Role Behaviours

The following case portrays the behaviours of the members of the 'Merit Pay Review Committee' of a large organization. The members are senior managers of different departments in the organization.

Your task is to identify the task and social roles performed by these senior managers. Indicate in the blank space beside each behaviour various task roles (e.g., information seeker, problem clarifier) and social roles (e.g., harmonizer, supporter) reviewed in this chapter.

Kate begins by stating the reason for the meeting and proposes that the group might first want to familiarize themselves with the theories and empirical work done on this subject (1._____). John warmly supports the idea (2._____). Joe questions how such a study will help the group (3._____). Cathy agrees with Kate about the value of the study but would like more details on how it is to be done given the limited time available (4._____). Jean explains that a reasonably sound understanding of why some systems work and others do not is useful in the type of problem-solving that faces the committee. She also offers to make available to the group a review of the literature on pay-for-performance which she had undertaken for her human resource management course (5._____).

Sharon senses that Joe is beginning to feel frustrated at this 'academic' talk and the failure to properly respond to his question. She therefore draws attention to the validity of Joe's question (6._____) and reminds the group that its objective is to review the merit pay system that now exists. Although an overview of the academic literature is helpful, it is essential that they do a survey of employees to determine what it is about the current system they do or do not like. In other words, Sharon's proposal seeks to look at both issues – the academic review as well as the current status in the organization (7._____). Kate notices that

Tom has not expressed his opinion so far and invites him to share the union's views on this subject (8._____).

Tom informs the group that the union's experience is that merit pay is often used to favour employees who do not support the union. Therefore, as a general policy, the union will not support such a programme. He also added that his sense is that this committee is serious about developing a fair programme. He is therefore willing not to take a doctrinaire approach to these issues. Despite his national union's policy on merit pay, his union local will support it if honest attempts are made to develop and administer a fair programme (9._____). Cathy welcomes Tom's comments (10._____) and expresses the hope that consistent with the values implicit in the organization's mission of treating employees fairly, this committee would strive to design and administer an equitable merit pay programme (11._____).

Kate notes that the views expressed so far seem to be that the group should review the literature on merit pay, survey employees to determine the current status of the programme and in the light of this information work towards developing a programme that is fair and equitable (12._____). Sharon then raises the question: 'Do I get the sense that our initial tasks, to be undertaken simultaneously, ought to be the literature review and the employee survey?' (13._____).

Leadership role behaviours:

1. Idea generator, 2. supporter, 3. information seeker, 4. information seeker, 5. information provider, 6. harmonizer, 7. problem clarifier, 8. gatekeeper, 9. comromiser, 10. supporter, 11. standard monitor, 12. summarizer, 13. consensus tester

Charismatic role

The leadership roles of managers in decision-making, task accomplishment and group maintenance are primarily directed toward achieving short-term operational objectives. This is done by using control strategies to ensure order and consistency in standard job behaviours of subordinates in the day-to-day operations of the organization. However, organizations need more than this in their leaders. Organizations need leaders who can formulate long-term objectives for the organization that are novel and different from the status quo. That way, organizations can change and develop in a competitive business environment. The model proposed by Conger and Kanungo (1998) suggests that the charismatic role provides such leadership.

In the **charismatic** role, the leader moves organizational members from an existing present state towards some future state. This dynamic might also be described as movement away from the status quo towards the achievement of desired longer-term goals. This process can be conceptualized into three specific stages and the behavioural components identified in each of those stages can enable us to distinguish the charismatic from the non-charismatic leadership (Table 5.3).

Stage 1. Evaluation of status quo. Leaders of organizations have to be highly sensitive to both the social and physical environment in which they operate. It is important that leaders are able to make realistic assessments of the environmental constraints and resources needed to bring about changes they advocate. A leader must also be sensitive to both the abilities and emotional needs of followers – a most important resource for attaining organizational goals. Such assessments are particularly important for these leaders because they often assume high risks by advocating radical changes. Their assessment of environmental resources and constraints then becomes extremely

Table 5.3   Distinguishing attributes of charismatic and non-charismatic leaders

Key Features of Charismatic Role	Critical Attributes	Non-Charismatic Leaders	Charismatic Leaders
Stage 1: Evaluation of Status Quo			
Assessment of environmental resources/constraints and follower needs. Realization of deficiencies in status quo	Environmental Sensitivity	Low	High
	Relation to Status Quo	Agree with and maintain status quo	Intolerance with shortcomings in status quo and search for opportunities to change it
Stage 2: Formulation of Organization Goals	Future Goals	Lack of vision or mission orientation	Strong vision or mission orientation
Formulation and effective articulation of inspirational vision that is highly discrepant from status quo yet within latitude of acceptance	Likableness	Shared perspective makes the leader likeable	Shared perspective plus idealized vision makes the leader adorable
	Articulation	Weak articulation of goals and motivation to lead	Strong articulation of goals and motivation to lead (inspirational)
Stage 3: Means to Achieve	Behaviour	Low risk, conventional and conforming	High risk, use of unconventional tactics
By personal example and risk, countercultural empowering, and impression management practices, leader conveys goals, demonstrates means to achieve, builds follower trust, motivates followers	Trustworthiness	Disinterested advocacy in persuasion attempts	Passionate advocacy through personal examples
	Expertise	Use of conventional means	Use of unconventional means and critiquing conventional means

important before planning courses of action. Thus, instead of launching a course of action as soon as a vision is formulated, a leader's environmental assessment may dictate that they prepare the ground and wait for an appropriate time, place and/or the availability of resources. This is where the knowledge, experience and expertise of the leader become critical.

In the assessment stage what distinguishes charismatic from non-charismatic leaders is their ability to recognize deficiencies in the present system. In other words, *they actively search out existing* or *potential shortcomings in the status quo.* For example, the charismatic manager might highlight the failure of a firm to exploit new technologies or new markets as a missed strategic or tactical opportunity. Deficiencies in a firm's strategic objectives are more readily detected by the charismatic, compared to non-charismatic leader. Likewise a charismatic leader might more readily perceive the unfulfilled needs of the marketplace and transform these into market opportunities for new products or services. Internal organizational deficiencies may be perceived by the charismatic leader as platforms for advocating radical change.

Because of their emphasis on deficiencies in the system and their high levels of intolerance for them, charismatic leaders are always seen as organizational reformers or entrepreneurs. In other words, they act as agents of innovative and radical change.

Stage 2. Formulation of organization goals. After assessing the environment a leader will formulate goals to achieve the organization's objectives. Charismatic leaders, however, can be distinguished from others by the nature of their goals and by the manner in which they articulate them. Charismatic leaders are characterized by a sense of strategic vision (Conger and Kanungo, 1998). Here the word 'vision' refers to some idealized goal which the leader wants the organization to achieve in the future. The more idealized or utopian the future goal advocated by the leader is, the more discrepant it becomes from the status quo. Moreover, by presenting a very discrepant and idealized goal to followers, the leader provides a sense of challenge and a motivating force for change. The idealized goal should represent a perspective shared by the followers and promises to meet their hopes and aspirations.

In their charismatic role, leaders not only need to have visions and plans for achieving them, they must also be able to articulate their visions and strategies for action in effective ways so as to influence their followers. Here articulation involves two separate processes: articulation of the context and articulation of the leader's motivation to lead. First, charismatic leaders must effectively articulate for followers the scenarios which represent the context:

- the nature of the status quo and its shortcomings,
- their future vision,
- how the future is realized when existing deficiencies are removed, and
- their plans of action for realizing their vision.

In articulating the context, the leader's verbal messages construct reality in such a way that only the negative features of the status quo are emphasized. The status quo is often presented as intolerable and the vision is presented as the most attractive and attainable alternative in clear specific terms.

Besides describing verbally the status quo, the future goal and the means to achieve the future goal, charismatic leaders must also articulate their own willingness to lead their followers. Using expressive modes of action, both verbal and non-verbal, they manifest their convictions, self-confidence and dedication to materialize what they advocate. In the use of rhetoric, words are selected to reflect their assertiveness, confidence, expertise and concern for followers' needs. These same qualities may also be expressed through high energy, persistence, unconventional and risky behaviour, heroic deeds and personal sacrifices – all these forms of manifest behaviour articulate their high motivation and enthusiasm. These leadership acts, which form part of a charismatic leader's impression management, are quite contagious and readily infect their followers.

Stage 3. Achieving the vision. Charismatic leaders build in followers a sense of trust in their abilities and clearly demonstrate the tactics and behaviours required to achieve the organization's goals. *The charismatic leader does this by building trust through personal example and risk-taking and through unconventional methods or behaviours.* It is critical that followers or subordinates develop trust in the leader's vision. Generally leaders are perceived as trustworthy when they advocate their position in a disinterested manner and demonstrate a concern for followers' needs rather than their own self-interest. However, in order to be charismatic, leaders must make these qualities appear extraordinary. They must transform their concern for followers' needs into a total dedication and commitment to the common cause they share with followers and express it in a selfless manner.

They must engage in exemplary acts that are perceived by followers as involving great personal risk, cost and energy. In this case, personal risk might include the possible loss of personal finances, the possibility of being fired or demoted and the loss of formal or informal status, power, authority and credibility. Examples of such behaviours entailing risk would be Lee Iacocca's reduction of his salary to one dollar in his first year at Chrysler or John DeLorean's confrontations with General Motors' (GM) senior management. The higher the manifest personal cost or sacrifice for the common goal, the greater is the trustworthiness of a leader. The more leaders are able to demonstrate that they are indefatigable workers, prepared to take on these high personal risks or incur high personal costs for achieving their shared vision, the more they would reflect charisma in the sense of being worthy of complete trust.

Finally, charismatic leaders must appear knowledgeable experts in their area of influence. Some degree of demonstrated expertise, as reflected in past successes, may be a necessary condition for the attribution of charisma; for example, Iacocca's phenomenal success with Ford Mustang. Furthermore, the attribution of charisma is generally influenced by the expertise of leaders in two areas. First, *charismatic leaders use their expertise in demonstrating the inadequacy of the traditional technology, rules and regulations of the status quo as a means of achieving the shared vision.*

Second, charismatic leaders show an expertise in devising effective but unconventional strategies and plans of action. Leaders then are perceived as charismatic when they demonstrate expertise in transcending the existing order through the use of unconventional or countercultural means. Iacocca's use of government-backed loans, money-back guarantees on cars, union representation on the board and advertisements featuring him are examples of unconventional strategic actions in the automobile industry.

CASE 5.3

How do they Differ in Charismatic Leadership?

Have you ever thought about whether male or female leaders are perceived to be more charismatic? How about leaders in public/government organizations vs. in private/multinational ones? Or political leaders vs. organizational leaders? Leaders of large vs. small organizations?

Let's find out!

The following is the Conger–Kanungo Scale of Charismatic Leadership (Conger et al., 1997).

Using this scale, ask as many respondents (e.g., students or employees of different various organizations) as you can their perception of charismatic leadership behaviours. We recommend that you ask at least 10 respondents.

Choose a pair of leadership for comparison (e.g., men vs. women leaders; leaders in public vs. private organizations; political vs. organizational leaders). Make sure that half of your respondents answer the survey thinking of one member of this pair (e.g., women), while the other half answers the survey thinking of the other member of this pair (e.g., men). Alternatively, you may ask the *same respondents* to answer the survey twice for each of the pairs.

The task of your respondents is to indicate the extent to which they perceive the specified leadership as charismatic. So, you will need to give your respondents the following instruction:

The following are various leadership behaviours. Based on your personal observations, please indicate if you think that _____ (*write one of the members of the pair in this blank, e.g. male*) leaders in general exhibit these behaviours.

(Continued)

(Continued)

We realize that there are large individual differences among leaders within this group, but we hope that you can make a gross generalization and respond to the survey thinking of the typical members of this group.

For each behaviour, please tick either 'yes', 'maybe' or 'not at all'.

	Yes	Maybe	Not at all
1. Provides inspiring strategic and organizational goals.			
2. Entrepreneurial; seizes new opportunities in order to achieve goals.			
3. Readily recognizes constraints in the physical environment (technological limitations, lack of resources, etc.) that may stand in the way of achieving organizational objectives.			
4. Readily recognizes constraints in the organization's social and cultural environment (cultural norms, lack of grass roots support, etc.) that may stand in the way of achieving organizational objectives.			
5. Often exhibits very unique behaviour that surprises other members of the organization.			
6. Exciting public speaker.			
7. Recognizes the abilities and skills of other members of the organization.			
8. Has vision; often brings up ideas about possibilities for the future.			
9. Recognizes the limitations of other members of the organization.			
10. Influences others by developing mutual liking and respect.			
11. Consistently generates new ideas for the future of the organization.			
12. Shows sensitivity for the needs and feelings of the other members in the organization.			
13. Often expresses personal concern for the needs and feelings of other members in the organization.			
14. Takes high personal risks for the sake of the organization.			
15. Inspirational; able to motivate by articulating effectively the importance of what organizational members are doing.			
16. Often incurs high personal cost for the good of the organization.			

	Yes	Maybe	Not at all

17. In pursuing organizational objectives, engages in activities involving considerable personal risk.

18. Readily recognizes new environmental opportunities (favourable physical and social conditions) that may facilitate achievement of organizational objectives.

19. Engages in unconventional behaviour in order to achieve organizational goals.

20. Use nontraditional means to achieve organizational goals.

The scale measures charismatic leadership behaviours on the following five dimensions:

Strategic vision and articulation (SVA): items 1, 2, 6, 8, 11, 15, 18

Sensitivity to the environment (SE): items 3, 4, 7, 9

Sensitivity to members' needs (SMN): items 10, 12, 13

Personal risk (PR): items 14, 16, 17

Unconventional behaviour (UB): items 5, 19, 20

To calculate the scores please give 2 points to 'yes', 1 point to 'maybe' and 0 points to 'not at all'.

You can now compute the average score of your respondents for these five dimensions generated for both members of the pair. To summarize your results, create a table similar to the following.

Average score of respondents	One member of the comparison group (e.g., male leaders)	Other member of the comparison group (e.g., female leaders)
SVA		
SE		
SMN		
PR		
UB		

(Continued)

(Continued)

- How do you observe the similarities and differences between the pairs of your comparison? Which dimensions are most similar, which ones are most different? Please speculate why.
- Feel free to repeat this exercise by comparing charismatic behaviours of those leaders who are perceived to be 'extremely successful' vs. 'unsuccessful'. For this exercise use the following instructions:

  Think of one of the most successful leaders in your organizations whose behaviours you have been able to observe. Please describe their behaviours using the following scale. Are these the typical behaviours of that leader? Answer 'yes', 'maybe', or 'not at all'. Now, think of one of the least successful leaders in your organizations and answer the same survey once again thinking of their behaviours.

Cross-cultural Approaches to Leadership

- Arabs worship their leaders – *as long as they are in power!* (House et al., 1997, p. 535)
- The Dutch place emphasis on egalitarianism and are sceptical about the value of leadership. Terms like leader and manager carry a stigma. If a father is employed as a manager, Dutch children will not admit it to their schoolmates. (House et al., 1997, p. 535)
- The Malaysian leader is expected to behave in a manner that is humble, modest and dignified. (House et al., 1997, p. 535)
- The Americans appreciate two kinds of leaders. They seek empowerment from leaders who grant autonomy and delegate authority to subordinates. They also respect the bold, forceful, confident and risk-taking leader as personified by John Wayne. (House et al., 1997, p. 536)
- For Europeans …. everything seems to indicate that leadership is an unintended and undesirable consequence of democracy. (Graumann and Moscovici, 1986, p. 241–2)
- Indians prefer leaders who are nurturant, caring, dependable, sacrificing and yet demanding, authoritative and strict disciplinarian. (Sinha, 1995, p. 99)

Source: Aycan (2008, pp. 219–20).

Leadership is in the eye of the beholder. That is why cultural values, norms and expectations play a key role in the perception of effective leadership. Is there a 'one best way' of managing and leading people that can be used across the globe? It seems not. However, organizations in countries with diverse cultural values and socio-economic development levels often import leadership development programmes based on US leadership theories. A group of Latin American mid-level managers participated in a leadership development training programme by a consulting firm. One of the participants wrote the following feedback about the programme:

> We learned some nice things in this program like participation, empowerment, open communication and all. Suppose that participants in this training are successful in implementing what we learn here and changed our style to be more participative and empowering. How would our subordinates AND our managers (who have not received this training) perceive us – as 'modern' managers or 'incompetent' ones? I wish our trainers had also told us how to get 'there' (the North American way of leading) from 'here' (the South American way of leading) and whether or not 'there' is a good place for us to be in.

This quote illustrates the importance of taking the cultural context into account in leadership development programmes. It also highlights the importance of the match between leader's behaviours and follower values and expectations. One of the authors of this book has recently developed a model of cross-cultural leadership that captured the dynamic interaction between the leader and follower. Dynamic Model of Leader–Follower Interaction (Aycan, 2008) integrates cultural values, assumptions and expectations at every phase of leader–follower interaction (Figure 5.3).

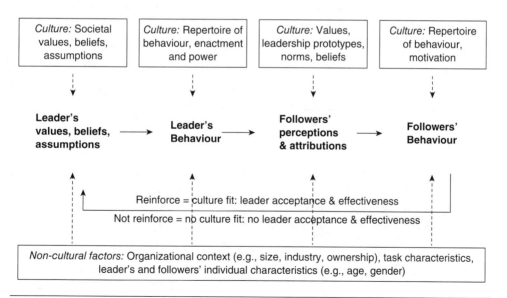

Figure 5.3 *Dynamic Model of Leader-Follower Interaction (Aycan, 2008, p. 224)*

The model postulates that leaders behave in accordance to their culturally based values, beliefs and assumptions. Followers react to leader's behaviours also in accordance to their culturally based values, beliefs and expectations from 'ideal leadership'. It should be noted that culture is not the only factor influencing leader–follower interaction. Leaders' and followers' values, beliefs, assumptions, expectations and behaviours would also be influenced by the non-cultural factors, including organizational context (e.g., size, industry), task characteristics (e.g., time urgency, complexity, novelty) and individual demographics (e.g., age, gender, personality). Consider the cases in Thinking across cultures 5.1 to demonstrate the cross-cultural interaction between the leader and followers.

Thinking across cultures 5.1

'Let's Keep Silent, let's Play Safe!'

Jyoto: What do you make out of the memo from Mr Abel; the one asking for our feedback for the candidates of the VP position?

Waira: Nothing really; it is weird. Why would the President ask employees' opinions about who should be the next VP? Doesn't he know what is best for the organization?

Jyoto: I don't know! Perhaps in his mind, he thinks that we would be pleased to give him feedback; look what he wrote in the memo: 'I am sure you would like to have your voices heard in this important decision concerning the future of our organization.'

Waira: I think he doesn't have the guts to make a decision. Or even worse, I think as a new expatriate manager he simply doesn't know what to do!

Jyoto: Hey, you know what I think: I think he is testing us! He has a favourite candidate in mind and those of us who would not support his candidate will be in his black books!!

Waira: Really? Wow, you may be right.

Jyoto: I tell you what – why take the risk? Let's keep silent and let's play safe ... Just write him that we have been busy with meeting several tight deadlines and did not have the time to attend the meeting with candidates! Sorry, no feedback from us...

• What do you think are the cultural backgrounds of Mr Abel and his subordinates Jyoto and Waira?

- According to the Dynamic Model of Leader–Follower Interaction, would you say there is a 'culture fit' between the leader and followers? Please explain why or why not.
- What would be the alternative way for Mr Abel to approach the situation? What would be the impact of this approach on followers?

In recent years there have been important advancements in the cross-cultural leadership literature. One of the most important developments is the **Project GLOBE** (Global Leadership and Organizational Behaviour Effectiveness), which is initiated by Robert House and his 128 colleagues from 62 cultural groups. In the following sections, we will present the key findings of the Project GLOBE and other studies to examine the impact of cultural context on leadership roles and behaviours.

Cultural Context and Decision-making Role of Leadership

The GLOBE Project has demonstrated that there are wide cross-cultural differences in the degree to which participative leadership was endorsed as an effective style. The cultural groups that highly endorse participative leadership are Germanic Europe, Nordic Europe and Anglo clusters. This is followed by Latin American, Latin European and Sub-Saharan African cultural groups. Those at the bottom of the list were Eastern European, Southern Asian, Confucian Asian and the Middle East, in that order (House et al., 2004, p. 683).

The data in this project also allow us to examine the cultural dimensions associated with the endorsement of participative leadership. Participative leadership was negatively associated with power distance, but positively associated with performance orientation and gender egalitarianism. In cultural contexts where there is power hierarchy, participative leadership is not strongly endorsed. On the other hand, in cultural contexts where high value is placed on performance and gender egalitarianism, participative leadership is perceived to be very effective (House et al., 2004).

Other studies demonstrated that the impact of participative leadership on performance and employee attitudes would vary across cultural contexts. Dorfman and Howell (1988) examined the effects of various leadership roles on employee job satisfaction, organizational commitment and job performance. They found that directive leadership behaviour (low participation and high close monitoring) was more effective in large power distance and collectivistic cultures. In a later study, Dorfman and colleagues (1997) found that directive leadership had a strong positive impact on job performance in Taiwan and Mexico, but had no impact in the US, Japan and South Korea. In a study conducted in Hong Kong, directive leadership was found to enhance employee performance, morale and satisfaction in large, compared to small power-distance contexts (Fellows et al., 2003). Leader participative behaviours were found to be counterproductive in Russia, a large power-distance culture (e.g., Welsh et al., 1993). In a study including 176 work units of a large US-based multinational operating in 18 European and Asian countries (e.g., Australia, Belgium, Denmark, France, Turkey, Hong Kong, and Japan), Newman and Nollen (1996) found that participative leadership practices improved the profitability of work units in small power distance, but not in large power distance cultures.

One of the most extensive investigations of leadership behaviour and practices is the Event Management project (Smith et al., 2002). In this programme of research, middle managers from 47 nations reported the ways in which they handled problematic work events by using rules, norms and people occupying various organizational roles to provide different sources of guidance. The events were (a) when a vacancy arises that requires appointment of a new subordinate in your department, (b) when one of your subordinates does consistently good work, (c) when one of your subordinates does consistently poor work, (d) when some of the equipment or machinery in your department seems to need replacement, (e) when another department does not provide the resources or support you require, (f) when there are differing opinions within your department, (g) when you see the need to introduce new work procedures into your department, and (h) when the time comes to evaluate the success of new work procedures.

The eight sources of guidance were listed in turn and described as follows: (a) formal rules and procedures, (b) unwritten rules as to 'how things are usually done around here', (c) my subordinates, (d) specialists outside my department, (e) other people at my level, (f) my superior, (g) opinions based on my own experience and training, and (h) beliefs that are widely accepted in my country as to what is right.

The findings confirmed that large power-distance was the strongest predictor of reliance on vertical sources of guidance – that is, superiors and rules within organizations. Small power-distance, on the other hand predicted reliance on one's own experience and on subordinates to solve problems (Smith and Peterson, 2005).

Sagie and Aycan (2003) also argued that power distance is a critical cultural dimension related to how well participative decision behaviour of leaders works in organizations. In high power-distance those higher in the hierarchy are *assumed* to be more knowledgeable and experienced than the rest of the people in the organization and therefore had to be respected and trusted to make the right decision. Decision-making is perceived as the right and privilege reserved to management cadres only. In such cultural contexts, employees may have a fear of punishment if they challenge or disagree with their management's decisions when their opinions are asked (see Thinking across cultures 5.1).

> No one wants to say, 'Boss, are you sure that's the way you want to do it?' They don't want to help you make decisions; they want to agree if you have an opinion. It is harder to find leaders with risk taking attitudes in Mexico. (Stephens and Greer, 1997, p. 110).

One of the reasons why participative behaviour does not result in uniform employee reactions may be that *participation* is understood differently in different cultural contexts. For example, asking employees' opinions and arriving at a decision that is contrary to the one provided by the employees may be perceived as participative leadership by employees in large power-distance cultures, but as non-participative in small power distance ones. As Kabasakal and Bodur (1998) explained, 'employees expect management to make decisions, although they prefer that the manager asks their opinion before making decisions' (p. 14). A senior worker in a Turkish company described his boss' participative style with the following example:

> You see this pen. The boss might have decided to buy this pen, but he does not just go ahead and buy it. He first asks our opinion. Does he not know what to do? Of course he does! He knows what is best for us and for the company. He is just showing courtesy of asking our opinion even though he may behave in the opposite direction of our suggestion. This is what we consider participation. (Sagie and Aycan, 2003, p. 462)

Cultural Context and Task and Social Role of Leadership

Researchers at Ohio State University proposed a two-dimensional structure of leadership role behaviours: initiating structure (task role) and consideration (social role). This two-dimensional structure has been found to replicate across cultures; behaviours of leaders have indeed been mapped onto these dimensions (e.g., Bond and Hwang, 1986; Misumi and Peterson, 1985). Additional role behaviours emerged in countries such as China, describing fairness and resistance to temptations for personal gains. Xu (1987) called this 'moral character' as a leadership role behaviour endorsed in the Asian context.

Misumi and colleagues (Misumi and Peterson, 1985; Smith et al., 1989) suggest that it is possible for task and social roles to be manifested in different ways depending on the cultural context. Accordingly, they used different behavioural descriptions for task and social roles in Japan, Hong Kong, the UK and the US to accommodate culture-specific behaviours belonging to these role categories. For example, a culturally specific item associated with social role in Japan described the supervisor as speaking about a subordinate's personal difficulties with others in his/her absence. In contrast, the item for social role in the US described the supervisor as being consultative and participative and not dealing with the problem through written memos.

Social and task roles of leaders have differential impact on employees (e.g., Agarwal et al., 1999). For example, employee commitment in the US is enhanced when leaders exhibit both task and social role behaviours, but commitment in India is associated only with leaders' social role behaviour. Employee commitment was higher in Hong Kong compared to Australia when leaders demonstrated social role behaviour (Lok and Crawford, 2004).

Cultural Context and Charismatic Role of Leadership

In all 62 nations included in the GLOBE Project, charismatic role of the leader was found to be universally endorsed as contributing to organizational effectiveness (see Figure 5.4). Despite its universal popularity the charismatic role may be perceived differently in different cultural contexts.

Although there is not much research on how charisma is perceived across cultures, available literature suggests that, for example, in China moral character, benevolence, sensitivity to others' needs, and a naturalistic approach (e.g., belief in the natural flow of life) contribute to the perception of charismatic leadership role (Wah, 2004). In India, following one's *dharma* (duty in life) was found to be an important indicator of fulfilling the charismatic role (Mehra and Krishnan, 2005). In Turkey perception of a leader's charisma is found to be inferred from the performance of the organization, whereas in the US it found to be driven from the fit of the leader to the characteristics of the ideal leader prototype (Ensari and Murphy, 2003).

What are the effects of charismatic role behaviour on employees across cultures? Charismatic leadership was found to be strongly associated with organizational commitment in all GLOBE cultural societies (Steyrer et al., 2008). Charismatic role enhanced creativity more in Korean employees holding liberal values than those holding conservative values (Shin and Zhou, 2003). The effect of charismatic role behaviour on job satisfaction, positive organizational attitudes and intention to remain in the organization is enhanced for employees with collectivistic orientation (Walumbwa and Lawler, 2003).

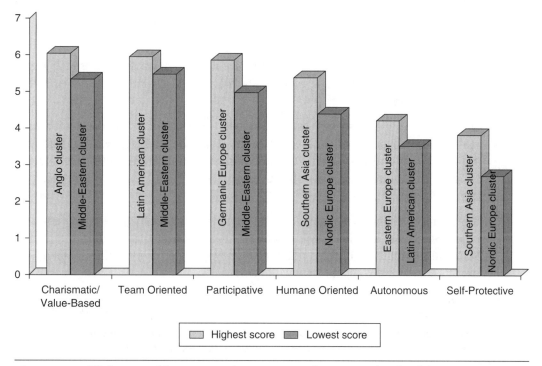

Figure 5.4 *Highest and lowest scoring country clusters on leadership prototypes included in the GLOBE Project (House et al., 2004).*

Note to the Figure. **Charismatic / value-based**: visionary, inspirational, self-sacrificial, integrity, decisive, performance-oriented; **Team-oriented**: team integrator, diplomacy, benevolent, administratively competent; **Self-protective**: self-centered, status-conscious, conflict-inducer, face saver, procedural; **Participative**: non-autocratic, participative; **Humane**: modest and humane oriented; **Autonomous**: individualistic, independent, autonomous, and unique.

Thinking across cultures 5.2

Charismatic Appeal

The following are end-of-year speeches of two imaginary CEOs. Please read them carefully and reflect on the questions at the end of the box.

Speech of Leader Y

Good morning and welcome. As in the past, the purpose of the meeting is to review and discuss the overall objectives for the coming year. Once again, the firms' principal

(Continued)

(Continued)

objective is to accomplish the sales goal while controlling operating expenses. This is the key to successfully reaching profitability goals, especially in light of the current economic environment.

Last week the operating and capital budgets were presented to the corporate staff for approval. I am pleased to report that the budgets were generally approved. If the desired goals for the company are achieved and if you show support for the organizational objectives, your efforts, of course, will be recognized and rewarded.

It is a duty of this firm's management and employees to work to achieve the desired objectives. If this is done, it will establish the position of this organization as a leader in this industry. If this is not done, it may very well threaten the company's existence in such a competitive environment.

I hope I have made clear to you the rewards associated with the accomplishment of the company's plans and the consequences of non-performance. Remember, if you deliver, you will be rewarded; and if you don't, you won't. Such an understanding is important so as to clarify your responsibilities and your rights in this organization.

Thank you very much for your time.

Speech of Leader X

As of today, our number-one priority is to help give the business in our nation a much needed shot in the arm. For some, our dream that 'anything is possible' is in question. The single most important key to the resurgence of that dream, to its vitality and the building of a positive vision of the future, is an innovative, vibrant, growing and highly productive business community.

What greater challenge is there? We have the talent; we have the skills; we have the commitment to help our nation assert its prominent position in the world economy. It will mean acting, on your own initiative, without hesitation, calling on all of your talents, skills, creativity and savvy, whenever and wherever it's required.

Too many think that our dream is impossible. Too many think it is unreal. We need not accept that view. Our problems are made by humans and thus can be solved by humans. You can be as big as you want. No problem of human destiny is beyond human beings. Our reasons and spirit have often solved the seemingly unsolvable and we believe that it can be done again.

In your hands my friends, more than mine, will rest the final success or failure of our course. Together, we are going to create something no one has ever done before. All of us, as members of this organization, will be responsible for this fundamental change.

I want people who want to win, who want to listen, who want to tell, who want to fulfill our dream. I am very much excited about what the future holds. Now let's get on with it.

Source: Adapted from Awamleh and Gardner (1999, pp. 368–9)

- Generate as many adjectives as possible to describe Leaders X and Y (e.g., honest, distant) and write them down. Pair up with one of your colleagues whose cultural or ethnic background is different from yours. Compare notes with your colleague. Observe that there are similarities as well as differences in the way you perceive these leaders – remember that leadership is indeed 'in the eyes of the beholder'.
- Which leader had more charismatic appeal to you? How about your colleague? Discuss the differences in your perception of charisma. What do you attribute these differences to?

Paternalistic (or *Parentalistic*) Leadership

Paternalism is a common and desired leadership style in collectivistic and large power-distance national cultures (e.g., Asian, Middle-Eastern, Latin American) where superior–subordinate relationship resembles the parent–child relationship: hierarchical, interdependent and emotional in nature. There is less emphasis on employees' privacy, self-reliance and proactivity. Superiors are assumed to know what is good for their subordinates and subordinates are, in return, expected to show loyalty, conformity and deference *voluntarily*.

In contrast, in individualistic and small power-distance national cultures, paternalism is considered undesirable and ineffective. In such national cultures characterized by values such as autonomy, privacy, individual accountability, self-reliance, proactivity, equality, reciprocity and emotional maturity and neutrality, paternalism may be perceived as exploitative and disempowering.

Thinking across cultures 5.3

Leader as the Surrogate Parent?

The following is the Paternalistic Leadership Questionnaire (PLQ) (Aycan, 2006; see Aycan et al., 2013 for the short version of PLQ). Please fill it out twice: 1. considering your current leader or manager (or one you have worked for in the past), 2. considering the ideal leader in your mind.

Remember; there are no right or wrong answers – your honest response is the most valuable!

Current leader: To what extent do you agree or disagree that your current leader or manager behaves in the following ways? Please write the appropriate number from the following scale under the Current leader column.

1	2	3	4	5

Strongly disagree	Disagree	Neutral	Agree	Strongly agree

Ideal leader: To what extent do you agree or disagree that an ideal leader should behave in the following ways? Please write the appropriate number from the following scale under the Ideal leader column.

1	2	3	4	5

Strongly disagree	Disagree	Neutral	Agree	Strongly agree

The scale measures paternalistic leadership behaviours on the following five dimensions:

Family atmosphere at work: items 1, 5, 9, 11, 15

Individualized relationships: items 2, 7, 10, 13

Involve in employees' non-work lives: items 4, 8, 14, 21

Loyalty expectation: items 6, 16, 17

Status hierarchy and authority: items 3, 12, 18, 19, 20

	Current Leader	Ideal Leader
1. Behaves like a family member (father/mother or elder brother/sister) towards his/her employees. (*)	_____	_____
2. Shows emotional reactions, such as joy, sorrow, anger, in his or her relationships with employees.	_____	_____
3. Believes that s/he knows what is best for his or her employees. (*)	_____	_____
4. Does not hesitate to take action in the name of his or her employees, whenever necessary.	_____	_____
5. Feels responsible for employees as if they are his or her own children. (*)	_____	_____
6. Expects loyalty and deference in exchange for his or her care and nurturance. (*)	_____	_____
7. Places importance to establishing one-to-one relationship with every employee.	_____	_____
8. Attends special events of employees (e.g. weddings and funeral ceremonies, graduations etc.). (*)	_____	_____
9. Provides advice to employees like a senior family member. (*)	_____	_____
10. Closely monitors the development and progress of his or her employees.	_____	_____
11. Creates a family environment in the workplace. (*)	_____	_____
12. Despite establishing close relationships with employees, keeps his or her distance.	_____	_____
13. Places importance to knowing every employee in person (e.g. personal problems, family life etc.).	_____	_____
14. Is prepared to act as a mediator whenever an employee has a problem in his or her private life (e.g. marital problems). (*)	_____	_____
15. Protects employees from outside criticisms.	_____	_____
16. Does not consider performance as the most important criterion while making a decision about employees (e.g. promotion, lay-off).	_____	_____
17. Places more importance to loyalty than performance in evaluating employees. (*)	_____	_____
18. Is disciplinarian and at the same time nurturant (tough & tender).	_____	_____
19. Asks opinions of employees about work-related issues; however, makes the last decision himself or herself.	_____	_____
20. Wants to control or to be informed about every work-related activity.	_____	_____
21. Is ready to help employees with their non-work problems (e.g. housing, education of the children, health etc.) whenever they need it. (*)	_____	_____

(*) Items in the PLQ-S (Short Version) (Aycan, Schyns, Sun, Felfe, & Saher, 2013).

(Continued)

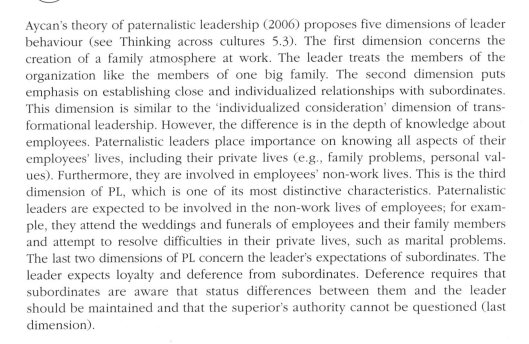

(Continued)

- On which of the dimensions of PLQ did you have the lowest and highest discrepancy between 'ideal' and 'current' leadership ratings? Please speculate on all the possible causes of the discrepancies.
- If you were to work with an expatriate manager who is not paternalistic, how do you think this would influence your commitment, satisfaction and job performance? Negatively or positively? Please explain why.

Aycan's theory of paternalistic leadership (2006) proposes five dimensions of leader behaviour (see Thinking across cultures 5.3). The first dimension concerns the creation of a family atmosphere at work. The leader treats the members of the organization like the members of one big family. The second dimension puts emphasis on establishing close and individualized relationships with subordinates. This dimension is similar to the 'individualized consideration' dimension of transformational leadership. However, the difference is in the depth of knowledge about employees. Paternalistic leaders place importance on knowing all aspects of their employees' lives, including their private lives (e.g., family problems, personal values). Furthermore, they are involved in employees' non-work lives. This is the third dimension of PL, which is one of its most distinctive characteristics. Paternalistic leaders are expected to be involved in the non-work lives of employees; for example, they attend the weddings and funerals of employees and their family members and attempt to resolve difficulties in their private lives, such as marital problems. The last two dimensions of PL concern the leader's expectations of subordinates. The leader expects loyalty and deference from subordinates. Deference requires that subordinates are aware that status differences between them and the leader should be maintained and that the superior's authority cannot be questioned (last dimension).

Cross-cultural Considerations for Managers

The importance and significance of leadership for organizational performance and survival cannot be denied. This truth is shared 'universally'. However, what constitutes an effective leader would differ substantially (see Video 5.3). Leadership development programmes should emphasize the role of culture in the leader–follower interaction. An effective global leader is someone who has high emotional and cultural intelligence (see also Chapter 9) to sense employee values, needs and expectations and adjust their leadership approach accordingly. Global leaders should question the applicability of Western theories of leadership, especially with respect to participative roles. As we discussed in this chapter, a participative decision-making role can take different forms in different cultural contexts. Also, social and task roles can be enacted in culturally appropriate ways.

We emphasize the importance of the fit between the cultural context and leaders' role behaviours. However, we should also question the assumption that the most effective leadership is always that which best fits the cultural context. It is quite possible that host country nationals expect expatriates to display a different leadership style so that they will have the opportunity to learn from them. In this regard, a distinction should be made between prevailing and effective leadership. For example, paternalistic leadership is a prevailing leadership style in large power-distance and collectivistic national cultures, but it may not be the most effective approach for employee and organizational outcomes. Prevailing leadership approaches probably increase leader acceptance, but not necessarily leader effectiveness in delivering important work outcomes, such as performance and innovation.

Expatriate managers are advised to consult the research findings to identify the values and expectations of employees in order to guide them in the right direction. One important resource to guide expatriate managers is the results of the GLOBE Project. It presents cultural values as they are perceived ('as is') and as they are espoused ('should be') by the employees of cultural societies. For example, according to GLOBE findings employees in societies with a large power-distance culture ('as is') wish to have small power-distance in organizations ('should be'). Expatriates who are aware of this expectation and adopt a participative style would be better appreciated than those who try to fit to the cultural norm and adopt an authoritarian style.

Related to this point is the question of how best to fill the gap between the actual and ideal leadership. Participative leadership may not be common in hierarchical cultures, but it may be desired by employees. In this case, a change in the organizational culture is needed to transform the leadership approach from authoritarian to participative. As we see in Chapter 8, change is easier said than done. The change process should be facilitated by the strong support and role modelling of top management as well as the HRM practices that are aligned to support the participative culture (e.g., training on participative leadership, hiring employees with strong participative leadership orientation, designing a reward system for the most participative leaders).

Most effective global managers are those who have multiple leadership approaches in their toolbox (i.e., participative, task-oriented, social-oriented, paternalistic) and who can use them (individually or in combination) at the right time and with the right employee groups. It should be remembered that among the leadership approaches discussed in this chapter, the charismatic role is always associated with positive employee and organizational outcomes. However, it may be necessary to 'flavour' the charismatic approach with the right dose of paternalism or performance orientation when the situation (task and employees) demands it.

Expatriate communities working in developing countries have increased over the years; let us end with some specific guidelines for them. The following are the characteristics of the most effective leadership approaches in a developing country context (from Aycan, 2004, p. 420):

An effective leadership approach includes being:

- Transformational and empowering.
- Participative, *but also* decisive.
- Friendly, *but not* a friend.
- Trustworthy: knowledgeable, skilfull and administratively competent.
- Nurturant/paternalistic, *but also* performance-oriented.
- Fair and just, especially in interpersonal relationships.
- Diplomatic.
- Status-conscious, *but also* modest and humble.
- Team integrator.

Chapter Summary

Leadership is a more intense and influential process than that experienced with managers. The chapter start with a brief discussion on the differences between leaders and managers. Leadership is discussed in light of four key leadership role behaviours required for positive employee and organizational outcomes. In relation to the decision-making role we discuss that the level of participation in decision-making should be contingent on several factors. Leaders should not ignore the employees' motivational state before engaging them in the decision process. All employees do not have the identical salient needs – in particular, the need to grow and accept responsibilities on the job. If the organization's mission is to develop a high-involvement organization, then the recruiting, selection and placement efforts should specifically be geared to seeking employees who desire to satisfy their growth needs on the job.

Supervisors should recognize that merely sharing power with subordinates through delegation does not guarantee that participative management will be effective. Since the effectiveness of participative management depends upon the personal self-efficacy beliefs of the subordinates, supervisors should adopt strategies to enhance these beliefs. Such strategies are: (1) the supervisor should function as coach and mentor to their subordinates; and (2) supervision practices which empower employees. In relation to the characteristics of the problem situation, the key is to develop the managers' analytical abilities, which are a critical competence, to effectively use the model proposed by Vroom and Jago. Specific training approaches in this area are: programmes designed to provide practice in case analysis, using the model, as well as feedback on the leadership style based on the individual's responses to the cases.

Regarding the task and social role behaviours, it is important to keep in mind that the appointed leader of the workgroup will be perceived as such (i.e., as a leader) to the extent that they perform both the task and social roles. This does not imply that the supervisor should 'hog' group meetings by constantly assuming all the roles. If the supervisor does this, then the reason for the group does not exist. The supervisor should create a climate in the group which allows members to participate fully as active members so that the supervisor can benefit from their expertise, talents and other resources in the group.

The supervisor's task and social roles are necessary for several reasons. First, it is the direct functional responsibility of the supervisor to ensure that the group attains its objective efficiently and effectively and the delegation of this responsibility can only be viewed as the supervisor abdicating their responsibility. Second, the reasons for the group's existence and its global objectives in relation to the work unit as well as to the other work units of the organization, can be known, in clear and specific terms, only to the supervisor. Third, the wealth of ideas and the high energy level generated in the group necessarily require someone to direct and channel these in a focused manner towards the group goals. When the needed coordination is not performed in the group, then the group runs the risk of the futile dissipation of its productive talents and energy.

The study of charismatic leadership role provides new insights into managerial behaviour. It brings into sharp focus a set of behaviours surrounding the formulation, articulation and realization of a vision – behaviours that are immediately noticed in managers to whom a profound transformation of the organization and its members is usually attributed. The influence of charismatic role behaviour on members of the organization is transformational in nature. Therefore, such leadership is viewed as transformational leadership as opposed to transactional leadership as discussed earlier in the chapter.

The chapter presents the Conger–Kanungo Model of Charismatic Leadership. According to the model in stage one, the charismatic leader displays considerable sensitivity to environmental constraints and follower needs and identifies the deficiencies in the status quo. In stage two, the charismatic leader formulates an idealized future vision and demonstrates an extensive use of articulation and impression management skills that sets them apart from other leaders. Finally, in stage three, the leader uses innovative and unconventional means for achieving the vision. According to this model, the followers attribute charisma to a leader based upon the frequency and intensity with which the leader performs the behaviours identified in each of the three stages. The model recognizes that the attribution of charisma to a leader will also depend on followers' perceptions that the leader's behaviour is congruent with their own values.

The last section of the chapter focuses on cross-cultural similarities and differences in the way leadership is understood and key leadership roles are enacted. One of the most important cross-cultural research programmes in this area is the Project GLOBE. According to this project charismatic role behaviour is 'universally' embraced as the key to outstanding organizational outcomes. The Dynamic Model of Leader–Follower Interaction proposes that leaders' assumptions and behaviours should match the followers' attributions and reactions. This match ensures leadership effectiveness and acceptance. Suppose that an Indian manager is assigned to Netherlands as an expatriate. Given their cultural background of high collectivism and high power-distance, they *assume* that employees want care and guidance in their personal and professional lives. Accordingly, they show interest in the personal lives of employees, making inquiries about the health problems in their families and so on. In other words, they show paternalistic leadership behaviour. Dutch employees *attribute* this behaviour to the leader's violation of privacy and avoid interacting with the new manager. This avoidant behaviour does not fit the initial assumption of the Indian expatriate manager and results in lack of cooperation between them and the team. The chapter concludes with specific suggestions to global managers working in a developing country context.

End of Chapter Reflection Questions

1. What do you think are the cultural conditions (national or organizational level) that promote and hamper development of effective leaders? Why do you think more (or more effective) leaders emerge in some countries or organizations rather than others?
2. How do you think behaviours and roles of leaders operating in a multicultural domestic workforce differ from a multinational workforce in different countries?
3. What do you think an ideal leadership development programme would look like? What would be the key components of the programme and how would it vary, if at all, depending on the cultural context for which leaders are developed?

Key Terms and Definitions

Leadership. The process through which an individual influences and motivates others to follow them towards achieving the (organizational) goals.

Participative decision-making. A process through which leaders encourage and solicit some level of participation of followers in the decisions concerning themselves or the organization.

Empowering leadership. Leadership that facilitates growth and development of followers by removing barriers to development and increasing follower self-efficacy.

Task role behaviour of leadership. Focus on problem identification and solutions, including resources allocation and monitoring of the behaviour of organizational members to accomplish the team and organizational goals.

Social role behaviour of leadership. Focus on people orientation, including the interpersonal relationships, which are conducive to building group cohesion and developing the quality of work life of its members.

Charismatic role behaviour of leadership. Focus on long-term objectives of the organization and formulating goals that are novel and different from the status quo.

Project GLOBE. Multicultural, multi-method project initiated by Robert House and his 128 colleagues from 62 cultural groups to investigate the effect of culture on leadership prototypes.

Paternalistic leadership. Leader–follower relationship resembles parent–child relationship in which the leader is caring, nurturant, authoritative and expecting loyalty and deference from followers.

Further Reading

Aycan, Z., Schyns, B., Sun, J., Felfe, J. and Saher, N. (2013) Convergence and divergence of paternalistic leadership: A cross-cultural investigation of prototypes. *Journal of International Business Studies*, 44 (9): 962–9.

De Pree, M. (2004) *Leadership is an Art*. New York: Currency Doubleday.

Harvard Business Review (2008) *Best of HBR (Harvard Business Review) on Emotionally Intelligent Leadership*, 2nd edn. (2008) http://www.proadvisorcoach.com/articles/3e-EmotionallyIntelligentLeadership.pdf.

Judge, T.A. and Piccolo, R.F. (2004) 'Transformational and transactional leadership: A meta analytic test of their relative validity'. *Journal of Applied Psychology*, 89 (5): 755–68.

Rhode, D.L. (ed.) (2004) *The Difference 'Difference' Makes: Women in Leadership*. London: Stanford University Press.

Shapiro, J.P. and Stefkovich, J.A. (2010) *Ethical Leadership and Decision Making in Education: Applying Theoretical Perspectives to Complex Dilemmas*. New York: Taylor and Francis.

Cases, Videos, Web Sources

Cases

The following cases focus on decision-making challenges of leaders in times of crises occurring at the cross roads of cultures.

Austen-Smith, D., Diermeier, D. and Zemel, E. (2011) *Unintended Acceleration: Toyota's Recall Crisis*. Kellogg School of Management Case, No: KEL598.

Ellington-Booth, B. and Cates, K.L. (2012) *Growing Managers: Moving from Team Member to Team Leader.* Kellogg School of Management Case, No: KEL629.

Isenberg, D.J. and Spence, S.M. (2009) *Leadership at Wild China (A).* Harvard Business School Case No: 807046-PDF-ENG.

Videos

Video 5.1 Sheryl Sandberg: *Why we Have too Few Women Leaders* (2010) www.ted.com/talks/sheryl_sandberg_why_we_have_too_few_women_leaders.html – As the Chief Operations Officer of Facebook, Sandberg gives a controversial insight into why there are few women leaders in the world.

Video 5.2 CNN: *Leading Women Series.* http://edition.cnn.com/SPECIALS/leading-women. This excellent series reveal the secrets of leadership from leading women around the world.

Video 5.3 Steve Ballmer, CEO Microsoft (2006) www.youtube.com/watch?v=wvsboPUjrGc – if the key to leadership is 'influence', this CEO seems to have it all. Do you think his style would be effective in different cultural contexts?

Web sources

www.ila-net.org/ – International Leadership Association.
www.emerging-leadership.com/aboutus.aspx – Emerging Leadership Association.
www.alp-leaders.net/ – Association of Leadership Programs.
www.gleam.org/ – Columbia Business School leadership tools.

References

Agarwal, S., Decarlo, T.E. and Vyas, S.B. (1999) 'Leadership behaviour and organizational commitment: A comparative study of American and Indian salespersons', *Journal of International Business Studies*, 30 (4): 727–43.

Awamleh, R. and Gardner, W.L. (1999) 'Perceptions of leader charisma and effectiveness: The effects of vision content, delivery and organizational performance', *Leadership Quarterly*, 10: 345–73.

Aycan, Z. (2004) 'Managing inequalities: Leadership and teamwork in developing country context', in H. Lane, M. Mendenhall and M. Maznevski, M. (eds), *International Handbook of Management*, pp. 406–23. New York: Blackwell.

Aycan, Z. (2006) 'Paternalism: Towards conceptual refinement and operationalization', in K.S. Yang, K.K. Hwang and U. Kim (eds), *Indigenous and Cultural Psychology: Understanding People in Context*, pp. 445–66. New York: Springer Publishing.

Aycan, Z. (2008) 'Leadership in cultural context', in P. Smith, M. Peterson and D. Thomas (eds), *Handbook of Cross-cultural Management Research*, pp. 219–39. London: Sage.

Aycan, Z., Shyncs, B., Sun, J., Felfe, J., and Saher, N. (2013) 'Convergence and divergence of paternalistic leadership: A cross-cultural investigation of prototypes', *International Journal of Business Studies*, 44: 962–969.

Bales, R.F. (1970) *Personality and Interpersonal Behavior.* New York: Holt, Rinehart and Winston.

Bandura, A. (1986) *Social Foundations of Thought and Action: A Social Cognitive Theory.* Englewood Cliffs, NJ: Prentice- Hall.

Bass, B.M. (1985) *Leadership and Performance Beyond Expectations.* New York: Free Press.

Bond, M.H. and Hwang, K.K. (1986) 'The social psychology of Chinese people', in M.H. Bond (ed.), *The Psychology of Chinese People*, pp. 213–66. New York: Oxford University Press.

Bryman, A. (1992) *Charisma and Leadership in Organizations*. London: Sage.

Burke, W. (1986) 'Leadership as empowering others', in S. Srivastra (ed.), *Executive Power*, pp. 51–77. San Francisco, CA: Jossey-Bass.

Conger, J.A. and Kanungo, R.N. (1998) *Charismatic Leadership in Organizations*. Thousand Oaks, CA: Sage.

Conger, J.A., Kanungo, R.N., Menon, S. and Mathur, P. (1997) 'Measuring charisma: Dimensionality and validity of the Conger-Kanungo scale of charismatic leadership', *Canadian Journal of Administrative Sciences*, 14 (3): 290–302.

Cowley, W.H. (1928) 'Three distinctions in the study of leaders', *Journal of Abnormal and Social Psychology*, 23 (2): 144–57.

Deci, E.L. (1975) *Intrinsic Motivation*. New York: Plenum.

Dorfman, P.W. and Howell, J.P. (1988) 'Dimensions of national culture and effective leadership patterns: Hofstede revisited', in E.G. McGoun (ed.), *Advances in International Comparative Management*, 3, pp. 127–49. Greenwich, CT: JAI Press.

Dorfman, P.W., Howell, J.P., Hibino, S., Lee, J.K., Tate, U. and Bautista, A. (1997) 'Leadership in Western and Asian countries: Commonalities and differences in effective leadership processes across cultures', *Leadership Quarterly*, 8 (3): 233–74.

Ensari, N. and Murphy, S.E. (2003) 'Cross-cultural variations in leadership perceptions and attribution of charisma to the leader', *Organizational Behavior and Human Decision Processes*, 92: 52–66.

Fellows, R., Liu, A. and Miu Fong, C. (2003) 'Leadership style and power relations in quantity surveying in Hong Kong', *Construction Management and Economics*, 21: 809–18.

Graumann, C.F. and Moscovici, S. (1986) *Changing Conceptions of Crowd Mind and Behavior*. New York: Springer.

House, R.J. (1988) 'Leadership research: Some forgotten, ignored, or overlooked findings', in J.G. Hunt, B.R. Baliga, H.P. Dachler and C.A. Schriesheim (eds), *Emerging Leadership Vistas*, pp. 245–60. Lexington, MA: Lexington.

House, R.J., Wright, N.S. and Aditya, R.N. (1997) 'Cross-cultural research on organizational leadership: A critical analysis and a proposed theory', in P.C. Earley and M. Erez (eds), *New Perspectives on International Industrial/Organizational Psychology*, pp. 535–625. San Francisco, CA: Jossey-Bass.

House, R.J., Javidan, M. and Dorfman, P. (2001) 'Project GLOBE: An introduction', *Applied Psychology: An International Review*, 50 (4): 489–505.

House, R.J., Hanges, P.J., Javidan, M., Dorfman, P.W. and Gupta, V. (2004) *Leadership, Culture and Organizations: The GLOBE Study of 62 Societies*. Thousand Oaks, CA: Sage Publications.

Kabasakal, H. and Bodur, M. (1998) *Leadership, Values and Institutions: The Case of Turkey*. Research Papers. Bogazici University, Istanbul, Turkey.

Kanter, R.M. (1979) 'Power failure in management circuits', *Harvard Business Review*, 57 (4): 65–75.

Kanter, R.M. (1983) *The Change Masters: Innovation for Productivity in the American Corporation*. New York: Simon and Schuster.

Lawler, E.E. (1986) *High Involvement Management: Participative Strategies for Improving Organizational Performance*. San Francisco, CA: Jossey-Bass.

Lok, P. and Crawford, J. (2004) 'The effects of organizational culture and leadership style on job satisfaction and organizational commitment', *Journal of Management Development*, 23 (4): 321–38.

Mehra, P. and Krishnan, V.R. (2005) 'Impact of Svadharma-orientation on transformational leadership and followers' trust in leader', *Journal of Indian Psychology*, 23 (1): 1–11.

Misumi, J. and Peterson, M.F. (1985) 'The performance-maintenance (PM) theory of leadership: Review of a Japanese research program', *Administrative Science Quarterly*, 30 (2): 198–223.

Newman, K. and Nollen, S. (1996) 'Culture and congruence: The fit between management practices and national culture', *Journal of International Business Studies*, 27 (4): 753–79.

Sagie, R. and Aycan, Z. (2003) 'A cross-cultural analysis of participative decision making in organizations', *Human Relations*, 56 (4): 453–73.

Shin, S.J. and Zhou, J. (2003) 'Transformational leadership, conservation and creativity: Evidence from Korea', *Academy of Management Journal*, 46 (6): 703–14.

Sinha, J.B.P. (1995) *The Cultural Context of Leadership and Power*. New Delhi: Sage Publications.

Smith, P. and Peterson, M.F. (2005) 'Demographic effects on the use of vertical sources of guidance by managers in widely differing cultural contexts', *International Journal of Cross Cultural Management*, 5 (1): 5–26.

Smith, P.B., Misumi, J., Tayeb, M., Peterson, M. and Bond, M. (1989) 'On the generality of leadership measures across cultures', *Journal of Occupational Psychology*, 62: 97–109.

Smith, P.B., Peterson, M.F. and Schwartz, S.H. (2002) 'Cultural values, sources of guidance and their relevance to managerial behavior', *Journal of Cross-cultural Psychology*, 33 (2): 188–208.

Stephens, G.K. and Greer, C.R. (1997) 'Doing business in Mexico: Understanding cultural differences', in H.W. Lane, J.J. DiStefano and M.L. Maznevski (eds), *International Management Behavior*, pp. 107–24. Cambridge, MA: Blackwell.

Steyrer, H., Schiffinger, M. and Lang, R. (2008) 'Organizational commitment – A missing link between leadership behavior and organizational performance?', *Scandinavian Journal of Management*, (24): 364–74.

Vroom, V.H. and Jago, A.G. (1988) *The New Leadership: Managing Participation in Organizations*. Englewood Cliffs, NJ: Prentice Hall.

Wah, S.S. (2004) 'Entrepreneurial leaders in family business organizations', *Journal of Enterprising Culture*, 12 (1): 1–34.

Walumbwa, F.O. and Lawler, J.J. (2003) 'Building effective organizations: Transformational leadership, collectivist orientation, work-related attitudes and withdrawal behaviors in three emerging economies', *International Journal of Human Resource Management*, 14: 1083–101.

Welsh, D.H.B., Luthans, F. and Sommer, S.M. (1993) 'Managing Russian factory workers: The impact of U.S.-based behavioral and participative techniques', *Academy of Management Journal*, 36 (1): 58–79.

Xu, L. (1987) 'A cross-cultural study of leadership behavior of Chinese and Japanese executives', *Asia Pacific Journal of Management*, 4 (3): 203–09.

Yukl, G. (1989) 'Managerial leadership: A review of theory and research', *Journal of Management*, 15 (2): 251–90.

Want to learn more? Visit the companion website at www.sagepub.co.uk/kanungo to gain access to videos from the end of each chapter, weblinks and flash cards of key terms.

6

Teamwork Effectiveness and Cross-cultural Perspectives

Chapter Outline

The most powerful team leading the world (2008–2012):

- President of the United States of America: Barack Obama. Born in Hawaii. His father is from Kenya.
- Secretary of Foreign Affairs: Hillary Clinton. Her origin is Irish.
- Secretary of Transportation: Ray LaHood. His origin is Arab. He is a Jordanian migrated from Lebanon.
- Secretary of Finance: Timothy Geithner. He spent his childhood in Zimbabwe, India and Thailand; went to high school in Bangkok and speaks Chinese and Japanese.
- Secretary of Justice: Eric Holder. He is black and origins are from Barbados.
- Secretary of Education: Arne Duncan. His mother established an institution to win African Americans to the society. His wife is from Australia. They met in Tasmania.
- Secretary of Energy: Steven Chu. His origins are Chinese. He won the Nobel Prize in Physics in 1997.
- Secretary of Labor: Hilda Solis. Her mother is from Nicaragua. Her father is from Mexico.

- Secretary of Homeland Security: Janet Napolitano. Originally Italian.
- Director of the Office of Management and Budget: Peter Orszag. He is originally Hungarian.
- Secretary of Veterans Affairs: Eric Shinseki. He was born in Kauai in the then Territory of Hawaii to a family of Japanese origin.
- Trade Representative: Ron Kirk. He is an African American.
- White House Chief of Staff: Rahm Israel Emanuel. As his name indicates he is originally from Israel.

Source: Ozdil (2009)

Working in teams is increasingly becoming the fact of organizational life. Like individual employees, work groups have to be managed to ensure their efficiency and effectiveness. The focus of this chapter is to understand several factors that contribute to the effective management of teams, with a special emphasis on multicultural teams.

We examine the nature and characteristic elements of work groups and the conditions of effectiveness – more specifically, group design and communication networks. We then explore the cross-cultural differences in teamwork processes and conditions under which multicultural teams work effectively. We conclude with the managerial implications outlining strategies to ensure efficient and effective work groups.

Learning Objectives

- To understand the nature of work groups and teams and the conditions required for their effectiveness.

- To distinguish between several communication networks in groups and teams; to develop an understanding of their characteristics and appropriateness for specific situations.

- To appreciate the importance of feedback as a communication skill necessary for effective team functioning.

- To become aware of the impact of cultural differences on attitudes towards teamwork.

- To understand advantages and disadvantages of multicultural teams.

- To review specific guidelines for effective management of multicultural and virtual teams.

The Nature of Groups and Teams

In general, a **group** can be defined as an entity composed of two or more persons who come together and communicate or interact with each other on matters of common interest. A **team** is usually smaller than a group, works on more specific tasks than groups and works together for a shorter period of time than groups. The critical elements of a group are members, purpose and interaction among members related to that purpose. The membership element can be examined in terms of numbers as well as the characteristics of members. A group with too large a membership might prove to be unwieldy, whereas one with a few members may be inadequate to accomplish the group task. Furthermore, the group members should be heterogeneous with regard to the knowledge, expertise and skills so that they can complement each other's efforts to complete the task and homogeneous with respect to their commitment to achieve the group's objective. A group without a purpose or an objective would be akin to an individual who is going nowhere. Finally, the interaction among members allows the group to work towards its stated task.

Work groups can be either formal or informal in terms of additional features such as lifespan, accountability, or degree of autonomy. The compensation section of the human resources department in an organization is a formal work group. It is part of the company's organization structure with objectives consistent with the organization's goals. Hence it tends to be more permanent in the sense that its lifespan is not determined by the membership of specific individuals. It is accountable to a specific person as indicated in the organization structure, and enjoys a degree of autonomy that is necessary to achieve the established objectives. In 'high-involvement' organizations, formal work groups might constitute 'self-regulating' or 'autonomous' work teams. Their unique characteristic lies in the fact that the members, as a collectivity, 'have the authority to manage their own task and interpersonal processes as they carry out their work' (Hackman and Oldham, 1980, p. 165). Formal work groups can also take the form of 'ad hoc' or 'taskforce' teams that are set up for a specific purpose. The lifespan of these teams is limited to the completion of the specific task for which it was set up; and the membership of such teams can be drawn from the different sections of a larger work group. For example, three sections in the human resources department – compensation, employee relations and recruitment and selection – might each depute a few of its members to study the issue of pay equity and report to the human resources department. The membership of ad hoc or taskforce committees or teams can also be drawn from different departments of the organization.

Informal work groups are made up of employees from the different departments who voluntarily come together because they believe that an informal setting might be more conducive to address procedural obstacles or minor problems of coordination that they experience in their work. They do not have an official status, but often such informal groups can become the nucleus for an ad hoc taskforce when such status becomes necessary in order to obtain the necessary mandate and resources to identify and develop solutions to problems affecting more than one functional area.

Teamwork effectiveness: team structure and communication

There are several conditions which are necessary for the efficiency and effectiveness of work groups and teams. Our discussion will focus on those which result from group structure (i.e., group design) and communication networks.

Hackman and Oldham (1980) identified three major criteria of group effectiveness which flow from group design: task-relevant effort by members; task-relevant knowledge, expertise and skills of members; and task-appropriate performance strategies.

Task-relevant effort by members

Think about your past teamwork experiences. What kept you (or other members) from giving all you can to the project at hand? The group objectives cannot be achieved if members do not put in the required effort to perform the behaviours that will lead to attaining the group's objectives. Although group members may have the necessary knowledge, skills and abilities their motivation to put in the required effort to perform may be adversely affected if their performance-to-outcomes expectancy is low and if they do not value the outcomes.

Let us examine some reasons why the group members' performance-to-outcomes expectancy and valence of outcomes might be low (Kerr, 1983). First, some group members might perceive that the group task is not considered to be particularly important or significant in relation to the organization's mission and objectives and, therefore, not experience meaningfulness of their effort and contributions. Such perceptions will lower their probability that performance will lead to the expected outcome of 'pride in work'. Remember from the motivation chapter that according to the job characteristics theory, when employees do not find their work to be very meaningful, their internal work motivation will be low. Second, some group members may not believe that they will receive the expected rewards. This perception that rewards are not contingent on performance also contributes to a low performance-to-outcomes expectancy. It may even affect the valence of outcomes should employees interpret the non-contingent rewards as being unfairly determined.

Third, group members might perceive that their efforts to perform lead to more outcomes with a negative rather than a positive valence. This relates to the group member's evaluation of the physical and psychological costs of contributing to enhance the group's performance. Examples of physical costs are long hours, and stress resulting from interpersonal relations. The major psychological cost is experiencing a type of inequity referred to as the '**sucker effect**' (Orbell and Dawes, 1981), when one feels that they are contributing to the collective good and when others do not. This has been found to be the case when some members do not feel compelled to put in the required effort because they believe that the group objectives can be attained by the efforts of the other members of the group. This is referred to as the '**free-rider effect**' (Kerr and Brunn, 1983). The members who put in the effort feel that the free riders are taking advantage of them and hence their feelings of inequity. Furthermore, being in a group or a team may result in the diffusion of responsibility. For some members, being in a group is a way to showcase their talents, while for others it is a way to reduce individual effort compared to working alone. The tendency to put less effort into a group environment than in an environment where they work alone is called the '**social loafing effect**' (Karau and Williams, 1993).

Task-relevant knowledge, expertise and skills of group members

The required level of task-relevant effort of group members will enable the group to achieve its objective only to the extent that this effort is accompanied and supported by knowledge, expertise and skills that are relevant to the task. Related to this condition are considerations such as the size of the group and the distribution of the knowledge, expertise and skills among the members. The size of the group should neither be large or small. As mentioned earlier, too many members make the group unwieldy – for example, effective communication and coordination becomes extremely difficult, if not impossible. Too few members could result in the group not having the required breadth or depth of knowledge and skills; besides, the small size might be inadequate to perform the numerous activities within the specified time limits.

The distribution of knowledge, expertise and skills among the members should be such that members complement each other and, at the same time, are able to fill in for another member should that be necessary. Furthermore, members should be perceived by their peers as having the ability to carry a fair share of the group load. When inequality is perceived to exist in this area, dysfunctional effects can follow leading to loss in productivity. On this point, recall our earlier discussion on the free-rider effect and the sucker effect.

In addition to the technical skills needed for task accomplishment, it is critical that group members possess interpersonal skills which help build group cohesion or help the group to work together. In other words, the ability of members to perform both the task role and social role behaviours will greatly facilitate the effective utilization of their expertise and skills in accomplishing the task.

Task-appropriate performance strategies

When a task is to be accomplished, decisions have to be made and activities performed on several aspects such as planning (e.g., setting objectives, developing policies and procedures); organizing (e.g., setting up a structure to achieve the objectives – that is, who does what activity, defining relationships within it, establishing coordination mechanisms); and directing and controlling (e.g., motivating, setting up a reporting system, providing for feedback).

Now there are several ways or approaches that group members can adopt in relation to the decisions and activities necessary to accomplish the task. These ways or approaches are referred to as performance strategies. For example, faced with a particular problem, the group might opt to have it resolved by the group as a whole, or depute a few of its members with specialized expertise to solve it or to bring a set of solutions for the group to decide. The appropriateness of the strategy that is adopted will be determined by criteria such as how well it contributes to the efficient and effective accomplishment of the task; how well it taps the group's knowledge, expertise and skill; or how well it contributes to building group cohesion or enabling members to work together as a group.

Communication Networks

The objective of a work group is to accomplish a given task with the full utilization of the intellectual, technical and social skills of its members. This implies that members do not work in isolation but in close interaction with each other as they contribute to decision-making and other group activities. Interpersonal communication is, therefore, an extremely important condition for group effectiveness. It basically supports the group effort in two ways. First, it allows for an exchange of ideas, views, proposals and related information in order that the resulting outcomes fully reflect the synergistic potential or capability of the group. Second, it provides the group with the mechanism and opportunity to develop and improve relationships among members; improved relationships greatly facilitate the task activities.

Communication networks, patterns of information exchange among members (Forsyth, 1990), have the potential to facilitate as well as to inhibit communication, depending upon whether it is appropriate for the nature of the group's task. The discussion that follows reviews the types of basic communication networks which work groups can use. The description of the network will also include the effects of communication networks as these relate to the degree of centralization in the flow of information; leader emergence potential; member satisfaction; and problem-solving efficiency.

Types of networks

The five basic communication networks are: the Star or the Wheel, the Y, the Chain, the Circle and the Comcon (Bavelas, 1950) ('Comcon' is the combination of two

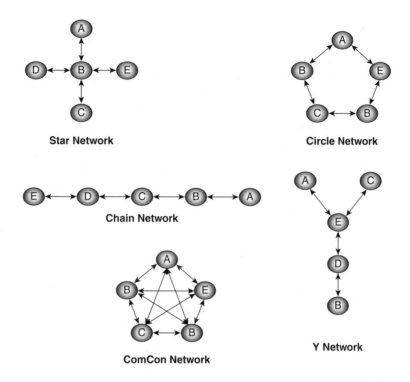

Figure 6.1 *Five communication networks (Bavelas, 1950)*

words: '*completely con*nected'). The five communication networks are illustrated in Figure 6.1 – the arrows in the illustration indicate the permitted direction of the flow of communication, or the access to communication channels.

Degree of centralization

The most important or central characteristic of networks is the degree of centralization. Centralized networks are those in which one position has the greatest number of linkages or access to communication channels. This position becomes the focal or central point in the network to and through which all information flows. Such key access allows this position to be more than a clearing house of information. It can process information – that is, perform the necessary analysis and synthesis – as no other position can; and then disseminate it to others. Decentralized networks, on the other hand, do not have any one position which is focal or central. On the contrary, any position can communicate with any other position. In terms of communication channels, each position in decentralized networks is linked or has access to an approximately equal number of channels.

On the continuum of centralization-decentralization, the Star network is an example of a communication network at one end of the continuum, with the greatest degree of centralization. In Figure 6.1, we see that 'B' is the hub position with access to the largest number of communication channels. The Y network has the next-highest degree of centralization, with 'E' being the hub position, but without the degree of centrality possessed by 'B' in the Star network. The Chain network falls into a more moderate category on the continuum. At the other extreme of the continuum, the Comcon network has the highest degree of decentralization. The Circle network is also decentralized but not to the same degree as the Comcon network. If we have to categorize the five networks in terms of centralization/decentralization, then the centralized communication networks are the Star, the Y and the Chain; the decentralized communication networks are the Comcon and the Circle.

Leader emergence potential

Information is the key to the success of the group's effort to achieve its objectives. A group member who has greater access to information and is in a position to control its flow in the group will, therefore, have a greater chance of being perceived as the leader of the group. Other things being equal, the person who occupies the hub or the central position in the communication network will have a greater probability of emerging as the leader in the group. Since the centralized communication networks have such central positions and the decentralized communication networks do not, the probability of leader emergence is higher in the centralized than in the decentralized networks. Among the centralized communication networks, the probability of leader emergence is the highest in the Star network and relatively high in the Y network.

Member satisfaction

In work groups with centralized communication networks, members can be viewed in terms of those who occupy the central or focal position and those who occupy the peripheral or outlying positions. Because the central or hub positions have greater access to and control of communication channels and, therefore, greater control of the information flow, the satisfaction of the person in the hub position is very high and the satisfaction of the members in the peripheral positions is low. Therefore, in centralized networks, the range in individual member satisfaction – that is, the difference between the member with the highest and the member with the lowest satisfaction – will be high. On the other hand, in work groups with decentralized communication networks, the difference among members in respect to the access and control of information is not as significant as in centralized networks. Therefore, in decentralized communication networks, the range in individual member satisfaction – that is, the difference between the member with the highest and the one with the lowest satisfaction – will be low.

Furthermore, compared to the decentralized networks, there are a smaller number of central positions and a larger number of peripheral positions in the centralized communication networks. Therefore, the total or overall member satisfaction in groups with centralized communication networks will be low when compared with the total or overall member satisfaction in groups with decentralized networks (Shaw, 1971).

Problem-solving efficiency

Research studies suggested that when groups work on relatively simple tasks, the centralized communication networks enabled them to be more efficient and effective than the decentralized communication networks. Examples of efficiency measures used were the ability to detect errors and take appropriate actions to correct them and time required to generate and decide on a solution. However, when groups work on relatively complex tasks, the decentralized communication networks proved to be more efficient (Leavitt, 1951; Shaw, 1971).

The reasons for the difference in network efficiency can be traced to the demands of simple versus complex tasks and the properties of networks to cope with these demands. The problem-solving process of a simple task does not require the elaborate activities relating to setting objectives and developing appropriate performance strategies; gathering and analysing information; generating alternative solutions and deciding on one course of action; developing implementation plans and determining measures to evaluate the success of these plans. In contrast, the successful accomplishment of a complex task requires the performance of these activities and, in addition, considerable attention must be paid to the interpersonal relations in the group in order that members work effectively as a group.

When we examine the properties of the networks in light of the task demands, we find that there is a better fit between the centralized networks and simple tasks and decentralized networks and complex tasks. The reason for this is differences in the degree of 'channel saturation' and 'message saturation' generated in the communication networks. Channel saturation occurs when a position in the network is linked to a large number of communication channels. Message saturation occurs when a position in the network is exposed to or receives a large number of messages (Shaw, 1971). In general, a position in a network can be subject to both types of saturation, but we can say that when a position is subjected to channel saturation, it is highly likely that position is also subjected to message saturation. On the other hand, the message saturation of a position need not imply that the position is also subjected to channel saturation.

When a group is faced with a complex task and uses the centralized communication network, the person in the central or focal position will experience both channel and message saturation. They will experience channel saturation because they are in a position that is structurally linked to a relatively larger number of communication channels. The person will also experience message saturation because the activities involved in a complex task, as identified earlier, will generate a relatively large amount of information from the different communication channels in the network and this volume of information will have to be processed by the person in the central position. The increased information saturation faced by the person in the central position will tend to have an adverse affect their performance efficiency and, as a result, reduce the performance efficiency of the group.

Interpersonal Communication in Teamwork

The interpersonal skills of providing feedback and active listening and behaving assertively are critical skills to promote group effectiveness and resolve conflicts. We discussed active listening and assertive behaviour in Chapter 4. In this chapter we focus on **feedback** as one of the key drivers of effective teamwork.

Reduced to its barest essentials, communication is the process in which an individual interacts with one or more other individuals. The interaction is a dynamic process, but it can be described in terms of a series of steps. First, the sender decides on the message to be communicated to a target recipient. This can be a piece of information, a set of instructions, an opinion, or a request for these from the recipient. Second, the message is encoded – that is, the message is put into a set of symbols such as pictures, words, diagrams, or mathematical equations. Third, the encoded message is transmitted through an appropriate medium, which might be in writing (e.g., a memo, letter, or e-mail) or orally (e.g., by telephone or face-to-face conversation). The fourth step is the receipt of the message by the intended recipient. This is an obvious step in the process, but it needs to be spelt out because its execution could easily be taken for granted. For example, if the message is transmitted by letter which is not delivered to the intended recipient, then communication fails. Likewise, if the message is delivered orally, but the intended recipient is not listening to the speech, then too communication fails. The last step is the decoding by the recipient. Here the recipient makes sense of or interprets the message which is a critical factor to the recipient's understanding of the message.

No one will deny the importance of the communication process in an organization. At the macro level, communication enables organizational members to become aware of the organization's mission, goals and objectives, its cultural values and assumptions, its opportunities and challenges and its policies and procedures. The communication process is used in much the same way at the interpersonal and team levels. Managers communicate to their employees the job objectives and performance standards, engage with them in problem-solving and decision-making and provide feedback on their performance. Team members coordinate their activities, create new ideas and solve conflicts through effective communication. Clearly, without communication, all organizational activity would grind to a halt. It is indeed an important means to influence individual and groups to achieve their objectives. The next section focuses on one of the key drivers of success in teams: feedback.

What is feedback?

Kurt Lewin adopted the notion of feedback as a corrective or adjusting mechanism in intragroup relations. Thus, when a group member's behaviour is not conducive to the attainment of the group objectives, the group will provide feedback to that member in order to make them aware of the dysfunctional behaviour and its undesirable effects. Such feedback allows the individual to evaluate their behaviour in the light of the group's perceptions and then make choices on modifying the behaviour as they deem appropriate.

In an exchange or a contractual relationship, which is the case in a work situation, it is expected that employees have perceptions of their obligations and their behaviour is intended to conform to those perceptions. For example, we can expect that John is aware of his obligations to meet the production target of 100 units a day and that in performing his work behaviours his intentions are to produce 100 units. Suppose that for the last week John has been making few calls to potential sponsors of the team project. After reviewing this record, one of John's teammates might say to him: 'The record of your calls clearly demonstrates that you have been goofing off, all of last week'. This feedback focuses on John's intentions, explicitly suggesting that he did not intend to meet his obligations.

Let us explore this feedback in the light of additional facts of John's situation: unavailability of sponsors due to the approaching holiday season and the work-related emergency that John had to attend, both of which were beyond his control. Although the teammate refers to the work behaviour, the focus is on John's intentions. The problem with such a focus is that we cannot read another's mind, only observe that person's behaviour and experience the effects of that behaviour. If we give feedback in terms of the person's intentions we inevitably risk reading the intentions incorrectly and, as a result, the feedback will invariably not achieve the desired objective. In this case, at best the feedback might be seen as totally incomprehensible, at worst, it could have unintended effects that can range from the employee's loss of respect and trust for the teammate to anger and dysfunctional work behaviours.

The key issue in giving feedback is to first determine the precise nature and extent of the obligations involved in the exchange relationship about which feedback is being given. Second, the feedback should focus on the behaviour consistent with the facts of the situation. If the facts of the situation cannot be determined, then the feedback should refer to the observed behaviours, point out their effects and seek information on what needs to be addressed in order that the desired behaviours are exhibited. Thus, in John's case, the teammate should draw John's attention to the production record, pointing out its undesirable effects on the work unit's effectiveness and should continue seeking information that led to such a situation. Feedback, in this form, will provide both John and the teammate with an opportunity to place themselves in a problem-solving mode and develop appropriate corrective measures. The next section discusses more specific guidelines for giving feedback.

Guidelines for feedback

The feedback guidelines are based on the assumption that an open relationship characterized by trust and a clear recognition and acceptance of the objectives of the relationship exists between the feedback provider (e.g., supervisor or team member) and the feedback recipient. In such a relationship, feedback is seen as a means to achieve mutually agreed goals, therefore, there is a greater acceptance of the feedback. Some of the specific guidelines for feedback are (Hanson, 1975):

- Describe behaviour rather than interpreting it; and focus on modifiable behaviour.
- Express feelings directly rather than indirectly.
- Do not evaluate the person.
- Be specific rather than general.
- Allow the receiver the freedom to modify their behaviour.
- Provide timely feedback.
- In intragroup relations, provide group-shared feedback.

Let us briefly comment on each of these points.

Descriptive feedback and focus on modifiable behaviour

Feedback should be descriptive and not interpretative. Feedback is descriptive when the giver focuses on the behaviour and states it as the giver perceives it. In the situation of John's low sponsorship search performance, the feedback would be descriptive if the teammate had said: 'John, here are the figures I have received for your weekly call record. As you can see, it is less than the agreed threshold for last week.' This allows John to examine and explain the discrepancy. On the other hand, if the teammate accuses John of 'goofing on the job', the feedback ceases to be descriptive and becomes *interpretative*: the teammate is now interpreting John's intentions and imputes motives to John's behaviour. Interpretative feedback is ineffective because it needlessly places two burdens on John: (1) to defend himself against what may be an unjust accusation; and (2) to explain the less than adequate performance. John's preoccupation with defending himself generally results in a loss of focus on the real issues.

In addition to being descriptive, the feedback should focus on modifiable behaviour. This means that it is within the feedback receiver capability to change the behaviour with reasonable effort and time. Suppose John had agreed to the goal of 80 calls a week believing that he could find the potential sponsors in their office and that he would be able to devote the majority of his time to this task. It now turns out that both of these assumptions failed for reasons beyond John's control. In these circumstances, providing John with feedback that he is not meeting the agreed goal clearly focuses on unmodifiable behaviour and therefore will not be effective.

Express feelings directly

The feedback guideline here cautions against the likelihood that when feelings are not expressed directly, there is ambiguity in the communication and the receiver might not get the intended message. For example, suppose Mary and Helen are working jointly on a project. For some reason, Mary was not regular in attending the meetings and suspecting that Helen is angry with her says: 'Helen, I sensed that you are angry because I could not attend the meetings regularly.' In this statement, Mary does not communicate directly how she feels in response to her perception that Helen is angry. A direct expression of feeling would be if Mary said: 'Helen, I am anxious because in the last meeting you looked angry when I came late.' The feedback provided by this statement communicates to Helen precisely how Mary feels and so gives Helen an opportunity to respond appropriately.

Do not evaluate the person

Returning to John's situation, suppose the teammate had said: 'John, you must be either incompetent or lazy.' This feedback shifts from John's behaviour and even from his intentions and constitutes a personal attack. It is true John might occasionally behave in a lazy or an incompetent manner, but that does not make him a lazy or an incompetent person. When feedback evaluates the person rather than the person's behaviour, it does not provide the receiver with information on their behaviour. Furthermore, such evaluations of the person might be in terms of a value system which the feedback receiver might not share: two undesirable effects can then follow. One is that the feedback is seen as an arbitrary imposition of values. The other is that the relationship is vitiated because the feedback receiver might perceive that their reluctance to share the other's values might lead to a lack of trust, openness, or acceptance in the relationship.

Specific rather than general feedback

Feedback would be characterized as 'general' if John's teammate were to say: 'John, your performance is totally unacceptable.' Such feedback does not clearly communicate to John what it is about the performance that needs to be modified. Is it the quantity; the quality; the delivery schedule; or all three? An example of specific feedback would be: 'John, the number of calls you made last week was half of what you were expected to do. Therefore, given the time pressure to fund our project this performance was unacceptable.' John now has a clear picture of the reasons why his work is unacceptable and can initiate appropriate actions to remedy the situation. Specific feedback thus improves communication and can contribute to improved performance.

Allow freedom of choice in accepting feedback

In situations where the required behaviour is critical or essential to attaining the job objectives, it is expected that descriptive and specific feedback on work behaviour should prompt the feedback receiver to modify their behaviour. The question of the feedback receiver's freedom of choice to change does not become an issue in these situations because the required behaviour is essential to attaining the job objectives.

On the other hand, in situations where the required behaviour is not relevant to attaining the job objectives (e.g., an employee's political views, dress, etc.) the receiver's freedom to accept or reject the feedback should be respected. In addition to the absence of criticality relative to job or organizational objectives, such behaviours are also characterized by the absence of agreed standards. Therefore, imposing feedback on these types of behaviours, besides being resented, might also communicate the message that the feedback giver's standards are superior when in fact it is merely a personal judgement. Interpersonal communications are greatly enhanced when feedback is not imposed in these situations.

Provide timely feedback

The effectiveness of feedback is considerably increased when it is given on time. The reason for this is that when the events are fresh in the minds of the giver and receiver of the feedback, the feedback giver is in a better position to follow the feedback guidelines such as being descriptive, specific and maintaining the focus on behaviours. In addition, the increased saliency of the event can make feedback more meaningful. For these reasons, timely feedback is likely to facilitate greater openness to and acceptance of the feedback by the receiver.

Group-shared feedback

The preceding feedback guidelines are also applicable to intragroup relations, but there are two that are particularly relevant to intragroup relations. The first guideline is that feedback to a member should focus on behaviour that has occurred in the group, for the obvious reason that all members have knowledge of it and can bring their perspective to bear in the feedback. This is referred to as **group-shared feedback**. The second guideline is that all members should contribute their perceptions when feedback is given. This point needs to be emphasized because there might be a tendency for members to remain silent when they concur with the contents of the feedback given by one member to another. The logic underlying the silence might be that since they will make the same points no useful purpose is served by repeating them.

However, let us examine how this silence might be interpreted by the feedback receiver. It is more than likely that the receiver might be inclined to believe that the feedback constitutes the perceptions of only one member of the group. Surely, if others felt the same way, they would have said so. Thus the silence of other group members can give the receiver a distorted picture of the situation. Repetition of the points by other group members helps the receiver to get a more complete and balanced picture. It also causes the receiver to take the feedback seriously, especially in situations where the receiver's perceptions are not congruent with the feedback content.

We conclude this section with two observations. First, the objective of giving feedback is not to hurt but to help the receiver. Whether it is a one-on-one relationship, as in the case of the supervisor and subordinate, or intragroup relations, the primary purpose of feedback must be kept in mind and respected if feedback is to be effective.

However, feedback needs to be practiced in a supportive climate which values trust, openness of and caring for people and their relationships. When feedback degenerates into fault-finding sessions and occasions for ego trips, it becomes an instrument that destroys communications and relationships. This leads us to the second observation. If the receiver manifests resentment or defensiveness when we give feedback, it is imperative that we step back to check if we have followed the proposed guidelines. A useful approach in this situation is to respond to the receiver's negative reaction by asking how they understood the feedback. This playback of the feedback should then be used as the basis to modify the feedback consistent with the proposed guidelines.

Cross-cultural approaches to teamwork

In the global work environment, teams or work groups comprised of members from different cultural backgrounds are becoming increasingly commonplace. As we saw at the beginning of this chapter, the team that was leading the world could not be more culturally diverse than this.

Teams with members from diverse cultural backgrounds either work in the same location (co-located multicultural teams) or across virtual borders (virtual multicultural teams). Co-located or virtual, multicultural teams have the potential to produce miraculous or disastrous results for organizations. Our focus in this section is on the conditions under which multicultural teams perform well, with a specific focus on the role of communication. But first we would like to discuss the advantages and disadvantages of multicultural teams for organizations.

Multicultural teams: advantages and disadvantages

Despite the many benefits of teamwork, managing interpersonal processes in teams is challenging. It is more so when the team members belong to different cultural backgrounds. Does cultural diversity bring significant benefits to organizations to justify the effort and resources spent to overcome the difficulties of managing it? Yes – but only if certain conditions are met. Some studies found that **multicultural teams** outperformed monocultural teams (e.g., Elron, 1997), while others found the reverse (e.g., Thomas, 1999). That's why a recent meta-analysis (Stahl et al., 2010) showed that the relationship of cultural diversity with team performance ranges from −0.60 to +0.48 (see Video 6.1).

Research in the last 20 years (e.g, Adler, 1997; Earley and Mosakowski, 2000; Elron, 1997; Thomas et al., 1996; Watson et al., 1993) suggest that, compared to monocultural teams, multicultural teams produce more creative ideas and more alternative solutions to problems. They are less likely to engage in **groupthink** (i.e., a lack of diversity of ideas in the team because the members are alike) and therefore more likely to search information from multiple sources, carefully examine objectives, alternatives, contingency plans and risks of preferred actions. In the UK, for example, teams with members of diverse backgrounds were found to perform better than those composed of high achievers or those with similar backgrounds (Schneider and Barsoux, 2003). There is evidence linking teams' cultural diversity to financial profits (Ng and Tung, 1998) and productivity (Townsend et al., 1998).

Research suggests that diverse teams perform particularly well under the following circumstances.

- Time: cultural diversity is found to bring increasing benefits to teamwork overtime (Watson et al., 1993). Comparing culturally homogenous and heterogeneous teams Watson and colleagues found that the former initially performed better than the latter, but in time the performance levels were the same. Time gives members the opportunity to develop a deeper understanding and appreciation of cultural diversities in the team. Also the team discovers ways to overcome interpersonal conflicts, thanks to the feedback they receive over time from within and outside of the team (Thomas, 1999; Watson et al., 1998). This can result in the development of a *hybrid* team culture (Earley and Mosakowski, 2000).
- Task: cultural diversity in teams is proven to be beneficial especially when the task allows autonomy and discretion to the team in decision-making and gives opportunities to influence the outcomes of teamwork. For example, tasks that require creative idea-generation and decision-making make better use of cultural

diversity than those require routine production (Thomas, 2002). Furthermore, tasks requiring diversity of skills, values and experiences are better suited to multicultural teamwork, compared to those requiring tacit coordination and consensus among members (e.g., production). The effectiveness of multicultural teamwork is maximized when the composition of diversity in the team matches the diversity required for the job (Halevy and Sagiv, 2008).

- Managerial and organizational support: Thomas and colleagues (2000) showed that management support is positively associated with task performance, member satisfaction, cohesiveness, commitment and trust and negatively associated with the amount of conflict in culturally diverse teams. Management support is important to create an organizational culture that respects and values cultural diversity; in such organizational cultures multicultural teams stand a better chance of succeeding (Cox, 1993). Management and organizational support to multicultural teams is also demonstrated in the ways in which HRM practices are designed for these teams, including training and development activities to improve cross-cultural understanding and effectiveness and performance management practices to recognize and reward successful teams (Cox, 1993).

Notwithstanding its advantages, multicultural teams also have disadvantages due to conflicts arising from differences among team members. Let us discuss some of the tension-creating conditions in multicultural teams.

- Differences in attitudes towards teamwork: team members from diverse cultures may hold different attitudes towards teamwork. Kirkman and Shapiro (1997, 2001) found that individualism was associated with resistance to working in teams. This is more so when members perform well individually, whereas their teams perform poorly (Chen et al., 1998). However, individualists are more committed to teamwork when rewards are allocated equitably (proportionate to each member's performance), while collectivistics are less committed to teamwork under the equity condition (Ramamoorthy and Flood, 2002).

  Kirkman and Shapiro (1997) also found that power distance was associated with resistance to **self-managed teams**. Gibson and Zellmer-Bruhn (2001) studied the metaphors used for teamwork in US, France, Puerto Rico and the Philippines. Metaphors convey expectations about the role, objectives and scopes of teams. For example, when the sports metaphor is used to describe teamwork it indicates that team members expect to have explicit role assignments (e.g., a coach, a player, a scorer) that are relatively non-hierarchical. For those using sports metaphor, teams are expected to have clear objectives with salient outcomes (e.g., winning and losing). However, a family metaphor implies hierarchical roles and a paternalistic authority in a team whose objective is either ambiguous or inherent to its members. A metaphor of community is endorsed in collectivistic settings implies roles that are informal, ambiguous and shared.

Employees from individualistic cultures preferred metaphors implying clear team objectives and voluntary group membership (e.g., sports metaphors); those from high power-distant cultures preferred metaphors implying roles that are hierarchical and objectives that are mandated (e.g., military metaphor); and those from collectivistic cultures preferred metaphors implying roles that are vague and objectives that are ambiguous and not oriented towards specific tasks (e.g., community metaphor).

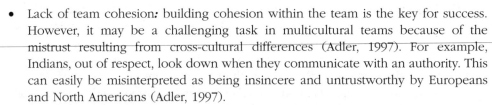

Thinking across cultures 6.1

The Team of Everybody, Somebody, Anybody and Nobody

This is a story of 'everybody', 'somebody', 'anybody' and 'nobody' working in a Zimbabwean firm. There was some very important work to be done and *everybody* was sure that *somebody* would do it. *Anybody* could have done it but *nobody* did it. People were very angry because it was *everybody's* job. *Everybody* thought that *anybody* could have done it, but *nobody* realized that *somebody* wasn't doing it. The story ends with *everybody* blaming *somebody* when *nobody* did what *anybody* could have done.

Source: modified from Granell (1997, p. 36).

- What do you think is experienced in this story: sucker effect, free-rider effect, or social-loafing?
- This story reflects a common experience of teamwork in some cultures of the world. Does that mean 'effective teamwork is not possible' in some cultures?
- What are some of your recommendations for this situation not to be experienced again?

- Lack of team cohesion: building cohesion within the team is the key for success. However, it may be a challenging task in multicultural teams because of the mistrust resulting from cross-cultural differences (Adler, 1997). For example, Indians, out of respect, look down when they communicate with an authority. This can easily be misinterpreted as being insincere and untrustworthy by Europeans and North Americans (Adler, 1997).

Collectivistic members shy away from working with those who they don't know or they don't like. If they are given the chance to self-select the team members, they make the choice not necessarily on the basis of the assessment of technical competence, but on the basis of the quality of interpersonal relationships. Harmony in teams weighs more than task competency in selecting members. It is difficult to form cohesion within the team if some members are perceived to belong to the out-group and not trusted by collectivistic members (Aycan, 2004; Earley, 1993; Gomez et al., 2000).

Thinking across cultures 6.2

Which Part of the Story was the Worst?

In her first year of teaching back at home, a US-educated Pakistani professor randomly assigned senior students into teams for their final class projects. This was a common practice back in the US. To her, it was an excellent opportunity for students to practice and learn how to work with different people in 'real life'. Soon after, a student came to her office *in tears* stating that 'Professor, you put me in the same team with someone who I have not been talking to since we were eight years old. Under the circumstances, I have no other choice but to drop the course.' The professor was in shock. Which was the worst? Was it that the student blamed the teacher for this coincidence (by saying that '*you* put me in the team with her'), or that the student was not talking to someone for more than 10 years, or that she dropped the course just because of this?

Source: Aycan (2004, p. 416).

- Which cultural characteristics do you think this story reflects?
- How do you think the professor should respond to the plea from this student? What would be the consequences of the professor's action?

Some status-conscious members from high power-distance cultures may be reluctant to cooperate, share information or criticise others so that they maintain their position in the team. This hurts the team's cohesiveness.

'There is a real fear about someone else taking over your job ... These feelings result in the control and retention of information ... people get hold of information hoping that this makes them indispensable' (Granell, 1997, p. 21).

Team cohesion is also damaged if some members hold negative stereotypes against each other. It is common knowledge that some nations have a history of hostility, such as Palestinians and Jews, Greeks and Turks, or Indians and Pakistanis. Given the historically rooted hostilities, it is difficult to build cohesion among members from such nations. There are also stereotypes pertaining to developing countries. Members from high status or economically developed countries may assume leadership in teams and leave the other members aside, assuming that they are incompetent.

- Communication problems: for multicultural teams, communication is the Achilles' heel. A study on teams composed of US and Russian managers showed that communication was a key to team performance: the correlation between cross-cultural communication competence of team members and team performance was 0.45 (Matveev and Nelson, 2004). Differences in languages and in the competence of using the common language (usually English) pose serious challenges to the works of diverse teams. Not being able to use one's own language can be frustrating, as put eloquently by an eastern European manager *'I can speak to you in your language, but I can't always tell you what I am thinking in my own'* (Lane et al., 2006, p. 56).

  Compounding the difficulties caused by language problems are cross-cultural differences in the communication styles, especially the high- vs. low-context communication. In high-context cultures, the message is embedded in the context and therefore there is no need to explain everything clearly. Subtlety in communication ensures that people do not lose face and harmony is not maintained. However in low-context cultures, rules, norms, roles, messages, conflicts,

"I agree with much of what you're saying, mostly the brief silent parts between the words."

Cartoon 6.1   A high-context communication. Copyright © Randy Glasbergen.

disagreements and all other key issues should be explained in detail to avoid the risk of misunderstandings. People are usually assertive and direct in their communication.

Thinking across cultures 6.3

'You **Must Understand What I Mean!**'

It was my first week in the project and I must admit that I had difficulties running some analyses. The first week is tough anyways – I felt homesick and worried about my family in Taiwan. I was fortunate enough to have nice and experienced people in the team and I was hoping that they would read my problems from my face and offer some help. But nobody did; nobody has asked me if everything was going well. One day I was struggling with the software and murmuring with anger. Having seen that, an Australian colleague, finally, asked if everything was OK. I said yes. How could I have said that I needed help? I was expecting him to understand the situation and insist on offering help. Instead, he said 'Are you sure?' What kind of a question was that? Am I supposed to say 'Well, I said "sure, everything is OK" a moment ago, but in the next moment I realize that I was not sure'? I simply nodded, confirming my response, and he left the room. He just left me like that! I lost a few nights sleep to think what I have done wrong? I guess I must have written SOS on my forehead for anybody to pay attention.

- How do you think the Taiwanese team member should behave next time a similar situation happens?
- In cultures where 'no' does not necessarily mean 'no' and 'yes' does not necessarily mean 'yes', how would one know the hidden meaning?

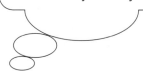

While the Taiwanese member felt frustrated about the response of his Australian colleague, the Australian colleague felt content with his behaviour. He did not offer help and advice without being asked for it and, therefore, did not patronize the junior member and impede his self-development.

The preference for the communication channel is also varied. In status conscious cultures communicating via e-mail can be offensive. Here is how a senior British manager expresses his feelings about it:

I hate e-mail... I am a bit status-conscious and e-mail is so bloody egalitarian. I suspect it is also because my surname beings with a T and I always find myself near the bottom of the list. It irritates me and it is so impersonal. It does not say 'Dear Peter, ... Regards, so and so'. It comes spitting out some code at the front and some codes at the bottom. (Schneider and Barsoux, 2003, p. 19)

Cross-cultural Considerations for Managers

Effective management of multicultural teams

To capitalize the full potential of multicultural teams one can simply recommend the enhancement of conditions associated with advantages and reduction of those associated with disadvantages of multicultural teams, as discussed in the previous section. But how? Here are some specific guidelines for effective management of cultural diversity in teams.

Pay close attention to team composition and team-building

There are three guidelines for members selection in multicultural teams. First, cultural backgrounds of team members should be selected purposefully. For example, if the purpose is to prepare a group of German mid-level managers for an expatriate assignment in Dubai, putting them in a virtual team comprised of Arab managers would serve the purpose of preparing them for the assignment. If a textile product is prepared for launch in Sweden, it would be wise to have a Swedish national in the R&D team. Cultural composition of the team is determined in accordance to the requirements of the task at hand. Second, team members should be selected not only because of their cultural backgrounds, but also because of their knowledge, skills (including language skills), abilities and expertise (Gluesing and Gibson, 2004). Multicultural teams that are comprised of technically competent members are less likely to be dominated by a subgroup, less likely to experience social loafing and more likely to have participation in decision-making, all of which, in turn, enhance team performance and effectiveness. Third, member selection to multicultural teams should also take proneness to work in culturally diverse teams into account. Gluesing and Gibson (2004, p. 211) recommend that tools such as Global Personality Inventory or Cross-cultural Adaptability Inventory could be used to determine the aptitude and willingness of members to work in diverse teams.

Adequacy of member selection strategies does not guarantee successful team building and functioning. Team-building requires relatively less time for members of cultures who are task- and performance-oriented, compared to those who are relationship-oriented (Adler, 1997). Members from the former group prefer to get down to business while members from the latter group prefer to get to know each other.

Team-building activities, such as climbing mountains or surviving the desert, may be perceived as manipulative and forceful for members who are not culturally accustomed to mix personal and professional relationships (Schneider and Barsoux, 2003). These activities can also be perceived as superficial and childish especially for those from a high power-distance culture. A French executive was furious when he was asked to wear the team t-shirt during the team-building activity 'forcing us to wear uniforms … was humiliating' (Schneider and Barsoux, 2003, p. 230).

The most important purpose of team-building is trust-building among members. However, there are vast cross-cultural differences in propensity to trust (see difference in the 'trust score' of countries in the World Values Survey; http://www.worldvalues-survey.org). There are also cross-cultural differences in the ways in which trust is built: 'Americans build trust by being friendly and informal. The Germans build trust by proving competence and demonstrating technical knowledge … Americans tend to trust first until proven wrong. For Germans the reverse is generally the case' (Schneider and Barsoux, 2003, p. 230).

Gluesing and Gibson (2004) emphasize the importance of *social processes* for successful team-building. They involve creating a safe environment to allow team members to express new ideas (e.g., start out working in small groups on tasks that are relatively less risky and less challenging), developing shared mental models (e.g., use metaphors and stories to allow team members the opportunity to share implicit knowledge) and creating a sense of community (e.g., develop a team logo to symbolize shared work values).

Lane and colleagues (2006) offer a useful framework for team-building, which is referred to as 'Mapping, Bridging and Integrating' (MBI). The first phase, mapping, involves recognizing and understanding cultural differences among team members; the second involves bridging cultural differences through communication and the third phase, integrating, involves managing differences for effective teamwork. We will discuss MBI in more depth later when we outline guidelines for communication.

Design the task to foster creativity and interdependence

To maximize the benefits of multicultural teams, tasks should be designed in such a way to foster *creativity* and *interdependence*. According to Adler:

> Cultural diversity provides the biggest potential benefit to teams with challenging tasks that require innovation. Diversity becomes less helpful when employees are working on simple tasks involving repetitive or routine procedures. With the advent of robots and

computer-aided manufacturing, the proportion of challenging, nonroutine tasks increases as does the need for and value of diversity. (1997, p. 139)

To increase the benefits of diversity, tasks should also be designed to foster each member's active participation. An ideal task is one which cannot be accomplished without the use of knowledge, skills and abilities of its members as well as the cultural perspectives they bring to the table. In such groups, members are indispensable because of their unique qualities. Therefore, common problems of diverse teams, such as some members resorting to social loafing or others dominating the group, would be less likely to occur. Such tasks bring the benefits of cultural diversity to the surface to the greatest extent.

The following guidelines by Menon (1994, pp. 110–11) explain how task characteristics influence the management of teams in non-Western cultures characterized by high collectivism, high power-distance and high uncertainty-avoidance.

- For routine, low-interdependence, low-tech jobs, the manager should:

  o clearly define the job roles and procedures;
  o physically group work stations into groups of six to eight employees; and
  o solicit input from employees on job procedures and targets and make the final decision to implement these suggestions.

- For routine, interdependent jobs as those involved in the production of low-tech, standardized items, the manager should form traditional work groups characterized by hierarchical supervisor–subordinate relationship.
- For non-routine, non-standardized, non-interdependent tasks such as high-tech jobs in design departments and management information systems teams MIS, the manager should adopt the 'nominal work group' approach. In this approach, several individuals performing independent tasks report to one manager, who assigns and evaluates tasks but delegates to each subordinate the responsibility for decision-making with regard to the actual task performance.
- For jobs characterized by high uncertainty and high interdependence such as in new product development teams, the manager should form work groups whose members participate to a considerable extent in problem-solving and decision-making situations. The manager would still make the final decision, but only after an exhaustive exploration of the issues with the group.

Provide a clear sense of purpose and direction

As we discussed above, teamwork has different connotations for members from diverse backgrounds. This may impede team cohesion. One of the key requirements to establish cohesion is to have a common purpose and direction. In low-context and performance-oriented cultures agreeing on a common purpose and direction usually accompanies setting specific performance criteria against which the team and its members are evaluated. However, this may be annoying to members who favour flexibility.

> Insisting on precise performance goals and objectives may be seen as too instrumental, too task-oriented and insensitive to individual member's needs, or the social needs of the group. Not enough time is devoted to relationship-building and developing a sense of rapport, including time for socialization … Furthermore, it is not obvious that team members share the same sense of priorities. For example, some members may feel that it is more important to achieve time deadlines, while others are more concerned with achieving higher quality despite delays. (Schneider and Barsoux, 2003, p. 224)

Our recommendation is to have superordinate goals at the initial stages of team formation, prior to setting specific strategies and performance standards (Adler, 1997; Thomas, 2002). Superordinate goals transcend cross-cultural differences, require interdependence and cooperation and are defined broadly enough to accommodate differences in perspectives and strategies. Superordinate goals provide a vision that give members a sense of purpose, direction, commitment and belongingness. Leaders (internal or external to the team) should convince the members that achieving the superordinate goal is more important than achieving the individual objectives of team members. For that, members should be prepared to work together despite differences, and make compromises if necessary to create outcomes they will all feel part of and proud of. Specific team objectives, strategies, performance and reward standards should be set collectively with participation of team members, after which they start establishing rapport and trust.

Division of roles and responsibilities

As discussed in the above section on attitudes towards teamwork, there are cross-cultural differences in how the roles and responsibilities are assigned in the team. Members from individualistic cultures expect roles to be clearly defined for each member, to work independently on individual assignments and aggregate the individual pieces at a later stage to produce team results. On the other hand, members from collectivistic cultures expect flexibility and vagueness in role assignments: 'One frustrated Swedish manager in Hungary complained that team members did not seem to realize that reaching a decision in the meeting was not enough – something had to be done between meetings' (Schneider and Barsoux, 2003, p. 228).

Specific role assignments are discomforting for members from cultures high on fatalism and power distance. For them, meeting role requirements may not be possible due to factors beyond an individual's control. They fear to lose face to the team members if they fail to meet their role requirements and receive negative evaluations from management. To protect members from criticisms within and outside the team, members from collectivistic, high power-distance and fatalistic cultures prefer to have vague and flexible role assignments. However, unclear role assignments and members' willingness to back up each other increase social loafing in the team. Therefore, it is recommended that team members are assigned to specific roles and responsibilities, but these assignments are done in a participatory manner. The team leader or coordinator (if one exists) should make sure that members take on roles and responsibilities in accordance to their competencies *and* willingness. As will be discussed in more detail below, each member's performance should be monitored. However, the monitoring system should not allow members to see each others' performance. Public posting of performance may increase evaluation anxiety for some members.

CASE 6.1

What Purpose does Teamwork Serve?

Whirlpool recommended that Vitro adopt Whirlpool's Worldwide Excellence System (WES), a total quality system that had proven highly successful in the US. However, after two years of attempts to introduce the system in the way it had been introduced in the US, virtually no change in performance had occurred. The joint venture concluded that they had failed to adapt the process to the Mexican work environment or to give the Mexican workers an incentive to comply with quality practices. The quality system was finally introduced successfully when Mexicans were involved through the use of hierarchical communication. In small groups, senior managers spoke to middle managers, middle managers to line managers and line managers to the workers. Overall, the evidence suggests that Mexican workers may be motivated by the shared responsibility that comes with teamwork, in contrast to workers in the US or Canada, who value the opportunity for individual expression and personal accountability. Teamwork in Mexico may appeal to workers as a way to reduce individual risk through collaboration.

Source: Nicholls et al. (1999)

What about the leadership role in culturally diverse teams? Cross-cultural differences are expected to surface in two ways. First, there are differences in how important the leadership role is perceived to be for effective functioning of teams. For members from low power-distance cultures the team can function very well without a leader, while for members from high power-distance cultures this is unconceivable. The first author of this book recalls how difficult it was to describe the *concept* of 'leaderless groups' in her MBA class in Turkey. Second, there are differences in the perception of 'who is qualified as a leader'. For Germans, the team leader must demonstrate technical competence to have credibility; for French or Italians, the team leader must have the power and political influence to get things done; for Nordic managers the leader is only a facilitator (Schneider and Barsoux, 2003). Our recommendation is to take the time to discuss the pros and cons of having a leader in the team, whether to have one, more than one or changing leaders in the team and the required characteristics of the leader vis-à-vis the task at hand. Based on this discussion, the team should arrive at an explicit or implicit agreement on a member to be the leader. It is *critical* that this process involves participation of all members, rather than have someone assume the leadership role because they have a better command of English compared to others in the team.

Foster effective communication and participation

The *raison d'etre* for multicultural teams is to use the benefits of diverse perspectives to enhance creativity and innovation. Multicultural teams do not actualize their potential when members cannot fully participate in team discussions and decision processes. One of the major barriers to participation is communication differences and difficulties (e.g., lack of language fluency).

Cross-cultural differences in communication style are well documented in the literature. Some cultures make excessive use of gestures (e.g., Latin Americans), while others use silence as a way to communicate the message (e.g., Japanese). In some cultures people interrupt each other and engage in parallel talk (e.g., Middle Easterners), while in others such behaviours are considered to be rude (e.g., Scandinavians). Some cultures prefer an indirect and subtle communication style (e.g., India); while others prefer a direct and open communication style (e.g., America).

> The entire production was relying on him and he knew it. When we asked him whether or not the production would be completed on time, he would not say 'yes', he would not say 'no'; he would just say 'inshallah' (things will happen if God is willing). We took it as a good sign and remained hopeful. Two hours before the delivery he called in and asked for an extension. We were blown away by this! He must have known that the delivery would be delayed. Why did he not tell us ahead of time?

Language fluency is a major barrier to equal participation in the team. 'Nonfluent team members may well be the most expert on the team, but their difficulty communicating knowledge makes it hard for the team to recognize and utilize their expertise' say Brett et al. (2006, p. 87).

> A Latin American member of a multicultural consulting team lamented 'Many times I felt that because of the language difference, I didn't have the words to say some things that I was thinking. I noticed that when I went to these interviews with the U.S. guy, he would tend to lead the interviews, which was understandable but also disappointing, because we are at the same level. I had many questions, but he would take the lead.' (Brett et al., 2006, p. 87)

The following suggestions would be useful to overcome communication barriers and facilitate participation.

- *Establish a group norm that requires soliciting opinion* of each member before an important decision is made (Lane et al. 2006).
- *Designate a team member to take the responsibility for monitoring team processes* and ensuring equal participation of all members (Lane et al., 2006).
- *Use different forms of communication to elicit participation.* For example, use of visual aids such as coloured cards to vote for agreement, or cue-cards to jot down ideas and circulate them in the team. Von Glinow et al. (2004) cites the case of a managing director using a garden metaphor and pictures to gain employees' acceptance of a vision.
- *Encourage members to express their opinions in environments where they feel the most comfortable.* For example, Finns say many things in a sauna that are unsaid in formal meetings (e.g., Lane et al., 2006; Schneider and Barsoux, 2003).
- *Encourage members to communicate in their own language, if necessary.* One manager of a global team offers the following suggestions:

> We make several rules for participation: speak slowly, ask for clarification at any point; and if anyone gets too frustrated in trying to make a point in English, the participant can revert to his or her native language and someone will translate … Even if there is no one to translate, the switch to native language releases pressure and frustration; and other participants often learn something about the individual's 'true personality'. There is an amazing transformation in body language, tone of voice, facial expression and confidence when someone switches to his/her native language. (Schneider and Barsoux, 2003, p. 232)

- *Develop an appreciation for and sensitivity to cross-cultural differences.* Lane et al.'s (2006) MBI framework provides a guideline to enhance communication in multicultural teams. In the first phase of mapping (M) members engage in discussing their cultural differences with respect to values, assumptions, expectations and preferences. In the second phase of bridging (B), members are required to find commonalities that would bind them together as a team. Developing empathy is critical in this phase. Members are required to communicate with the other person's perspective in mind, while also carefully considering the task and goals of the team. In the last phase of integration (I), members are required to communicate in a way that is 'blame-free'. The blame-free communication encourages participation and effective problem-solving (see Video 6.2 and 6.3).
- *Choose the right medium for communication.* According to research (e.g., Gluesing and Gibson, 2004) face-to-face meetings should be preferred when team members get to know one another, clarify the goals, norms and roles and when the team work on complex, sensitive and conflict producing issues. Computer-mediated communication would be appropriate when team members work on routine tasks.

Cross-cultural communication problems may naturally give rise to interpersonal conflicts in the team, which is a major barrier to effective teamwork.

Effective performance management

Performance management in multicultural teams involves three phases: setting performance standards, monitoring and evaluating performance, and rewarding performance. Culture has important impact on all aspects of performance management. In the above section, we alluded to differences in preferences of team members to set specific vs. broad performance standards. There are also vast cross-cultural differences in how performance is monitored and feedback is provided. For example, the majority of economically developing countries are characterized by cultures high on collectivism, power-distance, and uncertainty-avoidance and low on performance orientation. Team members from such cultures do not welcome negative performance feedback from other members (Aycan, 2004). Negative feedback is taken as a personal offence to the individual. Criticisms done openly, publicly, or representing teams' opinion are especially hurtful and intimidating. The member who receives such feedback may have feel tempted to quit the team. Performance feedback to such members should be given in a subtle way and in private. Negative feedback should always be balanced with positive. The feedback receiver should feel that they are not taking all of the blame for low performance. Extra care should be exercised to show that performance and personality are not mixed. For example, after giving negative feedback the team leader or team members can freely socialize with the low-performing team member, to show them that performance does not influence the relationships at the individual level. The team leader should tailor the style and frequency of performance feedback depending on team members' cultural background and preferences. This is easier said than done. It takes practice and tolerance for failure until the right balance is found between toughness and tenderness, directness and subtleness and professionalism and personalism. The exercise in Thinking across cultures 6.4 could be a first step to raise awareness about the sensitivities involved in giving feedback, especially in a culturally diverse team environment.

Finally, cultural context plays a major role also in the preference for individual vs. team-based rewards. It is recommended that a combination of individual- and team-based rewards is allocated to teams that achieve their objectives. Kirkman and Den Hartog (2004) propose the following guidelines to managers of global teams (pp. 255–6):

- Use a combination of individual- and team-based rewards to motivate team-related behaviour.
- Use a higher level of team-based rewards when the team requires a high level of interdependence.

- Use a higher level of individual-based rewards when the instability in the team increases.
- Use team-based rewards in teams dominated by members from collectivistic cultures, use individual-based rewards in teams dominated by those from individualistic cultures. If there is a cultural balance in the team, the reward system should be decided by the members.
- Take into account the importance of recognition (e.g., praise) to complement tangible reward systems and tailor recognition to the cultural values of team members (e.g., do not use recognition systems that single out the individual in the group for members with collectivistic values).

Thinking across cultures 6.4

Feedback to the Team Member

In one of your current assignments, you are required to evaluate a teammate and provide feedback to them in a face-to-face meeting. Evaluate your teammate using the following form (FORM A) and bring this form along with your notes to the feedback meeting.

After the feedback session is completed, give FORM B to your teammate to evaluate your feedback behaviour.

FORM A. Evaluating the 'feedback receiver' (La Fasto and Larson, 2001, p. 29):

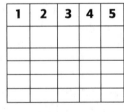

	1	2	3	4	5

1. Inexperienced

- Lacks understanding of the business
- Inappropriate technical background
- Unsure what needs to be done
- Narrow perspective

1. Experienced

- Understands the business issues
- Appropriate technical background
- Knows what to do
- Understands the broader picture

2. Unproductive problem solver

- Uncertain of direction or outcome
- Avoid seeking input
- Indecisive
- Does not volunteer information
- Drifts

2. Productive problem solver

- Clear direction and expectations
- Consults with others
- Decisive
- Shares information in timely manner
- Stays focused

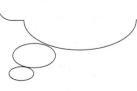

3. Closed
- Ignores issues
- Silent
- Guarded
- Biased
- Doesn't listen

3. Open
- Surfaces issues
- Talks it over
- Straightforward and candid
- Open minded
- Listens

4. Nonsupportive
- Defensive
- Withholds effort
- Finds fault with others
- Commanding and controlling
- Rigid and inflexible
- Intimidating and competitive

4. Supportive
- Challengeable
- Helps the team
- Encourages others
- Manages ego and control needs
- Adaptable to changing team needs
- Makes it safe to others to contribute

5. Passive
- Waits for others to act
- Gives up quickly
- More of a spectator
- Avoids risk
- Safety in numbers
- Seeks easy way out

5. Personal initiative
- Takes action
- Repeated efforts
- Likes being involved
- Takes risks
- Seeks personal accountability
- Sets high standards

6. Negative style
- Draining
- Creates tension
- Emotional
- Self-focused
- Insecure
- Cynical
- Cold and distant

6. Positive style
- Energizing
- Fun and relaxed
- Level headed
- Other oriented
- Confident
- Optimistic
- Warm and approachable

FORM B. Evaluating the 'feedback provider' (Mainiero and Tromley, 1994, p. 125).

When providing me with feedback, my teammate (chose either 'a' or 'b' in each pair):

1 a. Described my behaviour.
   b. Interpreted my behaviour.

2 a. Focused on the impact of my behaviour on my teammate's emotions.
   b. Told me what I should do or how I should behave differently.

3 a. Gave specific examples of my behaviours.
   b. Provided me with general statements about my behaviour without giving specific details.

(Continued)

(Continued)

4 a. Focused only on the behaviours that I can control and change.
   b. Sometimes focused on issues or behaviours I cannot control or change.

5 a. Provided me with timely feedback.
   b. Provided me with feedback on my performance or behaviour long after they occurred.

6 a. Focused on the impact of my behaviour on my teammate's emotions.
   b. Focused on why I behaved the way I did.

7 a. Balanced negative feedback with positive ones.
   b. Provided mostly negative feedback.

8 a. Made it clear to me that the purpose of feedback was to help me develop and improve teamwork effectiveness.
   b. Made it clear to me that the purpose of the feedback was to punish or patronize me.

Scoring: Count the number of 'a' options to find out the level of feedback provider's effectiveness. The higher the number of 'a's, the more effective was the feedback provided to you by your teammate.

- To what extent to you think 'feedback behaviour' of your teammate reflected their cultural, ethnic background in comparison to their gender, work experience, personality?
- Do you think behaving in alliance with 'effective feedback behaviour' would be discomforting to your teammate? Why, and why not?

Effective Management of Virtual Teams

There is an increasing trend of working in international, global or co-located teams virtually by leveraging the opportunities afforded by advanced technologies. According to a recent survey based on responses of 3,301 employees in 102 countries (Solomon, 2012), two-thirds of respondents reported working in **virtual teams**, mostly with colleagues in domestic and international work contexts, and one-quarter worked in virtual teams mostly with colleagues in international work contexts.

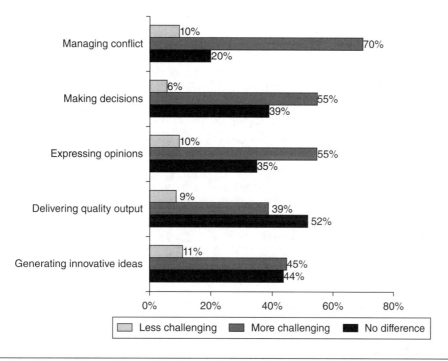

Figure 6.2 *Challenges experienced in virtual teams in comparison to face-to-face teams (Solomon, 2012, p. 12)*

Virtual teams have several important advantages over face-to-face teams, the most important of which is the opportunity to work with the best talents in the world without having to deal with the cost and hassle of frequent travelling. However, virtual teams may pose more challenges than co-located teams if not managed properly. Figure 6.2 demonstrates some of the differences in challenges experienced in virtual and face-to-face teams. As we can see, respondents perceive that managing the process (i.e., managing conflicts, making decisions and expressing opinions) is more challenging in virtual teams compared to face-to-face teams. However, they perceive that producing the results (i.e., delivering quality output and generating innovative ideas) is not necessarily more challenging in virtual teams.

The following are some guidelines to improve the effectiveness of virtual teams (e.g., Lane et al., 2009, pp. 106–08; Solomon, 2012, pp. 36–9):

• Use technologies that do not cause connection, audio-visual, or other technical problems. Encourage members to get out of the comfort zone (i.e., using the technologies they are familiar with) and upgrade or change technologies to improve the quality of connections among members.

- Avoid scheduling virtual meetings at inconvenient times as much as possible (e.g., extremely early or extremely late in the day). If you have to schedule a meeting in a time that is inconvenient for a particular team member, make sure that the schedule of the next meeting does not inconvenience the same person.
- Organize face-to-face meetings as frequently as required with as much participation as possible. Face-to-face meetings would be necessary at the beginning of teamwork to build cohesion and trust as well as a shared understanding of the goals, tasks, ground rules and norms. It would also be useful to hold face-to-face meetings to review the progress vis-à-vis goals and to discuss conflicts or process problems and inefficiencies surfaced during the teamwork process. Lane and colleagues (2009) call these 'heartbeat meetings' that pump oxygen to the team and bring alignment among team members.
- Get support for the virtual team from management. Make sure that management understands the importance of virtual teams and potential challenges associated with them. It may be necessary to receive training on how to work effectively in virtual teams and how to improve language skills, if necessary.

Chapter Summary

Teamwork is more than a group of individuals collectively working on a task. Teamwork requires interdependence among members and working in synergy so that the outcome is more than the collection of tasks completed by each member. This chapter begins by explaining differences among various types of teams. This is followed by a discussion on criteria for effectiveness in groups and teams, including task-relevant effort of members, task-relevant knowledge of members, complementarity of knowledge, skills and abilities of members and the task-appropriate performance strategies they use. While discussing task-relevant effort of members, we introduce the psychological processes keeping members from putting sufficient effort into teamwork, such as the sucker effect, free-riding and social loafing. Communication networks, when used effectively, are the key to the success of groups and teams. We discuss the degree of centralization in the flow of information, leader emergence potential, member satisfaction and problem-solving efficiency in five types of networks: a star network, Y network, chain network, circle network and completely connected network (Comcon). We introduce feedback as an essential communication skill to facilitate teamwork and presented specific guidelines for providing effective feedback especially in teamwork context. The last section of the chapter is devoted to cross-cultural approaches to teamwork with special focus on multicultural teams. Multicultural teams produce more creative ideas and more alternative solutions to problems; they are less likely to engage in groupthink. We present research findings suggesting that multicultural teams outperform monocultural teams if the conditions are right. Challenges facing multicultural teams are also outlined to raise awareness and to set realistic expectations for those working in or managing multicultural teams. We provide specific guidelines to manage multicultural teams, including suggestions for the design of the team, design of the task, allocation of roles and responsibilities and strategies to strengthen trust and communication networks. The chapter concludes with a discussion on managing virtual teams, which are becoming increasingly common in the global work context.

End of Chapter Reflection Questions

1. Organizations are keen to make the 'business case' for diversity. How would you build a compelling case for diversity other than a business case to convince the stakeholders and shareholders of organizations?
2. Do you think 'being a good team player' would increase the chances of being an effective member of a diverse team? Why, why not?
3. Giving feedback to a team member may hurt the relationship, especially in collectivistic cultures. Based on your personal experiences, how do you think the feedback process should be managed in such circumstances?

Key Terms and Definitions

Group. The social entity composed of two or more individuals coming together to communicate or interact with each other on matters of common interest.

Team. A team is usually smaller than a group, works on more specific tasks than groups and works together in an interdependent way for a shorter period of time than a group.

Sucker effect. A group or team member's feeling that they contribute to the collective process, while other members don't.

Free-rider effect. A group or team member's feeling that they are not compelled to put in the required effort because group objectives can be achieved by the efforts of other members.

Social loafing. The tendency to make less effort in a group environment than in an environment worked alone.

Communication networks. Patterns of information exchange among members in a group or team context.

Feedback. Information given to the group or team member by others about their performance vis-à-vis group objectives.

Group-shared feedback. Feedback to a member that focuses on their behaviour in the group, so that all members have knowledge of it and bring their perspective in the feedback.

Multicultural teams. Teams whose members represent different cultural backgrounds.

Virtual teams. Teams that are not located in the same place; they interact with the help of technology.

Groupthink. Lack of diversity of ideas in the team mainly because of the homogeneity of the member composition.

Self-managed teams. Teams whose members determine and manage their goals, strategies, activities and role assignments on their own.

Further Reading

Cook, S. (2009) *Building a High Performance Team: Proven Techniques for Effective Team Working*. London: IT Governance Publishing.

Davison, S.C. and Ekelund, B.Z. (2004) 'Effective team processes for global teams', in H.W. Lane, M.L. Maznevski, M.E. Mendenhall and J. McNett (eds), *The Blackwell Handbook of Global Management: A Guide to Managing Diversity*, pp. 134–51. Oxford: Blackwell.

Gibson, C.B. and Cohen, S.G. (eds) (2003) *Virtual Teams that Work: Creating Conditions for Virtual Team Effectiveness*. San Francisco, CA: Jossey-Bass.

Kirkman, B.L., Rosen, B., Gibson, C.B., Tesluk, P.E. and McPherson, S.O. (2002) 'Five challenges to virtual team success: Lessons from Sabre, Inc.', *Academy of Management Executive*, 18 (3): 67–72.

West, M. (2012) *Effective Teamwork: Practical Lessons from Organizational Research*. London: BPS Blackwell.

Cases, Videos and Web Sources

Cases

The following cases focus on managing diversity in teams.

Ahmad, S.S., Mishra, S. and Kumar, S. (2013) *Motivated reasoning, leadership and team performance*. IVEY Cases, No: 9B12C010.

Thomas, D.A. and Creary, S.J. (2009) *Meeting the diversity challenge at PepsiCo: The Steve Reinemund Era*. Harvard Business School Case No: 410024.

Videos

Video 6.1 *White men for Diversity: How PwC Spreads Diversity Managing* (2013) www.youtube.com/watch?v=3Q1JepjBaEMandfeature=player_embedded.

Video 6.2 *Accommodating Cultural Diversity* (2011) www.youtube.com/watch?v=_pSEni3LqEY.
Video 6.3 *Understanding and Respecting Others* (2010) www.youtube.com/watch?v= wxWtL48I8n8 – Would you consider using this video as part of the orientation for multi-cultural teamwork? Why and why not?

Web sources

www.diversityinc.com/ – The Diversity Inc. Foundation website.
www.prismdiversity.com/ – Prism International: Connecting Diversity for results.
www. amanet.org/ – American Management Association.
www.diversityicebreaker.com – An excellent way to raise awareness of differences that compliment each other.

References

Adler, N.J. (1997) *International Dimensions of Organizational Behavior*, 3rd edn. Cincinnati, OH: South-Western.

Aycan, Z. (2004) 'Managing inequalities: Leadership and teamwork in developing country context', in H. Lane, M. Mendenhall and M. Maznevski (eds), *International Handbook of Management*, pp. 406–23. New York: Blackwell.

Bavelas, A. (1950) 'Communication patterns in task oriented groups', *Journal of the Acoustical Society of America*, 57: 271–82.

Brett, J., Behfar, K. and Kern, C. (2006) 'Managing multicultural teams', *Harvard Business Review*, 84 (11): 84–91.

Chen, C.C., Chen, X. and Meindl, J.R. (1998) 'How can cooperation be fostered? The cultural effects of individualism-collectivism', *Academy of Management Review*, 23: 285–304.

Cox, T.H. (1993) *Cultural Diversity in Organizations: Theory, Research and Practice*. San Francisco, CA: Berrett-Koehler.

Earley, P.C. (1993) 'East meets Wests meets Mideast: Further explorations of collectivistic and individualistic work groups', *Academy of Management Journal*, 36: 319–48.

Earley, P.C. and Mosakowski, E.M. (2000) 'Creating hybrid team cultures: An empirical test of international team functioning', *Academy of Management Journal*, 43: 26–49.

Elron, E. (1997) 'Top management teams within multinational corporations: Effects of worker heterogeneity', *Leadership Quarterly*, 8 (4): 393–412.

Forsyth, D.R. (1990) *Group Dynamics*, 2nd edn. Pacific Grove, CA: Brooks/Cole.

Gibson, C.B. and Zellmer-Bruhn, M.E. (2001) 'Metaphors and meaning: An intercultural analysis of the meaning of teamwork', *Administrative Science Quarterly*, 46: 274–30.

Gluesing, J.C. and Gibson, C.B. (2004) 'Designing and forming global teams', in H.W. Lane, M.L. Maznevski, M.E. Mendenhall and J. McNett (eds), *Handbook of Global Management*, pp. 199–226. Malden, MA: Blackwell Publishing.

Gomez, C., Kirkman, B.L. and Shapiro, D.L. (2000) 'The impact of collectivism and in-group/out-group membership on the evaluation generosity of team members', *Academy of Management Journal*, 43 (6): 1097–106.

Granell, E. (1997) *Managing Culture for Success: Challenges and Opportunities in Venezuela*. Caracas: Refolit.

Hackman, J.R. and Oldham, G.R. (1980) *Work redesign*. Reading, MA: Addison-Wesley.

Halevy, N. and Sagiv, L. (2008) 'Teams within and across cultures', in M. Peterson, P. Smith and D. Thomas (eds), *Handbook of Cross-cultural Management Research*, pp. 253–68. Thousand Oaks, CA: Sage.

Hanson, P.G. (1975) Giving feedback: An interpersonal skill. In J.E. Jones and J.W. Pfeiffer (eds), *The 1975 Annual Handbook for Group Facilitators*, pp. 147-154. San Diego, CA: University Associates.

Karau, S.J. and Williams, K.D. (1993) 'Social loafing: A meta-analytic review and theoretical integration', *Journal of Personality and Social Psychology*, 65 (4): 681–706.

Kerr, N. and Brunn, S. (1983) 'Dispensability of member effort and group motivation losses: Free rider-effects', *Journal of Personality and Social Psychology*, 44: 78–94.

Kerr, N.L. (1983) 'Motivation losses in small groups: A social dilemma analysis', *Journal of Personality and Social Psychology*, 45: 819–28.

Kirkman, B.L. and Den Hartog, D.N. (2004) 'Team performance management', in H.W. Lane, M.L. Maznevski, M. Mendenhall and J. McNett (eds), *The Blackwell Handbook of Global Management*, pp. 250–72. Malden, MA: Blackwell.

Kirkman, B.L. and Shapiro, D.L. (1997) 'The impact of cultural values on employee resistance to teams: Toward a model of globalised self-managing work team effectiveness', *Academy of Management Review*, 22 (3): 730–57.

Kirkman, B.L. and Shapiro, D.L. (2001) 'The impact of cultural values on job satisfaction and organizational commitment in self-managing work teams: The mediating role of employee resistance', *Academy of Management Journal*, 44 (3): 557–69.

LaFasto, F. and Larson, C. (2001) *When Teams Work Best: 6,000 Team Members and Leaders Tell What it Takes to Succeed*. Thousand Oaks, CA: Sage.

Lane, H., DiStefano, J.J. and Maznevski, M.L. (2006) *International Management Behavior: Text, Readings and Cases*, 5th edn. Oxford: Blackwell.

Lane, H.W., Maznevski, M.L., DiStefano, J. and Dietz, J. (2009) *International Management Behavior: Leading with a Global Mindset*, 6th edn. Oxford: Wiley.

Leavitt, H.J. (1951) 'Some effects of certain communication patterns on group performance', *Journal of Abnormal and Social Psychology*, 46: 38–50.

Mainiero, L.A. and Tromley, C.L. (1994) *Developing Managerial Skills in Organizational Behavior*, 2nd edn. Englewood Cliffs, NJ: Prentice Hall.

Matveev, A.V. and Nelson, P.E. (2004) 'Cross cultural communication competence and multicultural team performance: Perceptions of American and Russian managers', *International Journal of Cross Cultural Management*, 4 (2): 253–70.

Menon, S. (1994) 'Designing work in developing countries', in R.N. Kanungo and M. Mendonça (eds), *Work Motivation: Models for Developing Countries*, pp. 84–114. Thousand Oaks, CA: Sage.

Ng, E.S.W. and Tung, R.L. (1998) 'Ethno-cultural diversity and organizational effectiveness: A field study', *The International Journal of Human Resource Management*, 9: 980–95.

Nicholls, C.E., Lane, H.W. and Brechu, M.B. (1999) 'Taking self-managed teams to Mexico', *Academy of Management Executive*, 13 (3): 15–25.

Orbell, J. and Dawes, R. (1981) 'Social dilemmas' in G. Stephenson and J.H. Davis (eds.), *Progress in Applied Social Psychology*, Vol. 1, pp. 37–65. Chichester, UK: Wiley.

Ozdil, Y. (2009) 'Here you have the globalization!' Hürriyet Newspaper, February 6.

Ramamoorthy, N. and Flood, P. (2002) 'Employee attitudes and behavioral intentions: A test of the main and moderating effects of individualism-collectivism', *Human Relations*, 55 (9): 1071–96.

Schneider, S.C. and Barsoux, J.-L. (2003) *Managing Across Cultures*, 2nd edn. London: Prentice Hall.

Shaw, M.E. (1971) *Group Dynamics: The Psychology of Small Group Behavior.* London: McGraw Hill Publishing.

Solomon, C. (2012) *Virtual Teams Survey Report. The Challenges of Working in Virtual Teams.* New York: RW³ LLC. Retrieved from http://rw-3.com/2012VirtualTeamsSurveyReport.pdf.

Stahl, G.K., Maznevski, M.L., Voigt, A. and Jonsen, K. (2010) 'Unraveling the effects of cultural diversity in teams: A meta-analysis of research on multicultural work groups', *Journal of International Business Studies,* 41: 690–709.

Thomas, D.C. (1999) 'Cultural diversity and work group effectiveness: An experimental study', *Journal of Cross-cultural Psychology,* 30 (2): 242–63.

Thomas, D.C. (2002) *Essentials of International Management: A Cross-cultural Perspective.* Thousand Oaks, CA: Sage.

Thomas, D.C., Ravlin, E.C. and Barry, D. (2000) Creating effective multicultural teams. *University of Auckland Business Review,* 2 (1): 10–25.

Thomas, D.C., Ravlin E.C. and Wallace, A.W. (1996) 'Effect of cultural diversity in work groups', *Research in the Sociology of Organizations,* 14: 1–33.

Townsend, A.M., DeMarie, S.M. and Hendrickson, A.R. (1998) 'Virtual teams: Technology and the workplace of the future', *Academy of Management Executive,* 12 (3): 17–29.

Von Glinow, M.A., Shapiro, D.L. and Brett, J.M. (2004) 'Can we talk and should we? Managers' emotional conflict in multicultural teams', *Academy of Management Review,* 29 (4): 578–92.

Watson, W., Johnson, L. and Merritt, D. (1998) 'Team orientation, self-orientation and diversity in task groups: Their connection to team performance over time', *Group and Organization Management,* 23 (2): 161–88.

Watson, W.E., Kumar, K. and Michaelsen, L.K. (1993) 'Cultural diversity's impact on interaction process and performance: comparing homogeneous and diverse task groups', *Academy of Management Journal,* 36: 590–602.

Want to learn more? Visit the companion website at www.sagepub.co.uk/kanungo to gain access to videos from the end of each chapter, weblinks and flash cards of key terms.

7

Organizational Attitudes and Work–Life Balance

Chapter Outline

Tarun Chopra came to the United Kingdom after finishing high school in India when his parents migrated there. After finishing his engineering education in computer science, he joined the product development department of a reputed IT company in London, in the year 2010 during the high-tech boom. Soon after, he married Monika, the daughter of his father's friend from India.

He earns a decent salary and lives comfortably in a London suburb with his wife and four-year-old son. In his job Tarun has to work for long hours. He loves his job and he is fully committed to it, which constantly prevents him from fulfilling his family commitments. On many occasions, he needed to sleep in his office rather than going home late and coming back to the office early in the morning. Monika often complains about Tarun's mental and physical absenteeism at home. Even when he is at home his work causes him to keep busy with his laptop, or he will be on the phone discussing work matters with co-workers. Monika also complains that Tarun spends very little time with his son and that he has never taken a vacation with his family. Tarun always justifies his behaviour by telling Monika that his company expects him to work long hours and to be always available whenever the work demands it. Lately, the situation got worsened and Monica's complaints have become louder and more frequent. As a result, Tarun is seriously exploring the best options to respond to this situation.

During a lunch-hour conversation with one of his friends, Tarun came to realize that organizations in the IT industry are becoming aware that more and more workers are considering work–life balance as a priority. With the increase in work demands, workers are looking for ways to cope with the demands of the workplace and of the family. His friend suggested that he might want to take a look at AT–XCL Technologies, which offers policies and programmes to encourage and enable employees to blend their professional and personal lives. For instance, it provides on-site childcare and emergency childcare assistance, flexible work arrangements to allow telecommuting, family leave policies, fitness facilities and seminars and workshops about health and wellness for the entire family.

Tarun took his friend's advice and applied for a position at AT-XCL Technologies. During the two hour interview with a manager of the company, he was grilled on a number of work-related issues. At the end, the manager asked if Tarun had any questions. Tarun replied: 'There is just one priority concern – my wife and my four-year-old son; I have to meet my family obligations in order to make my life work. I need your assurance that the company will help me meet this priority.' The manager addressed Tarun's concern by saying 'In this company, as long as the work gets done on time, management lets employees figure out their schedules. We are interested in fostering a work–life balance for our employees and, for this purpose, have included it in our company's operating framework.' After discussing some details of the company's policies on how to achieve work–life balance with the manager, Tarun decided to join the company.

Is Tarun's love for his current job and commitment to his company sufficient for a 'balanced' life? Would Tarun be more or less committed to his new employer, AT-XCL Technologies given that the organization supports flexible work arrangements? Is Tarun's and his wife's desire to balance work and life driven from their cultural background or is this a desire shared 'universally' in modern societies? In this chapter we explore some of these questions.

In this chapter, we first examine the **employee attitudes at work**, including job satisfaction, organizational commitment, organizational citizenship behaviour and organizational justice perception. We examine these topics from cross-cultural lenses and highlight universally shared patterns as well as culture-specific ones. We then discuss the phenomenon of worker alienation and involvement through Kanungo's Model of Work Involvement and Alienation. This is important to managers, because the effectiveness of their work unit is greatly affected by the extent to which their employees are involved in their work. The final discussion topic in this chapter is work–life balance. We present evidence suggesting that work, family and personal life interact in such a way that they can both harm and enhance each other, along with a summary of recent research in this area as well as policies and practices of organizations helping employees in their quest to have a more balanced life.

Learning Objectives

- To recognize the importance of positive employee attitudes for organizations.
- To review research findings pertaining to the antecedents and consequences of job satisfaction, organizational commitment, organizational citizenship behaviour, organizational justice perception and work alienation and involvement.
- To appreciate cross-cultural similarities and differences in the factors associated with positive and negative organizational attitudes.
- To familiarize the reader with concepts including work–family conflict, positive work–family spillover and life balance.
- To study cross-cultural similarities and differences in the prevalence of positive and negative work–family interface and coping strategies.
- To review organizational policies and practices to foster life balance and examine their usefulness.

Organizational Attitudes

An attitude is an evaluative tendency to respond to some specific object, situation, person, or category of people (e.g., Eagly and Chaiken, 1998). From this definition, we can see that the individual's belief and values forms the attitude which is likely to lead to behaviour towards an object, situation, or person. Clearly, attitudes relating to job satisfaction, organizational commitment, organizational citizenship behaviour and organizational justice perception can have a critical effect, positive (work involvement) and negative (work alienation), on employee performance and work behaviour.

Before discussing organizational attitudes in detail, let us first focus on the magnitude of the effect of employees' attitudes towards their organization on organizational outcomes. The attitude–performance link has been studied extensively in the literature. One of the meta-analytic studies investigating the causal relationship between organizational attitudes and performance of employees showed that employee attitudes (especially job satisfaction and organizational commitment) had a weak but significant impact on job performance (Riketta, 2008). The same study showed that there was no evidence for reverse causality (i.e., job performance impacting organizational attitudes). If an employee's positive attitude towards their organization makes a marginal contribution to their job performance, why should we be concerned with positive employee attitudes?

The answer is 'because it makes an important contribution to performance at the business unit level'. Recent research showed that the relationship between employee attitudes and performance is higher at the organizational level than at the individual level. According to a meta-analysis based on 7,939 business units in 36 companies (Harter et al., 2002), overall **job satisfaction** and work engagement of employees were associated with customer loyalty-satisfaction (0.32 and 0.33, respectively), employee turnover (–0.36 and –0.30), safety breaches (–0.20 and –0.32), productivity (0.20 and 0.25) and profitability (0.15 and 0.17) of the business unit. The correlation of job satisfaction with the composite business unit performance was 0.37, the correlation of employee engagement with the same was 0.38.

Remember that we spend one-third of our lives working! Feeling good about our work and the organization we work for are undoubtedly important for our psychological well-being and self-fulfilment. However, research shows that this is also important for organizations and the customers they serve. Let us now turn to each of the positive employee attitudes and discuss them in more detail.

Job satisfaction

Job satisfaction refers to a collection of attitudes that people have about their jobs – more specifically, in relation to the content and context of the job (e.g., Spector, 1997). Job content includes challenging assignments and opportunities for growth, whereas job context includes compensation and benefits, co-workers and supervisors, working climate and so on.

What are the factors which contribute to job satisfaction? Clearly, the individual's beliefs and values play a critical role in our understanding of the notion of job satisfaction, which can be viewed in two ways. First, satisfaction derives from receiving what one *desires* (i.e., values). For example, individuals experience job satisfaction when the job content offers challenging assignments and opportunities for growth that they desire and seek. As discussed in Chapter 2, these individuals have a high need to satisfy personal and professional growth at work.

Second, job satisfaction derives from receiving what one *perceives should be received* (i.e., beliefs and expectations). For example, individuals experience job satisfaction when the compensation they receive is fair – that is, equitable. As discussed in Chapter 2, the employee compares their perceived ratio of outcomes to inputs with their perceived ratio of the relevant other's outcomes to inputs. If the comparison reveals that the ratios are equal then the employee experiences satisfaction; if the ratios are unequal, then the employee experiences dissatisfaction.

What are the consequences of job satisfaction? They include the employee's involvement in work, which results in reduced absenteeism, reduced turnover and enhanced job performance. Hence job satisfaction leading to workers' involvement in their jobs significantly contributes to organizational effectiveness (e.g., Elias and Mittal, 2011; Judge et al., 2001).

Organizational commitment

Organizational commitment is an attitude that reflects the strength of the linkage between an employee and an organization. It moves beyond passive loyalty to an organization and is the result of a strong belief in an organization's goals and values, a willingness to exert considerable effort for the organization and a strong desire to maintain membership in the organization (e.g., Mowday et al., 1979).

Several meta-analyses found significant relationships of affective commitment with low employee turnover, low absenteeism, high job performance, low incidences of counterproductive work behaviour (e.g., theft, sabotage, vandalism) and an organization's ability to attract, retain and motivate key talent (e.g., Cooper-Hakim and Viswesvaran, 2005; Luchak and Gellatly, 2007; Michaels et al., 2001; Riketta, 2008).

Factors that contribute to organizational commitment have been summarized in a recent meta-analytical review of longitudinal research (Morrow, 2011). The review suggested that drivers of commitment ranged from individual factors (e.g., propensity to commitment, proactive personality, collectivistic values) to interpersonal (e.g., leadership, co-workers' support, mentoring) and organizational factors (e.g., training, group-based bonuses, involvement in HRM decision-making).

Organizational citizenship behaviour

Organizational citizenship behaviour (OCB) is entirely voluntary and spontaneous behaviour that goes beyond the call of duty to provide assistance, support and cooperation to address the unexpected needs of a colleague and to cope with the frustrations that are inevitable in organizational life (e.g., Organ, 1997). It entails employee behaviours such as altruism (e.g., helping voluntarily to others in need), conscientiousness (e.g., working hard and being reliable), sportsmanship (e.g., not complaining about trivial matters), courtesy (e.g., consulting with others before taking action) and civic virtue (e.g., keeping up with matters that affect the organization) (Organ, 1997).

The meta-analysis of LePine et al. (2002) showed that OCB was positively associated with other employee attitudes, including job satisfaction, organizational commitment and perception of fairness. They also found that personality (i.e., conscientiousness) and leadership support were correlated significantly with OCB. In another meta-analysis OCB was found to be negatively associated with role stressors, including conflict, ambiguity and overload in employees' roles in organizations (Eatough et al., 2011).

What are the consequences of organizational citizenship behaviour? Recent findings suggest a moderate correlation between OCB and performance at the team or business unit level (LePine et al., 2008). In organizations – in particular, in the large organizations – there is the likelihood of units/departments becoming more political than rational due to factors such as scarce and limited resources and organizational change brought about by a turbulent external environment. Organizational citizenship behaviour can greatly help to moderate the conflicting situations that are inevitable in these conditions because it is conducive to a culture of teamwork and an attitude of placing the 'interest of others before self'.

Organizational justice perception

Employees' **perception of organizational justice** mainly concerns the following types of justice (Colquitt, 2001):

- ***Distributive justice***: Perception of justice concerning distribution of resources. An employee perceives the outcomes they receive are fair if the ratio of the employee's outcomes (such as pay or status) to inputs (such as effort or time) are equal to the ratio of outcomes to inputs of the comparable other in the workplace.
- ***Procedural justice***: Perception of justice concerning the procedures in the organization. An employee perceives justice if the decision-making procedures are applied consistently across people and across time, free from bias and based on accurate information.
- *Interactional justice*: Perception of justice reflecting the quality of interpersonal treatment during the implementation of formal procedures of decisions.

As is the case in other employee attitudes, justice perception is influenced by both individual (e.g., demographic characteristics and personality traits such as negative affectivity) and organizational factors (e.g., transparency of rules and procedures, quality and frequency of communication with employees, assignment of valued outcomes) (Cohen-Charash and Spector, 2001).

Consequences of justice perception are also similar to those of job satisfaction, commitment and OCB. Employee perception of organizational justice strongly affects the attitude of workers, such as job satisfaction, turnover intentions, organizational commitment and absenteeism and organizational citizenship behaviour (Colquitt et al., 2001). Perceived organizational justice is also found to be an important antecedent of organizational citizenship behaviour (Bakhshi et al., 2009). In addition, research has also demonstrated the linkages between perceived organizational justice and individual work performance (Colquitt et al., 2001, Earley and Lind, 1987).

Involvement and alienation

The traditional approach to involvement and alienation was reinforced by two basic assumptions which characterized the writings of sociologists and psychologists, Karl

Marx and Abraham Maslow. The first assumption is that 'work is central to life'; through work alone individuals can realize the essence of their nature, i.e. self-actualization. The second is that 'growth needs are central to human development'. These assumptions explain why the traditional approach focused on involvement and alienation almost exclusively in the work context. According to the traditional approach, involvement in the work context is defined in two ways: (a) as a psychological identification with work; and (b) as performance → self-esteem contingency (i.e., one's self-esteem is enhanced by one's work).

In his critical review of the sociological and psychological literature on the subject, Kanungo (1990) has identified several limitations of the traditional approach to work involvement, such as the lack of empirical support for the universality of its assumptions (i.e., work is centrality in one's life and growth needs are central in one's work) and its neglect of contexts other than work.

According to the Kanungo model, involvement and alienation are cognitive beliefs about one's self-image in relation to a specific context. **Involvement** is related to the extent to which one identifies oneself with the context. For example, if a person is highly involved in the family context then that person will identify with the family context. Such identification makes that person think of themself as a 'family' person. Similarly, if a person is highly involved in the work context, then they will identify themself with the role in the work context, such as a machinist, bookkeeper, manager, lawyer, or doctor. The Kanungo Model defines job involvement as a cognitive state of identification, with the job based on its need-satisfying potential. This conceptualization is consistent with the expectancy theory of work motivation discussed in Chapter 2. **Alienation**, on the other hand, is the cognitive state of separation from a context. Thus, the Kanungo model defines *involvement* as the extent to which one psychologically identifies oneself with a context; and *alienation* as the extent to which one separates oneself from a context.

Involvement or its opposite, alienation, in a given context develops as a result of two factors. One is the need saliency or the perceived importance of needs in a given context. For example, an individual's belongingness need might be more salient in the family context, whereas their achievement need might be more salient in the work context. The sources of saliency or importance of certain needs in a given context are based on (1) our past socialization and (2) our current assessment of the context, our preset perceptions of the potential of the context for satisfaction of these salient needs. The other factor which determines involvement or alienation is the perceived potential of the context to satisfy the salient needs and expectations in the future.

Unlike the traditional approach, the Kanungo Model acknowledges that involvement and alienation can occur in different life domains (especially work and family) independent from one another.

Thinking across cultures 7.1

Involvement and Alienation in Multiple Life Domains

Below are a number of statements regarding the value one attaches to work and family as two distinct features of our lives. In these statements, work refers to work in general and not any specific job. Likewise family refers to family in general and not any specific family type.

  Please read each statement carefully and indicate your response to the statement by circling the appropriate number on the seven point scale.

1 (a) The most important things that happen in life involve the family.

   A great deal 7 6 5 4 3 2 1   Very little

  (b) The most important things that happen in life involve work.

   A great deal 7 6 5 4 3 2 1   Very little

2 (a) People should get involved in the family.

   Most of the time   7 6 5 4 3 2 1   Very little

  (b) People should get involved in work.

   Most of the time   7 6 5 4 3 2 1   Very little

3 (a) The family should be

   A large part of one's life   7 6 5 4 3 2 1   A small part of one's life

  (b) Work should be

   A large part of one's life   7 6 5 4 3 2 1   A small part of one's life

4 (a) The family should be considered as

   Most central to one's life   7 6 5 4 3 2 1   Least central to one's life

  (b) Work should be considered as

   Most central to one's life   7 6 5 4 3 2 1   Least central to one's life

5 (a) An individual's life goals should be

   Mainly family-oriented   7 6 5 4 3 2 1   Slightly family-oriented

(Continued)

(Continued)

 (b)   An individual's life goals should be

        Mainly work oriented   7 6 5 4 3 2 1   Slightly work oriented

6 (a)   Life is worth living only when people get

        Totally absorbed in family life   7 6 5 4 3 2 1   Slightly absorbed in family life

 (b)   Life is worth living only when people get

        Totally absorbed in work life   7 6 5 4 3 2 1   Slightly absorbed in work life

Scoring

Calculate your family involvement score by adding the numbers you circled for all statements starting with (a); calculate your work involvement score by adding the numbers you circled for all statements starting with (b).

42–29: high involvement; 28–19: medium involvement; 18–6: low involvement

- Compare your family and work involvement scores with two of your colleagues. What are the reasons for similarities and differences among you?
- To what extent do you think the similarities and differences among your colleagues can be attributed to differences in gender, age, marital status, ethnic or cultural background, work experience and so on?

Cross-cultural Perspectives to Organizational Attitudes

Let us discuss cross-cultural similarities and differences in the employee experiences of organizational attitudes in the areas of job satisfaction, organizational commitment, organizational citizenship behaviour and justice perception. In this section we summarize the key findings based on recent reviews of the literature (i.e., Aycan and Gelfand, 2012; Gelfand et al., 2007). Please be reminded that cross-cultural issues in job satisfaction and organizational justice are also discussed in Chapter 2. Cross-cultural perspectives on involvement and alienation will be highlighted in the next section on work–life balance.

CASE 7.1

China's Disengaged Workforce

China will become the global economic leader sometime in the next 10 to 25 years, according to many economists. This means China – and not the United States – will have the largest GDP in the world, which will, of course, be a global game-changer. She who has the gold makes the geopolitical rules. But China faces some serious challenges on its road to dominance. Some obvious ones:

- Enormous environmental problems that will require billions of dollars to fix.
- The family planning policy, which will create a scenario of far too few workers supporting far too many retirees.
- Economic uncertainty, if China's GDP – increasing at more than 8 percent – continues to grow at a decreasing rate.
- Rising factory wages, which may cause China to lose its huge competitive advantage over other countries, some that may offer labor at a lower cost.

To this list of well-known woes and concerns, let me add one you probably don't know, but which is perhaps the most serious of all: low workforce engagement.

I know that sounds soft at first, but human beings spend at least one-third of their lives at work and because of this, one could argue that a person's quality of life is driven by their life at work. And the working citizens of China are doing horribly.

Barely 6 percent of the people who work for an organization report being engaged at their jobs. In addition, about 26 percent are flat-out miserable – what Gallup researchers call actively disengaged. To put that into perspective, the US workforce is about 30 percent engaged and 20 percent actively disengaged.

If you were to ask me what the most dangerous state of mind in China is right now, I'd say it's this active disengagement in the workplace, because it is so widespread.

The cause of this disengagement is the same in China as it is in every workplace around the world: the workers despise their immediate boss. And the reason they hate their boss is because the wrong person was hired to be boss. It is really that simple.

(Continued)

(Continued)

How does this happen? Well, I know just enough about the Chinese workplace to know that control is of huge cultural importance. The type of people who are named boss in China command and control their 'underlings', and those underlings do as they're told. People are not named manager for their ability to develop and engage employees.

But this command-and-control approach doesn't work in the new global workplace, where employees demand more autonomy, want more freedom of thought and action and desire to be more empowered and engaged.

Old top-down management, the type that's entrenched in China, just doesn't work anymore. Plus, increasing globalization and access to media gives more workers in China a look at what life is like in other places. This, no doubt, creates a dangerous gap between their world and what they see is happening outside of their country ... China's national workforce will be transformed – becoming highly productive and engaged – when its organizations hire and develop managers who inspire employees.

Source: Excerpt from Clifton (2013, p. 17).

- How do you think Chinese employees' disengagement in their work is associated with their job satisfaction, organizational commitment, organizational citizenship behaviour, justice perception and work alienation?
- What would your advice be to the local Chinese and expatriate managers working in China to increase **employee engagement** and positive organizational attitudes?

Job Satisfaction

- Employee-related factors such as positive self-concept and internal locus of control (i.e., belief that what happens in life is controlled by the individual, rather than external forces, such as fate) are associated with higher job satisfaction across a wide range of cultures (Piccolo et al., 2005; Spector et al., 2002).
- Extrinsic job characteristics (e.g., pay, benefits) are associated with job satisfaction across cultures, but intrinsic job characteristics (e.g., opportunity to learn and grow) are more strongly associated with job satisfaction in economically developed and individualistic countries than in economically developing and collectivistic ones (Huang and Van de Vliert, 2003; Hui et al., 2004).

- Satisfaction is positively related to self-referent performance motives (e.g., motivation to demonstrate mastery and improvement in challenging situations) and negatively related to other-referent performance motives (e.g., motivation to demonstrate superiority to others). This pattern is stronger in economically developed countries (Van de Vliert and Janssen, 2002).
- Job level is related to job satisfaction in individualistic compared to collectivistic cultures. In collectivistic cultures employees in high-level jobs are dissatisfied if they feel underemployed (Huang and Van de Vliert, 2004).
- Work environments with warm interpersonal relationships facilitate job satisfaction among employees with a collectivistic orientation, but low satisfaction among those with an individualistic orientation in China (Hui and Yee, 1999).
- The negative relationship between job satisfaction and withdrawal from work (e.g., absenteeism and turnover) is stronger in individualistic compared to collectivistic cultures (Posthuma et al., 2005; Ramesh and Gelfand, 2010; Thomas and Au, 2002).

Organizational Commitment

- In a meta-analysis, normative commitment was found to be more strongly associated with perceived organizational support and less strongly associated with employee demographics (e.g., age, education, tenure) in studies conducted non-US sample, compared to those with US samples (Meyer et al., 2002).
- In the same meta-analysis commitment was found to be negatively associated with job-related factors such as role conflict and role ambiguity within the US compared to other countries.
- Satisfaction with work and promotions were the strongest predictors of organizational commitment among individualists, whereas satisfaction with supervisors was an important predictor among collectivists (Wasti, 2003).
- Material job values (e.g., job quality, autonomy at work) are more predictive of organizational commitment in individualistic societies whereas post-materialistic job values (e.g., helping others, meaningful work) are more predictive of organizational commitment in collectivistic societies (Andolšek and Stebe, 2004).
- Opinions of in-group members (e.g., family, close friends) about the organization are strongly related to continuance commitment, particularly among those with collectivistic values (Wasti, 1999).
- In a meta-analytical review (Jaramillo et al., 2005) organizational commitment was shown to be a stronger correlate of job performance in nations scoring high on collectivism than those high on individualism.
- In another meta-analysis, job outcomes (e.g., withdrawal, performance, extra-role behaviour) were associated with affective commitment in studies with US samples,

whereas they were associated with normative commitment in studies with non-US samples (Meyer et al., 2002).

- Power distance was positively associated with commitment to the organization, supervisor and work group (Clugston et al., 2000).

Organizational Citizenship Behaviour

- OCB as the extra-role employee behaviour was found to include other indicators in addition to altruism, conscientiousness, civic virtue, courtesy and sportsmanship in different cultural contexts. For example 'interpersonal harmony' and 'protecting company resources' are cited as important OCB dimensions in Taiwan (Farh, Earley and Lin, 1997). Furthermore, some dimensions of OCB (e.g., courtesy, sportsmanship) are considered to be in-group behaviours in Japan and Hong Kong (Podsakoff et al., 1990).
- In a recent investigation of employee motives for engaging in OCB Dávila de León and Finkelstein (2011) found that those with high collectivistic values engage in OCB out of concern for the organization (pride in and positive affect toward the organization) and prosocial concern (desire to help others and to be accepted by others). Those high on individualistic values engage in OCB out of concern for impression management (desire to maintain a positive image and avoid negative impressions, so that one receives special benefits in the organization).
- In individualistic team cultures *directive leadership* was more negatively and *supportive leadership* was less positively associated with OCB at the group level, compared to collectivistic ones (Euwema et al., 2007).
- In an in-depth investigation of Chinese employees and managers, ten OCB behaviours at four levels (societal, organizational, group, and individual) were identified (Figure 7.1.) (Farh et al., 2004).
- A meta-analysis by Meyer et al. (2002) found that normative commitment was more strongly associated with OCBs in non-Western contexts compared to Western ones.
- Compared to other organizational attitudes, commitment to one's *supervisor* is a more powerful predictor of OCBs in Chinese organizations (Cheng et al., 2003).

Organizational Justice Perception

- Do employees perceive equity or equality as the fair method of reward allocation? In a meta-analytic study, the equity principle was found to be preferred in reward distribution by those high on individualistic value, whereas the equality principle was favoured by those high on collectivistic values, especially when it is applied to in-group members (Sama and Papamarcos, 2000).

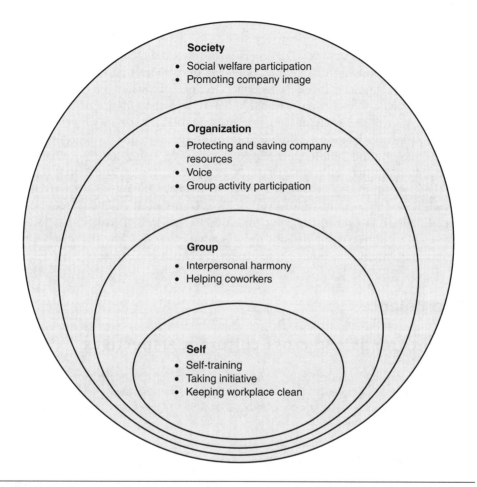

Figure 7.1 *Organizational citizenship behaviour in China (Farh, Zhong and Organ, 2004, p. 250)*

However, later meta-analytic review found no relationship of equity-equality preference to individualism and collectivism (Fischer and Smith, 2003). Scholars explained this discrepancy among findings through the role of the 'reward allocator': if the reward allocator was also the reward recipient, the above-cited individualism-collectivism effects of preference for equality with in-groups and equity with out-groups is expected (e.g., Leung, 1997).

- Employees in high power-distance cultures preferred equity over equality (Fischer and Smith, 2003).
- In a recent meta-analysis Fischer (2013) examined the relationship of organizational justice perception with job satisfaction, organizational citizenship behaviour

and withdrawal. The associations of justice with other attitudes were stronger in countries of high income inequality and collectivism. Power distance also intensified the relationship between interpersonal justice and OCB. It was concluded that fairness is important in all cultural contexts, but its effect gets stronger especially when there is greater income inequality, leaders and institutions are expected to foster loyalty and individuals strongly identify with their in-groups (p. 25).

- Is distributive or procedural justice more important for employees' sense of fairness in organizations? The literature presents no pattern suggesting systematic cross-cultural differences. While distributive justice had dominance over procedural justice in countries such as Taiwan, Hong Kong and India, the reverse was the case in countries such as Korea, China and Russia (e.g., Fahr et al., 1997; Pillai et al., 2001; Yoon, 1996; Leung et al., 1996; Giacobbe-Miller et al., 1998). However, the joint effect of both types of justice was such that procedural justice compensated the negative effects of low distributive justice especially in collectivistic cultures (e.g., Brockner et al., 2000).

Work–Life Balance

Current trends and cross-cultural perspectives

We want work–life balance, we encourage people to have work–life balance, but finally it is the attitudes of the employers, it is the attitudes of the individuals who are pursuing their careers, it is a social norm, everybody is working, so I feel I have to work long hours too and so we are stuck in that position.

So first work–life balance, I think we need to do more to promote flexible work arrangements and we can help to help employers to go in this direction.

We also have to improve work culture and employer attitudes so that you have certain new norms which are set and maybe we should take seriously the idea of having one day a week when you close shop at six o'clock and if you are seen in the office after that, then that is a minus for promotion purposes!

Source: Loong, 2012

Work–life balance is at the top of the agenda of leaders in business and politics. World leaders realize that lack of work–life balance is not only a threat to individual and organizational well-being, but it is also harmful for societies at large. Singapore's Prime Minister Mr. Loong, for example, attributed alarmingly low birth rates to families' difficulties balancing work and family responsibilities.

There are numerous studies showing substantial correlation of work–life imbalance to employees' health problems (psychological and physiological) as well as organizations' challenge in attracting, keeping and motivating talent (e.g., Amstad et al., 2011; Shockley and Singla, 2011).

Work–life imbalance is generally confined to work and family domains and referred to as **work–family conflict** (WFC). Work–family conflict is defined as an 'interrole conflict' experienced by individuals having difficulties in fulfilling responsibilities in one domain of life (e.g., family) because of the role pressures in the other domain of life (e.g., work) (Greenhaus and Beutell, 1985).

Remember the case of Tarun at the beginning of this chapter; he and his wife were complaining about him spending too much time at work and consequently not being able to fulfil his family responsibilities. He was experiencing work–family conflict. In his case, work was interfering with family (WIF). Consider the case of Allen taking care of his ageing parents, who are also cancer patients. Allen takes his parents to hospital every week for treatment; he also needs to take them to the nearby clinic for blood tests in the morning of every other day. Because of the time and stress demands in his family, he finds it very difficult to catch up with work and meet performance expectations of his team. In Allen's case family was interfering with work (FIW).

Let us go back to Tarun's case and ponder on the 'causes' and 'consequences' of his work–family conflict. What do you think are some of the key factors leading to work–family conflict? In a recent meta-analytical summary of the literature accumulated over several decades, the following are found to be associated with high levels of WIF and FIW (Michel et al., 2011).

"It's important to live a balanced life:
8 hours for sleeping, 8 hours for working
and 8 hours for working harder!"

Cartoon 7.1 Life balance from the manager's perspective. Copyright © Randy Glasbergen

- Job stressors are the strongest predictors of WIF. Job stressors associated with WIF the most to the least are work role overload (i.e., having more work than one thinks one can handle), work role conflict (i.e., having conflicting demands in work) and work role ambiguity (i.e., having uncertainties in work) respectively.
- Work characteristics mildly associated with WIF are task variety, lack of job autonomy and family-unfriendly organizational culture.
- Low social support at work and in the family (i.e., organizational, supervisory, co-worker, family and spousal support) is moderately associated with WIF and FIW.
- Family stressors (i.e., family role overload, conflict and ambiguity) are the strongest predictors of FIW. Number of children or dependents had a mild association with FIW.
- Negative affectivity, neuroticism and external locus of control (belief that what happens in life is controlled by external forces such as fate, rather than by the individual) as personality characteristics are associated with both WIF and FIW.
- The relationship of job and family stressors with WFC is weaker for those who are female, married, or having children:

  It seems that incorporating additional roles into one's life (e.g., marital roles, parental roles) and thus increasing self-complexity, may provide a protective buffer for role stressors' negative influence on work–family conflict … having high self-complexity (i.e., more roles) prevents stressors or stressful events from one domain spreading or spilling over into other self-aspects or roles; thus protecting the overall positive self-view of the individual. (Michel et al., 2011, p. 710)

Let us now turn to the consequences of WFC. Meta-analytical summaries of research findings allude to the following robust findings regarding health and performance outcomes associated with WIF and FIW (Amstad et al., 2011).

- WIF and FIW are strongly associated with low levels of organizational citizenship behaviour and high levels of work-related stress and burnout/exhaustion. They are moderately associated with low levels of job satisfaction and organizational commitment and intention to quit one's job. They are mildly associated with work-related performance; FIW's correlation with performance is higher than that of WIF's.
- WIF and FIW are moderately associated with family-related stress and low levels of marital satisfaction.
- WIF is correlated strongly with psychological stress, moderately correlated with low levels of life satisfaction, high levels of health and psychosomatic problems, depressive symptoms and anxiety. It has low but significant correlation with substance abuse. FIW's correlation with the health-related outcomes is lower than WIF's correlation with the same.

Decades of research show that stressors in the work and family domains (especially the feeling of overload, which is the perception that one has too much to handle) increase the likelihood of work–family conflict. Social support and personality characteristics help employees buffer the negative effects of WFC. Research also shows that WFC is a serious health hazard; it is associated with high levels of psychological stress and health problems caused by stress. WFC has negative consequences also for work-related outcomes because it is associated with stress and burnout at work, negative attitudes towards organization (especially low OCB, job satisfaction, intention to remain in the organization) and low job performance.

It is important to note that gender differences in the level of WFC are usually found not to be significant, but the association of WFC with the antecedents and outcomes tend to be significant across genders (e.g., Aycan and Eskin, 2005; Duxbury and Higgins, 1991; McElwain et al., 2005).

How about cross-cultural differences? Do cultural values have an impact on the ways in which the work and family interface is experienced? According to research findings the answer seems to be yes. Work and family domains are perceived to be segmented in the US, but integrated in China (Yang, 2005). Because of the perception of segmentation, work and family roles are considered to be incompatible, rather than congruent. Role incompatibility leads to experiences of conflict (e.g., US), whereas role integration leads to experiences of balance (e.g., Hong Kong) (Joplin et al., 2003).

Thinking across cultures 7.2

Work and Family Across Cultures

'Work and family – almost a conflict in terms' (Australian woman)

'Work and family: salt and pepper of life' (Taiwanese woman)

'I work for my own personal well-being. I cannot waste my years of education' (American woman)

'My family is my priority; I do everything for them – I work like crazy so that they don't have to go through the difficulties that I have gone through in life' (Chinese man)

'I come back tired from work and my neighbours come in to drink coffee and to check how I manage my home duties' (Arab woman)

(Continued)

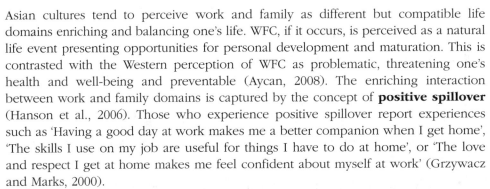

(Continued)

'My mother-in-law said when we had our first child, "Do the tigers give their babies to the elephants to get raised? Do the elephants ever give their babies to the lions to get raised?" I thought "Oh gosh, I better stay at home with my own kids"' (American woman; from Joplin et al., 2003, p.322)

'My mother-in-law almost got fainted when I told her that I wanted to give my child to daycare. She took it as the biggest insult to herself' (Turkish woman)

Source: Aycan (2008, p. 359)

- The above interview excerpts are from cross-cultural research on the work–family interface. What do you think are the cultural and non-cultural factors (e.g., age, gender, education of respondents, or industrial development and job market conditions of countries) influencing differences in experiences expressed in these quotations?

Asian cultures tend to perceive work and family as different but compatible life domains enriching and balancing one's life. WFC, if it occurs, is perceived as a natural life event presenting opportunities for personal development and maturation. This is contrasted with the Western perception of WFC as problematic, threatening one's health and well-being and preventable (Aycan, 2008). The enriching interaction between work and family domains is captured by the concept of **positive spillover** (Hanson et al., 2006). Those who experience positive spillover report experiences such as 'Having a good day at work makes me a better companion when I get home', 'The skills I use on my job are useful for things I have to do at home', or 'The love and respect I get at home makes me feel confident about myself at work' (Grzywacz and Marks, 2000).

One of the most comprehensive cross-cultural projects on work–family conflict is Project 3535, initiated and coordinated by the first author of this book. It includes ten countries (http://www.workfamilyconflict.ca). According to the preliminary findings of the project there are cross-cultural differences in the way work and family interaction is experienced (Figure 7.2). In economically developing and collectivistic countries (e.g., Indonesia, Turkey, India) positive spillover is experienced to a greater extent than in economically developed and individualistic countries (e.g., Australia, US, Canada). Furthermore, the former group of countries report having higher or equal

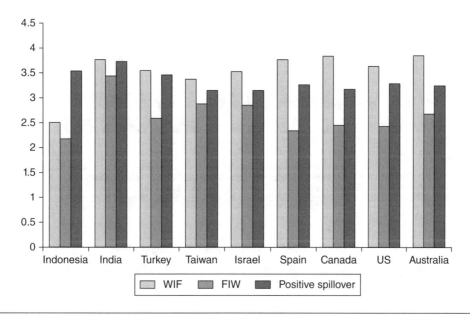

Figure 7.2 *Experiences of positive and negative spillover between work and family across cultures (scores out of 5 points) (Aycan, 2012)*

levels of positive spillover as negative spillover (WIF or FIW), whereas the latter group of countries report having less positive spillover than WIF. Notwithstanding these differences, the so-called 'universal' trend appears to be that WIF is experienced more than FIW (see also Spector et al., 2007).

There are also cross-cultural differences in the ways employees cope with work and family demands and leverage organizational policies and practices to improve their work–family balance. Based on the Project 3535 data set, Somech, and colleagues (2013) showed that employees in individualistic cultures with egalitarian gender role ideologies (i.e., Australia, Canada, USA, Spain) have different coping strategies than those in collectivistic cultures with traditional gender role ideologies (i.e., China, India, Indonesia, Turkey). Employees in the former group of countries use a delegation strategy at work and at home the most and to a greater extent than those in the latter group of countries. They also settle with doing things just good enough, especially at home (Figure 7.3).

On the other hand, employees of collectivistic cultures with traditional gender role ideologies adopt a perfectionist strategy, both at work and at home, to keep the balance in their life (i.e., they insist on doing, on their own, all duties perfectly from the least important to the most important). They use this strategy to a greater extent than employees in individualistic cultures with egalitarian gender role ideologies. They also

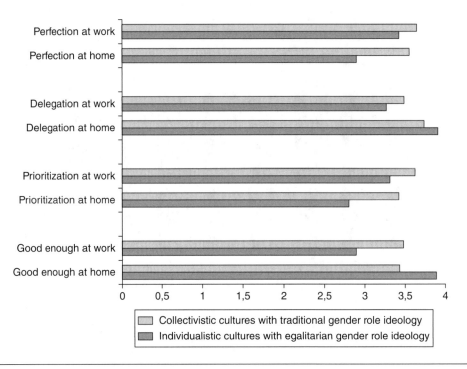

Figure 7.3   *Cross-cultural differences in the use of coping strategies to balance work and family (scores out of 5 points) (Somech et al., 2013)*

use prioritization strategy more than employees in individualistic cultures with egalitarian gender role ideologies.

Cross-cultural differences exist not only in regards to how employees handle demands, but also what kind of support mechanisms they use. In Thinking across cultures 7.3 we present the case of China, where grandparents (or other members of the extended family) are an important source of childcare support to dual-earner families. In addition to informal social networks, organizational policies and practices help employees to balance their work and family lives. Included in the organizational practices enhancing work–life balance are flexible work arrangements (e.g., flexible schedule, compressed work week, telecommuting), maternity and/or paternity leaves beyond legal requirements, subsidized childcare, emergency leave allowance and so on. Project 3535 findings suggest that these organizational policies and practices appear to help employees around the world by reducing their level of WIF (rather than FIW). Employees who find them useful report higher levels of life satisfaction (an indicator of psychological well-being) and lower levels of turnover intention, compared to those who don't find them useful (Korabik, Lero, Aycan and Bardoel, 2013).

Thinking across cultures 7.3

'The Grandparent Trap': The Double Blessing of Social Support in Collectivistic Cultures

Despite the sandy wind and terrible air quality on Saturday, more than one hundred parents and grandparents got up early and hurried to the Beijing Women and Children Social Center in Jinsong, Chaoyang district to take classes on grandparenting held by the Beijing Women's Federation.

Zhang Xianglan, a retired college professor in her 50s, came because she was concerned about how to care for her granddaughter and does not want her son and daughter-in-law to blame her 'if anything goes wrong'.

Source: Lu (2013, p. 6)

- To what extent do you think social support provided by the extended family helps parents in their work–family balance?

'What About Me?'

This was the question posed by one of the participants in a training session on work–family balance. At the end of our training this participant, in her 50s, raised her hand and asked 'You talked about balancing work and family. All my life I tried to balance them. Now that I am almost retired and have adult children, I ask myself what I have done for *myself* for all these years.' This was a wake-up moment leading to the development of the three-dimensional **life balance** model (Aycan et al., 2007). The life balance model includes three domains of life: work, family and self.

Just like the work and family domains, the 'self' domain also has *demands*, such as doing things to please oneself (e.g., spending time on hobbies or with friends from college), to enhance one's health and well-being (e.g., a regular workout and annual check-up) and to develop one's knowledge, skills and abilities in different areas (e.g., attending self-development training other than that related to work).

Research suggests that letting work or family interfere with 'self' may have negative psychological health consequences (Erkovan, 2008). Employees report high levels of burnout if they experience work-to-personal life conflict (e.g., not being able to spend time on themselves because of the demands at work). Experience of family-to-personal life conflict is associated with high levels of anxiety and low levels of life satisfaction.

It appears that life balance can only be achieved if the self is also being attended to. Organizations that help their employees balance work, family and personal life are those that will attract and keep the best talent in today's global competition.

Cross-cultural Considerations for Managers

The work we do and the organization we work for are important parts of who we are. This is true regardless of our age, gender or ethnic/cultural background. Therefore, *what we think* and *how we feel* about our work and organization (i.e., employees' organizational attitudes) have significant impact on the well-being of employees and organizations.

Research shows that negative organizational attitudes are strongly associated with employees' intention to quit their jobs. What is lost is not only the talent, but also the reputation of the organization as well as valued customers or the entire team of employees who decided to quit. Research in recent years shows that positive organizational attitudes foster task performance, extra-role behaviour (e.g., helping others, voluntary involvement in tasks beyond one's own), customer satisfaction, health and safety, unit productivity and organizational profitability.

Given the robust research findings, the importance of fostering positive organizational attitudes for global learning organizations cannot be overestimated. Global leaders should be aware of cross-cultural differences in the factors leading to job satisfaction, organizational commitment, justice perception, citizenship behaviour and job involvement. The policies and practices of multinational organizations to foster positive employee attitudes should be adjusted according to the values and needs of employees in different cultures. For example, having an interesting and challenging job with ample opportunities for learning and personal development would be the primary factors fostering job satisfaction, organizational commitment and organizational citizenship in economically developed nations with individualistic value orientations, while having job security (e.g., satisfactory pay, benefits, employment guarantee), harmonious work relationships and supportive leaders would be the primary factors in economically developing nations with collectivistic value orientations.

Global leaders should also recognize the importance of procedural and interpersonal justice in collectivistic and hierarchical cultures, especially when they have limited resources to distribute among employees. Employees in individualistic cultures tend to feel justice is violated when resources are not distributed on the basis of merit, whereas those in collectivistic cultures tend to feel violated when they are not treated with dignity and respect and when critical information concerning them is deliberately withheld from them.

Learning organizations in cross-cultural context are strongly advised to conduct periodical assessment of employee attitudes to identify problems and progresses. The good news is that there are reliable and cross-culturally valid measures of job satisfaction, organizational commitment, organizational citizenship behaviour, work involvement and organizational justice, which can be used or adopted to fit the specific needs of the organization. Plotting organizational attitudes against organizational outcomes (e.g., productivity, sales, turnover, customer satisfaction/loyalty) and comparing the results across different cultural/geographical units would provide an invaluable insight about how the diversity should be managed in the organization. It would also be useful to benchmark organizational practices with and learn from those listed in *Fortune* or Forbes '100 Best Companies to Work For' published every year.

Global leaders should also pay attention to employee lives beyond work (see Video 7.1). Work–life balance is at the top of top business and political leaders' agendas. Organizations clearly realize that helping employees balance their lives is in fact helping themselves. Decades of research document clearly that problems in managing work–life balance are associated with high turnover, low productivity and negative organizational attitudes. The number of organizations initiating work–life balance programmes has been increasing (see Video 7.2).

The list of companies that 'know what it takes to keep their employee mums productive and engaged both at work and at home' is called 'The Working Mother 100 Best Companies'. Organizations such as Proctor and Gamble and Unilever have flexibility programmes (e.g., agile workplace programme) to facilitate work–life balance for all employees, not only working mothers. Organizations also have wellness programmes for their employees to facilitate a balance between work and self.

Among the three domains captured by the Life Balance model discussed in this chapter, the self is probably the most important, because without a healthy and happy self, one cannot achieve work and family balance. It recalls the (almost counterintuitive) announcement on the airplanes for passengers travelling with small children: 'make sure to attend to yourself before helping others'.

Learning organizations in cross-cultural context should know that employees from diverse backgrounds may have different demands, especially in their family, and different coping mechanisms. For example an Indian working mother may feel the pressure from her extended family (e.g. mother-in-law) to fulfil spousal and parental duties. The way she tries to balance work and family may be to fulfil both work and family responsibilities in a *perfect* way and on her own (i.e., without delegating or lowering standards). A cross-culturally competent manager is expected to realize these pressures and support this employee in the best way possible (e.g., allowing her to work at home one day in every two weeks), before she experiences burnout and contemplates leaving her job.

Chapter Summary

We dedicate this chapter to employee experiences that are not only critical for employees, but also for organizations: attitudes towards organization and work–life balance. We start with a discussion of why organizational attitudes are key to the sustainability and performance of organizations. We present findings of meta-analytical research summaries conducted over several decades to demonstrate that job satisfaction, organizational commitment, organizational citizenship behaviours, organizational justice and involvement and engagement in a job are significant correlates of low turnover, high performance and productivity and good records of health and safety and customer loyalty and satisfaction. If positive employee attitudes are so important for an organization, what are the factors that foster positive attitudes and what are the factors that reduce negative attitudes in organizations? We addressed these questions through findings of the literature. What seems to lie behind all of the positive organizational attitudes are enriching work content (e.g., opportunity for development, a challenging job) and positive work context (e.g., supportive supervision, cooperative work climate, satisfactory pay and benefits). The importance of these factors for positive organizational attitudes appears to vary depending on the cultural values and needs of employees (see Video 7.3).

The second part of the chapter is devoted to work–life balance. We discussed why work–life balance is important for employees and organizations. We argue that sustainable organizations must address lives of employees beyond work. Families and societies are key stakeholders for organizations. Inappropriate work hours and excessive workload not only harm these external stakeholders (e.g., families, children, society at large), but also threaten the sustainability of the organization. Working long and inconvenient hours with a heavy workload results in work–family conflict and makes it very difficult for organizations to attract and keep talent (see Video 7.4). The three-dimensional life balance model suggests that it is also important to attend to oneself and satisfy the needs of employees at the personal level. The chapter concludes with specific suggestions for global managers and leaders for life balance programmes to benefit all stakeholders involved.

End of Chapter Reflection Questions

1. Organizations want to promote employee commitment, but some scholars would argue that too much commitment may harm the organization. Do you agree with this argument; why and why not?
2. We suggested in this chapter that the 'self' domain should take precedence over work and family domains, because without the self, neither work nor family exists. Some people may believe that this is selfishness and that the demands of self domains will clash sooner or later in close relationships (e.g. in marriage or a subordinate–superior relationship). What is your take on this issue? What are the conditions that would allow self domains to peacefully coexist in close relationships?
3. Do you think there are generation differences in employee attitudes and that Generation X is more prone to tolerate injustice, more committed to the organization and easier to feel satisfied with their job than Generation Y? If yes, how should organizations manage possible conflicts arising from these differences?

Key Terms and Definitions

Employee organizational attitudes. Positive or negative evaluation of how employees think and feel about their work and organization.

Job satisfaction. Positive evaluation of one's job, including work, supervision, co-workers, organizational policies and practices, development and promotion opportunities, financial and non-financial benefits and so on.

Organizational commitment. Positive attitudes towards the organization and what it stands for.

Organizational citizenship behaviour. Voluntary and spontaneous behaviour that goes beyond the call of duty to provide assistance, support and cooperation as needed in the organization.

Organizational justice perception. Positive perception and feeling that an organization treats its employees fairly and with justice.

Distributive justice. Perception of justice based on the judgement that resources are distributed according to merit or proportionate to employee inputs.

Procedural justice. Perception of justice deriving from the application of rules and procedures uniformly without nepotism or favouritism.

Alienation and involvement. Alienation is the extent to which employees feel cognitively separated from the work or family context, whereas involvement is the psychological identification with the context.

Employee engagement. Satisfaction, commitment and involvement in one's job; concern with organizational well-being; willingness to develop and perform.

Work–family conflict. Inability to fulfil role demands in family or work due to pressures (especially time and stress) experienced in the other domain of life.

Positive spillover. Feeling enriched at work or in the family due to positive experiences in the other domain of life.

Life balance. Ability to attend the needs and demands from work, family and self to a level that satisfies the individual and keeps them healthy and happy while doing so.

Further Reading

Carr, J.C., Boyar, S.L. and Gregory, B.T. (2008) 'The moderating effect of work-family centrality on work-conflict, organizational attitudes and turnover', *Journal of Management*, 34 (2): 244–62.

Dasborough, M.T., Ashkanasy, N.M., Tee, E.Y. and Tse, H.H. (2009) 'What goes around comes around: How meso-level negative emotional contagion can ultimately determine organizational attitudes towards leaders', *Leadership Quarterly*, 20 (4): 571–85.

Gambles, R., Lewis, S. and Rapoport, R. (2006) *The Myth of Work–life Balance: The Challenge of our Time for Men, Women and Societies.* London: John Wiley and Sons.

Kidwell, R.E. and Martin, C.L. (2005) *Managing Organizational Deviance.* London: Sage.

Loehr, J. and Schwartz, T. (2003) *The Power of Full Engagement: Managing Energy, not Time, is the Key to High Performance and Personal Renewal.* New York: Free Press.

Merrill, A.R. and Merrill, R.R. (2003) *Life Matters: Creating a Dynamic Balance of Work, Family, Time and Money.* New York: McGraw Hill.

Shockley, K.M. and Singla, N. (2011) 'Reconsidering work–family interactions and satisfaction: A meta-analysis', *Journal of Management*, 37 (3): 861–86.

Yang, L., Spector, P., Sanchez, J.I., Allen, T.D., Poelmans, S. et al. (2012) 'Individualism-collectivism as a moderator of work demands-strains relationship: A cross-level and cross-national examination', *Journal of International Business Studies*, 43 (4): 424–43.

Cases, Videos and Web sources

Cases

The following cases present challenging situations facing today's organizations concerning employee satisfaction, engagement and work–life balance.

Mishra, A.K. and Bharadwaj, S.S. (2013) *Work from Home: Curse or Boon.* IVEY Cases, No: 9B13C008.

Groysberg, B. and Sherman, E. (2008) *Sloan and Harrison: The Associate Challenge.* Harvard Business School Case No: 409032-PDF-ENG.

Videos

Video 7.1 Nigel Marsh: *How To Make Work-Life Balance Work* (2011) www.ted.com/talks/nigel_marsh_how_to_make_work_life_balance_work.html – if you think that work–life balance is an issue only for women, watch this entertaining talk.

Video 7.2 Stefan Sagmeister: *The Power of Time Off* (2009) www.ted.com/talks/stefan_sagmeister_the_power_of_time_off.html – Sagmeister talks about perils of taking corporate sabbaticals!

Video 7.3 *China's Lack of Commitment* (2012) www.youtube.com/watch?v=8HbKcGgtkTs.

Video 7.4 OMFInternational: *Live to Work Japan: Below the Surface* (2009) www.youtube.com/watch?v=5Ms5q6D7V6c – first 5.30 minutes of this video features the relationship between culture and work–life balance.

Web sources

www.shrm.org/about/foundation/products/Pages/EmployeeEngagement.aspx – Society for Human Resource Management's website for employee engagement and commitment.

http://workplaceflexibility.bc.edu/workFlex – workplace flexibility by Sloan Center on Aging and Work at Boston College.

www.bc.edu/centers/cwf/ – Center for Work and Family Caroll School of Management.

www.awlp.org/awlp/home/html/homepage.jsp – Alliance for Work–life Progress website.

www.workfamilyconflict.ca/ – multinational work–family research project website.

References

Amstad, F.T., Meier, L.L., Fasel, U., Elfering, A. and Semmer, N.K. (2011) 'A meta-analysis of work-family conflict and various outcomes with a special emphasis on cross-domain versus matching-domain relations', *Journal of Occupational Health Psychology*, 16 (2): 151.

Andolsěk, D.M. and Stebe, J. (2004) 'Multinational perspectives on work values and commitment', *International Journal of Cross-cultural Management*, 4 (2): 181–209.

Aycan, Z. (2012) *Cross-cultural cross-domain, and cross-over effects in work-life interface*. International Congress of Psychology, July, Cape Town.

Aycan, Z. (2008) 'Cross-cultural perspectives to work-family conflict', in K. Korabik, D. Lero and D. Whitehead (eds), *Handbook of Work-Family Integration*, pp. 359–71. Cambridge: Cambridge University Press.

Aycan, Z. and Eskin, M. (2005) 'Relative contributions of childcare, spousal support and organizational support in reducing work–family conflict for men and women: The case of Turkey', *Sex Roles*, 53 (7–8): 453–71.

Aycan, Z. and Gelfand, M.J. (2012) 'Cross-cultural organizational psychology', in S. Kozlowski (ed.), *Oxford Industrial and Organizational Psychology Handbook* (pp. 1103–1160). New York: Oxford University Press.

Aycan, Z., Eskin, M. and Yavuz, S. (2007) *Hayat Dengesi: İş, Aile ve Özel Hayatı Dengeleme Sanatı* (Life balance: the art of balancing work, family and private life). İstanbul: Sistem Press.

Bakhshi, A., Kumar, K. and Rani, E. (2009) 'Organizational justice perceptions as predictor of job satisfaction and organization commitment', *International Journal of Business and Management*, 4 (9), 145–154.

Brockner, J., Chen, Y.R., Mannix, E.A., Leung, K. and Skarlicki, D.P. (2000) 'Culture and procedural fairness: When the effects of what you do depend on how you do it', *Administrative Science Quarterly*, 45 (1): 138–59.

Cheng, B.S., Jiang, D.Y. and Riley, J.H. (2003) 'Organizational commitment, supervisory commitment and employee outcomes in the Chinese context: proximal hypothesis or global hypothesis?', *Journal of Organizational Behavior*, 24 (3): 313–34.

Clifton, J. (2013) 'China's disengaged workforce', *China Daily*, February 23.

Clugston, M., Howell, J.P. and Dorfman, P.W. (2000) 'Does cultural socialization predict multiple bases and foci of commitment?', *Journal of Management*, 26 (1): 5–30.

Cohen-Charash, Y. and Spector, P.E. (2001) 'The role of justice in organizations: A meta-analysis', *Organizational Behavior and Human Decision Processes*, 86 (2): 278–321.

Colquitt, J.A. (2001) 'On the dimensionality of organizational justice: A construct validation of a measure', *Journal of Applied Psychology*, 86 (3): 386–400.

Colquitt, J.A., Conlon, D.E., Wesson, M.J., Porter, C.O. and Ng, K.Y. (2001) 'Justice at the millennium: a meta-analytic review of 25 years of organizational justice research', *Journal of Applied Psychology*, 86 (3): 425.

Cooper-Hakim, A. and Viswesvaran, C. (2005) 'The construct of work commitment: testing an integrative framework', *Psychological Bulletin*, 131 (2): 241.

Dávila de León, M.C. and Finkelstein, M.A. (2011) 'Individualism/collectivism and organizational citizenship behavior', *Psicothema*, 23 (3): 401–06.

Duxbury, L.E. and Higgins, C.A. (1991) 'Gender differences in work-family conflict', *Journal of Applied Psychology*, 76 (1): 60.

Eagly, A.H. and Chaiken, S. (1998) 'Attitude structure and function', in D.T. Gilbert, S.T. Fiske and G. Lindzey (eds), *The Handbook of Social Psychology*, 4th edn, Vols 1 and 2, pp. 269–322. New York: McGraw-Hill.

Earley, P.C. and Lind, A.E. (1987) 'Procedural justice and participation in task selection: The role of control in mediating justice judgments', *Journal of Personality and Social Psychology*, 52 (6): 1148–60.

Eatough, E.M., Chang, C.H., Miloslavic, S.A. and Johnson, R.E. (2011) 'Relationships of role stressors with organizational citizenship behavior: A meta-analysis', *Journal of Applied Psychology*, 96 (3): 619.

Elias, S.M. and Mittal, R. (2011) 'The importance of supervisor support for a change initiative: An analysis of job satisfaction and involvement', *International Journal of Organizational Analysis*, 19 (4): 305–16.

Erkovan, H.E. (2008) *Work-family-personal life conflict: Testing of a three-dimensional model.* Unpublished Masters Dissertation. Koc University, Istanbul.

Euwema, M.C., Wendi, H. and Emmerik, H.V. (2007) 'Leadership styles and group organizational citizenship behavior across cultures', *Journal of Organizational Behavior*, 28: 1035–57.

Farh, J.L., Earley, P.C. and Lin, S.C. (1997) 'Impetus for action: A cultural analysis of justice and organizational citizenship behavior in Chinese society', *Administrative Science Quarterly*, 42 (3): 421–44.

Farh, J.L., Zhong, C.B. and Organ, D.W. (2004) 'Organizational citizenship behavior in the People's Republic of China', *Organization Science*, 15 (2): 241–53.

Fischer, R. (2013) 'Belonging, status or self-protection? Examining justice motives in a three-level cultural meta-analysis of organizational justice effects', *Cross-Cultural Research*, 47 (1): 3–41.

Fischer, R. and Smith, P.B. (2003) 'Reward allocation and culture a meta-analysis', *Journal of Cross-cultural Psychology*, 34 (3): 251–68.

Gelfand, M.J., Erez, M. and Aycan, Z. (2007) 'Cross-cultural organizational behavior', *Annual Review of Psychology*, 58: 479–514.

Giacobbe-Miller, J.K., Miller, D.J. and Victorov, V.I. (1998) 'A comparison of Russian and US pay allocation decisions, distributive justice judgments and productivity under different payment conditions', *Personnel Psychology*, 51 (1): 137–63.

Greenhaus, J.H. and Beutell, N.J. (1985) 'Sources of conflict between work and family roles', *Academy of Management Review*, 10 (1): 76–88.

Grzywacz, J.G. and Marks, N.F. (2000) 'Reconceptualizing the work-family interface: An ecological perspective on the correlates of positive and negative spillover between work and family', *Journal of Occupational Health Psychology*, 5 (1): 111–26.

Hanson, G.C., Hammer, L.B. and Colton, C.L. (2006) 'Development and validation of a multidimensional scale of perceived work-family positive spillover', *Journal of Occupational Health Psychology*, 11 (3): 249.

Harter, J.K., Schmidt, F.L. and Hayes, T.L. (2002) 'Business-unit-level relationship between employee satisfaction, employee engagement and business outcomes: A meta-analysis', *Journal of Applied Psychology*, 87 (2): 268–79.

Huang, X. and Van De Vliert, E. (2003) 'Where intrinsic job satisfaction fails to work: National moderators of intrinsic motivation', *Journal of Organizational Behavior*, 24 (2): 159–79.

Huang, X. and Vliert, E.V.D. (2004) 'Job level and national culture as joint roots of job satisfaction', *Applied Psychology: An International Review*, 53 (3): 329–48.

Hui, C.H. and Yee, C. (1999) 'The impact of psychological collectivism and workgroup atmosphere on Chinese employees' job satisfaction', *Applied Psychology: An International Review*, 48 (2): 175–85.

Hui, M. K., Au, K. and Fock, H. (2004) 'Empowerment effects across cultures', *Journal of International Business Studies*, 35 (1): 46–60.

Jaramillo, F., Mulki, J.P. and Marshall, G.W. (2005) 'A meta-analysis of the relationship between organizational commitment and salesperson job performance: 25 years of research', *Journal of Business Research*, 58 (6): 705–14.

Joplin, J.R., Shaffer, M.A., Francesco, A.M. and Lau, T. (2003) 'The macro-environment and work-family conflict development of a cross cultural comparative framework', *International Journal of Cross Cultural Management*, 3 (3): 305–28.

Judge, T.A., Thoresen, C.J., Bono, J.E. and Patton, G.K. (2001) 'The job satisfaction–job performance relationship: A qualitative and quantitative review', *Psychological Bulletin*, 127 (3): 376.

Kanungo, R.N. (1990) 'Culture and work alienation western models and eastern realities', *International Journal of Psychology*, 25 (3–6): 795–812.

Korabik, K. Lero, D., Aycan, Z. and Bardoel, A. (2013) 'HR policies to enhance work-family balance: Fostering organizational sustainability in global context.' Paper presented at the Sustainable Organizations: Human and Social Dimensions Conference, February, Sydney.

LePine, J.A., Erez, A. and Johnson, D.E. (2002) 'The nature and dimensionality of organizational citizenship behavior: A critical review and meta-analysis', *Journal of Applied Psychology*, 87 (1): 52–65.

LePine, J.A., Piccolo, R.F., Jackson, C.L., Mathieu, J.E. and Saul, J.R. (2008) 'A meta-analysis of teamwork processes: Tests of a multidimensional model and relationships with team effectiveness criteria', *Personnel Psychology*, 61 (2): 273–307.

Leung, K. (1997) 'Negotiation and reward allocation across cultures', in P.C. Earley and M. Erez (eds), *New Perspectives on International Industrial/Organizational Psychology*, pp. 640–675. San Francisco, CA: New Lexington.

Leung, K., Smith, P.B., Wang, Z.M. and Sun, H.F. (1996) 'Job satisfaction in joint venture hotels in China: An organizational justice analysis', *Journal of International Business Studies*, 27: 947–62.

Loong, L.H. (2012) Singapore Prime Minister Mr. Lee Hsien Loong's National Day Rally Speech, August. Retrieved from http://www.pmo.gov.sg/content/ pmosite/mediacentre/speechesninterviews/primeminister/2012/August/prime_minister_leehsienloongsnationaldayrally2012speechinenglish.m.html on May 6, 2013.

Lu, Y. (2013, March 12) 'The grandparent trap', *Global Times*. Retrieved from http://www.globaltimes.cn/content/767633.shtml#.UknEw4ZrTyU.

Luchak, A.A. and Gellatly, I.R. (2007) 'A comparison of linear and nonlinear relations between organizational commitment and work outcomes', *Journal of Applied Psychology*, 92 (3): 786.

McElwain, A.K., Korabik, K. and Rosin, H.M. (2005) 'An examination of gender differences in work-family conflict', *Canadian Journal of Behavioural Science*, 37 (4): 283–98.

Meyer, J.P., Stanley, D.J., Herscovitch, L. and Topolnytsky, L. (2002) 'Affective, continuance and normative commitment to the organization: A meta-analysis of antecedents, correlates and consequences', *Journal of Vocational Behavior*, 61 (1): 20–52.

Michaels, E., Handfield-Jones, H. and Axelrod, B. (2001) *War for Talent*. Boston, MA: Harvard Business Press.

Michel, J.S., Kotrba, L.M., Mitchelson, J.K., Clark, M.A. and Baltes, B.B. (2011) 'Antecedents of work–family conflict: A meta-analytic review', *Journal of Organizational Behavior*, 32 (5): 689–725.

Morrow, P.C. (2011) 'Managing organizational commitment: Insights from longitudinal research', *Journal of Vocational Behavior*, 79: 18–35.

Mowday, R.T., Steers, R.M. and Porter, L.W. (1979) 'The measurement of organizational commitment', *Journal of Vocational Behavior*, 14 (2): 224–47.

Organ, D.W. (1997) 'Organizational citizenship behavior: It's construct clean-up time', *Human Performance*, 10 (2): 85–97.

Piccolo, R.F., Judge, T.A., Takahashi, K., Watanabe, N. and Locke, E.A. (2005) 'Core self-evaluations in Japan: Relative effects on job satisfaction, life satisfaction, happiness and dysfunctional thinking', *Journal of Organizational Behavior*, 26: 965–84.

Pillai, R., Williams, E.S. and Tan, J. J. (2001) 'Are the scales tipped in favor of procedural or distributive justice? An investigation of the U.S., India, Germany and Hong Kong', *International Journal of Conflict Management*, 12 (4), 312–332.

Podsakoff, P.M., MacKenzie, S.B., Moorman, R.H. and Fetter, R. (1990) 'Transformational leader behaviors and their effects on followers' trust in leader, satisfaction and organizational citizenship behaviors', *The Leadership Quarterly*, 1 (2): 107–42.

Posthuma, R.A., Campion, M.A. and Vargas, A.L. (2005) 'Predicting counterproductive performance among temporary workers: A note', *Industrial Relations*, 44 (3), 550–554.

Ramesh, A. and Gelfand, M.J. (2010) 'Will they stay or will they go? The role of job embeddedness in predicting turnover in individualistic and collectivistic cultures', *Journal of Applied Psychology*, 95 (5): 807–23.

Riketta, M. (2008) 'The causal relation between job attitudes and performance: A meta-analysis of panel studies', *Journal of Applied Psychology*, 93 (2): 472.

Sama, L.M. and Papamarcos, S.D. (2000) 'Culture's consequences for working women in corporate America and Japan, Inc.', *Cross-cultural Management: An International Journal*, 7 (2): 18–29.

Shockley, K.M. and Singla, N. (2011) 'Reconsidering work–family interactions and satisfaction: A meta-analysis', *Journal of Management*, 37 (3): 861–86.

Somech, A., Drach-Zahavy, A., Aycan, Z., Korabik, K., Ayman, R., Bardoel, A., Poelmans, S., Rajadhyaksha, U., Mawardi, A., Huang,T., Lero, D., Desai, T., Hammer, L. and Li, Z. (2013) *Understanding the role of personal strategy in decreasing work and family conflict: a cross-cultural perspective*. Fifth International Conference on Work and Family, Barcelona, July.

Spector, P.E. (1997) *Job Satisfaction: Applications, Assessment, Causes and Consequences*. Thousand Oaks, CA: Sage.

Spector, P.E., Allen, T.D., Poelmans, S.A.Y., Lapierre, L.M., Cooper, C.L., O'Driscoll, M., Sanchez, J.I., Abarca, N., Alexandrova, M., Beham, B., Brough, P., Ferreiro, P., Fraile, G., Lu, C. Q., Lu, L., Moreno-Veláquez, I., Pagon, M., Pitariu, H., Salamatov, V., Shima, S., Suarez, Simoni, A., Siu, O.L. and Widerszal-Bazyl, M. (2007) 'Cross-national differences in relationships of work demands, job satisfaction and turnover intentions with work-family conflict', *Personnel Psychology*, 60: 805–35.

Spector, P.E., Cooper, C.L., Sanchez, J.I., O'Driscoll, M., Sparks, K., Bernin, P., Büssing, A., Dewe, P., Hart, P., Lu, L., Miller, K., Renault de Moraes, L., Ostrognay, G.M., Pagon, M., Pitariu, H., Poelmans, S., Radhakrishnan, P., Russinova, V., Salamatov, V., Salgado, J, Shima, S., Siu, O.L., Stora, J.B., Teichmann, M., Theorell, T., Vlerick, P., Westman, M., Widerszal-Bazyl, M., Wong, P. and Yu, S. (2002) 'A 24-nation/territory study of work locus of control in relation to well-being at work: How generalizable are western findings?', *Academy of Management Journal*, 45: 453–66.

Thomas, D.C. and Au, K. (2002) 'The effect of cultural differences on behavioral responses to low job satisfaction', *Journal of International Business Studies*, 33 (2): 309–26.

Van de Vliert, E. and Janssen, O. (2002) '"Better than" performance motives as roots of satisfaction across more and less developed countries', *Journal of Cross-cultural Psychology*, 33 (4): 380–97.

Wasti, A.S. (1999) *Organizational commitment in a collectivist culture: The case of Turkey*. Unpublished Ph.D. thesis, Urban-Illinois, University of Illinois.

Wasti, A.S. (2003) 'The influence of cultural values on antecedents of organisational commitment: An individual-level analysis', *Applied Psychology: An International Review*, 52 (4): 533–54.

Yang, N. (2005) 'Individualism-collectivism and work-family interface: A Sino-US comparison', in S.A.Y. Poelmans (ed.), *Work and Family: An International Research Perspective*, pp. 287–319. London: Lawrence Erlbaum.

Yoon, J. (1996) 'Fairness issues and job satisfaction among Korean employees: The significance of status value and procedural justice in work orientation', *Social Justice Research*, 9: 121–43.

Want to learn more? Visit the companion website at www.sagepub.co.uk/kanungo to gain access to videos from the end of each chapter, weblinks and flash cards of key terms.

8

Organizational Structure and Organizational Change

Chapter Outline

I'se the boy that builds the boat, I'se the boy that sails her, I'se the boy that catches the fish and brings 'em home to Eliza.

Every Newfoundlander in Canada learns this ditty at his mother's knee. It vividly captures the enterprise and self-reliance of a Newfoundland outport fisherman. But it could well be a picturesque description of the organization structure of The Joe Bart Fishing Company – a one-man operation, in Joe Bart's Arm, Newfoundland. Undoubtedly, Joe Bart is more than your everyday entrepreneur; he builds the boat (a capital formation activity – therefore, an investor), he sails the boat (equipment operator), he catches the fish (producer) and brings the fish home to Eliza (marketer). This verse does not refer to the outcomes, but one can surmise that Eliza will be mighty proud of her husband. Joe Bart plans, organizes and performs all the activities needed for a successful business operation. Therefore, there is an organization structure of some sort – not on paper, but in Joe Bart's mind.

Suppose we catch up with Joe Bart a few years later. *The Joe Bart Fishing Company* has now grown and has several fishing boats. Joe Bart cannot, obviously, sail all the boats himself, market the fish and attend to the many chores of running the company. He hires employees, assigns tasks and personally supervises each one of them to ensure that the fish is caught, sold and the dollars brought home to Eliza.

The organization structure of *The Joe Bart Fishing Company* is now becoming visible. Joe Bart has divided the work among the employees and is coordinating and directing their efforts to achieve his objectives. The company continues to prosper and expand with a bigger fleet and many more employees. Joe Bart realizes that he can no longer manage the operation on a person-to-person basis, as he had done hitherto. He needs a better structure, systems and policies. More importantly, he needs to spell them out. These structures, systems and policies are an attempt to do through others whatever he would have done by himself – on a person-to-person basis, if the size and complexity of the operations had not prevented him from doing so. The organization structure and its component elements, then, is the device Joe Bart uses to relate people and work to achieve the organizational objectives.

In this chapter, we shall consider organizational structure and design, which we will treat in two parts. In the first part, we take a look at the building blocks of organizational structure. We explore the component elements of organization structure – the authority and task structures and the principles that govern them. We then examine the characteristics of organizational structure and their impact on the behaviour of individuals and groups vis-à-vis the objectives of the organization. In the second part, we focus on management beliefs and assumptions about the work attitudes and behaviour of employees, which inform and influence organizational design. We discuss the implications of these beliefs and assumptions for the policies and practices relating to the organization, direction, communication and control of work and workers.

We then examine the impact of the sociocultural environment on the design of the organizational structure. We discuss whether there is converge in organizational structures across the globe or divergence remains because of the cultural context. The non-cultural vs. cultural factors influencing organizational design and structure are outlined. The critical question we raise is whether some organizations in non-Western contexts are successful *despite* their structure (i.e., they could be even more successful had they changed their structure) or *because of* their structure. Following this discussion is another critical question: how to change organizational structure and culture. The challenges and facilitators of organizational change are discussed with specific managerial suggestions to foster 'learning organizations'.

Learning Objectives

- To identify and understand the nature, characteristics and principles of authority and task structure as building blocks of organizational structures.

- To become aware that the specific design of the organizational structure is influenced by management's beliefs and assumptions about the work and employees.

- To distinguish between the traditional, human relations, human resources and human resource development models capturing managerial assumptions and beliefs.

- To become aware of the impact of the sociocultural environment on the design of the organizational structure.

- To become familiar with the cultural factors associated with resistance to change.

- To critically evaluate whether or not organizations around the world can and must change to converge into a structure required for global competition.

Organizational Structure

Organizational structure is intended to replace the face-to-face interaction with employees, something that is no longer possible because of the increasing size and complexity of the organization. In face-to-face interaction the owner communicates specific job objectives to each employee and monitors progress in resolving problems. In larger corporations, however, the owner delegates this task to professional managers, who are accountable to the owner. The professional managers (or even the owner-manager, if directly involved) use an organizational structure to relate people and work. An organizational structure, then, is 'a relatively stable framework of jobs and departments that influences the behavior of individuals and groups toward organizational goals' (Ivancevich and Matteson, 1987, p. 470). *People* and *work* are the basic building blocks of organizational structure. The building block relating to people and the relationships among them is referred to as the authority structure or hierarchy; the one relating to work is referred to as the task structure. The sections that follow discuss the characteristics of authority and task structures.

The Authority Structure

The basic principles which apply to authority structures are ***unity of command, span of control,*** *delegation, decentralization* and *line-staff.* These principles ensure that the authority of a position is, indeed, of a type and extent which enhances organizational effectiveness. We shall briefly consider each of these concepts.

The first principle, *unity of command,* states that an employee should not have more than one superior. This principle serves to avoid a situation in which an employee is receiving conflicting orders. It also serves to ensure personal accountability. Is this principle adhered to in a modern organization? Some say that it is not and cite examples of everyday situations where an employee is subject to their own line manager and also to the functional specialists who have the responsibility and authority to offer *advice* and *recommendations.*

The second principle relates to *the span of authority or control,* which refers to the number of employees that can be effectively supervised by a manager. Traditionally, this number was limited to five or six. The reason for this limit is that the number of potential relationships between the superior and subordinates increases geometrically as the number of subordinates increases arithmetically. Other aspects of the job which affect the span of control are specialization and complexity. For example, a simple, routine and repetitive operation could easily have a wider span of control.

Delegation is the third principle of authority structure and states that a decision which can be effectively handled at the lower hierarchical level should be transferred to a position at that level. Delegation permits managers to make full use of the expertise and ability of their subordinates. Delegation essentially is the transfer of authority from the manager to the subordinate, but not the transfer of the responsibility, which still remains with the manager. In some organizations with a strong centralized authority structure, employees complain about the task being given to them by the management without the authority to execute it (e.g., being given the responsibility to make a purchase, but having no authority in spending decisions in the budget). Having both the authority and responsibility brings us to the next principle: decentralization.

Thinking across cultures 8.1

Can you Delegate or are you a 'Control Freak'?

Think about yourself in a teamwork environment or a manager you know in an organization. Here is a test to tell if you or a manager you know is a 'control freak'; i.e., experiences difficulties in delegating tasks to others. Feel free to fill it out to evaluate yourself or a manager you know or have worked with. Put one of the appropriate numbers from the following scale in spaces at the beginning of each statement.

1	2	3	4	5
Strongly disagree	Disagree	Neutral	Agree	Strongly agree

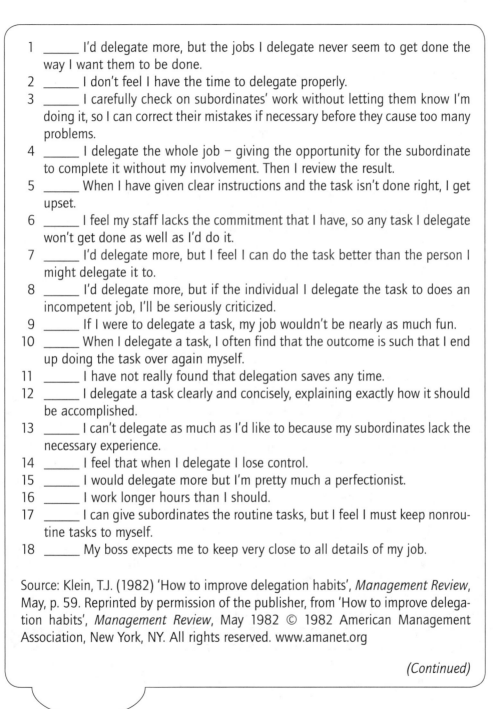

1 _____ I'd delegate more, but the jobs I delegate never seem to get done the way I want them to be done.

2 _____ I don't feel I have the time to delegate properly.

3 _____ I carefully check on subordinates' work without letting them know I'm doing it, so I can correct their mistakes if necessary before they cause too many problems.

4 _____ I delegate the whole job – giving the opportunity for the subordinate to complete it without my involvement. Then I review the result.

5 _____ When I have given clear instructions and the task isn't done right, I get upset.

6 _____ I feel my staff lacks the commitment that I have, so any task I delegate won't get done as well as I'd do it.

7 _____ I'd delegate more, but I feel I can do the task better than the person I might delegate it to.

8 _____ I'd delegate more, but if the individual I delegate the task to does an incompetent job, I'll be seriously criticized.

9 _____ If I were to delegate a task, my job wouldn't be nearly as much fun.

10 _____ When I delegate a task, I often find that the outcome is such that I end up doing the task over again myself.

11 _____ I have not really found that delegation saves any time.

12 _____ I delegate a task clearly and concisely, explaining exactly how it should be accomplished.

13 _____ I can't delegate as much as I'd like to because my subordinates lack the necessary experience.

14 _____ I feel that when I delegate I lose control.

15 _____ I would delegate more but I'm pretty much a perfectionist.

16 _____ I work longer hours than I should.

17 _____ I can give subordinates the routine tasks, but I feel I must keep nonroutine tasks to myself.

18 _____ My boss expects me to keep very close to all details of my job.

Source: Klein, T.J. (1982) 'How to improve delegation habits', *Management Review*, May, p. 59. Reprinted by permission of the publisher, from 'How to improve delegation habits', *Management Review*, May 1982 © 1982 American Management Association, New York, NY. All rights reserved. www.amanet.org

(Continued)

(Continued)

Scoring: Add up the numbers you assigned for each statement .

52–65: High level of difficulty in delegating.

39–51: Medium level of difficulty in delegating.

13–38: Low level of difficulty in delegating.

- Speculate on the factors (e.g., age, personality, cultural values) that enable or disable a person's delegation ability.
- Based on the analysis of the results given to the above assessment, which areas do you think need improvement and what would be your recommendation to strengthen the delegation behaviour.

The fourth principle of authority structure is **decentralization**. Decentralization is a management strategy or philosophy which transfers to separate organizational units such as plants, divisions, and branches the authority and responsibility to make decisions for their units (e.g., Koontz and O'Donnell, 1972). What is the difference between **delegation** and decentralization? Delegation involves the transfer of authority but not the responsibility from a manager to the subordinate. Decentralization involves the transfer of both authority and responsibility from one organizational unit (e.g., headquarters) to another (e.g., subsidiaries).

The last principle of authority structure is line-staff. This concept has basically two meanings. The first is that the line functions are those which are essential to the core of the business and its operations; the staff functions are those which support the essential functions. By this definition, production and sales would be regarded as line functions of a typical manufacturing company; whereas human resources, IT, accounting and design would be staff functions. One can see that this distinction does not always reflect organizational reality. For instance, in some manufacturing companies, the design of the product may be critical, which would make the design department absolutely essential to the business and, therefore, a line function. The second meaning refers to the authority versus advisory relationship. The line represents an authority (superior–subordinate) relationship; staff represents an advisory relationship.

The Task Structure

The task structure of an organization reflects the basis upon which work or jobs are grouped. The key criterion for the grouping is organizational efficiency and effectiveness. Jobs can be grouped according to function, product/service, project, customer and territory. We shall explore, in some detail, the *functional, product/service* and *project bases* of organization and briefly touch upon the *matrix organization* as well as *customer and territorial bases* of organization.

The functional basis of organization

When work or jobs are grouped along functional lines, the organization is structured on the basis of the major activities it must engage in to fulfil its mission. Thus, for a typical manufacturing company the major activities (functions) are production, marketing, finance, accounting and personnel. For a hospital, the functional divisions would also include surgery, radiology, psychiatry, personnel, accounting and so on. The operative principle is **specialization** – the related skills and responsibilities are grouped into one department.

The major advantage of the functional departmentalization is the efficiency arising from specialization. Specialists working in the same department can share their expertise and provide mutual support in resolving departmental problems. Also, resource-efficiency is achieved because equipment and related facilities need not be duplicated. However, the functional basis also has disadvantages. The chief disadvantage is that the departmental interest often tends to override the organizational interest. For example, when scarce organizational resources are to be rationed, it is not uncommon for departments to fight with each other in the most unseemly manner, totally disregarding any consideration of what would best serve the organization as a whole. Coordination can also become a problem, especially if information-processing or the technology, creates an interdependence between departments.

The product/service basis of organization

In this form of organization, the jobs are grouped according to their contribution to producing a product or providing a service. Thus, all the functions (e.g., production, design, marketing, sales) needed to produce *Product A* will be grouped together in one unit. There will, ordinarily, be as many units as there are products. Sometimes, the related products may be grouped in the same unit. The functions that are not specific to any one product (e.g., HR) may remain at the corporate level.

The product form of organization has several advantages. It allows the organization to develop the expertise in the functions specific to a product and to develop and use efficiently the highly specialized equipment needed for the product. Coordination between functions within a product division is relatively easy. Another advantage is that since each product division has complete control of its operations, it can be set up as a profit centre and held accountable. The chief disadvantage is the possibility of services being duplicated in each division, resulting in increased costs. Also related to costs is the consideration as to whether the product volume will justify the costs of this form of organization.

The project basis of organization

In the project basis of organization, all the jobs that contribute directly to a project are grouped together. Several projects might be under way in an organization at any one time of varying duration – from a few months to several years. Each project has its own organization headed by the project manager who is assigned the necessary facilities, resources and personnel – many of whom are 'on loan' from the regular line and staff departments. There are several variations of the project form of organization. The variations are marked by the control exercised by the project manager over the activities, personnel and resources.

The advantage of the project form of organization is that it permits a heightened focus on the project, which makes for an efficient mobilization of the organizational resources. But this form has to overcome severe managerial challenges. The people 'loaned' to the project come from different organizational units with varying norms and patterns of behaviour. The relatively short duration of projects adds to the difficulty of the project manager's job; it also does not give much time for the project organizations to develop the appropriate behavioural norms. In these circumstances, the effectiveness of the project manager will depend on the extent to which they draw upon their competence and leadership abilities, rather than on line authority. The project manager also faces the usual challenge of dealing with the regular staff departments, but these relationships tend to be particularly stressful when the staff departments fail to appreciate the critical and urgent nature of the requests from the project organization.

A special type of project-based organization is the **matrix organization**. It is a type of organization where employees or project teams report to more than one unit manager. Individual employees or teams work with different units and managers to accomplish the task at hand. The matrix structure essentially combines the features of organizations structured on the basis of function (i.e., employees belong to a specific functional unit), product or service (i.e., employees or teams may be specialized on a particular product or service) and project (i.e., they form teams to work on a specific project and report to one or more managers concerning that particular project). For example, a group of employees in the HRM department may form a team with engineers in the organization to work on projects on employee health and safety. These groups are required to report to the manager of the HRM department as well as the manager of the quality control department for the duration of the projects.

The key advantage of matrix organization is that it allows employees to be **boundary-spanners**. Working across boundaries not only benefits the organization, but also widens the career scope of employees. However, if managed poorly, matrix organization may pose severe disadvantages to organizations. One obvious disadvantage is the role conflict employees may face working on multiple and sometimes conflicting tasks. Working with more than one 'master' (i.e., manager) may also create emotional tensions and uncertainties of loyalties.

The customer and territorial bases of organization

In addition to the three forms of organization we explored, jobs can also be grouped on a customer and territorial basis. An example of grouping on a customer basis would be the divisions of a publishing company. It has the school textbook division and college textbook division. Another example is a manufacturing company organized along the lines of serving the industrial, government, hospital and consumer sectors. A territorial form of organization is exemplified by the national retail chain stores which are grouped on a regional basis. The store managers report to a regional manager, the regional manager reports to the national president. In both the customer and territorial forms, each division has the people and resources to meet the needs of the customer and territory it serves.

So far we have considered the basic authority structure and the task structure of an organization. These two structures are combined to form the organizational structure of an organization. Organizations can choose from among several combinations of these structures which will be effective in achieving their goals. This process of choosing the appropriate organizational structure is called organizational design.

In order to understand organizational design and its end result (i.e., the organizational structure), we need to address two questions: (1) what are the significant characteristics of an organizational structure? (2) what considerations inform and influence the process of organizational design? The answer to the first question leads to the identification of the significant characteristics of an organizational structure, which is helpful to understand the nature of the structure and its impact on employee behaviour. We explore this question in the next section. The answer to the second question will lead to an examination of the managerial beliefs and assumptions about employees' work attitudes and behaviours, which significantly influence the process of organizational design. This answer, fully discussed in a later section, will also provide the rationale for the choice of a specific organizational structure.

Characteristics of Organizational Structure

An organizational structure can be characterized in several ways. We will focus on four structural characteristics which have been found to have significant impact on employee motivation and work behaviour. These characteristics expressed in contrasting pairs are: *specialized versus general, tall versus flat, independent versus interdependent, tight versus loose* (Coffey et al., 1975).

Specialized vs. general

This characteristic relates to the way work is designed. At one extreme is specialization. Organizations which choose specialization design the jobs to include simple, repetitive movements. The jobs have little, if any, skill variety and task identity and absolutely no opportunity for initiative or creativity. At the other extreme are organizations which believe in designing work to include skill variety, skill identity, task significance, autonomy and feedback as much as possible. The structural characteristic in these organizations will be general, as opposed to specialized. Between these two extremes, several degrees of specialized and general jobs exist. Specialization is known to improve productivity, but the fact that organizations need to introduce job enlargement, job rotation, job enrichment and 'quality of working life' programmes, indicates that the impact of specialization on work motivation and behaviour is not positive.

Tall vs. flat

This characteristic literally describes the shape of the organization structure. A tall structure is one in which there are many hierarchical levels. This generally occurs when the spans of control are narrow. By contrast, a flat structure has fewer hierarchical levels which are brought about by wider spans of control. A flat structure would provide employees more opportunity for enriched work and, to that extent, have a positive impact on work behaviour (Worthy, 1950). A tall structure, on the other hand, gives managers more control and, consequently, would tend to limit the amount of autonomy which employees could have in their work.

Independent vs. interdependent

In this characteristic the focus is on the independence or interdependence of work units. The work of a unit can be structured in a specialized or general way. If it is done in a specialized manner, then it causes greater interdependence. If specialization is not used, then the work unit will be relatively independent. In an interdependent system if one work unit goes on a wildcat strike or, for some reason, is unable to perform its function, then the other units will remain idle and production will come to a standstill.

Tight vs. loose

Tight or loose is also referred to as the degree of **formalization** in the organization. A high degree of formalization makes it a tight organization; a low degree of formalization results in a loose organization. Formalization refers to the extent and the manner in which policies, procedures and rules are spelt out in the organization. Tight organizations will not have a positive effect on individuals who value autonomy and are competent in their jobs. However, a tight structure is appropriate for some areas such as organizational security and also for some employees who do not seek autonomy or discretion.

The terms **mechanistic** and **organic** are also used to describe tight and loose, respectively. The distinction between mechanistic vs. organic structures is brought out by Woodward in his earlier writing (see also Thinking across cultures 8.2):

> Mechanistic systems are characterized by ... precise definition of duties, responsibilities and power and a well developed command hierarchy through which information filters up and decisions and instructions flow down. Organic systems are more adaptable, jobs lose much of their formal definition and communications up and down the hierarchy are more in the nature of consultation ... In this type of situation, the chief executive is not regarded as omniscient. (Woodward, 1965, p. 230)

Thinking across cultures 8.2

What is the Structure of your Organization/work Unit?

Think of the organization or the work unit you are familiar with; e.g., your university or college, your faculty, library in the university, the organization you worked or interned for. Evaluate the characteristics of that workplace to the best of your ability by using the statements below. Number 1 indicates that the characteristic is most similar to the statement on the left hand side, whereas number 7 indicates that it is most similar to the one on the right hand side; 4 implies that it is in the middle. You may also ask the employees in that unit to check the realism of your observations.

(Continued)

(Continued)

In general operating management philosophy in this unit/organization favours:

Highly structured channels of communication and a highly restricted access to important financial and operating information	1 2 3 4 5 6 7	Open channels of communication with important financial and operating information flowing freely throughout the organization
A strong insistence on a uniform managerial style throughout the organization	1 2 3 4 5 6 7	Managers' operating styles allowed to range freely from the very formal to the very informal
A strong emphasis on giving the most say in decision-making to formal line managers	1 2 3 4 5 6 7	A strong tendency to let the expert in a given situation have the most say in decision-making even if this means temporary bypassing of formal line authority
A strong emphasis on holding fast to tried and true management principles despite any changes in business conditions	1 2 3 4 5 6 7	A strong emphasis on adapting freely to changing circumstances without too much concern for past practices
A strong emphasis on always getting personnel to follow the formally laid down procedures	1 2 3 4 5 6 7	A strong emphasis on getting things done even if it means disregarding formal procedures
Tight formal control of most operations by means of sophisticated control and information systems	1 2 3 4 5 6 7	Loose, informal control: heavy dependence on informal relationships and the norm of cooperation for getting things done
A strong emphasis on getting line and staff personnel to adhere closely to formal job descriptions	1 2 3 4 5 6 7	A strong tendency to let the requirements of the situation and individual's personality define descriptions

Source: Khandwalla (1977)

Evaluation: Smaller numbers on the scales represent mechanistic or tight organizational structures, while larger numbers represent organic ones. How many statements did you have with a value of 1, 2 or 3 (mechanistic) and how many did you have with a value of 5, 6 or 7 (organic)? If you have more statements with smaller values than those with larger values, then the organization or work unit you evaluated was mechanistic. If the condition is reverse, then the organization or work unit was organic.

- Why do you think the organization or work unit you evaluated was mechanistic or organic? What are the key factors that may influence the choice of the organizational structure?
- Which type of organizational structure do you think best represents a 'learning organization'? You may refer back to the definition of learning organization in Chapter 1: 'where people continuously expand their capacity to create the results they truly desire, where new and expansive patterns of thinking are nurtured, where collective aspiration is set free and where people are continually learning how to learn together' (Senge, 1990, p. 7).
- How is it possible to change the organizational structure from mechanistic to organic? (See also Case 8.3)

We conclude this section with two observations. First, the contrasting pairs of structural characteristics that we have discussed ought to be viewed as the extreme ends of a continuum and it is more likely that, in reality, organizational structures will lie between these two extremes. The second observation relates to the fact that managers, based on their beliefs and assumptions, have the decision-making latitude to judge who has the authority, discretion, flexibility in the organization, regardless of the organizational structure.

Impact of Managerial Beliefs and Assumptions on the Design of the Organizational Structure

Managerial beliefs and assumptions play a crucial role in the choice of structures and characteristics and in the formulation and enforcement of policies, rules and regulations that flow from the chosen structure (Schein, 1985). As discussed in

Chapter 1, four major models have contributed significantly to managerial beliefs and assumptions:

1. Traditional model based on Frederick Taylor's (1911) scientific management.
2. Human relations model based on the work of Elton Mayo (1949) and the findings of the classic Hawthorne experiments.
3. Human resource model based on the works of Abraham Maslow (1954) and Douglas McGregor (1960).
4. Human resource development model based on systems thinking and lending itself to the learning organization perspective.

We discuss each model in terms of its underlying assumptions and how organizational design based on these assumptions will influence organizational goals, policies and procedures relating to job design, decision-making, communication, control of behaviour, rewards and managerial role.

The Traditional Model

Assumptions and goals. The traditional model operates on three basic assumptions. First, workers are naturally lazy, greedy, selfish and uncooperative; they find work to be inherently distasteful. Second, few workers want or can handle autonomy and responsibility; on the contrary, they have a natural tendency to avoid responsibility. Third, the only way an organization can overcome the workers' dislike for work is to offer monetary rewards.

Organizational design based on this model results in an organizational structure which is specialized, tall, interdependent and tight. The primary organizational goal is high productivity. The organization will also attend to its employees but only to the extent that such attention will lead to increased productivity. Consequently, the secondary organizational goal will be to provide its workers with economic security and safe working conditions.

Job design. Since workers are assumed to be lazy and disinclined to accept responsibility, the entire organizational effort is basically divided into two sets of jobs: those that require 'thinking' and others that require 'executing'. Management is assigned the jobs which require planning, organizing, problem-solving, etc. The workers are assigned simple, repetitive, easy-to-learn operations. For this purpose, the workers' jobs are broken down into simple, routine, programmable tasks. The specialized tasks lend themselves to repetitive operations which will make the workers skilled, in spite of their reluctance to learn and hence improve productivity. The work routines and procedures are spelt out in minute detail, leaving absolutely no room for any initiative by the worker.

Decision-making. The decision-making style, not surprisingly, is autocratic. If employees are assumed to lack expertise and to dislike autonomy and responsibility, then the manager cannot be expected to consult them. Besides, it is assumed that the manager has all the necessary information for decision-making, that the acceptance of the decisions by the subordinates is not critical to their implementation and that the subordinates do not necessarily have to share the organizational goals to execute the orders.

Communication. The communication pattern is top-down, which is perfectly consistent with the basis of job design – management 'thinks' and the worker 'does.' Even so, the workers have limited access to information because the detailed procedures that are provided are considered to be more than adequate for the simplified tasks. Furthermore, there is no need for a two-way communication, because the workers are not expected to have information which is worth passing up to management. If they had, it is assumed that their lack of interest in work and in organizational goals and their uncooperative attitude would not motivate them to share it with management

Control of behaviour. Employee compliance with the required job behaviours is obtained through organizational controls. The degree of hierarchical control is extremely high because the model assumes that workers are not interested in, much less committed to, the organizational goals of high productivity. Therefore, only if workers are closely monitored and controlled will they produce up to standard.

Rewards. The underlying approach to the rewards system design is best captured by the expression 'carrot and stick approach'. The model's strong belief in the *economic man* concept leads management to expect that workers can and will *tolerate* (not enjoy) work if they receive good monetary rewards. Hence, there is a strong emphasis on extrinsic rewards. The reward system is designed to ensure that rewards are closely tied to performance and are contingent on specific levels of output.

Managerial role. The role of the manager is one of controlling and monitoring the different mechanisms and processes which ensure that employees perform the required tasks and comply with the established rules and procedures. The task role receives the greatest emphasis functioning as information-provider, problem-solver and, above all, as controller. The manager does select and train their subordinates, but these activities have an exclusive task-orientation – to describe clearly the tasks and the methods and procedures subordinates must use to perform them.

The Human Relations Model

Assumptions and goals. The human relations model operates upon two assumptions. First, human beings have a natural desire to belong, to feel useful and to be recognized. The second is a corollary of the first – that above a reasonable salary, fulfilment of these natural desires is more important than money. Since the human relations model tacitly accepted the assumptions of the traditional model, organizational design in organizations under this model did not substantially differ from those under the traditional model, i.e., specialized, tall, interdependent and tight. There were, however, some differences in the implementation of policies and practices, which we highlight below.

The organizational goal is still high productivity, but it is believed that it can be achieved only through high employee morale. The emphasis, therefore, is on maintaining high employee morale, which becomes the main concern because of the underlying implications of the model that 'a happy worker is a productive worker'.

Job design. As noted earlier, the basic job design principles of the traditional model prevail. Management continues to 'think' and the worker continues to 'do'. Also, the tasks are fractionated, programmable and routine. The main difference is that work is now organized in groups – not for any consideration of efficiency, but because of the belief that groups contribute to satisfying the workers' natural desire to belong, to interact and to possibly feel useful to one's peers.

Decision-making. The decision-making style continues to be autocratic as was the case under the traditional model. Yet there is a slight but important twist. Managers now listen to their subordinates before the decision is announced. However, they do so not to obtain input for their decisions which, more often than not, they have already made. Managers want to give their employees the satisfaction that they are useful, that they are recognized, that they belong to the work unit. Generally, managers are advised to use the consultative process in a genuine manner for issues which are peripheral to the job (e.g., design of staff recreational facilities, new year party, lighting and painting of work areas).

Communication. The pattern continues to be top-down and limited access to information – as in the traditional model. The difference is that the manager listens in the same manner and for the same reasons as they do in decision-making discussed above. There is also an abundance of communication, however, about a variety of topics which range from the birth of new products to new babies, from mergers to marriages; from employee successes in bowling leagues to achievement in training programmes. Maintaining and boosting high employee morale is the sole objective of the communications programme.

Control of behaviour. Employee compliance of the required job behaviours is obtained through organizational controls in the same manner and for the same reasons as the traditional model. However, the organization is careful to ensure that the controls are properly communicated and explained. This paternalistic approach helps because the improved communication is the sugar which makes the bitter medicine go down.

Rewards. The reward system is a key departure point from the traditional model. The rewards system focuses only on the 'carrot', which is not contingent on performance. Managers who subscribe to the human relations model believe that employee satisfaction must precede employee performance; hence, the model's emphasis is on unconditional rewards. Social rewards such as being listened to, public praise and recognition in organizations' magazines, for instance, form an important component of the reward system. The management of the reward system is highly paternalistic; the manager is the caring and concerned parental figure and the work unit is one, big, happy family.

Managerial role. The manager, as the executor of these policies and practices, must obviously adopt a social role. They listen to problems, provide praise and recognition, consult on routine and inconsequential matters – in a word, give the employees the 'feeling' that they are important, they belong and they are needed. The effect of the manager's social role is to promote high morale and elicit cooperation so that organizational objectives are attained with the least possible disruption and cost.

The Human Resource Model

Assumptions and goals. The human resource model has three basic assumptions. First, workers do not find work to be inherently distasteful, if it gives them an opportunity to achieve their own goals through a meaningful contribution to the achievement of organizational goals. Second, although an equitable compensation package is essential, growth in the job is more important than just making money. Third, most workers seek and can handle challenge, autonomy and responsibility. Organizational design results in an organizational structure which is fundamentally different from that of the earlier models: general, flat and loose. The characteristic of independent/interdependent would depend on the technology used by the organization. The policies and practices, discussed below, reflect the organic view of the organization.

The human resources model recognizes that the organization is an open system operating in an environment that is subject to frequent and often rapid and turbulent changes. The organizational goals, then, are productivity, process control, and learning and adaptation, which will enable the organization to respond effectively to both new opportunities and challenges. The model also recognizes that an organization can progress to this state of effectiveness only through the full utilization of its human resources.

Job design. The rigid distinction between 'thinking' and 'doing' is eliminated. The focus of management jobs is on strategic planning for the organization. The worker 'thinks' and 'does' in areas in which they have the most expertise. The jobs are not fractionated and routinized. Instead, every effort is made to provide, to the fullest extent feasible, skill variety, task identity and significance, autonomy and feedback. Autonomous work teams in organizations with QWL (Quality of Working Life) programmes illustrate the job design concept under the human resources model. These teams are fully responsible not only for the operations of their unit, but also for management and activities (e.g., equipment maintenance, purchasing, quality control, selection and training of team members).

Decision-making. The decision-making style and process is consultative and participatory. Managers consult with their subordinates with the genuine desire to tap their expertise, unlike the charade perpetrated in the human relations model. Employee participation and involvement is genuinely encouraged in all matters and issues that affect the job tasks and the unit in which these tasks are performed. Such participation is a natural outcome of the model's recognition that most workers seek and can handle challenge, autonomy and responsibility and that they have the know-how and competence to improve organizational performance and effectiveness.

Communication. Under the human resources model, there is two-way communication between managers and subordinates. There is free and open access to information which is first provided to those who need it. The uninhibited sharing of information is imperative if workers are to exercise autonomy and responsibility in a meaningful and productive manner. Informed employees are usually better prepared to sense and to make sense of untoward occurrences affecting their job and work unit and to generally develop appropriate coping mechanisms.

Control of behaviour. The human resources model obtains employee compliance with the required job behaviours not through organizational controls but through employee commitment to the job. The various policies and practices we have discussed under this model contribute to creating a job environment in which the worker is seen and treated as a mature, self-directing, self-controlling and autonomous person. This is very evident in high-involvement organizations which have designed work along the lines of autonomous work teams.

Rewards. The reward system under the human resources model places a heavy emphasis on growth needs and self-actualization. This follows the managerial beliefs that employees regard growth in the job as more valuable than just making money. Therefore, career development plans together with opportunities for training and development and being assigned to challenging projects receive special attention in the human resources model. The manager plays a pivotal role as a coach and mentor to ensure that participation and involvement by the subordinates are always opportunities for growth and development.

Managerial role. The human resources model offers the manager a unique opportunity to create just the right balance between the task and social roles (see Chapter 5). The manager believes that their subordinates seek and are capable of autonomy and self-control. Therefore, they believe that it is essential to give them the autonomy and responsibility for the performance of their job tasks. The manager is also acutely aware that they are ultimately responsible for the unit's objectives. In the event of failure the manager cannot explain it away by attributing it to the failure of their subordinates. How does the manager reconcile this conflict – to give autonomy and self-control to his subordinates and, at the same time, monitor them to ensure that the unit objectives are attained? A good approach is for the manager to function as coach and mentor to their subordinates. As a coach and mentor the manager will collaborate with his subordinates to clarify roles, establish objectives, provide support and feedback, and remove or minimize constraints to effective performance.

Human Resource Development Model and Learning Organizations

Assumptions and goals. Human resource development (HRD) model advocates long-term learning and development to enhance the work-related capacity of individuals, groups and organizations (Watkins and Marsick, 1995). The basic assumption that applies to individuals, groups and organizations is 'development through learning'. Other fundamental assumptions of this approach include:

1. Humans individually and collectively have an infinite capacity to learn and develop,
2. The primary goal of the organization is to provide every opportunity to individual and team learning, and
3. Organizations are successful to the extent that learning is fostered at all levels (Swanson and Holton, 2001).

The most important difference between the human resource model and the human resource development model is the way employees are perceived. In the HR model employees are critical 'resources' for the bottom line of the organization, whereas the HRD model employees are valued 'for their intrinsic worth as people, not just as resources to achieve outcomes … Thus, learning and development should be a means to enhance people and their humanness, not to accomplish performance goals' (Swanson and Holton, 2001, p. 135). Organizational design is similar to that of the previous model: general, flat and loose to foster double-loop learning and development.

Learning organizations fully embrace the assumptions of HRD. In a famous quotation Senge (1990, p. 7) defined learning organization as 'an organization where people continuously expand their capacity to create the results they truly desire, where new and expansive patterns of thinking are nurtured, where collective aspiration is set free and where people are continually learning how to learn together'.

Job design. In learning organizations jobs are not fractionated and routinized. Instead, every effort is made to provide, to the fullest extent feasible, skill variety, task identity, task significance, autonomy and feedback, which will enable the organization to respond effectively to its every changing environment, bringing both new opportunities and challenges. Job design fosters employees' feeling of empowerment and personal mastery (i.e., sense of expertise, control and contribution). Job design also includes 'autonomous work teams' – fully responsible not only for the operations of their unit, but also for activities such as: equipment maintenance, purchasing, quality control and even for the selection and training of team members.

Decision-making. Decision-making is similar to that in the human resource model: consultative and participatory; a natural outcome of the model's recognition that most workers have the capacity to learn, develop and contribute to strategic decisions of the organization. As mentioned above, autonomous work teams have decision-making latitude on operational and strategic matters.

Communication. The unrestricted flow of information facilitating learning and adaptation processes is encouraged. There is a culture of open discussion and dialogue that creates a supportive atmosphere which allows employees to develop their ability to be assertive in advocating their views and ideas, engage in 'active listening' and have the courage to accept and build on the views and ideas of others when one finds these to be more valid and germane to the situation.

Control of behaviour. The focus is on self-control and self-regulation. This gives employees a real sense of ownership of the job and, as a consequence, increases their stake in and commitment to the job. Employees are expected to have the control and responsibility of their own learning and development, rather than relying solely on organizational resources and guidance for learning.

Rewards. The most important reward is the ultimate achievement of learning and development. Organizational policies and practices to foster learning and development, such as stretch assignments, expatriate assignment, and cross-functional teamwork are considered rewarding. These opportunities for growth and development are not merely for a climb up the rungs of the hierarchical ladder, but rather to increased autonomy and responsibility.

Managerial role. The manager believes that subordinates seek and are capable of, autonomy and self-control. Therefore, they give them the autonomy and responsibility for the performance of their job tasks. At the same time, the manager coaches and mentors subordinates towards the attainment of the unit objectives. In a learning organization, the leader's vision is not dictated to or imposed upon the employees; rather, it is *internalized* by the employees. Such internalization changes the employees' attitudes, values and behaviour in the direction of the goals, beliefs and values that are inherent in the vision. All the policies and practices of the human resources model are conducive to the internalization of the leader's vision. However, it is the managerial role that is critical to the process of building as shared vision. As coach and mentor, the manager empowers subordinates as they collaborate with subordinates to clarify roles, establish objectives, provide support and feedback, remove or minimize constraints to effective performance.

Impact of Sociocultural Environment on Organizational Structure

American management is '*informal within a formalized frame*', whereas British management is '*formal within a non-formalized customary pattern*'. (Mallory et al., 1983, cited in Hickson and Pugh, 1995, p. 62)

French firms run more bureaucratically, with orders and procedures set from above, while German work organizations rely more on the professional expertise which derives from the trained knowledge and skills of more junior employees. (Hickson and Pugh, 1995, p. 103)

Organizations are complex systems operating in complex environmental forces. Organizational structure and design are influenced by environmental forces internal to the organization, including size, industry, workforce composition, technology and life cycle. The environment external to the organization include political, legal, educational, institutional and sociocultural context. Before we focus on the role of the sociocultural context vis-à-vis other environmental forces, let us first present an overview of **convergence**, **divergence** and cross-vergence approaches in relation to organizational structure.

Since early 1960s comparative management studies of organizations have focused on non-cultural factors (i.e., factors that are not directly associated with the cultural context). Among the most popular non-cultural approaches was that of contingency approach. One stream within this approach argued that industrialization had a homogenizing effect on organizations around the world (Harbison and Myers, 1959). According to this approach, organizations in industrialized economies have increasing specialization, size and complexity, which lead to managerial decentralization, professionalism and formalized management. In their large-scale comparative study of 1000 organizations in 14 countries (Algeria, Canada, Egypt, France, Germany, India, Iran, Israel, Japan, Jordan, Poland, Sweden, the UK and the USA) Hickson and associates (Hickson et al., 1969, 1974) found that size was positively related with specialization and formalization, whereas dependence was positively related with centralization.

One of the most important non-cultural approaches is the institutional theory (DiMaggio and Powell, 1983). According to this theory, organizational structures especially within the same industry (e.g., finance, health) have to be alike (i.e., isomorphic) because they function under similar environmental pressures. These pressures include governmental regulations leading to *coercive isomorphism*, norms developed and promoted by professional bodies leading to *normative isomorphism and* competitors that are proven to be successful leading to *mimetic isomorphism.*

Among other non-cultural approaches the political economy perspective has emphasized the importance of two major forms of economic systems of production, namely capitalism and socialism, are contrasted. Organizations in the same sociopolitical systems were assumed to have similar characteristics, especially with respect to organizational objectives, control strategies and degree of centralization and decision-making. Finally, the societal effect approach focused on the role of the state, education system and labour relations of a country in shaping organizational structures.

Common to all of these non-cultural perspectives is the convergence assumption, proposing that organizations go through similar structural phases, regardless of cultural differences. Divergence assumption, on the other hand, argues that organizational structures remain different, because culturally embedded managerial values, beliefs and assumptions result in variations in responses to environmental demands. Indeed, the strong effect that managerial assumptions and beliefs have on the organizational structure was discussed in the previous section.

Critics of the non-cultural approach are concerned with its deterministic orientation as well as underestimation of the role of culture in explaining the variations in organizational structures. For example, within the capitalist system, there is vast variety among organizational and management practices. Trade union movements (which have strong implications in the structure of organizations) in Britain, France and the United States are fundamentally different despite the similarity in their socio-economic system (i.e., capitalism) (cf., Gallie, 1978).

A relatively recent third avenue, cross-vergence, proposes that organizations would adopt a hybrid structure influenced by the interaction of non-cultural and cultural factors. For instance, Tayeb (1988) studied British and Indian organizations that are matched in many ways, such as industry, size and age. She found that while contingency variables influenced formal characteristics of the organizations (e.g., centralization, specialization, span of control, etc.), cultural variables influenced the interpersonal aspects such as power and authority structure, delegation, consultation and communication patterns. Others asserted that culture has a moderating effect on organizations (e.g., Child, 1981). Even though the contingent factors may influence the organizational structure, culturally driven preferences influence the exercise of choice between alternative structures.

Culture and Organizational Structure

As we discussed in the previous section, organizational structure is strongly affected by prevailing managerial assumptions and beliefs. We know that culture is a key factor influencing managerial assumptions and beliefs (see also Chapter 9). It would not be wrong to expect traditional model to be common in high power-distance cultures, the human relations model in humane and collectivistic cultures, and human resource and human resource development models in performance-oriented individualistic cultures.

Among the cultural dimensions that influence organizations, the one that is closely related to organizational structure is power distance. Lane et al. (2000) argue that organizations in hierarchical cultures support vertical differentiation (i.e., sharp managerial–non-managerial role differentiations), while those in non-hierarchical and collectivistic cultures support horizontal differentiation (i.e., departmental specialization). They also suggest that organizational structures in individualistic cultures are generally informal and flexible.

Asian organizations are characterized by tall structures and a network of extended family relationships and this is mainly due to cultural characteristics derived from Confucianism (i.e., respect for hierarchy based on seniority and position; benevolence and cultivation of harmony) (Pearson and Entrekin, 1998).

Organizations' structures also tend to differ across cultures with respect to formality. Lane et al. (2000) attribute organizational flexibility to the cultural characteristic of individualism. Hampden-Turner and Trompenaars (2000) asked managers across many countries the following question: 'Is an organization a set of tasks, payments, machines and objectives, etc., or a web of social relationships?'

Figure 8.1 shows cross-cultural variations in the extent to which organization is seen as a network of social relationships as opposed to a bundle of specific rules, guidelines and objectives. It appears that preference for social networks over rules and regulations increases with cultural collectivism.

Three successful organizational structures rooted in the cultural context are worth mentioning here: Japanese *zaibatsu* and *keiretsu* and Korean *chaebol*. *Zaibatsus* played an important role in the Japanese economy between the end of the nineteenth century and the Second World War (Chen, 1995). Among the four biggest *zaibatsus* were the Yasuda group (banking), Mitsubishi (shipping and mining), Mitsui (commerce) and Sumitomo (copper mining and refining) (Tipton, 2007). In the pyramidal structure of *zaibatsu*, founder family is at the top and in control of all the subsidiaries, including a bank that finances the member subsidiaries (Figure 8.2). Zaibatsus did not observe the division between ownership and operational control as in Western organizations (Tipton, 2007). The family was in control but the 'family' had a particular meaning.

In Japanese, 'family' can be either *kazoku* (those connected by blood relationship) or *ie* (the household, including those not related by blood). Historically, noble households could include retainers who were treated very much as family members. In addition it

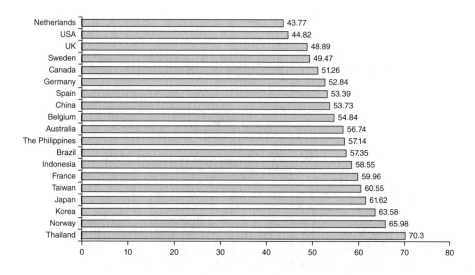

Figure 8.1 *Percentage of respondents perceiving organizations as a web of social relationships rather than a bundle of specific rules, guidelines, and objectives (selected countries from Hampden-Turner, 2003, p.182)*

has continued to be quite common for wealthy Japanese families to adopt sons, or for a son-in-law to take the wife's family name, to preserve the *ie*. In the prewar *zaibatsu*, active managers were hired and promoted on the basis of their competence. In addition, however, as members of the company group, they were 'adopted' into the family, considered as members of the extended household. The entire group could be seen as an extended family, closed against outsiders, but willing to adopt new employees in this symbolic sense. (Tipton, 2007, p. 33)

Korean *chaebols* make up 20 per cent of Korea's GDP, with the five largest *chaebols* including Hyundai, Samsung, LG, Daewoo and Sunkyong (Chen, 1995, p. 166). As in *zaibatsus*, *chaebols* also have a hierarchical structure with the family ownership at the top. However, in *chaebols* family only involves those who have blood relationship. Family members play a very important role in management of *chaebols*. It would be rare but possible to see professionals who are non-family members in management as the size of the *chaebol* increases (Chen, 1995).

In the postwar period of high speed national development, *zaibatsus* were dissolved thanks mainly to the introduction of the antimonopoly law, and *keiretsus* emerged (Tipton, 2007). *Keiretsus* did not have the hierarchical structure of *zaibatsus* (Figure 8.3). Member organizations were linked to each other by cross-shareholdings and the lead bank. Presidents held regular and frequent meetings to exchange information and facilitate coordination. The difficulty with the structure was that it was difficult to respond to crises resulting from low-speed development or economic downturns by diversifying or shutting down a member firm.

There is no hierarchy and members have moral obligation to support each other. The firm is a community or family, including managers and workers and the extended family includes employees of other firms in *keiretsu* group ... Firms may find the cost of continued membership outweigh the benefits. (Tipton, 2007, p. 53)

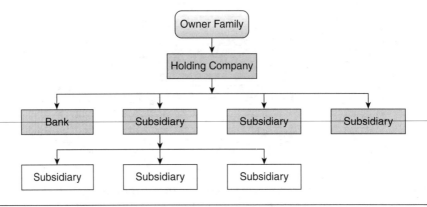

Figure 8.2 *Zaibatsu pyramidal structure (Tipton, 2007, p. 32)*

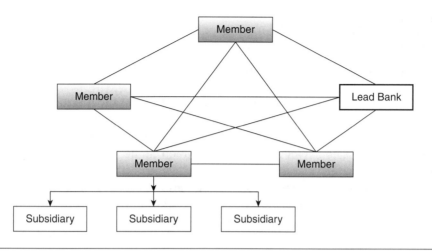

Figure 8.3   *Keiretsu non-hierarchical structure (Tipton, 2007, p. 40)*

Organizational Change

According to the convergence thesis, organizations have to be similar to be success-ful, i.e., they have to be flatter, flexible and team-oriented. However, divergence thesis argues that different structures could equally be successful in different cul-tural contexts so long as there is congruence between the organization and its context.

Divergence Thesis: 'Change is not Necessary or Possible'

The majority of Chinese organizations' structure remains hierarchical and family-like, despite environmental pressures for more professional management and decentralized structures. One such environmental pressure that strongly influences organizational structure is uncertainty (i.e., the change of simple and stable envi-ronment to a complex and unstable one): 'To meet the demands imposed by the uncertainty, organizations will increase their horizontal complexity by adopting "buffering", or boundary spanning departments and replacing mechanistic elements such as standardization and centralization with organic structural mechanisms' (Head, 2005, p. 83).

Head (2005) studied the structural change of nine mid-size Chinese organizations to cope with uncertainty and found that while some organizations try to adopt their structures, others find it very difficult to change because of the cultural context. In the latter case organizations try to minimize environmental uncertainty, rather than change their organizational structure. This is demonstrated in Case 8.1.

CASE 8.1

Change the organizational structure: *No can do!*

Organization ABC is a chemical company that was one of the first in its region to be taken private through a Hong Kong–China joint venture 14 years ago. Before going private it had a mass production/low-cost strategy. After the acquisition it changed to a custom production/differentiation strategy. However, it did not change its structure.

The organization has about 1000 employees organized in 8 departments by function. There are five levels in the hierarchy, starting with a very powerful and controlling board. Reporting to the board is the general manager, vice-general managers, department heads and finally the non-managerial workers. It is a highly mechanistic structure. There is a significant amount of formalization, for example all managers must fill out five reports daily to communicate information to top management. Decision-making is highly centralized, even to dictating what changes are required to adjust the projection process for particular orders. Jobs are highly specialized and standardized.

The general manager recognizes the inappropriateness of the structure. He would like to create a flatter organization by decentralizing decision-making and increasing employee participation. He would like to encourage the workers to act more independently. He also feels that the current structure is creating coordination problems between departments. Unfortunately he has not been able to convince the board of the desirability of these changes ... The organization decided to change its strategy and technology, rather than its structure.

Source: Head (2005, pp. 87, 90)

There are many organizations in China, India and other emerging economies with hierarchical or informal and non-professional structures that compete at the global scale. The question to reflect on is: are they successful in spite of their structure or because of their structure? This dilemma is demonstrated in Case 8.2.

According to the first view, organizations could be even more successful had they adopted the Western organizational and management model, whereas according to the second view, they would not be less successful had they adopted the Western model. Pearson and Entrekin (1998) found that Chinese-dominated organizations in Singapore and Malaysia retained their tall and bureaucratic structure with mechanistic control systems. They were as successful as Singaporean organizations adopting Western organizational structures and management systems. The authors concluded that 'There may be a dynamic operating within these organizations (i.e., Chinese-dominated) that allows them to accomplish informally what is done by deliberate design in Western organizations' (emphases added, p. 1301).

One can argue that organizational structure (especially in domestic organizations) should be congruent with the cultural context to some extent, because organizations function with people (i.e., employees) and for people (i.e., customers) sharing the same cultural characteristics. For example, people in high power-distance cultures would find it difficult to manage their relationships in a decentralized organization (e.g., addressing the manager by their first name). Or customers raised in a particularistic culture (e.g., rules are bent for some individuals, under some circumstances, sometimes) would find it difficult to deal with an organization which is highly formalized and rule-based. 'Many and possibly most Korean firms "look" very Western. But, it is said, looks can be deceiving. "We talk the talk, Western-style", said one executive, "but we walk the walk, Confucian-style"' (Tipton, 2007, p. 88).

CASE 8.2

'You sing my friend and I forget about your debt'!

Here I am, a professional manager for 20 years, watching this most awkward scene in shock!

This is a medium-size trading company selling products imported from Egypt to local and international customers. Its annual turnover is US$60 million! Employees are trusted family members, but it mainly is a 'one man show' ... and what a show he runs!

Two months ago I visited him to talk about our services of international freight forwarding and logistics. He greeted me warmly and respectfully. Following small talk and exchange of good wishes, we started talking about the organization. After all, he was the owner of a multimillion dollar business and I was eager to learn how he managed it.

As I was listening to him I heard the Friday Prayer from the nearby mosque. I did not pay attention to it at first, but I was distracted by the sight of him getting off his shoes and socks. Seeing my puzzlement he said 'I have to get clean and pray now, my friend; please feel at home and drink some tea waiting for me.' I said 'sure' as if there was anything else I could say.

He came back and we resumed our conversation. It was my turn to talk about our organization and the services we offer, not knowing that we would be distracted again in the most unusual way! The secretary came in with a man saying

(Continued)

(Continued)

that he wanted to see the boss. The man was sort of shy and reluctant to take a seat. 'Where were you, my friend?' the boss said. 'I've been looking for you all over the place.' The man murmured something, looking down and avoiding eye contact with me and the boss. 'This guy sings very well, you know!' said the boss. 'Let us hear one of your songs, my friend; see I have a guest here and I would like to entertain him.' The poor man did not know what to do. The boss insisted 'You sing, my friend and I defer the payment of your debt – what do you say?'

I was *sure* that it was a joke, only it wasn't. The man indeed started to sing a folk song and the boss started to dance. As he was pulling my arm to join his dance, I said I had to catch my train, which was about to arrive in five minutes. He insisted that I paid him another visit soon to talk about 'business'.

I left in complete shock and thought to myself 'how is it possible that he makes so much money? Is it because of the way he organizes and manages his business?' I still wonder what would happen if he changes his organizational structure and culture and runs it more professionally with managers like me.

Convergence Thesis: 'Change is Necessary and Possible!'

In today's turbulent environment only those organizations that are flexible, adaptive, participative, and innovative will survive and prosper. Hence, the need for **organizational change** and development – a planned and continuous effort that effectively integrates the organization's sociotechnical system and the environment – is more pronounced than ever.

The effectiveness of approaches to organizational change and development can be gauged by the extent to which these are conducive to single-loop learning or double-loop learning. In single-loop learning the organization adapts to environmental changes without significant change in its basic assumptions; as a result, it improves the organization's capacity to achieve known objectives. Examples of organizational approaches in the single-loop learning category include Quality of Work Life (QWL); sociotechnical approach to job design; Total Quality Management (TQM). On the other hand, double-loop learning goes beyond adapting and anticipates change; it involves changing the organization's culture and learns from that process. The learning organization requires double-loop learning. It is an organization where 'people continually expand their capacity to create the results they truly desire, where new and expansive patterns of thinking are nurtured, where collective aspiration is set free and where people are continually learning how to learn together' (Senge, 1990, p. 3).

If we accept the proposition that 'change is the only thing that does not change', then the next obvious question is 'change in what direction?' Recent research (e.g., Erez and Gati, 2004) show that global work environment dictates change in the following direction:

- High employee involvement and empowerment (i.e., low power-distance)
- Openness to change and willingness to learn
- High interdependence and trust
- Team orientation
- Quality orientation
- Innovation
- Performance orientation
- Diversity and inclusion.

It has been argued that organizations that do not adopt these values have little chance to survive and prosper in global competition. However, changing organizational culture to fit to these values would be a challenge, mainly because these values go counter to the cultural context of the organization (i.e., values of employees).

The process of organizational change *itself* is culture-bound. Some cultures are more comfortable with change, while others resist it. The following cultural characteristics are likely to create resistance to change.

1. ***Uncertainty avoidance***. Change is difficult in cultures where people are threatened by change, rather than perceiving it as an opportunity for growth and development.
2. ***Fatalism***. People in fatalistic cultures believe that the control of things is not in their hands and therefore efforts to change are futile. Fatalistic people also have the tendency to believe that humans, by nature, cannot change.
3. ***Past (as opposed to future) orientation***. People in past-orientated cultures focus on traditions and achievement of the past and consider change unnecessary.
4. ***Power distance***. Those holding power may prevent change from happening, fearing that they would lose power. Those under their supervision, on the other hand, do not question the authority's decision and do not initiate the change process themselves.

How is change possible in cultural contexts that show resistance to change? Change is managed successfully to the extent that leaders are aware of the resistance-producing cultural context and yet courageous enough to *resist the resistance*.

> Global managers have exceptionally open minds. They respect how different countries do things and they have the imagination to appreciate why they do them that way. But they are also incisive, they push the limits of the culture. Global managers don't passively accept it when someone says 'You can't do that in Italy or Spain'... They sort through the debris of cultural excuses. (Taylor, 1991, p. 94)

Let us examine Case 8.3 and discuss the keys to a successful and sustainable organizational change.

CASE 8.3

New Rules in the Old Town

Dear Armane,

I hope you are well. I am sorry I could not find the opportunity to write you sooner. Time ran fast as I tried to catch up with everything I have missed (family, friends, food ...) and to get adjusted to my new job. How is your family? The girls must have grown tall; I would very much like to see you all as soon as possible.

My friend, now that I mentioned the new job, let me tell you a bit more about it and ask your advice. It has been six months since I have started here and I still can not get the hang of what is going on in the company. I have attended the best possible universities abroad believing that I would be a very successful manager when I came back home. But now I am losing confidence in myself. This is my country of origin but it seems to be a different world and I feel like an alien!

It is impossible to make people work independently here. Nobody does anything unless I tell them so. They expect direct orders from their supervisors or managers. The other day one of our hotel guests complained about the radiator that was overheating in his room. That room's heating system is the same with three other rooms on that floor. When you change the heat in one room all of them change. Our technician's response to the guest's complain was that he had to 'ask his supervisor'. When he did, the supervisor said he had to get my approval before doing anything about the problem and put it on hold. I was away from the office that day for a sales visit. So, the problem could not be solved and the guest had to leave the hotel that evening, leaving me a letter of complaint!

When I read about this incident the next day and talked to the technician he told me he had no authority to make a decision at the time. There were surely alternative ways to solve the problem. 'Are you trying to please the customer or the manager?' I asked. He looked at me in the strangest way. I ask you, what was wrong with what I asked?

Last week I announced that I would organize a big meeting and I expected everyone to attend. Only the department managers attended the meeting! I found this rather curious, but I did not want to cancel the meeting at the last minute. I told everyone that, as the new Assistant General Manager, I wanted to know what managers' and employees' expect from this organization to improve job satisfaction and performance. No one spoke up; not a single soul! After few superficial remarks and exchange of good wishes, the meeting was adjourned. I thought 'oh well, how nice that everyone is satisfied with their work', not knowing that I would soon find out that I was naive.

(Continued)

(Continued)

Half an hour later the manager of the food and beverages division, Mr Archen, called and told me he wanted to speak with me. By the time he left my office, I felt that the coffee which I had so enjoyed hardened in my stomach. It turned out there were so many bitter issues concerning employees I was not aware of. And why have I not been made aware of them in the meeting? It was because everyone was too shy to speak up. Why? Apparently because they did not want to *lose their jobs*. Why would they be afraid of losing their jobs? Because, they did not want to be the ones to complain about the organization (so called *trouble-makers*); so, they pretended that all was well!

I was literally speechless. After I recovered from my astonishment, all I could ask him was 'How do you guys focus on your jobs, while worrying about losing face and losing your job? Who will be accountable for any problems that may arise from lack of communication in this organization?' His response was 'We trust *you*, sir!' I did not get it; what was it that they trusted me for? Before I could ask, he ran out and left my office.

I am not sure what to do my friend. I am open to any ideas which may enlighten me. I wish we could return to our school days when life was not so complicated. Please give my love to your wife and the girls.

Hope to see you very soon,

Sabin

Dear brother,

How are you? Don't you worry about us. My mother has been doing better since you left. She takes her medication regularly, of course rather unwillingly. This is to be expected, so we don't complain.

I have no complaints about the family, but it is the job that is killing me. Like the work pressure was not overwhelming enough, now we have to deal with this new Assistant General Manager. He means well, but he seems a bit naïve. He was educated in top schools in the US and now he is trying to apply what he'd learnt here in the organization. He keeps talking about 'open management': everyone should speak freely and openly and take personal responsibility for their jobs. So, what am I sup- posed to do, shoot off whatever comes to my mind just to be open and honest? This is an invitation to chaos. Things should be done in the right manner.

Let me tell you what happened the other day. He reprimanded a poor technician, because he did not do what the customer wanted him to do. What was the guy supposed to do? He had no authority in the matter. The Assistant GM thinks that he should have taken the initiative and been creative enough to solve the customer's problem. If some- thing had gone wrong, the technician was to blame for it, right? Yeah, but who cares! The customer filed a complaint and the Assistant GM was looking for a scapegoat, that's

(Continued)

(Continued)

all. These guys are always like that. They tell you to take responsibility and that they would always back you up, but once you do as they say and things go wrong they pretend that they don't know who you are. I learned the hard lesson years ago and now I don't do anything without a written order from the top.

This guy also has an interest in meetings. He wants us to gather around a table and speak about everything openly. This sounds like a nice idea, but things do not work that way around here. Last week, he invited everyone to the meeting and we went. It seemed like he was expecting all employees for a general evaluation of the workplace. He wanted us to talk about our job satisfaction. For what? To keep the 'satisfied' and fire the 'dissatisfied'?! Anyway, he asked whether there were any problems with cooperation and teamwork. There are of course problems like in any other organization, but these are not to be discussed openly in a general meeting. An administrator is supposed to sense such problems and fix them silently. If we are the ones to point them out and find solutions, what good are you as a manager?

Dear brother, I am sorry I took much of your time. Do such things happen also in your workplace? Like I said, the new boss is really well-intentioned, but he is very young. I hope he will learn about life and its complications soon.

Stay in touch and don't you worry about us.

Love, Barnal

Dear Ms Marhane,

I hope you are doing well. I have received your new year gift; thanks. Congratulations on your promotion and new office; I would like to visit you as soon as I can.

The reason I am writing to you is to seek advice on the latest organizational change we have been going through. We are experiencing some tension between the hotel management and employees and I am not sure why. About six month ago I hired a bright and dynamic new Assistant General Manager educated in the top MBA programmes. As you know, we are in the process of transforming our culture and structure from family-owned organization to a more professional one. We have been trying to attract the best and the brightest and I was very happy to convince this guy to take the position. I was certain that he would make the transition a success. However, things did not go as I had expected. The new manager is just not compatible with the team he works with. Both sides are right in their own terms but they don't understand each other.

I would very much like to talk to you about this matter in detail. The audit is around the corner and things need to get back to normal very fast. Please let me know the earliest date possible to meet you.

Thanks and best regards,

Kayatram Arhan

Founder and President

- List the 'current' cultural characteristics (e.g., high power-distance) and 'desired' cultural characteristic of the organization (e.g., participative).
- What was the President's plan to make the change from the 'current' to the 'desired' organizational structure and culture? Why was the plan not successful?
- What should have been done to prevent the tension from building between the new manager and employees? Is there anything that can be done to save the situation now?

What was missing in the change process described in the case was strong leadership with a clear vision and articulation of where the organization is heading. This had to be the task of the President who was also the respected and trusted founder of the organization. Instead, the leadership role was 'delegated' to the inexperienced and distrusted newcomer (i.e., the young Assistant GM).

In high power-distance and uncertainty-avoiding societal or organizational cultures, leadership plays a particularly important role to explain: 1. why change is necessary, 2. where the organization is heading and 3. what should and should not be expected during the process of change (e.g., some position titles may change but no one will lose their job). The leader not only talks the talk but walks the walk. They should be the role model practicing the new cultural values. For example, if more participation is encouraged, the leader should be the one exercising and demonstrating it publicly.

The leadership style required to successfully implement change is a mixture of transformational and nurturant-task leaderships (see Chapter 5). Transformational leaders question the status quo and intellectually stimulate employees to think out of the box, while nurturant-task leaders provide the emotional support and nurturance to elicit and reward desired employee behaviours.

As discussed above, global competition requires adoption of key competencies including participation, teamwork, openness, quality, innovation, performance-orientation and diversity. Organizational cultures should change to promote these competencies and the change process is initiated by strong leaders who show the way and energize people to walk through it. However, leadership itself is not sufficient to successfully implement a sustainable new work culture and structure.

The role of HRM practices is the key here. If leadership is the engine of change, HRM is the fuel. To strengthen the new organizational culture and structure HRM practices should be all aligned and geared towards the new competencies as the building blocks of the organization. For example, in *employee selection*, job applicants should be evaluated specifically for their ability and willingness to participate, to work in teams, or to innovate. *Job descriptions* should be revised and changed from fixed and narrow description of tasks to flexible and dynamic description of competencies and processes allowing for more participation, teamwork and innovation.

Performance appraisal should include evaluation criteria such as participation, teamwork and innovation. *Training and development* activities should be designed to promote participation, teamwork and innovation. *Compensation and reward management* criteria should include participation, teamwork and innovation.

Cross-cultural Considerations for Managers

'As the world becomes more interconnected and business becomes more complex and dynamic, work must become more *learningful*' (Senge, 1990, p. 4).

As discussed in this chapter, the organization that is successful and continues to endure in today's global and turbulent environment is the learning organization. It is equally appealing to employees – striving to achieve extraordinary performance together with the satisfaction and fulfilment that flow from a job well done. To become a learning organization, there should be openness to new and diverse approaches and encouragement of participation and empowerment. Cultural characteristics such as high power-distance, high uncertainty-avoidance, high fatalism or low performance-orientation may be barriers to change from the 'traditional model' to the 'human resource development model' (e.g., learning organizations) adopted by organizations (See Video 8.1). However, these cultural characteristics are not fate that cannot be changed.

Culture at the organizational level is easier to change than culture at the societal level. Leadership and HRM practices are the keys to facilitate this transformation process. In such cultural contexts, change is initiated and energized by transformational and nurturant-task leaders. The new structure, values and practices are instated in the organization with the help of HRM practices. A strategic HRM approach makes sure that employees with the new and desired set of values and behaviours are attracted to the organization and maintained, and existing employees are trained and rewarded to modify their behaviours.

The paradigm of the learning organization is best suited to cope with the demands and challenges of rapidly changing technology and increasing globalization of business in a world with artificial borders. Organizational design, based on the underlying assumptions of the human resource development model, will result in an organizational structure which is most conducive to implementing the learning organization. We briefly outline how the policies and practices of the human resources development model provide a sound foundation for the effective implementation of *systems thinking; personal mastery;* and *team learning* – some of the essential dimensions of the 'learning organization' (Senge, 1990).

- Systems thinking. All human endeavours, including organizations, are 'systems' – a set of interconnected/interrelated actions. In an attempt to make sense of the complexity that is involved in systems, we often tend to view and analyse each part, action, or activity in isolation from the rest. The specialization involved in this process may increase our expertise, but it also results in a 'silo mentality' which causes us to lose sight of the total picture or system – as would be the case when departments in an organization seek to optimize themselves in isolation at the expense of the organization. 'Systems thinking' avoids the inefficiencies of the silo mentality through cross-functional teams which bring together the different departments. Systems thinking is 'concerned with a shift of mind from seeing parts to seeing wholes, from seeing people as helpless reactors to seeing them as active participants in shaping their reality, from reacting to the present to creating the future' (Senge 1990, p. 69).

- Personal mastery. Personal mastery at all levels is one of the critical disciplines of the learning organization because it is not organizations but people who learn. To achieve this objective the leader first acquires personal mastery and then assists and empowers all employees to do the same. We briefly explore the critical behaviours of personal mastery – *shared vision, objective assessment, focused energies, creative tension* (Senge, 1990).

  o *Shared vision*: Leaders with high personal mastery devote much effort and care to ensure a shared vision for the organization – one that incorporates the beliefs, values and aspirations of the employees. When this is created, there is no trade-off between economic success and moral principles. Such a broad vision promotes among employees a better understanding and appreciation and empathy for each other that moves them away from self-centredness.

  o *Objective assessment*: Leaders with high personal mastery cultivate a culture of openness that permits a meaningful dialogue and testing of assumptions pertaining to acceptable behaviour and practices in the organization. At the same time, they enable employees to assess their work situations objectively, recognize the interdependencies that exist and thereby better understand and appreciate the structures, practices and relationships in the organization. Underlying the objective assessment is a deep commitment to a continuous search for truth in the sense of desire to recognize reality as it currently exists.

  o *Focused energies*: Leaders with high personal mastery see an intrinsic value in the vision – as an expression of the organization's purpose, as the *raison d'être* of the organization. They pursue the vision with focused energies and total dedication of their talent, ability and efforts. Even when their efforts to realize the vision suffer serious setbacks and failures they do not abandon the principles implicit in the vision, despite possible personal costs to them.

  o *Creative tension*: The discrepancy between the vision and current reality can lead to discouragement, anxiety, fear of failure and even hopelessness. This uncomfortable, if not painful, experience can generate in leaders considerable pressure to compromise the integrity of the vision. Leaders with high personal mastery will not succumb to seeking relief from the emotional tensions by following the line of least resistance and avoiding the pressures to struggle towards the vision.

- Team learning. 'How can a team of committed managers with individual IQs above 120 have a collective IQ of 63?' (Senge, 1990, p. 9). To prevent this undesirable situation, team members need to learn to perform the task and social role behaviours. The combined effect of the leaders' task and social role behaviours is to permit a free flow of ideas and relevant information in the group, which enables the group to develop insights and synthesis of ideas and proposals that could not be attained individually.

Chapter Summary

In this chapter we present a relatively brief overview of the vast domain of organizational structure and change. We touch on the basic components of an organizational structure, namely task and authority structure, the principles which govern them and the features which characterize organizational structures. Features of authority structure include chain of command or reporting structure (i.e., unity of command and unit of command principles), the level of delegation of tasks and centralization of decision-making authority and differentiation of core and support functions. Organizations are structured also according to their task structure. Tasks are organized either according to their function or according to the products or services offered, or customers/regions served. Project-based or matrix organizations use a combination of these features. Based on these structural features organizations can be classified as tall vs. flat, specialized vs. general, independent vs. interdependent and tight vs. loose. We examined the managerial beliefs and assumptions about employee work attitudes and behaviour influencing the choice of organizational structure (see Video 8.2).

We explored four managerial approaches: the traditional, human relations, human resource and human resource development models. Each model adopted by top management leads to a certain type of organizational structure and culture. We argue that sociocultural environment (e.g., societal values, beliefs, assumptions) played an important role in managerial approaches/models adopted and in the organizational design and structure commonly observed in different countries. We also argue that culture was not the only factor; included in the societal forces other than culture are the level of industrialization, political and economic structure, education and labour relations system of a country. The most important question we pose is whether or not organizations around the world should and could change their structure and culture to be competitive and sustainable in the globalized world. We suggest that the learning organization model should be adopted. Organizational change is possible with strong leadership and strategic HRM practices to support the new structure and culture (see Video 8.3).

End of Chapter Reflection Questions

1. Suppose that one of the largest organizations in Taiwan resists the idea of organizational change, arguing that they are already the market leader. How would you build a case for change to those who think they need it the least?

2. There are family-owned business organizations among the giants of the world. A closer look at their organizational structure and culture suggests that they are still quite 'traditional'. How can you explain this, given the association between organizational structure and performance? Do you think they need to change? Why and why not?

3. If you adopt the famous principle of 'survival of the fittest' to change management, is it possible and desirable to say that 'those who can survive the organizational change process will remain in the organization, while others who cannot adapt should leave'?

Key Terms and Definitions

Organization structure. The way organizations arrange tasks, employee roles and responsibility to function effectively and respond in a timely fashion to environmental demands.

Unity of command. One of the principles of authority structure in organizations concerning the hierarchical positioning of jobs and the reporting structure among them.

Span of control. The principle of authority structure concerning the size of the units under the control and supervision of managers at different levels.

Delegation. Transfer of or sharing managerial **authority** to lower cadres, while keeping the **responsibility** in the hands of those at management levels.

Decentralization. Transfer of top management authority and responsibility of decision-making to all units in the organization.

Specialization. Structuring organizations according to specialized jobs held by expert units or teams.

Matrix organization. Organizational structure allowing for flow of skills and information among units and employees, who can work on projects under more than one manager at a time.

(Continued)

(Continued)

Boundary-spanning. Boundary-transcending flow of employees and information within or outside the organization to create open systems and to facilitate innovation.

Formalization. Organizational structure and culture favouring close adherence to rules, regulations and procedures.

Mechanistic and organic organizations. Mechanistic organizations are characterized by precise and fixed rules, responsibilities and hierarchical structures, whereas organic ones are flexible, adaptable, and participative.

Convergence vs. divergence thesis. The convergence thesis argues that organizational structures in particular industrial, economic, political and social environments look alike, whereas the divergence thesis argues that differences among organizations in similar environments is possible.

Organizational change. A series of planned actions to facilitate transformation in the organizational structure and/or strategies.

Further Reading

Argyris, C. (1993) *Knowledge for Action: A Guide to Overcoming Barriers to Organizational Change*. San Francisco, CA: Jossey-Bass Inc.

Cameron, K.S. and Quinn, R.E. (1999) *Diagnosing and Changing Organizational Culture: Competing Values Framework*. Reading, MA: Addison-Wesley.

Carter, L., Giber, D. and Goldsmith, M. (eds) (2001) *Best Practices in Organization Development and Change: Culture, Leadership, Retention, Performance, Coaching Case Studies, Tools, Models*. San Francisco, CA: Jossey-Bass.

De Caluwe, L. and Vermaak, H. (2003) *Learning to Change: A Guide for Organizational Change Agents*. Thousand Oaks, CA: Sage.

Garvin, D.A. (2000) *Learning in Action: A Guide to Putting The Learning Organization to Work*. Boston, MA: Harvard Business School Press.

Tobin, D.R. (1998) *The Knowledge-enabled Organization: Moving from 'Training' to 'Learning' to Meet Business Goals*. New York: AMACOM.

Tsang, E. (1997) 'Organizational learning and the learning organization: A dichotomy between descriptive and prescriptive research', *Human Relations*, 50 (1): 73–89.

Weick, K.E. and Quinn, R.E. (1999) 'Organizational change and development', *Annual Review of Psychology*, 50: 361–86.

Cases, Videos and Web Sources

The following cases present issues concerning the 'growing pains' in organizations, such as transformation from paternalistic to professional structure and managing resistance to change.

Cases

Beer, M., Khurana, R. and Weber, J. (2005) *Hewlett-Packard: Culture in Changing Times*. Harvard Business School Case No: 404087-PDF-ENG.

Lowe, J.Y. (2013) *Goran Kapicic at Actavis China*. IVEY Case No: 9B13C001.

Saini, D.S. (2007) *Flaxo-Exports: Managing People in a Small-to-medium-size Enterprise*. Harvard Business School Case No: HKU668-PDF-ENG.

Videos

Video 8.1 Clay Shirky: *Institutions vs. collaboration* (2008) www.ted.com/talks/clay_shirky_on_institutions_versus_collaboration.html - Shirky challenges the institutional structures and proposes alternatives.

Video 8.2 Dan Heath: *Want Your Organization to Change? Put Feelings First* (2010). www.youtube.com/watch?v=JhBzxy7CneM.

Video 8.3 IBM Study: *Making Change Work* (2008) www.youtube.com/watch?v=2ol9zYw4Chg.

Web sources

www.acmpglobal.org/ – Association for Change Management Professionals.
www.iodanet.org/ – International Organizational Development Association.
www.odnetwork.org/ – Organizational Development Network.

References

Chen, M. (1995) *Asian Management Systems*. New York: International Thomson Business Press.

Child, J. (1981) 'Culture, contingency and capitalism in the cross-national study of organizations', *Research in Organizational Behaviour*, 3: 303–56.

Coffey, R.E., Athos, A.G. and Raynolds, R.A. (1975) *Behavior in Organization: A Multi-dimensional View*. Upper Saddle River, NJ: Prentice Hall.

DiMaggio, Paul J. and Powell, Walter W. (1983) 'The iron cage revisited: Institutional isomorphism and collective rationality in organizational fields', *American Sociological Review*, 48, 147–60.

Erez, M. and Gati, E. (2004) 'A dynamic multi-level model of culture: From the micro-level of the individual to the macro level of a global culture', *Applied Psychology: An International Review,* 53 (4): 583–98.

Gallie, W.B. (1978) *Philosophers of Peace and War: Kant, Clausewitz, Marx, Engels and Tolstoy. The Wiles Lectures, delivered at Belfast University in May 1976*. Cambridge: Cambridge University Press.

Hampden-Turner, C. (2003) 'Culture and management in Singapore', in M. Warner (ed.), *Culture and Management in Asia*, pp. 171–86. London: Routledge Curzon.

Hampden-Turner, C. and Trompenaars, F. (2000) *Building Cross-cultural Competence: How to Create Wealth from Conflicting Values*. New Haven, CT: Yale University Press.

Harbison, F.H. and Myers, C.A. (1959) *Management in the Industrial World: An International Analysis*. New York: McGraw-Hill

Head, T.C. (2005) 'Structural changes in turbulent environments: A study of small and mid-size Chinese organizations', *Journal of Leadership and Organizational Studies*, 12 (2): 82–93.

Hickson, D.J. and Pugh, D.S. (1995) *Management Worldwide: The Impact of Societal Culture on Organizations Around the Globe*. London: Penguin.

Hickson, D.J., Hinings, C.R., McMillan, C.J. and Schwitter, J.P. (1974) 'The culture-free context of organization structure: A tri-national comparison', *Sociology*, 8 (1): 59–80.

Hickson, D.J., Pugh, D.S. and Pheysey, D.C. (1969) 'Operations technology and organization structure: An empirical reappraisal', *Administrative Science Quarterly*, 14: 378–97.

Ivancevich, J.M. and Matteson, M.T. (1987) *Controlling Work Stress: Effective Human Resource and Management Strategies*. San Francisco, CA: Jossey-Bass.

Koontz, H.D. and O'Donnell, C.J. (1972) *Principles of Management: An Analysis of Managerial Functions*. New York, McGraw-Hill.

Khandwalla, P.N. (1977) *The Design of Organizations*. New York: Harcourt, Brace, Jovanovich.

Lane, H.W., DiStefano, J.J. and Maznevski, M.L. (2000) *International Management Behavior*. Cambridge, MA: Blackwell.

Maslow, A.H. (1954). *Motivation and Personality*. New York, NY: Harper.

Mayo, E. (1949). *The Social Problems of An Industrial Civilisation*. Oxon, UK: Routledge.

McGregor, D. (1960) *The Human Side of Enterprise*, New York: McGraw-Hill.

Pearson, C. and Entrekin, L. (1998) 'Structural properties, work practices and control in Asian businesses: Some evidence from Singapore and Malaysia', *Human Relations*, 51: 1285–307.

Schein, E.H. (1985) *Organizational Culture and Leadership*. San Francisco, CA: Jossey-Bass.

Senge, P.S. (1990) *The Fifth Discipline: The Art and Practice of the Learning Organization*. New York: Doubleday Currency.

Swanson, R.A. and Holton, E.F. (2001) *Foundations of Human Resource Development*. San Francisco, CA: Berrett-Koehler.

Tayeb, M.H. (1988) *Organizations and National Culture: A Comparative Analysis*. London: Sage.

Taylor, F. (1911) *The Principles of Scientific Management*. New York and London: Harper & Brothers.

Taylor, W. (1991) 'The logic of global business: An interview with ABB's Percy Barnevik', *Harvard Business Review*, 69 (2): 90–95.

Tipton, F.B. (2007) *Asian Firms: History, Institutions and Management*. Cheltenham: Edward Elgar.

Watkins, K.E. and Marsick, V. J. (1995) 'The case for learning', in E.F. Holton (ed.), *Academy of Human Resource Development Conference Proceedings*, pp. 1–7. Austin, TX: Academy of Human Resource Development.

Woodward, J. (1965) *Industrial Organization: Theory and Practice*. Oxford: Oxford University Press.

Worthy, James C. (1950) 'Organizational structure and employee morale', *American Sociological Review*, 15: 169–79.

Want to learn more? Visit the companion website at www.sagepub.co.uk/kanungo to gain access to videos from the end of each chapter, weblinks and flash cards of key terms.

9

Human Resource Management in Cross-cultural Context

The Moscow Aerostar Hotel was a joint venture between Aeroflot, the national airline of Russia, and an aerospace multinational, IMP Group Limited in Nova Scotia. The four-star hotel had a reputation as an 'oasis of Western efficiency in the midst of the Russian economic and political hurricane'. However, one of the key challenges facing the hotel was the transfer of Western HRM practices to Russia. Despite the initial success in attracting qualified applicants, there was a decline in good applicants. The hotel management had to rely solely on network-based recruitment by initiating a 'hire-a-friend' campaign. The application forms included many questions that are illegal or unethical in North America, such as applicant's age, number of children, whether their parents belonged to the Communist Party and their military service.

The interviews conducted for selection purposes proved to be difficult because the applicants were not used to answering such standard questions in the Western context as 'Why should we hire you?' or 'Why should we hire you instead of someone else?'. Similarly, in reference checks no one was willing to give an honest answer. The training sessions during the orientation did not work well, either. Employees preferred lectures and memorizing facts, rather than interactive sessions involving role plays and active participation.

The most challenging issue in managing Russian employees was meeting their expectations and motivating them for career advancement. Although they were paid much more than their colleagues in the country, their expectation was to match their salaries with the Western standards. No matter what kinds of rewards were offered, there was always a lack of appreciation. Higher salaries were preferred instead of performance-based bonuses. There was avoidance of responsibility and workload 'In the West, promotion to line management was viewed as prestigious, but in Russia it just seemed to mean extra work.' None of the Western best-practices worked the way they were intended in Russia and the HR department did not know why and what to do about it (source: adapted from Lane and Shea, 2006).

Why do you think the Canadian hotel chain could not replicate the successful business model in Russia? Based on this case, do you think that the so called Western HRM practices would not work in non-Western contexts? If not, what needs to be done to make it work? Would you recommend changing the practice to fit into the national/ organizational culture or changing the organizational culture to make it congruent with the HRM practices? What are the advantages and disadvantages of the approach you chose?

Competitive and sustainable advantage in the global context is possible only if organizations manage their human resources effectively, and to achieve this cultural factors must be taken into consideration. This chapter is comprised of two parts: cross-cultural approaches to HRM and international HRM. In the first part, the specific focus is on the effect of cultural context on HRM practices (employee selection, performance appraisal, training and development, compensation and reward management, human resource planning and career management). This part will present findings pertaining to differences in HRM practices in the above-mentioned areas and provide a systematic examination of how cultural values and assumptions can explain these differences. In the second part, the focus will be on the HRM practices of multinational corporations to manage the mobile workforce (i.e., expatriates). We will discuss the factors that are associated with expatriate adjustment and performance, followed by HRM practices to facilitate expatriate success.

Learning Objectives

- To become familiar with HRM strategies, approaches and practices in different organizational and cultural contexts.
- To understand how cultural context, vis-à-vis other structural factors (e.g., economic, political, legal, industrial) influence HRM practices.
- To develop strategies for effective HRM practices that fit the local context and meet the challenges of global competitiveness.
- To examine factors associated with expatriates' adjustment and performance.
- To understand HRM practices to enhance expatriate adjustment and performance.

In today's work environment, human resource management (HRM) has a strategic role in growth and survival of the organizations facing increasing competition at a global scale. As the case at the beginning of the chapter illustrates, the main challenge for many organizations is the design and implementation of HRM practices to fit the global *as well as* the local context. This is critical for both multinational and domestic organizations. The multinational corporations (MNCs) feel the pressure to ensure standardization of HRM practices on the one hand and localization on the other to increase the fit with the economic, demographic, legal, sociopolitical and cultural context of the local country. Domestic organizations with a multicultural workforce try to accommodate cultural differences in designing HRM activities. Organizations in the non-Western part of the world strive to adopt culturally appropriate HRM systems that enable them to compete globally. The tension between global integration and local differentiation has dominated the international HRM literature for more than 20 years.

Convergence vs. Divergence in HRM Practices

Earlier writings purported the existence of 'one best way' (i.e., North American) of managing human resources and suggested that HRM practices are converging in the world (see Ruona and Gibson, 2004). However, some researchers and practitioners argue that HRM practices in the world are far from converging. In fact, HRM as a concept is not relevant in countries where there is still heavy reliance on agriculture, an informal sector and unstructured labour markets. The current literature clearly shows that convergence is not possible, at least in the near future, given the multitude of environmental forces influencing HRM practices.

There are three large-scale efforts to document the differences in HRM practices around the world. First, the Routledge Global Human Resource Management Series (edited by Schuler, Jackson, Sparrow and Poole) examines HRM practices in depth in regions of the world including Africa, Asia-Pacific, Latin America, Europe and the Middle East. Differences in HRM practices around the world can be attributed to a multitude of factors exerted by the external and internal environment surrounding organizations.

Second is the best known research on the HRM practices in Europe carried out by the The Cranfield Network (Cranet Project www.cranet.org) established in 1989. The network is a collaboration among 39 universities and business schools in Europe coordinated by the Centre for European Human Resource Management at Cranfield School of Management. The first wave of data was collected between 1990–95, the second wave between 1999–2000 from 8,050 organizations in Europe. Figures 9.1 and 9.2. show similarities and differences among countries in various HRM practices including employee selection and compensation. In relation to the convergence

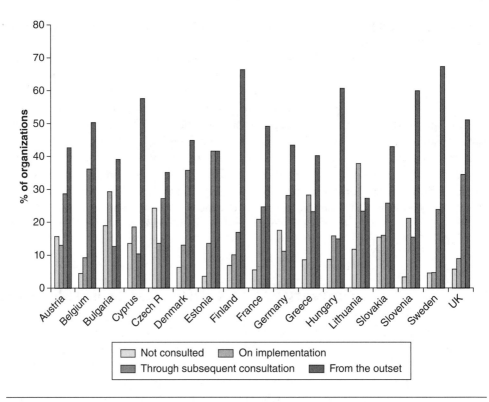

Figure 9.1 *Stage at which HR is involved in development of business strategy (Cranet, 2011, International Executive Report 2011, www.cranet.org, p. 19)*

issue, the authors analysed the trend over time: 'Overall, a broad conclusion might be drawn that while there are some signs of convergence between countries in Europe in the direction of trends, there remain very substantial differences, perhaps even continuing further divergence, in terms of final convergence' (Mayrhofer, Morley and Brewster, 2004, p. 434).

Last but not least is the research commonly referred to as the 'Best Practices Project' (Von Glinow et al., 2002) aimed at documenting attitudes towards various HRM practices in the areas of selection, performance appraisal, training and development, compensation and the strategic role of HRM practices. The countries included in this study were Australia, Canada, USA, China, Indonesia, Japan, Korea, Taiwan, Mexico and several countries in Latin America. The innovation in this research is the assessment of not only how the practices are currently employed in the country ('as is'), but also how they should be employed in the future ('should be'). Authors concluded that there are some common themes as well as differences across cultures in the way HRM practices are approached (Von Glinow et al., 2002).

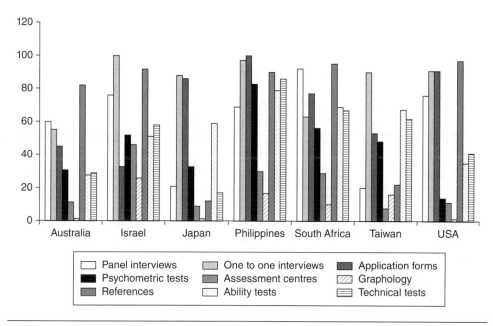

Figure 9.2   *Percentage of organizations utilizing different employee selection methods for professionals (Cranet , 2011, International Executive Report 2011, www.cranet.org, p. 43)*

For example, in employee selection what appears to be 'universal' is the importance between the fit between employees' values and the corporate culture. In performance appraisal, all countries were in agreement that the current performance appraisal practices in their organizations fell short of the strategic purposes of the process, such as evaluating goal accomplishment and planning for development activities. Another finding shared by all countries was that the primary use of training and development was to improve employees' technical skills. The findings also alluded to some country-specific approaches, such as China's and Taiwan's desire to use individual-based incentive systems to motivate employees, Japan's emphasis on evaluating a person's potential to do the job in the hiring practices, and Mexico's use of training and development as a reward to employees.

Why Divergence?

Given that HRM practices are far from being converged across the globe, what do you think accounts for the differences? To what extent does culture play a role? How about labour laws, availability of skilled workforce, typical size and ownership of organizations? Let's examine some of the findings of the Best Practices Project and speculate on the factors accounting for differences in trying to answer the following questions:

- Why do you think 'having the right connections' is more important as an employee selection criterion in Mexico, China and Taiwan than it is in Australia and Canada?
- Why do you think 'documentation of performance' is a more important purpose of performance appraisal in Australia than it is in China?
- Why is 'providing skills to do different jobs' the purpose of training most emphasized by Taiwan?
- Why do countries differ in the importance assigned to seniority in compensation?
- Do countries differ more widely in the ratings of practices 'as is' or 'should be'? Why?

As discussed in Chapter 8, there are a host of factors influencing the design and implementation of HRM practices. These include external environmental factors, such as labour laws and regulations, politics, unions, labour markets and level of industrial development as well as internal environmental factors (i.e., organizational characteristics), such as size, industry, organizational life cycle, strategy and technological infrastructure (see Jackson and Schuler, 1995). Is it possible that culture influences certain aspects of HRM practices more than others? The study of Papalexandris and Panayotopoulou (2004) examined the relationship between HRM practices in the **Cranet project** and GLOBE study findings in 19 countries. They found that cultural values were most strongly associated with HRM practices concerning the management of 'internal communication', and least strongly associate with HRM practices concerning the management of rewards and benefits.

Let us summarize findings of research alluding to differences in HRM practices in the areas of employee selection, performance appraisal, training and development, job analysis and job design, HR planning and career management and compensation and benefit management (based on the reviews by Aycan, 2005; Aycan and Gelfand, 2012). While reading these findings, please think about the cultural, institutional, organizational and legal contexts that might underlie these differences.

Employee Selection

- Employment tests are commonly used in North America to increase the organizational bottom line. However, in some European countries testing for employment has a negative connotation, because it is perceived as invasion of privacy, violation of individuals' rights to control their own careers and a barrier to the holistic representation of individuals (cf., Levy-Leboyer, 1994; Shackleton and Newell, 1997; Sparrow and Hiltrop, 1994; Steiner and Gilliland, 1996).
- In North America, strategic human resource planning is geared towards recruiting the right number of people with the best qualifications to do the job, whereas in

economically underdeveloped countries it is geared towards combating poverty and unemployment (Herriot and Anderson, 1997; Sinha, 1997). In such contexts, the strategic goal of organizations is to meet societal as well as economic needs.

- In some countries employee selection criteria are more interpersonal (e.g., good connection) than individual (e.g., good educational credentials, appropriate knowledge and skills). For example, criteria heavily weighted for employee selection include team members' favourable opinions about the candidate in Japan; agreeableness, good interpersonal relations and trustworthiness in Islamic Arab countries; similarity with the background of the manager in India (e.g., the same family background or homeland); positive attitudes towards family life in Latin America; close relationship with influential government officials in China; and age and social status in Korea (e.g., the *yon-go* system) (Ali, 1989; Lee, 1999; Huo and Von Glinow, 1995; Lu and Bjorkman, 1997; Sinha, 1997: see also Ryan et al., 1999 for the relationship between culture and selection methods).

Performance Appraisal

- The North American approach to performance appraisal is to identify individual differences and make career and reward decisions accordingly (e.g., promotion, training, layoffs, salary increase, benefits). Unlike individualistic cultures, collectivist cultures downplay individual differences; the primary purpose of performance appraisal is to justify the decisions of managers (e.g., Triandis and Bhawuk, 1997). In cultures where favouritism and nepotism are common, there is cynicism and mistrust towards the performance appraisal process. Employees believe that it is pointless if personnel decisions are based on favouritism (e.g., low-performing employees are protected if they have good relations with power holders) rather than merit (cf. Vallance, 1999).
- What constitutes 'good performance' may be culture-bound. Performance-orientated individualistic cultures create an evaluation system that is based on employee productivity, timeliness, quality of output and job-related knowledge and competence (e.g., Harris and Moran, 1996). In collectivist cultures, loyalty, good manners, respectfulness, and citizenship are valued more than productivity (e.g., Blunt and Popoola, 1985; Tung, 1984). In fact, high-performing employees who stand out in the group are disliked because this may disturb group harmony and invoke jealousy (e.g., Kovach, 1995). Seddon (1987) reports that in some African countries, employees' off-the-job behaviours are also included in the appraisal process to protect the company image in public.
- Giving and receiving performance feedback could also be a major challenge in some cultural contexts. Multi-source feedback (e.g., 360-degree performance appraisal) is a method that requires low power-distance (Fletcher and Perry, 2002). In high power-distance cultures, performance appraisal is a top-down process. In

collectivist cultures, 360-degree evaluation may disturb group harmony due to constant monitoring of the behaviour of one's colleagues. There is also a positive leniency bias in peer evaluations because of in-group favouritism and loyalty among colleagues. Finally, self-appraisal in the 360-degree evaluation is neither desirable nor appropriate for collectivistic cultures. The emphasis on the self and personal achievements is disturbing in cultures where humility in self-presentation is the norm (Wiersman and van den Berg, 1999).

- There is a tendency to avoid giving negative feedback to save the employee from losing face (e.g., Seddon, 1987). Positive feedback on performance may also not be well-received in collectivist cultures. Triandis (1994) argues that positive feedback serves the purpose of facilitating interpersonal relations. As such, it may be necessary at the initial stages of entry to the group. Once group acceptance is ensured, there is less need to give positive feedback. Positive feedback to individual performance could also disturb group harmony because it may induce jealousy and resentment among those who did not receive such feedback. Also, in collectivist cultures, positive feedback is expected to come from the outside. If a manager praises their own employees, this could be perceived as self-serving.

Training and Development

- The importance of training and development is undermined in fatalistic cultures where managers assume that employees, by nature, have limited capacity and improvement is not likely (Aycan et al., 2000). In performance-oriented cultural contexts, training and development is primarily geared towards improvement of individual or team performance. However, in collectivistic cultures, such activities serve additional purposes including increasing loyalty and commitment to the organization (e.g., Wong et al., 2001) and fostering team building in work units (Drost et al., 2002).
- There is in-group favouritism based on kinship or tribal ties in collectivist cultures in selecting employees for training and development. In individualistic and low power-distance cultures, training needs are usually determined jointly by the employee and their superior (Wilkins, 2001). In paternalistic cultures, supervisor's guidance is expected and appreciated, because the manager/leader is trusted to know what is best for the employees (Aycan, 2006).
- Cross-cultural variation in cognitive style has to be taken into account when designing training. Allinson and Hayes (2000) found that managers in economically developing countries were the most analytical group, while Anglo, Northern and Latin Europeans were the most intuitive ones. Accordingly, those with an analytical style typically seek certainty, while those with an intuitive style are more likely to question norms and assumptions. The former group prefers trainers who are powerful and knowledgeable experts, while the latter group prefers trainers who encourage questioning and the participation and interaction of the trainees.

Job Analysis and Job Design

- Job analysis is the process in which job description (i.e., listing of job duties and responsibilities) and employee characteristics (i.e., job specifications) are specified. In high uncertainty-avoiding cultures, jobs are defined in specific rather than broad terms in order to reduce role ambiguities (Wong and Birnbaum-More, 1994). In high power-distance cultures, jobs are defined in broader terms, so that superiors have more latitude to ask employees to do a variety of different jobs. There is also a heavy reliance on supervisory guidance in performing jobs and this may reduce the necessity to have specific job descriptions.

- In individualistic cultures, it is expected that job descriptions are for individual workers, whereas in collectivistic cultures they are defined for teams or work groups. Individual accountabilities are blurred in the latter case, and there may be more emphasis on within-job activities among team members (cf. Sanchez and Levine, 1999).

- Raghuram et al. (2001) conducted a cross-cultural study comparing work schedules of selected European countries that differ significantly on Hofstede's four cultural dimensions. Results revealed that shift work and contract work were related to high uncertainty-avoidance, high power-distance and high collectivism. Shift work is preferred the most in high uncertainty-avoidance cultures, because employers seek structured and predictable work arrangement to control the worker output. It is easier to maintain the authority structure and monitor the workers closely in shift work, compared to part-time or telework where worker autonomy and discretion is high. Hence shift work is prevalent also in high power-distance cultures. Because shift work and contract work reinforce solidarity among work groups, it is preferred more in collectivistic rather than individualistic cultures. Finally, it was found that temporary work, telework and part-time work is more common among countries scoring high on femininity rather than masculinity, because workers prefer to have work flexibility to be able to spend time with their families and socialize with their acquaintances.

Human Resource Planning and Career Management

- Human resource planning (HRP) and career planning is not carried out in such a systematic and evidence-based way in all cultural contexts. In past-oriented cultures staffing practices are an extension of the past practices; in present-oriented cultures, short-term staffing plans are made based on current workforce supply and demand; and in future-oriented cultures, long-term plans are implemented to achieve the strategic goals (cf. Lane et al., 1997). In fatalistic sociocultural environments, work culture is reactive, rather than proactive (Aycan et al., 2000). Future planning (i.e., proactivity) is deemed to be unnecessary and useless when events are perceived to be beyond the control of the individuals. In such a cultural context, the common approach is that 'we'll fix the problem (e.g., shortage of employees) when it occurs' (i.e., reactivity). In high power-distance cultures, systematic and participative human resource planning is rare, because as in all other decisions, the HRP decision-making process is centralized. For example, despite succession plans the nephew of a high-level manager, as a new graduate, may be unexpectedly appointed to a managerial position (see Bian and Ang, 1997 for more discussion on *guanxi* networks and job mobility), or an unsuccessful family member is 'promoted' to a position where they are given a passive role; this way they do not lose face.

- It may be wrong to assume that career decisions are made by employees in accordance to their own values, competencies and career orientations. Aycan and Fikret-Pasa (2003) demonstrated that career decisions in collectivistic cultures are based on the opinions of significant others, especially the family. In some countries, parents accompany their adult child in the job interview. They sit in the interview and negotiate job conditions, salary and benefits on behalf of their son or daughter. For employees under the pressure of parental and societal expectations, career management should also serve the function of helping them to find what they really want for their own career and how to make the move in this direction from where they are.

- There are significant differences in promotion criteria. Evans (1993) reports that 'seniority' is the most important promotion criterion followed by job performance in Japanese enterprises. This is similar in other Confucian Asian cultures. In an excellent analysis of employee categorization and promotion likelihood in Chinese organizations, Cheng and Sethi (1999) described the process by which promotion decisions are made. The first criterion is the 'relationship' of the candidate to the top manager (whether they are an in-group or an out-group member, based on kinship or other salient factors); next comes the 'loyalty' criterion; this is followed by the 'competence' criterion. According to this categorization, even an employee with high competence and high loyalty is not able to make it to the top if they are not related to the power holders. Schaubroeck and Lam (2002) found that similarity in personality and good relationships with *peers* was a significant predictor of the promotion decision in individualistic cultures, while similarity in personality and good relationships with *superiors* was a significant predictor of the promotion decision in collectivistic cultures.

Compensation and Benefits

- In the North American HRM context, compensation management, especially determination of the base salary, begins with the process of 'job evaluation', which is the objective, formal and systematic comparison of jobs to determine the worth of one job relative to another. In cultures characterized by high power-distance and particularism, wage and salary determination is based on subjective evaluations of managers who reserve the right to assign differential salaries to employees recruited for the same job (cf., Kanungo and Mendonça, 1997). As such, wages and salaries reflect the 'value' of people (i.e., in-group members are valued higher than the out-group members), rather than the value of the job itself.

- Seniority is a widespread criterion in compensation in collectivistic and hierarchical cultural contexts. There are numerous studies pointing to the tension between seniority vs. merit-based pay schemes, especially in Asian countries, which are becoming more and more performance-oriented with a strong collectivistic and hierarchical cultural orientation (e.g., Björkman and Lu, 1999; Budhwar and Khatri, 2001; Lowe et al., 2002). Pay-for-performance and focus on individual performance in compensation are more common in individualistic than in collectivistic cultures (Schuler and Rogovsky, 1998). Lowe et al. (2002) found that in China, Indonesia and Taiwan, pay is contingent on the group's performance, more so than it is in Australia and USA. Wage differential is narrow even among the lowest and highest ranking (e.g., 4:1) officials in collectivistic cultures, whereas this is very high in individualistic performance-oriented cultures (e.g., ranging from 20:1 to 40:1) (Easterby-Smith et al., 1995).
- Differences also exist with respect to indirect compensation, namely, benefits and allowances. Milliman and colleagues (1998) found a strong positive correlation between the femininity cultural dimension and flexible benefit plans, workplace childcare practices, maternity leave programmes and career-break schemes and a strong positive correlation between collectivism and such benefits. Employees in feminine and collectivistic cultures seek for more flexibility and organizational support to accommodate their non-work responsibilities. Other benefits for collectivistic cultures include welfare programmes such as housing, contribution to education of children, or heating support (e.g., Quinn and Rivoli, 1991; Sparrow and Budhwar, 1997).

How does Culture Influence HRM Practices?

As our brief review of the comparative literature suggests, culture plays a significant role in HRM practices. How does it influence HRM practices? In an attempt to answer this question Kanungo and colleagues developed the Model of Culture Fit (MCF) (Kanungo and Jaeger, 1990; Mendonça and Kanungo, 1994; Aycan, Kanungo and Sinha, 1999) and tested it in ten countries including the USA, Canada, Germany, Russia, Romania, Israel, Turkey, Pakistan, India and China (Aycan et al., 2000).

According to the MCF (Figure 9.3), organizational culture is shaped by managerial beliefs and assumptions about two fundamental organizational elements: the task and the employees. Managerial assumptions pertaining to the task deal with the nature of the task and how it can best be accomplished, whereas those pertaining to the employees deal with the employee nature and behaviour. Managers implement HRM practices based on their assumptions on the nature of both the task and the employees.

Task-driven assumptions are influenced by characteristics of the organization, such as sector, size, industry, strategy, market competitiveness and resource availability. ***Employee-related assumptions*** are influenced by the sociocultural context. For example, managers who assume that employees by nature cannot change (as in the saying 'A 70-year-old is the same person as he was at the age of 7') would provide less training to their employees than the manager who assumes that 'sky is the limit'. Managers' assumptions, in turn, are influenced by the cultural values with which they were socialized. Managerial assumptions include the following:

- Malleability – whether or not the employees' nature can be changed.
- Future orientation – whether or not employees take a futuristic stance in planning their actions.
- Proactivity/reactivity – whether employees take personal initiatives or simply react to external demands while trying to achieve their job objectives.
- Responsibility-seeking – whether or not employees accept and seek responsibility in their job.
- Participation – whether or not employees prefer delegation at all levels and like to be consulted in matters that concern them.
- Obligation towards others – whether or not employees feel obliged to fulfil their responsibilities towards others in workplace.

There were some interesting patterns observed in the cross-cultural study comparing 10 countries. For example, managers in cultures high on paternalism values assumed that employees could not be proactive in their jobs and that they needed close guidance and supervision. Based on this assumption, they did not allow autonomy and provide feedback to employees which would enrich their jobs and empower them. Managers from cultures valuing fatalism assumed that employees by nature cannot change and improve (the malleability assumption). Accordingly, they did not reward employees on the basis of their performance. Rewarding employees on the basis of good performance is a technique to change behaviour and shape it in such a way that is desirable for the organization. Managers socialized in fatalistic cultures believe that employee nature and behaviour cannot be changed; therefore they do not use behavioural modification techniques such as performance-based rewards.

Cultural Orientations and HRM Practices

The MCF Framework has been extended to include more HRM practices by Aycan (2005) (Table 9.1). According to the framework there are three overarching cultural orientations that account for variations in HRM practices: (1) relationships vs. performance, (2) hierarchy vs. participation and (3) stability vs. change.

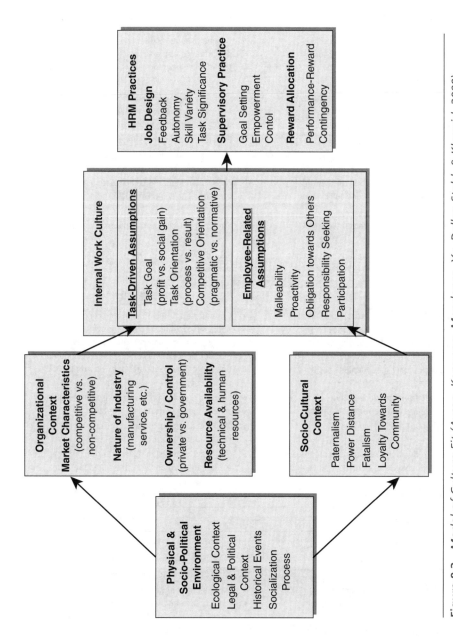

Figure 9.3 *Model of Culture Fit (Aycan, Kanungo, Mendonca, Yu, Deller, Stahl, & Khursid, 2000)*

HRM Practices

Job Design
Feedback
Autonomy
Skill Variety
Task Significance

Supervisory Practice
Goal Setting
Empowerment
Contol

Reward Allocation
Performance-Reward
Contingency

Internal Work Culture

Task-Driven Assumptions
Task Goal
(profit vs. social gain)
Task Orientation
(process vs. result)
Competitive Orientation
(pragmatic vs. normative)

Employee-Related Assumptions
Malleability
Proactivity
Obligation towards Others
Responsibility Seeking
Participation

Organizational Context
Market Characteristics
(competitive vs. non-competitive)
Nature of Industry
(manufacturing service, etc.)
Ownership / Control
(private vs. government)
Resource Availability
(technical & human resources)

Socio-Cultural Context
Paternalism
Power Distance
Fatalism
Loyalty Towards Community

Physical & Socio-Political Environment
Ecological Context
Legal & Political Context
Historical Events
Socialization Process

Table 9.1   Cultural orientations (national or organizational) and corresponding HRM practices (Aycan, 2005, pp. 1110–12)

Relationship ←→ Performance	
• Criteria used in recruitment, selection, and performance appraisal emphasize ability to maintain good interpersonal relationships and work in harmony with others	• Criteria used in recruitment, selection, and performance appraisal emphasize job-related and technical competencies
• Subjective evaluations in recruitment, selection, and performance appraisal; indirect, subtle and non-confrontational feedback	• Objective and systematic evaluations in recruitment, selection, and performance appraisal; direct and explicit feedback
• Preference for internal or network-based recruitment	• Preference for formal, structured and widespread use of recruitment channels
• Criteria used in need assessment for training, career planning, and compensation and reward management emphasize loyalty and seniority	• Criteria used in need assessment for training, career planning, and compensation and reward management emphasize performance outcomes and merit
• Job descriptions, rewards, and performance feedback are team-based	• Strong emphasis on training and development
• Strong emphasis on employee welfare programmes and intrinsic rewards	• Awards, recognition, and bonuses for good performance

Hierarchy ←→ Participation	
• Criteria used in recruitment, selection, performance appraisal, training and development need assessment, and compensation and reward management emphasize good interpersonal relationships with higher management, social class, seniority, and age	• Criteria used in recruitment, selection, performance appraisal, training and development need assessment, and compensation and reward management emphasize job-related competencies and merit. Equal employment opportunity is encouraged
• Differential criteria and methods used in recruitment, selection and performance appraisal	• Uniform criteria and methods used in recruitment, selection and performance appraisal
• Top-down performance appraisal	• Multiple assessors and multiple criteria in performance appraisal
• Non-participative decision making in training need assessment, job analysis, and human resource and career planning	• Participative decision making in training need assessment, job analysis, and human resource and career planning
• One-way lecturing; role-modelling of superiors	• Participative, interactive training

Stability ←→ Change	
• Preference for internal or network-based recruitment	• Preference for external recruitment
• Low performance-reward contingency	• High performance-reward contingency
• Process-oriented performance evaluation (intention, effort, motivation to do the job)	• Results-oriented performance evaluation
• One-way lecturing; hands-on-training	• Participative and interactive training
• Detailed, narrowly defined, fixed job desciptions	• Strong emphasis on training and development
• Employee security plans	• Broad, flexible, dynamic job descriptions
	• Equity principle in compensation and reward management; individual bonuses / commissions

There are two caveats to keep in mind when interpreting this framework. First, the framework applies to cultures at the national or organizational level. If applied at the national level, it would be wrong to assume that in a country all organizations have, say, oriented towards maintaining status hierarchy; some may promote status hierarchy, while others may promote egalitarianism and participation. As discussed in the Model of Culture Fit, this would depend partly on the organizational context, such as size, industry, ownership status and so on. Second, it would be wrong to place organizations at the extremes presented in the Table 9.1 and assume that, say, an organization is either oriented towards maintaining status hierarchy or promoting egalitarianism and participation – it may be somewhere in between and that is why we have double-headed arrows to represent a continuum, rather than a category.

The first orientation towards 'relationship vs. performance' represents a loosely coupled combination of cultural value dimensions, including performance-orientation, future-orientation and individualism-collectivism. On the one hand, a strong value is placed upon improving performance and on the other, on maintaining good interpersonal relationships and in-group harmony. Although these two orientations do not necessarily contradict or compete with one another, being high on one usually denotes being low on the other. In societies or organizations that are high on performance orientation, HRM practices are designed to improve employee performance and organizational bottom line. There is strong emphasis on training and development; criteria for recruitment, selection, performance appraisal, training and development, compensation and reward management are based on performance outcomes and merit. On the other hand, in societies and organizations that are high on relationship orientation, HRM practices are geared towards attracting, maintaining, developing and rewarding people who fit well to the social networks in the organization. Individual-based rewards and recognitions such as employee of the month are to be avoided. Performance feedback is given in a highly subtle way so as not to hurt the feelings of employees, which would harm the relationship.

Thinking across cultures 9.1

Double the Effort – Why?

What is going on here? As I was prepared to talk to Jade about her low performance in the last year, she told me that she received very high evaluations from her manager. She has just e-mailed me the performance evaluation ratings from her manager and I could not believe my eyes – it

(Continued)

(Continued)

was different from the one submitted to the HR department! Did the manager fill out two forms for every employee: one to be given to the employee and the other to be submitted to the HR department? Why would he double the effort? Which evaluation should I trust?!

The second orientation refers to 'hierarchy vs. participation' (characterized by cultural values of power distance and particularism). It is concerned with the degree of status hierarchy a society or an organization likes to maintain. In societies and organizations that value maintaining the status hierarchy, HRM practices are designed to attract, maintain and reward only those who come from a 'privileged' background or who have good relationships with power holders in the organization. Differential treatment and favouritism are commonplace in selection, performance appraisal, training and development, compensation and reward management and career planning. There is centralized decision-making in almost all HRM practices. Performance evaluation and promotion decisions are top-down. Training occurs as a didactic delivery of information by people perceived to be the authority in the subject; interactive and participative training are not appreciated.

At the other end of the continuum, in societies and organizations that promote egalitarianism and participation, uniform procedures are administered to everyone evaluated on the basis of objective criteria, such as education, performance, work experience and so on. HRM practices are geared towards minimizing discrimination on the basis of age, gender or group membership (social class, caste, alumni, home town etc.). Decisions in key HRM areas are made with the participation of employees. Feedback on employee performance is collected from multiple sources using multiple criteria. Training and development activities are engaging; two-way learning is encouraged.

Thinking across cultures. 9.2

There is no 'Inappropriate' Question Here!

The following are the type of questions in job application forms or interviews asked by the majority of organizations in a particular country. Can you guess the cultural characteristics of the country?

- Applicant's mother's and father's occupation.
- Marital status of the applicant.
- Marital status of the mother and father of the applicant (e.g., whether or not they are separated).
- Occupation of the spouse.
- Number of siblings.
- Applicant's order of birth.
- Intention to get married and have children.
- Names of schools attended starting with the primary school.
- Membership to social clubs.
- Hobbies.
- Books most recently read.
- Photo of the applicant.

The final orientation referred to as 'stability vs. change' is a loose combination of cultural values including uncertainty avoidance and fatalism. In societies or organizations that are inflexible and do not believe in change and development, HRM practices promote stability and maintenance of status quo. Typical HRM practices in stability-oriented cultures include preference for an internal candidate for promotion who would not rock the boat. Because these cultures tend to be risk-averse, job descriptions will be detailed, outlining the specific roles, duties and expectations of employees. The absence of belief in change results in a low priority being given to employee training and development; performance-based rewards are not perceived to be useful to improve performance.

Fatalistic beliefs lead to rewarding 'effort' even though the goals are not achieved. Employees are upset when their effort is not rewarded in cases when they could not deliver results because of reasons they believe to be out of their control. On the other hand, in organizations that value flexibility, change and development, HRM practices are geared towards increasing change, dynamism and innovation. In promotion decisions, bringing in new blood is more important than 'inbreeding'. Organizational culture and climate encourages interaction and exchange of ideas at all levels. Job descriptions are flexible enough to enable employees to work in stretch assignments, enlarged jobs, cross-functional teams and rotations in different departments. Employees typically believe that they can control the outcome of their efforts. Therefore, they are motivated when rewards are contingent upon their performance.

Cross–cultural Considerations for Managers

How is it possible to implement HRM practices on the right-hand side of Table 9.1 (e.g., multisource performance feedback, participative training, performance-reward contingency) to organizations oriented towards maintaining harmonious relationships, hierarchy and the status quo? Case 9.1 illustrates the challenge of this transformation.

CASE 9.1

Acarel TR*: 'For years I nurtured snakes in my heart, instead of friends'

Everyone was excited about the new performance evaluation system. People called it 'open and all around', meaning open feedback from everyone within the work unit. This would be *the* opportunity to talk freely about what is great about working in the team and what is not so good about it.

Yes there were sceptics, but given the strong support from top management, employees remained hopeful that the new system would enable them to meet the ambitious strategic plan of the coming years. The champion of this project, naturally, was the HR department. The HR manager was extremely excited and proud to initiate this process, which will make Acarel the pioneering company implementing a 360-degree open feedback performance evaluation system for the first time in Turkey. The Dutch CEO, who took up his expatriate position in Turkey eight months ago, was equally excited. He thought this was the right thing to do and expected no glitches.

A large group of consultants were hired to facilitate the open feedback sessions to take place in each department. Prior to feedback sessions, employees filled out questionnaires anonymously evaluating the competencies of their unit managers and colleagues in key roles. The scores were averaged and fancy graphs were generated to show the current vs. desired levels of required competencies. Consultants held lengthy training sessions with employees and managers about the rules of giving and receiving feedback. Handouts featured the so-called golden rules.

The first open feedback session was held between the CEO and the functional managers. The purpose was to demonstrate how the CEO, himself, would take and respond to feedback from his direct reports. The session was extremely successful. He listened to each and every criticism carefully, took notes and showed appreciation of the opportunity for receiving candid feedback from his subordinates. The meeting was the first successful step!

The next day, functional managers were to meet with their employees. Everyone was prepared: they knew the rules, they (at least the managers) had first-hand experience of such a session, they studied the graphs before coming to the meeting and they knew the gaps between the 'actual' and 'ideal'. No problems were expected.

Managers met with their own subordinates in separate meeting rooms. A consultant was assigned to each group to facilitate the meeting. The doors were closed, meetings started. A peaceful 20 minutes into the meeting, the corridors were shaken by the crying and yelling of the HR manager! She, of all the managers, was the one who could not take the feedback from her subordinates! 'I nurtured snakes in my heart for years instead of friends,' she bawled.

Everyone came out of the meeting rooms, shocked and upset. No one was able to resume the meeting with such a bad example of morale. After all, if the HR manager could not take it, how could anyone expect the rest of the managers to take it!

* The real name of the organization is disguised.

- Why do you think the project was not successful?
- What could have been done differently to prevent the crisis?
- Based on this case, can we conclude that 'Western' HRM practices cannot work in non-Western contexts?

As Case 9.1 illustrates, organizations must take the cultural context into account, especially when transferring Western (mostly North American) practices to other countries. This is the challenged faced by many MNCs who try to keep the same HRM systems in their foreign subsidiaries, while realizing that they may lose their competitive advantage in the labour market by not localizing their practices. The following are the strategies we recommend to deal with this dilemma.

- Culture plays a more important role in determining 'how' an HR practice is implemented, rather than 'what' is implemented (e.g. Tayeb, 1995). For example, in performance appraisal 'what' is evaluated, namely, behavioural competencies, may be the same in all subsidiaries of MNCs. However, 'how' they are evaluated should be sensitive to the cultural context. As discussed earlier in the chapter, in high power-distance cultures superiors do not like to be evaluated by their subordinates and in collectivistic cultures employees do not like to be evaluated by their colleagues. Therefore, in such cultural contexts performance evaluation should be initially conducted as a top-down process (i.e., only supervisors evaluate employees). Later the process may involve colleagues, but the feedback from colleagues should be used as information used for personal development, rather than for performance evaluation. As employees get used to the initial applications of the multisource feedback system, the MNC can gradually implement the full 360-degree performance evaluation. The key is to implement the so called 'culturally inappropriate' HR systems gradually in the organization and avoid radical and quick changes over night!

- An alternative strategy is to regionalize HRM practices – that is to design and/or implement different HRM systems for different country/cultural regions. This strategy is midway between 'global standardization' and 'localization' and seems to be adopted by the majority of MNCs. HRM practices are the same within the region but different across the regions.

- Managers should remember that changing HRM practices essentially means changing the organizational culture. Therefore, the change process should be managed well (see Chapter 8). It not only requires persistence and patience, but also requires full support and championship of the top- and mid-level managers. It may also mean upgrading the workforce (e.g., hiring new employees and training the existing ones) to fit to the new cultural context created by the new HRM policies and practices.

- MNCs are strongly recommended to adopt the learning organizational perspective in transferring HRM practices to local subsidiaries. According to a recent research on subsidiaries of 23 MNCs (Isik, 2012), those promoting 'participation in decision-making' and 'knowledge transfer' among HRM units of subsidiaries found that employees perceived HRM practices to be more responsive to their needs and expectations. In turn, this was associated positively with employee satisfaction with HRM practices, higher organizational identification and lower turnover intention.

Expatriate Management: How to Enhance Adjustment and Performance

Expatriates are employees of multinational organizations working in overseas subsidiaries on temporary assignments that usually take more than six months and less than five years in one term (Aycan and Kanungo, 1997). The key benefits of expatriation include knowledge transfer among organizations, control of the local unit and contribution to local unit's performance and human resource development (e.g., Harzing, 2001; Hébert et al., 2005; Minbaeva and Michailova, 2004; Selmer, 2004). Global expansion of business organization has become the norm. Multinational business organizations not only have subsidiaries, but also headquarters in diverse locations. For example, according to a recent survey (Brookfield Global Relocation Services, 2012), 42 per cent of business organizations have their headquarters located in the Europe, Middle East and Africa region (EMEA) in 2007 compared to only 10 per cent in 2000. Growing geographical expansion of business activities parallels a growing expatriate population. Although, depending on the purpose of the assignment, alternative forms of overseas assignments are proposed including short-term assignments, frequent flyers, international commuters, flexpatriates, international itinerants and inpatriates (employees from an international subsidiary working in the headquarter for a temporary period), expatriation is still the most common form of overseas assignments (see Banai and Harry, 2004; Mayerhofer et al., 2004; Minbaeva and Michailova, 2004). Sixty-three per cent of the 123 multinational organizations participated in the Global Relocation Trends (Brookfield Global Relocation Services, 2012) survey reported that their expatriate population are expected to increase from the previous year, whereas only 8 per cent reported an expectation of decrease. This trend is attributed to commercial growth within the European Union, the growth in the Chinese economy and high cost of doing business in the US.

HSBC Bank's International Expat Explorer Survey (2008) of 2,155 expatriates showed that the top three destinations that Western expatriates preferred were the United Arab Emirates, Singapore and India, bottom of this list were the UK and France. This indicates that expatriates in growing numbers work in countries that are culturally dissimilar to their own. Hence, finding the right candidate for expatriation, preparing them for the assignment and retaining and motivating them are at the top of international human resource management (IHRM) agendas of multinational organizations. Before presenting specific IHRM practices to improve the success of expatriation, let us first discuss what we mean by expatriate success and failure.

Reports show that 12 per cent of expatriates leave the assignment and come back to the country of origin before their term is over, and 6 per cent failed during their assignment (Brookfield Global Relocation Services, 2012). Why do you think some expatriates prematurely terminate their assignment or fail in their assignment?

There is consensus in the literature to define successful expatriation on the basis of two criteria: cross-cultural adjustment and job performance (e.g., Harzing, 2004). An expatriate's 'failure' implies failure to adjust to the host country (adjustment criterion) and/or failure in the assigned job (performance criterion). The majority of expatriates who *fail* suffer from adjustment problems rather than job-related incompetence.

Factors associated with expatriate adjustment

An expatriate's **adjustment** to the new culture refers to their progress in becoming fully effective in the host society by meeting requirements of daily life and engaging in and maintaining positive interpersonal relations with the members of the host society (Black et al., 1991).

Characteristics of the expatriate

- Good interpersonal skills (Hechanova et al., 2003).
- Good command of the native language (Bhaskar-Shrinivas et al., 2005).

- Willingness and ability to adjust to a different cross-cultural context (Selmer, 2004).
- Willingness to communicate with host nationals (Takeuchi et al., 2002).
- Positive attitudes towards learning the new culture, while maintaining the cultural characteristics of their home country (i.e., integrating the best of both worlds: home and host country cultural characteristics) (Tung, 1998).
- Gender of the expatriate. Female expatriates were found to have better adjustment in their social interactions with locals than male expatriates (Hechanova et al., 2003). Although females constitute a small portion of expatriates, they are reported to have high success rates (e.g., Caligiuri and Cascio, 1999). Indeed females are deemed to be more appropriate for overseas assignments because of their coping skills with coping-mediated stress, boundary-spanning ability and interpersonal sensitivity (Selmer and Leung, 2003). Moreover, they are reported to have an advantage over their male colleagues for receiving positive attitudes from the business community in the host country, largely due to the fact that they are trusted and respected by host-country nationals and better remembered by business associates (e.g., Caligiuri, Joshi and Lazarova, 1999). Males and females did not differ in their level of willingness to accept international assignments; but females are found to accept posts in hardship places (Hofbauer and Fischlmayr, 2004; Haines and Saba, 1999; Tung, 2004). (see Video 9.2.)
- Learning orientation of expatriates (Palthe, 2004).
- High self-efficacy (Hechanova et al., 2003; Bhaskar-Shrinivas et al., 2005; Palthe, 2004).
- Effective coping strategies focusing on solving the problem rather than getting rid of the symptoms of discomfort (e.g., Stahl and Caligiuri, 2005; Selmer, 2002).
- Personality characteristics, including extroversion, agreeableness and emotional stability (Caligiuri, 2000).

Nature of the assignment

- Prior work experience in a similar culture (Bhaskar-Shrinivas et al., 2005; Shaffer, et al., 1999). It should be noted that some studies shed doubt on the importance of cultural similarity (e.g., Palthe, 2004). For example, Finnish expatriates had difficulty adjusting to European countries (Suutari and Brewster, 1998); Indian expatriates living overseas had more difficulty adjusting to work in India than in Oman (Deosthalee, 2002); Hong Kong expatriates to China had more adjustment problems than Chinese expatriates in Hong Kong (Selmer, et al., 2003). It appears that cultural similarity or dissimilarity, by itself, is not a factor significantly influencing the adjustment process.
- Duration of the assignment. Generally, the U-curve hypothesis is supported to depict the dynamic nature of adjustment (honeymoon period, followed by a period of discomfort, ending with high degree of adjustment), but a sideways S appeared

to be a better-fitting model (U curve followed by a period of decline) (Bhaskar-Shrinivas et al., 2005).

- Longer duration of the assignment and autonomy in the expatriate's role (role discretion) enhanced adjustment, whereas role ambiguity lowers it (Hechanova et al., 2003). However, Palthe (2004) reports that role discretion lowers interaction adjustment. These contradictory findings suggest that too little and too much discretion increases adjustment difficulties.

Organizational support

- Socialization and orientation programmes in the host country (Palthe, 2004).
- Support from the co-workers in the host country and resources provided by the parent company (the company that sends the expatriate to overseas assignment) (Bhaskar-Shrinivas et al., 2005; Shaffer et al., 1999).
- Support from the supervisor in the local unit. It is interesting to note that if the expatriate had no prior expatriation experience, supervisory support in the unit has a negative impact on adjustment, presumably because the expatriate expects more support coming from the *parent company*, whereas if the expatriate had prior international work experience, supervisory support is correlated positively with adjustment (Shaffer et al., 1999).
- Cross-cultural training is recognized to have high importance for the expatriation process and 81 per cent or organizations provide training to some or all of their expatriates (Brookfield Global Relocation Services, 2012). There are some inconsistencies among studies investigating the effectiveness of cross-cultural training. For example, two meta-analyses found positive but modest correlations between cross-cultural training and expatriate adjustment and performance outcomes (Mendenhall et al., 2004; Morris and Robie, 2001), while another one found a low but surprisingly negative relationship with adjustment (Hechanova et al., 2003). These inconsistencies can be attributed to the diversity in the type and duration of trainings offered.
- The large size and cultural diversity of expatriates social networks as well as frequent interactions with them enhances expatriates' adjustment and psychological well-being (Wang and Kanungo, 2004).

Family-related factors

- Adjustment of the spouse for married expatriates was found to be one of the most important factors for expatriate premature termination of the assignment (e.g., Bhaskar-Shrinivas et al., 2005; Hechanova et al., 2003; Palthe, 2004). (see Video 9.1.)

Factors associated with expatriate performance and job satisfaction

- Language competence enhances work performance more for non-native speakers of English going to English-speaking Anglo-Saxon countries, compared to English speaking expatriates going to countries whose native language they cannot speak (Bhaskar-Shrinivas et al., 2005).
- Role clarity, role discretion, months on the assignment, positive outcome expectancy (i.e., belief that the international assignment will benefit their career) and amount of interaction with host nationals are positively associated with job performance (e.g., Hechanova et al., 2003; Bhaskar-Shrinivas et al., 2005; Palthe, 2004), whereas role ambiguity, role conflict and role novelty are negatively associated with it (e.g., Shaffer et al., 1999; Kraimer and Wayne, 2004).
- Personality was found to be a factor both directly influencing and moderating performance ratings. Caligiuri (2000) found that conscientiousness correlated positively with supervisory ratings of expatriate performance and Caligiuri and Day (2000) found that high self-monitoring correlated negatively with contextual performance, especially when expatriate and their supervisor are from different nationalities.
- Expatriate job satisfaction is enhanced with increasing task significance, job autonomy, job authority (control and discretion), job similarity, teamwork, consensus-based decision-making, organizational support (Yavas and Bodur, 1999), mentorship and boundary-spanning activities (Au and Fukuda, 2002; Downes et al., 2002; Jackson et al., 2000).
- Personal factors such as cultural sensitivity, good interpersonal relationships, cultural openness, flexibility and adaptability also enhance job satisfaction (Yavas and Bodur, 1999).
- **Meta-analyses** (e.g., Bhaskar-Shrinivas et al., 2005; Hechanova et al., 2003) revealed that there is a strong relationship among expatriate adjustment, job satisfaction, organizational commitment and turnover intention. Sinangil and Ones (1997) found that adjustment to living abroad correlated strongly with all dimensions of performance rated by the host country nationals.

Cross-cultural Considerations for Managers

Successful management of the expatriation process depends on the effectiveness of international HRM practices (see Video 9.2). Western European and Japanese organizations have more successful expatriates than North American organizations because the IHRM practices (especially selection and performance management) of the former are more developed and effective than that of the latter (Tung, 1982). According to the most recent survey of IHRM practices (Brookfield Global Relocation Services, 2012), critical challenges to manage expatriation were reported to be finding suitable candidates by 15 per cent of organizations, reducing assignment costs (13 per cent), career management (9 per cent) and retention of expatriates (9 per cent).

Selection of expatriates

Selecting the right candidate for the job may be a daunting task in all work contexts, but it is more so for overseas assignments. Selection criteria and methods for expatriates should predict high job performance *as well as* cross-cultural adjustment. Therefore, it is not sufficient to rely on technical competence on the job as the only criterion for selection. Based on what we know from research findings above, what do you think should be the selection criteria for expatriates and how would they differ from those for domestic employees?

Job performance of expatriates depends on their technical competence, cognitive ability and conscientious personality. However, cross-cultural adjustment depends on their potential to establish good interpersonal relationships with employees from different cultures, to adjust to new and ambiguous contexts and to tolerate uncertainties. The following selection criteria should be used to evaluate candidates for expatriation (e.g., Caligiuri, 2000; Harzing, 2004; Tung and Varma, 2008; Mendenhall and Oddou, 1985):

- Knowledge of how work behaviours are influenced by culture and how cultures differ.
- Knowledge of the sociocultural, political and economic context of the host country as well as historical trends and future projections.
- Willingness to learn about the new culture and integrate the host and home country values.
- Ability to establish effective relationships with culturally different members of workgroups.
- Extraversion, openness to new experiences and flexibility as personality characteristics.
- Effective coping with stress and uncertainties and social problem-solving skills.
- High self-esteem and self-efficacy.

One of the most important but overlooked criteria is the candidate's willingness to work in an overseas assignment. Research finds that willingness to work overseas enhanced adjustment (Selmer and Leung, 2003). Expatriation is considered to be an opportunity for acquiring unique skills and experiences, developing personally and professionally, developing of global self-identity and broadening the family's experience (Shaffer et al., 1998; Harvey et al., 2004; Kohonen, 2005; Richardson and Mallon, 2005). Willingness to accept an expatriate assignment is *positively* associated with perceived benefit of expatriation for career success, availability and effectiveness of the company's relocation policy, interest in internationalization, entrepreneurial characteristics and spousal support (Hui et al., 2003) and *negatively* associated with having responsibilities towards relatives, having children at school age, or having a spouse with career involvement (Hui et al., 2003).

Another strong predictor of expatriate success used in selection is **cultural intelligence**. The simplest definition of cultural intelligence is a person's ability to adapt effectively to a new cultural context (Earley and Ang, 2003). Thomas and colleagues (2008) provided a more complete definition of cultural intelligence as a '*system* of interacting knowledge and skills, linked by cultural metacognition, that allows people to adapt to, select and shape the cultural aspects of their environment' (p. 127). Cultural intelligence includes three key components: *knowledge* (both general knowledge of how culture plays a role in behaviour and specific knowledge about the cultural characteristics of the host country); *skills* (perceptual skills such as open-mindedness and being non-judgemental, relational skills such as flexibility and adaptive skills such as exhibiting culturally appropriate behaviour); and *metacognition* (knowledge of and control over one's thinking and learning) (Thomas et al., 2008). The metacognition allows that the person actively reflects on available knowledge and skills regarding, say, gift giving; monitors how this relates to intended outcomes (e.g., pleasing the co-worker) and, if need be, regulates behaviour by formulating alternative course of behaviour (Thomas et al., 2008, p. 133). It involves conscious monitoring and regulating one's behaviours and emotions. Thinking across cultures 9.3 presents a short test of cultural intelligence that you can use for self-assessment.

Thinking across cultures 9.3

Assess Your Cultural Intelligence

Please write one of the appropriate numbers from the following scale in the space at the beginning of each statement.

1	2	3	4	5
Strongly disagree	*Disagree*	*Neutral*	*Agree*	*Strongly agree*

1 _____Before I interact with people from a new culture, I ask myself what I hope to achieve.

2 _____It's easy for me to change my body language (for example, eye contact or posture) to suit people from a different culture.

3 _____I have confidence that I can deal well with people from a different culture.

4 _____I modify my speech style (for example, accent or tone) to suit people from a different culture.

5 _____When I come into a new cultural situation, I can immediately sense whether something is going well or something is wrong.

6 _____I can alter my expression when a cultural encounter requires it.

7 _____I am certain that I can befriend people whose cultural backgrounds are different from mine.

8 _____I can adapt to the lifestyle of a different culture with relative ease.

9 _____I plan how I'm going to relate to people from a different culture before I meet them.

10 _____I am confident that I can deal with a cultural situation that's unfamiliar.

11 _____I easily change the way I act when a cross-cultural encounter seems to require it.

12 _____If I encounter something unexpected while working in a new culture, I use this experience to figure out new ways to approach other cultures in the future.

Source: Earley and Mosakowski (2004, pp. 139–46)

What about the demographic characteristics of expatriates; should they be included in the selection criteria? Organizations used to recruit relatively older candidates for expatriate assignments to reduce the risk of failure (Brookfield Global Relocation Services, 2012). It seems that the trend is reversed in more recent years. According to 2012 report (Brookfield Global Relocation Services, 2012) the percentage of young expatriates (aged between 20–29) jumped from 9 per cent to 13 per cent, while the percentage of expatriates in the age group between 40–49 decreased to 34 per cent.

The same report reveals that there is a slight increase in female expatriates in 2012. The percentage of married expatriates was reported as 60 per cent and those accompanied by their children as 43 per cent. Both spouse and children are invaluable sources of social support for expatriates as well as one of the key reasons for premature return to home country. Therefore, organizations are strongly advised to raise the family issues in the selection process. Some organizations interview also with the spouse to evaluate their fit and readiness for the assignment.

Expatriate Training and Performance Evaluation

After the selection of the expatriates, the next critical step is to provide them with cross-cultural training (CCT). CCT is not 'nice-to-have', but a 'must-have' (Brislin et al., 2007, p. 400). Indeed, the majority of MNCs offered formal cross-cultural preparation for relocation (81 per cent, Brookfield Global Relocation Services, 2012). CCTs are particularly important for expatriates assigned to locations that are culturally distant from their own. More than half of organizations also offered CCT to the entire family of the expatriate.

If you were to design a cross-cultural training programme, what would you aim at developing? Let us consider the following topics in an ideal CCT (Black and Mendenhall, 1990; Brislin et al., 2008; Tarique and Caliguiri, 2004):

- Awareness of the impact of culture's influence on behaviour and understanding of cross-cultural differences.
- Knowledge of the key characteristics of the local country (e.g., culture, sociopolitical and economic context; history, geography).
- Awareness of and coping strategies with possible difficulties while interacting with host nationals.
- Skills to facilitate interpersonal relationships such as relationship-building and negotiation.
- Self-maintenance skills, such as stress and time management.

Cross-cultural training utilizes both didactic and experiential methods, including lectures, cases and role plays. A special technique called 'cultural assimilator' has been developed by Brislin (1981). Cultural assimilator presents trainees with a set of situations that they may encounter during the assignment. Trainees are required to choose from possible responses in these situations. They receive feedback on the appropriateness of their response with an explanation telling them why the response was inappropriate. Cultural assimilator can be web-based. There is an increasing trend to use web- or media-based CCT programmes because they are cost-effective and allow flexibility for trainees to use them at their own pace of learning. As part of a training or selection process, some organizations send their expatriates for a field visit to the local culture, so that they spend a short period of time getting a feel for what it is like to live and work in the new culture. In recent years, some organizations have assigned mentors to each expatriate who meet with them on a regular basis before, during and after the assignment to make sure that the expatriates receive the necessary support from the parent and host organization (Brookfields Global Recruitment Services, 2012).

Effectiveness of CCT has been an issue of concern. It would be wrong to conclude that CCT is not much use without knowledge of the content and method used. There is strong support to suggest that longer training that includes experiential learning activities predicts better adjustment and performance than one-day training with outdated information (e.g., Deshpande and Viswesvaran, 1992). Follow-up training sessions with expatriates and their families after their move to the new location would also be extremely useful. It is also recommended that CCT is offered to host country nationals to raise awareness of cross-cultural difference and develop skills to work in a culturally diverse team (Arman and Aycan, 2012). Expatriate performance evaluation should be based on multiple criteria. Objective criterion such as expatriates' value creation (i.e., contribution to financial success) for their organization as a whole or for the local unit is an important aspect of performance. However, expatriate performance evaluation should not be limited to the objective work outputs for two reasons. First, it may be difficult for the expatriate to contribute to profit and competitiveness of the organization for reasons beyond their control. Expatriates may not produce the expected outcomes due to lack of resources allocated to the local unit by the headquarters or volatility in the international and local markets. It is also possible that the organization makes a strategic decision to compromise the performance of the local unit in the short term to boost the performance of the overall organization (Dowling et al., 1999). Contextual factors such as economic and political constraints influencing the local country, region or the world as a whole (e.g., the global recession) should be taken into consideration to evaluate the performance of the expatriate.

> An American expatriate working in Chile was able to stop a strike that would have closed the plant for months. At the same time, due to exchange rate fluctuations, the subsidiary experienced a significant downturn in sales. When evaluating this manager, headquarters decided to ignore his achievement of averting the strike and instead focused on the sales data giving him a slightly better than average rating. (Francesco and Gold, 2005, p. 163)

Evaluating expatriate performance on the basis of objective work outcomes is problematic because this is not only biased (there are constraints influencing expatriate performance in international work contexts), but also incomplete. There must be other performance criteria specific to expatriate assignments. Expatriate-specific performance criteria include (e.g., Arthur and Bennett, 1995; Caligiuri, 1997; Varma et al., 2002):

- Ability to transfer knowledge between the parent company and the local unit.
- Relational skills; i.e., establishing good interpersonal relationships and teamwork with host-country nationals.
- Fostering commitment to the parent company as well as the local unit.
- Competencies including flexibility, uncertainty tolerance and openness.

Performance criteria and methods differ depending on who evaluates performance. Cross-cultural differences in performance evaluation criteria and methods are surfaced when expatriates are evaluated by their peers in the local unit (e.g., Sinangil and Ones, 1997). There are also variations in the way expatriates are evaluated by MNC of different origin (e.g., US, Dutch, Japan, Korean, Taiwanese) (Shih et al., 2005). Expatriates perceive the performance management system to be fair when formal appraisals take place against the preset performance goals, when the evaluator is geographically closer to the expatriate and when feedback is received from both host- and home-country managers (Gregersen, Hite and Black, 1996; Suutari and Tahvanainen, 2002).

Expatriate Compensation

Expatriation is a costly process. The cost of an assignment is usually three-to-five-times the employee's annual salary (e.g., Schell and Solomon, 1997). A typical expatriate compensation package includes the base salary, benefits, cost of living adjustment, allowances and tax equalization. There is a long list of allowances for expatriates, including hardship, foreign service, housing, utility, furnishing, education, home leave, relocation, rest and relaxation, car and driver, club membership, stopover, temporary living allowances and so on. The final component of expatriate compensation is tax equalization. The objective of this procedure is to ensure that expatriates do not pay more or less than they would have paid in the home country.

Despite all the investment and expenses, neither expatriates nor HR managers are fully satisfied with overseas compensation packages. Expatriates expect to be better compensated, whereas companies believe that expatriate demands are extravagant. Over the years, MNCs have been experimenting with a number of different approaches to overseas compensation to attract, retain and motivate their expatriate managers and to enhance their sense of equity.

Literature on global compensation suggests four major approaches to expatriate compensation (e.g., Black, Gregersen and Mendenhall, 1992; Harvey, 1993; Hodgetts and Luthans, 1993; Schell and Solomon, 1997; Swaak, 1995). The first and the most common is what is referred to as the balance sheet approach. The main objective of this approach is to maintain the standard of living before, during and after the assignment by covering actual cost of living differentials between the two countries. The second is the home country-based approach in which all US expatriate employees are paid exactly the same in every location. In contrast to this approach is the host country-based approach. Here, salary and benefits are determined as if the expatriate is a local national. Finally, the fourth approach is the regional approach to expatriate compensation. In this approach, companies design compensation packages on the basis of a salary and standard of living index of a designated group of countries.

Expatriates expect compensation packages to recognize their education, skills and abilities and job performance. They also expect compensation to be consistent with their expectations and motivation in accepting the assignment. As far as the parent company is concerned, overseas compensation should be cost-effective and consistent with the business strategy. Its main objective should be to attract, retain and motivate expatriates. In designing compensation, the parent company is also concerned with maintaining equity among the expatriate employees in the home country and other expatriates in different locations. The local unit's concern, on the other hand, is to establish equity between the expatriate and host country co-workers, so that cooperation and productivity are enhanced. Chen et al. (2002) found that Chinese locals perceive less fairness when comparing their compensation with expatriates than when they are comparing it with other locals. Perceived unfairness of local country co-workers would have a negative impact on their teamwork with the expatriate. Finally, an expatriate family expects compensation to meet their needs and provide support before, during and after the assignment.

Research conducted by the first author in an American-Indonesian joint venture in Kazakhstan examined the extent to which expatriates perceived their compensation to be fair considering the work conditions and their expectations (Thinking across cultures 9.4). Results revealed that the largest discrepancy between what is expected and what is obtained was found when expatriates consider the factors that were related to their job. Considering the work conditions and job responsibilities, expatriates found their compensation less than what it should be. However, when they considered parent company strategies in designing their compensation package, the perceived discrepancy disappeared. Expatriates appreciated that the current compensation package was cost-effective, efficient in attracting, retaining, motivating employees and establishing equity with locals and other expatriates, but at the same time they found it unsatisfactory under the present work conditions. An important finding of this research was that perceived fairness was associated with expatriates' commitment to the organization (see Video 9.3).

Thinking across cultures 9.4

Everything is Different – Even the Food!

Although expatriates on both sides were well paid in terms of base salary, there were differences between American and Indonesian expatriates with regards to other benefits and allowances. For instance, Indonesian expatriates worked eleven weeks and took a week of vacation, whereas American expatriates worked nine weeks and took two weeks of vacation. Another disturbing difference was the canteen facilities. Indonesian and American canteens were separated. Indonesian expatriates were eating with Kazakhs and other workers in a dining hall of 1000 people. On the other hand, American expatriates were eating in a smaller dining hall where no one else was allowed to enter. On the American side, there were four different choices of main dish as well as a salad bar. On the Indonesian side, there was one main dish on a fixed menu. Although the Indonesian workers were well fed, it was disappointing for them to experience such differences in benefits.

Management of Repatriation

Returning home may be as difficult as leaving home for expatriates and their families. Living overseas may mean that expatriates lose ties with the business and social community at home. Home may no longer be the same place as they leave. Hence, expatriates face the 'reverse culture shock'. Furthermore, expatriates often find that their overseas experience is not appreciated and effectively utilized by the parent company. They do not get the promotion they expected and deserved. They may not even return to their original position and therefore experience 'status loss'.

Due to the mismanagement of **repatriation** turnover after repatriation is possible and sometimes common. Suutari and Brewster (2003) reported that 60 per cent of those who stayed in their parent organizations were seriously considering leaving. The decision to quit surely results from the frustration of unmet expectations, but also from the desire to adapt a 'boundaryless career' (e.g., Bossard and Peterson, 2005). Expatriates consider turnover when:

- the assigned task after repatriation is not challenging,
- they see limited career prospects in the parent company,
- they receive job offers from other organizations,
- there is lack of clarity in their new job in the parent company, and
- they are dissatisfied with the repatriation treatment (Suutari and Brewster, 2003).

When the repatriate has no or little opportunity to use the acquired knowledge, skills and abilities from overseas, their commitment to the parent company also decreases (Stroh et al., 2000). To minimize the repatriation problems, organizations now have a written repatriation policy and clear statement of post-assignment duties (Brooksfield Global Recruitment Services, 2012).

Chapter Summary

Despite the forces of globalization, HRM practices seem to continue to differ across the globe. In this chapter, we first demonstrated that HRM practices were far from converging and that there was no 'one best way' of designing and implementing HRM practices. We discussed that HRM practices are influenced by a multitude of factors, including the legal, political, economic, cultural context, labour market conditions, size of the organization, industry, ownership status (public, private, family owned) and organizational life stage. Among these factors, we focused specifically on the effect of culture on HRM practices. We provided a brief literature review on the cross-cultural differences in HRM practices in the areas of employee selection, performance appraisal, training and development, job analysis and job design, compensation and benefits and human resource planning and career management. The framework presented in this chapter attributed differences in HRM practices to three broad cultural orientations that can occur both at the societal and organizational levels: relationship vs. performance; hierarchy vs. participation; stability vs. change. Managerial implications of adopting North American HRM practices in other cultural contexts have been discussed extensively with specific suggestions for multinational corporations. Expatriate management issues can be considered as part of the general field of cross-cultural HRM. Expatriates are foreign managers assigned to overseas operations. Their 'success' is usually defined as the adjustment and performance in the host country. The chapter reviewed factors relating to expatriate adjustment, performance and job satisfaction. Managerial implications included guidelines on how to select and train expatriates and how to evaluate their performance, design their compensation package and manage their repatriation.

Key Terms and Definitions

Convergence vs. divergence in HRM practices. A discussion pertaining to whether HRM practices become similar or remain distinct in the globalized work context.

Cranet project. A collaborative effort coordinated by the Cranfield School of Management to document HRM practices in European countries based on data collected periodically and nation-wide.

Task-driven and employee-related assumptions. Managerial assumptions that form the internal work culture and are related to questions including what should the critical tasks and goals be in an organization and how should they be achieved; what is the nature of employees and how do they behave.

Expatriate managers. Foreign managers assigned to local subsidiaries of multinational corporations for a temporary period.

Adjustment. Expatriates' progress in becoming fully effective in the host society by meeting the requirements of daily life and engaging in and maintaining positive interpersonal relations with members of the host society.

Meta-analysis. A statistical method of providing a quantitative summary of the findings of various published or unpublished studies investigating a particular research question (e.g., the relationship between cross-cultural training and expatriate adjustment).

Cultural intelligence. 'System of interacting knowledge and skills, linked by cultural metacognition, that allows people to adapt to, select and shape the cultural aspects of their environment' (Thomas et al., 2008, p. 126).

Repatriation. Expatriates who return to the home country and home organization after completing their overseas assignment.

End of Chapter Reflection Questions

1. Multinational organizations struggle to strike the balance between administering local and global HRM practices. What would be two examples of HRM practices that require both global integration and local adaptation?
2. What are the challenges facing HRM departments in their quest to manage diversity on the one hand and ensure fairness among employees on the other?
3. Do you think findings in the expatriation literature apply and explain adjustment and performance of internationally mobile students (e.g., exchange students or those pursuing their graduate degrees in a different country)? Why and why not?

Further Reading

Budhwar, P.S. and Sparrow, P.R. (2002) 'An integrative framework for understanding cross-national human resource management practices', *Human Resource Management Review*, 12 (3): 377–403.

Caligiuri, P. (2012) *Cultural Agility: Building a Pipeline of Successful Global Professionals.* Somerset, New Jersey: Wiley.

Harzing, A.W. and Pinnington, A. (2010) *International Human Resource Management.* London: Sage.

Pudelko, M. and Harzing, A.W. (2007) 'Country-of-origin, localization, or dominance effect? An empirical investigation of HRM practices in foreign subsidiaries', *Human Resource Management*, 46 (4): 535–59.

Sparrow, P., Schuler, R.S. and Jackson, S.E. (1994) 'Convergence or divergence: Human resource practices and policies for competitive advantage worldwide', *International Journal of Human Resource Management*, 5 (2): 267–99.

Tayeb, M. (2004) *International Human Resource Management: A Multinational Company Perspective.* Oxford: Oxford University Press.

Cases, Videos and Web Sources

Cases

The following cases present the HRM challenges for managing the global talent.

Beamish, P.W. and Newendham-Kahindi, A. (2007) *Human Resource Management in Multinational Banks in Tanzania.* IVEY Business School Case, No: 9B07C040.

Ellement, G., Lane, H.W. and McNett, J.M. (2012) *Ellen Moore (B): Living and Working in Korea.* IVEY Business School Case No: 9B12C011.

Lane, H. W. and Shea, C. (2006) *Moscow Aerostar.* In H. W. Lane, J. J. Distefano and M. L. Maznevski (eds) *International Management Behaviour: Text, readings and cases*, pp. 320–30. Malden, MA: Blackwell Publishing.

Videos

HRM Video Series – www.shrm.org/multimedia/video/Pages/default.aspx.

Video 9.1 *Expat Women in Hong Kong* (2009) www.youtube.com/watch?v=-5Mk6o_QXlQ – Expat spouses sharing their experiences.

Video 9.2 *The Expat Experience* (2011) www.youtube.com/watch?v=V5xhRx2pgRs.
Video 9.3 *2011/12 Global Talent Management and Rewards Study* (2012). www.youtube.com/watch?v=z8tT5ewwLQo.

Web sources

www.brookfieldgrs.com/– Brookfield Global Relocation Services.
www.shrm.org/ – Society for Human Resource Management.
www.imaa-institute.org/ – Institute for Mergers, Acquisitions and Alliances.
www.talentmanagers.org/ – Talent Management Association.
http: cranet.org – The Cranfield Network on International Human Resource Management.

References

Ali, A. (1989) 'A comparative study of managerial beliefs about work in the Arab States', *Advances in International Comparative Management*, 4: 95–112.

Allinson, C.W. and Hayes, J. (2000) 'Cross-national differences in cognitive style: Implications for management', *International Journal of Human Resource Management*, 11 (1): 161–70.

Arman, G. and Aycan, Z. (2012) 'Host country nationals' attitudes towards expatriates: Development and validation of a measure', *International Journal of Human Resource Management*, 24 (15), 2927–47.

Arthur, W. and Bennett, W. (1995) 'The international assignee: The relative importance of factors perceived to contribute to success', *Personnel Psychology*, 48: 99–114.

Au, K.Y. and Fukuda, J. (2003) 'Boundary spanning behaviors of expatriates', *Journal of World Business*, 37 (4): 285–96.

Aycan, Z. (2005) 'The interplay between cultural and institutional/structural contingencies in human resource management', *International Journal of Human Resource Management*, 16 (7): 1083–120.

Aycan, Z. (2006) 'Human resource management in Turkey', in P. Budhwar and K. Mellahi (eds), *Managing Human Resources in the Middle East*, pp. 160–80. Oxon, UK: Routledge.

Aycan, Z. and Fikret-Pasa, S. (2003) 'Career choices, job selection criteria and leadership preferences in a transitional nation: The case of Turkey', *Journal of Career Development*, 30 (2): 129–44.

Aycan, Z. and Gelfand, M.J. (2012) 'Cross-cultural organizational psychology', in S. Kozlowski (ed.), *The Oxford Handbook of Organizational Psychology*, pp. 1103–60. New York: Oxford University Press.

Aycan, Z. and Kanungo, R.N. (1997) 'Current issues and future challenges in expatriate management', in Z. Aycan (ed.) *Expatriate Management: Theory and Practice*, vol. 4, pp. 245–60. Greenwich, CT: JAI Press.

Aycan, Z., Kanungo, R.N. and Sinha, J.B.P. (1999) 'Organizational culture and human resource management practices: The model of culture fit', *Journal of Cross-cultural Psychology*, 30 (4): 501–27.

Aycan, Z., Kanungo, R.N., Mendonça, M., Yu, K., Deller, J., Stahl, G. and Khursid, A. (2000) 'Impact of culture on human resource management practices: A ten country comparison', *Applied Psychology: An International Review*, 49 (1): 192–220.

Banai, M. and Harry, W. (2004) 'Boundaryless global careers: The international itinerants', *International Studies of Management and Organization*, 34 (3): 96–120.

Bhaskar-Shrinivas, P., Harrison, D.A., Shaffer, M.A. and Luk, D.M. (2005) 'Input-based and time-based models of international adjustment: Meta-analytic evidence and theoretical extensions', *Academy of Management Journal*, 48 (2): 257–81.

Bian, Y. and Ang, S. (1997) 'Guanxi networks and job mobility in China and Singapore', *Social Forces*, 75 (3): 981–1005.

Björkman, I. and Lu, Y. (1999) 'The management of human resources in Chinese-Western joint ventures', *Journal of World Business*, 34 (3): 306–24.

Black, J.S. and Mendenhall, M. (1990) 'Cross-cultural training effectiveness: A review and a theoretical framework for future research', *Academy of Management Review*, 16 (2): 113–36.

Black, J.S., Gregersen, H.B. and Mendenhall, M. (1992) *Global Assignments: Successfully Expatriating and Repatriating International Managers*. San Francisco, CA: Joscy-Bass.

Black, J.S., Mendenhall, M. and Oddou, G. (1991) 'Toward a comprehensive model of international adjustment: An integration of multiple theoretical perspectives', *Academy of Management Review*, 16 (2): 291–317.

Blunt, P. and Popoola, O.E. (1985) *Personnel Management in Africa*. Reading, MA: Addison-Wesley Longman.

Bossard, A.B. and Peterson, R.B. (2005) 'The repatriate experience as seen by American expatriates', *Journal of World Business*, 40 (1): 9–28.

Brislin, R., MacNab, B. and Nayani, F. (2008) 'Cross-cultural training: Applications and research', in P. Smith, M. Peterson and D. Thomas (eds), *Handbook of Cross-cultural Management Research*, pp. 397–410. Thousand Oaks, CA: Sage.

Brislin, R.W. (1981) *Cross-cultural Encounters: Face-to-face Interaction*. New York: Pergamon Press.

Brookfield Global Relocation Services (2012) Global relocation trends, 2012 survey report. Retrieved from http:\\knowledge.brookfieldgrs.com\\content\\insights_ideas-2012_GRTS.

Budhwar, P.S. and Khatri, N. (2001) 'A comparative study of HR practices in Britain and India', *International Journal of Human Resource Management*, 12 (5): 800–26.

Caligiuri, P. (2012) *Cultural Agility: Building a Pipeline of Successful Global Professionals*. Somerset, NJ: Wiley.

Caligiuri, P.M. (1997) 'Assessing expatriate success: Beyond just "being there"', in Z. Aycan (ed.), *Expatriate Management: Theory and Practice*, Vol. 4, pp. 117–140. Greenwich, CT: JAI Press.

Caligiuri, P.M. (2000) 'The Big Five personality characteristics as predictors of expatriate success', *Personnel Psychology*, 53: 67–88.

Caligiuri, P.M. and Cascio, W. (1998) 'Can we send her there? Maximizing the success of Western women on global assignments', *Journal of World Business*, 33 (4): 394–416.

Caligiuri, P.M. and Day, D.V. (2000) 'Effects of self-monitoring on technical, contextual and assignment-specific performance: A study of cross-national work performance ratings', *Group and Organization Management*, 25 (2): 154–75.

Caligiuri, P.M., Joshi, A. and Lazarova, M. (1999) 'Factors influencing the adjustment of women on global assignments', *International Journal of Human Resource Management*, 10 (2): 163–79.

Chen, C., Choi, J. and Chi, S.C. (2002) 'Making justice sense of local-expatriate compensation disparity: Mitigation by local referents, ideological explanations, and interpersonal sensitivity in China-foreign joint ventures', *Academy of Management Journal*, 45 (4), 807–17.

Cheng, F. and Sethi, S.P. (1999) 'A periodic review inventory model with demand influenced by promotion decisions', *Management Science*, 45 (11): 1510–1523.

Deosthalee, P.G. (2002) 'Are Indian expatriates in Sultanate of Oman under stress?', *Journal of Managerial Psychology*, 17 (6): 523–8.

Deshpande, S.P. and Viswesvaran, C. (1992) 'Is cross-cultural training of expatriate managers effective: A meta analysis', *International Journal of Intercultural Relations*, 16 (3): 295–310.

Dowling, P.J., Welch, D.E. and Schuler, R.S. (1999) *International Human Resource Management: Managing People in a Multinational Context*. Cincinnati, OH: South-Western College Publishing.

Downes, M., Thomas, A.S. and Singley, R.B. (2002) 'Predicting expatriate job satisfaction: The role of firm internationalization', *Career Development International*, 7 (1): 24–36.

Drost, E., Frayne, C., Lowe, K.B. and Geringer, M. (2002) 'In search of "best" training and development practices: A ten country comparative analysis', *Human Resource Management*, 41 (1): 67–86.

Earley, P. and Ang, S. (2003) *Cultural Intelligence: Individual Interactions Across Cultures*. Stanford, CA: Stanford Business Books.

Earley, P.C. and Mosakowski, E. (2004) 'Cultural intelligence', *Harvard Business Review*, 82 (10): 139–46.

Easterby-Smith, M., Malina, D. and Yuan, L. (1995) 'How culture-sensitive is HRM? A comparative analysis of practice in Chinese and UK companies', *International Journal of Human Resource Management*, 6 (1): 31–59.

Evans, C.L. (1993) 'Human resource management in the Japanese financial institution abroad: The case of the London office', *British Journal of Industrial Relations*, 31 (3): 347–64.

Expat Explorer Survey 2008 (2008) HSBC Bank International. Retrieved from http://blog.just-landed.com/wp-content/uploads/2008/10/expat-explorer-offshore-offspring.pdf.

Fletcher, C. and Perry, E.L. (2002) 'Performance appraisal and feedback: A consideration of national culture and a review of contemporary research and future trends', in N. Anderson, D.S. Ones, H. Kepir-Sinangil and C. Viswesvaran (eds), *Handbook of Industrial, Work and Organizational Psychology*, Vol. 1. pp. 127–45. London: Sage.

Francesco, A.M. and Gold, B.A. (2005) *International Organizational Behavior: Text, Cases and Skills*, 2nd edn. Upper Saddle River, NJ: Pearson/Prentice Hall.

Gregersen, H.B., Hite, J.M. and Black, J.S. (1996) 'Expatriate performance appraisal in US multinational firms', *Journal of International Business Studies*, 27: 711–34.

Haines, V.Y. and Saba, T. (1999) 'Understanding reactions to international mobility policies and practices', *Human Resource Planning*, 22 (3): 40–52.

Harris, P.R. and Moran, R.T. (1996) *Managing Cultural Differences*, 4th edn. Houston, TX: Gulf.

Harvey, M. (1993) 'Designing A global compensation system – The logic and a model', *The Columbia Journal of World Business*, 28 (4): 56–72.

Harvey, M., Novicevic, M.M. and Garrison, G. (2004) 'Challenges to staffing global virtual teams', *Human Resource Management Review*, 14 (3): 275–94.

Harzing, A.W. (2004) 'Composing an international staff', in A.W. Harzing and J. Van Ruysseveldt (eds), *International Human Resource Management: An Integrated Approach*, pp. 251–82. London: Sage.

Harzing, A.W.K. (2001) 'Of bears, bumble-bees and spiders: The role of expatriates in controlling foreign subsidiaries', *Journal of World Business*, 36 (4): 366–79.

Hébert, L., Very, P. and Beamish, P.W. (2005) 'Expatriation as a bridge over troubled water: A knowledge-based perspective applied to cross-border acquisitions', *Organization Studies*, 26 (10): 1455–76.

Hechanova, R., Beehr, T.A. and Christiansen, N.D. (2003) 'Antecedents and consequences of employees' adjustment to overseas assignment: A meta-analytic review', *Applied Psychology: An International Review*, 52 (2): 213–36.

Herriot, P. and Anderson, N. (1997) 'Selecting for change: How will personnel and selection psychology survive?', in N. Anderson and P. Herriot (eds), *International Handbook of Selection and Assessment*, pp. 1–38. Chichester: Wiley.

Hodgetts, R.M. and Luthans, F. (1993) 'US multinationals' compensation strategies for local management: Cross-cultural implications', *Compensation and Benefits Review*, 25 (2): 42–8.

Hofbauer, J. and Fischlmayr, I.C. (2004) 'Feminization of international assignments: conquering empty castles?', *International Studies of Management and Organization*, 34 (3): 46–67.

Huo, Y.P. and Von Glinow, M.A. (1995) 'On transplanting human resource practices to China: A culture-driven approach', *International Journal of Manpower*, 16 (9): 3–15.

Isik, D. (2012) *Local vs. global balance in HRM practices of multinational organizations*. Unpublished MA thesis. Koc University, Istanbul, Turkey.

Jackson, D.W. Jr, Naumann, E. and Widmier, S.M. (2000) 'Examining the relationship between work attitudes and propensity to leave among expatriate sales people', *Journal of Personal Selling and Sales Management*, 20: 227–41.

Jackson, S.E. and Schuler, R.S. (1995) 'Understanding human resource management in the context of organizations and their environments', *Annual Review of Psychology*, 46: 237–64.

Kanungo, R.N. and Jaeger, A.M. (1990) 'Introduction: The need for indigenous management in developing countries', in A.M. Jaeger and R.N. Kanungo (eds), *Management in Developing Countries*, pp. 1-19. London: Routledge.

Kanungo, R.N. and Mendonça, M. (1997) *Compensation: Effective reward management*, (2nd edn.). Toronto: John Wiley & Sons.

Kohonen, E. (2005) 'Developing global leaders through international assignments: An identity construction perspective', *Personnel Review*, 34 (1): 22–36.

Kovach, R.C. (1995) 'Matching assumptions to environment in the transfer of management practices', *International Studies of Management and Organization*, 24 (4): 83–100.

Kraimer, M.L. and Wayne, S.J. (2004) 'An examination of perceived organizational support as a multidimensional construct in the context of an expatriate assignment', *Journal of Management*, 30 (2), 209–37.

Lane, H.W. and Shea, C. (2006) 'Moscow Aerostar', in H.W. Lane, J. J. Distefano and M.L. Maznevski (eds) *International Management Behavior: Text, Readings, and Cases*, pp. 320–30. Malden, MA: Blackwell Publishing.

Lane, H.W., DiStefano, J.J. and Maznevski, M.L. (1997) *International Management Behavior*. Cambridge, MA: Blackwell.

Lawler, J.J., Zaidi, M. and Atmiyanandana, V. (1989) 'Human resource strategies in Southeast Asia: The case of Thailand', in A. Nedd, G. Ferries and K. Rowland (eds) *Research in Personnel and Human Resource Management*, pp. 201–22. Greenwich: JAI Press.

Lee, H. (1999) 'Transformation of employment practices in Korean business', *International Studies of Management & Organization*, 28 (4): 26–39.

Levy-Leboyer, C. (1994) 'Selection and assessment in Europe', in H.C. Triandis, M.D. Dunnette and L.M. Hough (eds), *Handbook of Industrial and Organizational Psychology*, pp. 173–90. Palo Alto, CA: Consulting Psychologists Press.

Lowe, K.B., Milliman, J., De Cieri, H. and Dowling, P.J. (2002) 'International compensation practices: a ten-country comparative analysis', *Human Resource Management*, 41 (1): 45–66.

Lu, Y. and Bjorkman, I. (1997) 'HRM practices in China-Western joint ventures: MNC standardization versus localization', *International Journal of Human Resource Management*, 8 (5): 614–28.

Mayerhofer, H., Hartmann, L.C., Michelitsch-Riedl, G. and Kollinger, I. (2004) 'Flexpatriate assignments: A neglected issue in global staffing', *The International Journal of Human Resource Management*, 15 (8): 1371–89.

Mayrhofer, W., Morley, M. and Brewster, C. (2004) 'Convergence, stasis or divergence?', in C. Brewster, W. Mayrhofer and M. Morley (eds), *Human Resource Management in Europe: Evidence of Convergence?*, pp. 415–36. Burlington, MA: Elsevier Butterworth-Heinemann.

Mendenhall, M. and Oddou, G. (1985) 'The dimensions of expatriate acculturation: A review', *Academy of Management Review*, 10 (1): 39–47.

Mendenhall, M.E., Stahl, G.K., Ehnert, I., Oddou, G., Osland, J.S. and Kühlmann, T.M. (2004) 'Evaluation studies of cross-cultural training programs', in D. Landis, J. Bennett and M. Bennett (eds), *Handbook of Intercultural Training*, pp. 129–43. Thousand Oaks, CA: Sage Publications.

Mendonça, M. and Kanungo, R.N. (1994) 'Managing human resources the issue of cultural fit', *Journal of Management Inquiry*, 3 (2): 189–205.

Milliman, J., Nason, S., Gallagher, E., Huo, P., Von Glinow, M.A. and Lowe, K. (1998) 'The impact of national culture on human resource management practices: The case of performance appraisal', in J.L.C. Cheng and R.B. Peterson (eds), *Advances in International Comparative Management*, pp. 157–83. Greenwich, CT: JAI Press.

Minbaeva, D.B. and Michailova, S. (2004) 'Knowledge transfer and expatriation in multinational corporations: The role of disseminative capacity', *Employee Relations*, 26 (6): 663–79.

Morris, M.A. and Robie, C. (2001) 'A meta-analysis of the effects of cross-cultural training on expatriate performance and adjustment', *International Journal of Training and Development*, 5: 112–25.

Palthe, J. (2004) 'The relative importance of antecedents to cross-cultural adjustment: Implications for managing a alobal workforce', *International Journal of Intercultural Relations*, 28 (1), 37–59.

Papalexandris, N. and Panayotopoulou, L. (2004) 'Exploring the mutual interaction of societal culture and human resource management practices: Evidence from 19 countries', *Employee Relations*, 26 (5): 495–509.

Quinn, D.P. and Rivoli, P. (1991) 'The effects of American- and Japanese-style employment and compensation practices on innovation', *Organization Science*, 2 (4): 323–41.

Raghuram, S., London, M. and Larsen, H. (2001) 'Flexible employment practices in Europe: Country versus culture', *International Journal of Human Resource Management*, 12: 738–53.

Richardson, J. and Mallon, M. (2005) 'Career interrupted? The case of the self-directed expatriate', *Journal of World Business*, 40 (4): 409–20.

Ruona, W.E. and Gibson, S.K. (2004) 'The making of twenty-first-century HR: An analysis of the convergence of HRM, HRD and OD', *Human Resource Management*, 43 (1): 49–66.

Ryan, A.M., McFarland, L., Baron, H. and Page, R. (1999) 'An international look at selection practices: Nation and culture as explanations for variability in practice', *Personnel Psychology*, 52: 359–91.

Sanchez, J.I. and Levine, E.L. (1999) 'Is job analysis dead, misunderstood, or both? New forms of work analysis and design', in A.I. Kraut and A.K. Korman (eds), *Evolving Practices in Human Resource Management*, pp. 43–69. San Francisco, CA: Jossey-Bass.

Schaubroeck, J. and Lam, S.S. (2002) 'How similarity to peers and supervisor influences organizational advancement in different cultures', *Academy of Management Journal*, 45 (6): 1120–36.

Schell, M.S. and Solomon, C.M. (1997) *Capitalizing on the Global Workforce: A Strategic Guide for Expatriate Management*. New York, NY: Irwin Professional Publishing.

Schuler, R.S. and Rogovsky, N. (1998) 'Understanding compensation practice variations across firms: The impact of national culture', *Journal of International Business Studies*, 29 (1), 159–77.

Seddon, J. (1987) 'Assumptions, culture and performance appraisal', *Journal of Management Development*, 6 (3): 47–54.

Selmer, J. (2002) 'Practice makes perfect? International experience and expatriate adjustment', *Management International Review*, 42 (1), 71–87.

Selmer, J. (2004) 'Psychological barriers to adjustment of Western business expatriates in China: newcomers vs long stayers', *International Journal of Human Resource Management*, 15 (4–5): 794–813.

Selmer, J. and Leung, A.S. (2003) 'Personal characteristics of female vs male business expatriates', *International Journal of Cross Cultural Management*, 3 (2): 195–212.

Selmer, J., Ling, E.S.H., Shiu, L.S.C. and de Leon, C.T. (2003) 'Reciprocal adjustment? Mainland Chinese managers in Hong Kong vs. Hong Kong Chinese managers on the mainland', *Cross Cultural Management*, 10 (3), 58–79.

Shackleton, N.J. and Newell, S. (1997) 'International assessment and selection', in N. Anderson and P. Herriot (eds), *International Handbook of Selection and Assessment*, pp. 81–96. Chichester: Wiley.

Shaffer, M.A. and Harrison, D.A. (1998) 'Expatriates' psychological withdrawal from international assignments: work, nonwork and family influences', *Personnel Psychology*, 51 (1): 87–118.

Shaffer, M.A., Harrison, D.A. and Gilley, K.M. (1999) 'Dimensions, determinants and differences in the expatriate adjustment process', *Journal of International Business Studies*, 30 (3) 557–81.

Shih, H.A., Chiang, Y.H. and Kim, I.S. (2005) 'Expatriate performance management from MNEs of different national origins', *International Journal of Manpower*, 26 (2): 157–76.

Sinangil, H.K. and Ones, D.S. (1997) 'Empirical investigations of the host country perspective in expatriate management', in Z. Aycan (ed.), *Expatriate Management: Theory and Research*, pp. 173–205. London: JAI Press.

Sinha, J.B. (1997) 'A cultural perspective on organizational behavior in India', in P.C. Earley and M. Erez (eds), *New Perspectives on International Industrial/Organizational Psychology*, pp. 53–75. San Francisco, CA: The New Lexington Press.

Sparrow, P. and Hiltrop, J.M. (1994) *European Human Resource Management in Transition*. Hemel Hempstead: Prentice Hall.

Sparrow, P.R. and Budhwar, P.S. (1997) 'Competition and change: mapping the Indian HRM recipe against world-wide patterns', *Journal of World Business*, 32 (3): 224–42.

Stahl, G. and Caligiuri, P.M. (2005) 'The relationship between expatriate coping strategies and expatriate adjustment', *Journal of Applied Psychology*, 90 (4): 603–16.

Steiner, D.D. and Gilliland, S.W. (1996) 'Fairness reactions to personnel selection techniques in France and United States', *Journal of Applied Psychology*, 81 (2): 134–42.

Stroh, L.K., Gregersen, H.B. and Black, J.S. (2000) 'Triumphs and tragedies: expectations and commitments upon repatriation', *International Journal of Human Resource Management*, 11 (4): 681–97.

Suutari, V. and Brewster, C. (1998) *Expatriate Management Practices and their Perceived Relevance: Evidence from Finnish Companies*. Discussion papers 247. Vaasa: University of Vaasa.

Suutari, V. and Brewster, C. (2003) 'Repatriation: empirical evidence from a longitudinal study of careers and expectations among Finnish expatriates', *International Journal of Human Resource Management*, 14 (7): 1132–51.

Suutari, V. and Tahvanainen, M. (2002) 'The antecedents of performance management amongst Finnish expatriates', *International Journal of Human Resource Management*, 13 (1), 1–21.

Swaak, R.A. (1995) 'Expatriate failures too many, too much cost, too little planning', *Compensation and Benefits Review*, 27 (6): 47–55.

Takeuchi, R., Yun, S. and Russell, J.E.A. (2002) 'Antecedents and consequences of the perceived adjustment of Japanese expatriates in the USA', *International Journal of Human Resource Management*, 13 (8): 1224–44.

Tarique, I. and Caligiuri, P.M. (2004) 'Training and development of international staff', A.W. Harzing and J. Van Ruysseveldt (eds), *International Human Resource Management*, pp. 283–306. London: Sage Publications.

Tayeb, M. (1995) 'The competitive advantage of nations: the role of HRM and its socio-cultural context', *International Journal of Human Resource Management*, 6 (3): 588–605.

Thomas, D.C., Elron, E., Stahl, G., Ekelund, B.Z., Ravlin, E.C., Cerdin, J.L. and Lazarova, M.B. (2008) 'Cultural intelligence domain and assessment', *International Journal of Cross Cultural Management*, 8 (2): 123–43.

Triandis, H.C. (1994) 'Cross-cultural industrial and organizational psychology', in H.C. Triandis, M.D. Dunnette and L.M. Hough (eds), *Handbook of Industrial and Organizational Psychology*, Vol. 4, pp. 103–72. Palo Alto, CA: Consulting Psychologists Press.

Triandis, H.C. and Bhawuk, D.P.S. (1997) 'Culture theory and the meaning of relatedness', in P.C. Earley and M. Erez (eds), *New Perspectives on International Industrial/Organizational Psychology*, pp. 13–53. San Francisco, CA: New Lexington Press.

Tung, R. (1984) 'Human resource planning in Japanese multinationals: a model for US firms?', *Journal of International Business Studies*, 15 (2): 139–49.

Tung, R.L. (1982) 'Selection and training procedures of US, European and Japanese multinationals', *California Management Review*, 25 (1): 57–71.

Tung, R.L. (1998) 'American expatriates abroad: From neophytes to cosmopolitans', *Journal of World Business*, 33(2): 125–144.

Tung, R.L. (2004) 'Female expatriates: A model for global leaders', *Organizational Dynamics*, 33 (3): 243–53.

Tung, R.L. and Varma, A. (2008) 'Expatriate selection and evaluation', in P. Smith, M.F. Peterson and D.C. Thomas (eds), *Handbook of Cross-cultural Management Research*, pp. 367–75. Thousand Oaks, CA: Sage.

Vallance, S. (1999) 'Performance appraisal in Singapore, Thailand and the Philippines: A cultural perspective', *Australian Journal of Public Administration*, 58 (4): 78–95.

Von Glinow, M.A., Drost, E.A. and Teagarden, M.B. (2002) 'Converging on IHRM best practices: Lessons learned from a globally distributed consortium on theory and practice', *Human Resource Management*, 41 (1): 123–40.

Wang, X. and Kanungo, R.N. (2004) 'Nationality, social network and psychological well-being: Expatriates in China', *International Journal of Human Resource Management*, 15 (4–5): 775–93.

Wiersma, U.J. and van den Berg, P.T. (1999) 'Influences and trends in human resource practices in The Netherlands', *Employee Relations*, 21 (1): 63–79.

Wilkins, S. (2001) 'Management development in the Arab Gulf States – the influence of language and culture', *Industrial and Commercial Training*, 33 (7): 260–5.

Wong, C.S, Wong, Y.T., Hui, C. and Law, K.S. (2001) 'The significant role of Chinese employees: organizational commitment implications for managing employees in Chinese societies', *Journal of World Business*, 36 (3): 326–40.

Wong, G.Y. and Birnbaum-More, P.H. (1994) 'Culture, context and structure: A test on Hong Kong banks', *Organization Studies*, 15 (1): 99–123.

Yavas, U. and Bodur, M. (1999) 'Satisfaction among expatriate managers: correlates and consequences', *Career Development International*, 4 (5): 261–9.

Want to learn more? Visit the companion website at www.sagepub.co.uk/kanungo to gain access to videos from the end of each chapter, weblinks and flash cards of key terms.

10

Corporate Social Responsibility and Ethics

Chapter Outline

We need more from business than just profit.

Ben Verwaayen, Alcatel-Lucent

Ethics is the new competitive environment.

Peter Robinson, Mountain Equipment Co-op

Sustainability started as a moral obligation, but has now become a key differentiator for consumers.

Sung-joo Kim, Sungjoo Group

We need partnerships, both public-private and also between developed and emerging economies.

PM Telang, Tata Motors

A theme that will become increasingly apparent in the coming years is the role that emerging countries will play in shaping sustainability.

Carlos Ghosn, Renault Nissan Alliance

In the largest CEO survey on sustainability conducted to date, top executives stated that sustainability had the highest priority in their business agenda and that ethics and corporate social responsibility (CSR) were key strategies to achieve it (Lacy et al.,

2010). The quotations of CEOs from this report (Lacy et al. 2010, pp. 27–30) demonstrate the importance of ethical and socially responsible business practices, as well as the necessity to raise commitment to such practices across cultures. Movement towards CSR is not without its critics, such as that of Professor Aneel Karnani of Ross Business School:

> The idea that companies have a responsibility to act in the public interest and will profit from doing so is fundamentally flawed … Very simply, in cases where private profits and public interests are aligned, the idea of corporate social responsibility is irrelevant: Companies that simply do everything they can to boost profits will end up increasing social welfare … In circumstances in which profits and social welfare are in direct opposition, an appeal to corporate social responsibility will almost always be ineffective, because executives are unlikely to act voluntarily in the public interest and against shareholder interests.

Take a moment to think about the case *for* and *against* CRS and ethics in business. Which of the above quotations is your position closest to and why?

The concept of corporate social responsibility (CSR) originated in the 1950s, as business corporations rapidly increased in size and power. Until this time, the principal responsibilities of business corporations were *economic* responsibilities and *legal*. In the 1960s and 1970s, in the context of emerging social problems such as poverty, unemployment, race relations and pollution, there was increasing recognition that apart from wealth creation business also has responsibilities beyond its economic and legal responsibilities. With the rapidly changing global economy, companies with valuable brand names began to allocate more resources to CSR programmes to better cope with potential complaints and organized protests. As a result, the concept has evolved today into a CSR movement – an industry in itself (Boatright, 2009).

In this chapter, we discuss the meaning of CSR; the basic questions and issues involved in CSR; and the theories of ethics which serve as a sound foundation for CSR. We also examine the elements of implementing a successful CSR programme. Finally, we discuss the cross-cultural differences in the approaches to ethics and CSR and provide guidelines for international business executives.

Learning Objectives

- To explore the concept of corporate social responsibility (CSR) and its importance for sustainable business practices in the global world.

- To consider criteria for ethical decision-making through the lenses of three theoretical approaches: utilitarianism, the Kantian imperative and personalism.

- To understand the challenges faced by cross-cultural managers in situations requiring ethical decision-making.
- To explore cross-cultural differences in the approaches to ethics and CSR.
- To identify the position of cultural relativism in ethical decision-making.
- To understand the key principles and guidelines in ethical decision-making and CSR for cross-cultural managers.

Corporate Social Responsibility

Corporate social responsibility (CSR) is the selection and evaluation of corporate goals and outcomes based not only on profitability and organizational well-being, but also on ethical standards or judgements of social desirability. It also includes the capacity of a company to respond to social pressures (Frederick, 1994) – consistent with the 'principles of social responsibility, processes of response to social requirements and policies, programs and tangible results that reflect the company's relations with society' (Wood, 1991, p. 693).

CSR goes well beyond: (1) the economic responsibility of earning a profit by producing goods and providing services, (2) the legal responsibilities, i.e., the fiduciary responsibility of managing the corporation in the interests of the shareholders, and (3) legal compliance as it relates to the corporation's customers, suppliers, employees and local communities.

As can be seen from the following examples (Boatright, 2009), CSR involves behaviours and activities that are not necessarily codified into law, but demonstrates social responsibility and judgements using high ethical standards.

- Choosing to operate the corporation on a level higher than that which the law requires – e.g., the majority of MNC's codes of ethics prohibit payments to a government official even when a local law permits it.
- Providing benefits such as flexible work, for employees and improving the quality of life in the workplace beyond economic and legal requirements.
- Contributing to civic, charitable organizations and non-profit institutions to support worthy causes.
- Taking advantage of an economic opportunity that is judged to be less profitable but more socially desirable than some alternatives – e.g., Starbucks pays an above-market rate for Fair Trade coffee that benefits growers in poor countries.
- Using corporate resources to operate a programme that addresses a major social problem – e.g., Merck developed and now gives away (free) a drug in Africa for treatment of river blindness.

- In the social issue of environmental concerns, packaging: recognizing an obligation to change packaging to protect the environment, working with environmentalists to develop new packaging and switch to the new packaging.

Arguments for and against corporate social responsibility

We examine the main approaches to CSR through two theoretical frameworks: shareholder value theory or fiduciary capitalism and stakeholder theory.

The shareholder value theory or fiduciary capitalism

The major challenge to the idea that corporations should be socially responsible comes from the **shareholder value theory** or fiduciary capitalism. This theory argues that 'the only one responsibility of business towards the society is the maximization of profits to the shareholders, within the legal framework and ethical custom of the country' (Friedman, 1970, p. 122). According to this theory, corporate officials are the agent and bear fiduciary duties towards the principal – the owners of the corporation. Although Friedman acknowledges that corporations ought to seek profit within the framework of the law, he argues that it is the job of society to establish the required legal framework. He also acknowledges that the corporation's socially responsible actions are legitimate so long as these actions ultimately benefit the shareholders and are not purely philanthropic.

Shareholder value theory has several weaknesses (based on Boatright, 2009).

- Corporations have a responsibility to function in a manner that prevents specific harms from occurring. If the law has stipulated a minimum level of conduct, then corporations are vulnerable to intervention by external forces, including pressure from special interest groups and government regulation. Through recognition of its social responsibility, corporations are enabled to *internalize* the expectations of society and, thereby, retain control over decision-making and avoid the costs associated with government regulation.
- As corporations have become large and powerful, they are not effectively restrained by market forces and government regulation. Hence, by accepting social responsibility, corporations exercise the self-imposed restraint that is needed.
- Managers are obligated to earn a profit for shareholders, but they have a moral obligation to be sensitive to the social impact of their actions. For example, expenditure on product safety may reduce shareholders' return; but failure to provide product safety threatens the well-being of others in society.

"Now that we've embraced our diversity, celebrated our
pioneering spirit, made a fresh commitment to excellence
and given something back to the community, does
anyone remember what we do to make money?"

Cartoon 10.1 *Organizational cynicism about CSR. Copyright © Randy Glasbergen*

- Maximization of shareholder value frequently reflects short-term profits rather than long-term profitability. Economic success in the long run is achieved when management takes into account the interests of the shareholders and also the interests of the other stakeholders of the corporations – i.e., employees, customers, suppliers, local communities and other relevant groups. Such an approach is conducive to building trust, good relationships and cooperation with all the stakeholders. Earning a maximum return for shareholders in the long run requires corporations to act in a socially responsible manner and to satisfy the legitimate expectations of society (Mele, 2008).
- Because shareholders are consumers, citizens of communities and even environmentalists, they may, in fact, favour a certain amount of socially responsible conduct. In this situation, managers who exercise social responsibility would be using shareholders' money to serve the interests of the shareholders.

The stakeholder theory

Stakeholder theory is concerned with individuals or groups with a 'stake' in the corporation. Hence, the corporation ought to be managed for the benefit of its stakeholders – its customers, suppliers, owners, employees and local communities and to maintain the survival of the firm (Evan and Freeman, 1988). Figure 10.1 shows the main stakeholder groups that CEOs believe will have the greatest impact on the way they manage social expectations over the next five years.

The stakeholder theory is based on ethical principles of respect for persons – more specifically: 'the corporation and its managers may not violate the rights of others to determine their future ... the corporations and its managers are responsible for the effects of their actions on others' (Evan and Freeman, 1988, p. 79).

Unlike shareholder value theory, the stakeholder theory has several strengths:

- It views a good business as a community with purpose, a community with members who have rights, including the right to vote or express their views on major issues (Handy, 2002).
- The agenda and target of CSR activities are clearly outlined. They identify concrete interests, practices and specific responsibilities to specific groups of people affected by business activity (Blair, 1995; Clarkson, 1995).
- Shareholders are key players and CSR is not inherently against increasing shareholder benefits. As aptly put by Freeman and colleagues this approach is not against shareholders because:

  (i) the goal of creating value for *stakeholders* is *pro-shareholder*; (ii) creating value for stakeholders creates appropriate incentives for managers to assume entrepreneurial risks; (iii) having one objective function will make governance and management difficult, if not impossible; (iv) it is easier to make stakeholders out of shareholders rather than vice versa; and (v) in the event of a breach of contract or trust, shareholders, compared with stakeholders, have protection (or can seek remedies) through mechanisms such as market price per share. (Freeman et al., 2004, p. 365)

The preceding review of the two main approaches to CSR suggests that stakeholder theory provides a better understanding of the business–society relationship and, as a result, the social responsibility of the corporation. The results of a two-year study (Cappelli et al., 2010) of the 100 largest companies in India were striking:

- The most important goal of these companies was to serve a social mission rather than maximizing shareholder value – despite the fact that many executives were major shareholders of the company; the social mission enables employees to discover meaning in their work – a powerful source of employee motivation.
- The most distinctive feature of corporate governance is to balance the interests of diverse stakeholders. In addition, the interests of the broader community, extending to the entire nation, is emphasized.
- The companies take the development of human capital seriously by investing in employee training and development and employee empowerment and recognition practices. Measurement of the effectiveness of these practices was especially important.
- The companies' approach to business strategy was internal. It was based on innovations in the companies' value chains – that is the result of the social mission and investment in the employees.

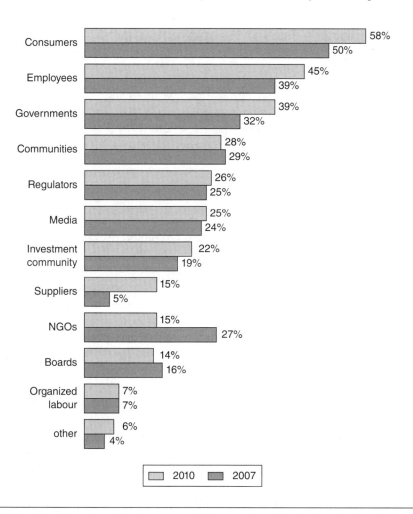

Figure 10.1 *Changing trends in the ways CEOs perceive stakeholders having the greatest impact on the way organizations manage social expectations*

Source: United Nations Global Compact CEO Survey 2010 and McKinsey UN Global Compact survey 2007 (cited in Lacy et al., 2010, p. 23)

There is a major concern that the potential for pluralistic interpretations in the stakeholder approach can 'lead to different distribution of benefits and burden, of pleasures and pain, of values, rights and interests' (Hummels, 1998, p. 1404). Hence, it is essential that the stakeholder theory is supported by a sound ethical foundation, which we discuss in the next section.

Ethics and Corporate Social Responsibility

Theories of ethics

Moral principles provide a conceptual framework to guide the making of moral decisions – to distinguish right actions from wrong actions. We explore utilitarianism, Kantian categorical imperative and personalism. In the light of these theories, we also examine the shareholder value theory and the stakeholder theory.

Utilitarianism

In essence, this moral doctrine prescribes that we should always act so as to produce the greatest possible balance of good, pleasure, or comfort over bad, pain, or discomfort for everyone affected by our action. Thus, in utilitarianism, the primary rule of human morality is the maximization of pleasure for the greatest possible number of people with a minimum of discomfort for the same number. The theory implicitly accepts that the 'end justifies the means'; hence, it is morally acceptable to produce the end (consequences or results) by any means (act) regardless of how abhorrent the act might be. Furthermore, no act is inherently objectionable; rather, it is objectionable only when it leads to a lesser amount of *good* than that which could have been produced.

Utilitarianism, in reality, involves two principles: greatest good, greatest number. It is not uncommon to be in a situation in which an act can produce the greatest good, but may not produce it for the greatest number; and vice-versa. Utilitarianism does not provide a means of determining which act is the morally right act.

Shareholder theory is consistent with utilitarian moral philosophy emphasizing an *enlightened self-interest*. The work of Milton Friedman (1963) advocates the notion that a free and competitive market contributes not only to the profitability of the most efficient organization, but also to the good of society. Human selfishness in this context is considered divine providence. Thus the concept of the economic human (*homo economicus*) has evolved from these intellectual traditions.

Guided by the desirability of a competitive free market characterizing the external environment and the economic human characterizing the internal environment, organizations consider it ideal to create conditions that facilitate individual autonomy and complete freedom of choice. In addition, it is acceptable to use information to one's own advantage and to compete intensely among individuals to maximize personal benefits.

Although organizations promote selfish and egoistic (rather than unselfish and altruistic) behaviours on the basis of the dual assumptions of free competition and the economic human, both of these assumptions have been found to be untrue. As early as the 1960s economists such as Galbraith (1967) were arguing that American corporations do not operate in an ideal free-market environment. Markets do not control the corporations; rather the corporations control the markets and consequently are able to engage in monopoly pricing, price-cutting to eliminate competition, employment and customer discrimination, deceptive advertising, environmental pollution and so on.

This state of affairs continues today – as evident from the 'unending (as of this date) stream of corporate financial scandals that began in the mid-1990s in which we saw executives manipulating finances to improve share prices and pad their pockets' (Cappelli et al., 2010, p. 7). All of these forms of self-serving behaviour at the organizational level directly produce many social 'evils' rather than social 'goods'. They have led to public criticism of business ethics and a public demand for corporate altruism and social responsibility.

Kantian categorical imperative

As a rational being I have an obligation to act. This obligation leads me to ask 'what is the act that is morally right?' **Kant's categorical imperative** states that *my act is morally right in a given situation if and only if I am willing that every person could act in the same way for the same reason.* The underlying logic or major test of a morally right act is whether its principle can be applied to all rational beings and in a consistent way. The test is not whether people in fact accept it; but whether all rational beings, thinking rationally, would accept it regardless of whether they are the doers or the receivers of the actions. Contrary to utilitarianism, Kant's idealism prescribes that the end does not justify the means. Hence, we cannot treat a person as means to an end. To treat a person simply as means would be to view the person as a 'thing' and, thereby, fail to recognize the dignity of the human person.

As stated in the discussion of stakeholder theory, the corporation and its managers: (1) are responsible for the effects of their actions on others and (2) may not violate the rights of others to determine their future.

These principles are consistent with Kant's dictum of respect for persons. In addition, stakeholder theory is also consistent with the principle of *solidarity* which enables a person to fulfil themselves through participation with others: a critical element of the theory of personalism, which is discussed next.

Personalism

Personalism – the philosophy of Karol Wojtyla, synthesized the two approaches: the metaphysical realism of Aristotle and Thomas Aquinas and the sensitivity to human experience and human subjectivity of Max Scheler's phenomenology (Kupczak, 2000). Through this synthesis, we can think through the relationship between the objective truth of things as they are and our subjective or personal experience of that truth. This approach provides two profound insights on the nature and uniqueness of the human person and serves as a sound foundation of ethical behaviour.

As we reflect on the nature of human experience, we find that it can, in essence, be reduced to the experience of: (1) 'things that happen to me'; and (2) 'I make things happen'. In the former experience, I am the object of the action. In the latter experience I assess the truth of the subject matter and then make a decision that conforms to the truth. In acting freely and in conformity with the truth, I experience myself as the efficient cause of my actions and grow as a *person* – from the person-I-am to the person-I-ought-to-be (Weigel, 2001). It is not the freedom to do what I feel like doing, but the freedom to do what I ought to do.

A person fulfils themself through free and responsible actions, but a person also has a social nature and lives in a world with many other persons. This fact necessitates that the person acts together with others in such a way that the person can fulfil themself through participation with others. Clearly, the person's participation – that is, acting together with others – ought to serve both the individual and the common good. What attitude will foster such participation and nurture a truly human society? Wojtyla (1979) analyses four 'attitudes': conformism; non-involvement; opposition or resistance; solidarity. Two of these attitudes – conformism and non-involvement, serve neither the individual nor the community. Conformism denotes a tendency to comply with the accepted practices and to assimilate with the community which could be a sign of solidarity with the community. But, if compliance with the accepted practices is solely to acquire benefit to self, then it is a servile attitude that does harm to both the person as well as the community. The attitude of non-involvement reflects a lack of concern for the common good. Participation is a fundamental good of a community; the attitude of non-involvement would prevent persons from fulfilling themselves in acting 'together with others'.

The other two attitudes – opposition and solidarity – serve both the individual and the common good. Opposition is an authentic attitude when out of a deep concern for the common good one resists the injustice that exists. In such a situation, those who oppose do not cut themselves off from their community. Rather, they engage in a dialogue in order to bring to light what is right and true and develop a constructive resolution of the differences. Solidarity is, indeed, the primary authentic attitude toward society.

> Solidarity means a constant readiness to accept and to realize one's share in the community because of one's membership within that particular community. In accepting the attitude of solidarity man does what he is supposed to do not only because of his membership in the group, but because he has the benefit of the whole in view: he does it for the *common good*. The awareness of the common good makes him look beyond his own share; and this intentional reference allows him to realize essentially his own share. Indeed, to some extent, solidarity prevents trespass upon other people's obligations and duties and seizing things belonging to others ... It is this attitude that allows man to find the fulfillment of himself in complementing others. (Wojtyla, 1979, pp. 284–5)

The personalist philosophy is indeed a solid ethical foundation for CSR. By accepting the attitude of solidarity, individuals, starting with corporation executives and managers, are enabled to do what they are supposed to do for the 'common good': 'to view economic life as an exercise of human responsibility, intrinsically oriented towards the promotion of the dignity of the person, the pursuit of the common good and the integral development – political, cultural and spiritual – of individuals, families and societies' (Benedict XVI, 2010).

Indeed, there is a need for good leaders with strong virtues in corporations. As Bass and Steidlmeier (2004, p. 181) observed:

> An approach to ethics based upon moral character and virtue enjoys an extraordinarily broad cross-cultural base ... that guides ethical discourse in cultural settings as diverse as Western and Confucian traditions. It constitutes an inner-directed and habitual strength of mind and will. The acquisition of such habitual strength, also known as the practice of virtue, is greatly facilitated by the individual's moral mentors who guide both by precept and example. (p. 181)

The idea of virtue as signifying human rightness was taken for granted by the contemporaries of Socrates. Plato first formulated the four **cardinal virtues** – *prudence, justice, fortitude* and *temperance*. We briefly discuss each cardinal virtue in the context of its importance to moral behaviour in leadership.

Prudence

The practice of this virtue requires habitual assessment, in the light of right standards, of the situation or issue on which a decision is to be made. The assessment also includes the likely favourable and unfavourable consequences of the decision for oneself as well as for others. The leader who is in the habit of practicing prudence will not abdicate their responsibility for unethical behaviour by followers in messages such as: *do whatever you have to do, just don't tell me about it*. The prudent person will not resent that others disagree with their views and will actively seek such information to better assess the situation and exercise sound judgement.

Justice

The virtue of justice requires the individual to strive constantly to give others what is their due. The 'due' means more than the legalistic notion of the contractual rights of others. It includes whatever others might need to fulfil their duties and exercise their rights as persons, that is, the right to life, to cultural and moral goods, material goods and so on. In the leadership context, it means the exercise of a sense of responsibility that balances, in a fair manner, the rights of all the stakeholders – customers, suppliers, government and community – as well as of the owners.

Fortitude

This is the courage to take great risks for an ideal that is worthwhile. A courageous leader faces difficult situations and strives to act positively to overcome obstacles to do what is good and noble. One of the underlying characteristics of fortitude is persever-ance and endurance against great odds. 'Determined people try to make it happen because they believe in it, not because the odds are on their side' (Leavitt, 1986, p. 95).

Temperance

The practice of temperance involves distinguishing between what is reasonable and necessary and what is self-indulgent. Although it includes the reasonable use and satisfaction of one's sense appetites, it also involves the efficient and effective alloca-tion of one's time, effort and resources. In essence, temperance means the exercise of self-control that, in general, would lead one to avoid and resist the temptation to overindulge in hedonistic behaviours.

Managerial Implications

Implementing CSR and creating an ethical corporate environment

> The old thinking was that if you make money you can do this positive social and environ-mental stuff – but I think the true philosophy of sustainability is the interdependence. It's not about charity; it's about the fact that if you do the right things in the community, the community will do the right things for you. If you do the right things for the environment, you'll have a stronger business so that you can make more money. (Manufacturing Execu-tive, 2005, cited in Kurucz et al., 2008, p. 83, emphasis added)

Clearly, there are advantages in exercising CSR. It is good for business, because the market rewards responsible behaviour and punishes corporate lapses. Also, firms are able to attract investment more easily if they are socially responsible. We explore the following issues and components of programmes in implementing CSR:

- Programme selection and design
- Vision statement
- Code of ethics
- Reporting and accountability.

Programme selection and design

Porter and Kramer suggest that if corporations

> were to analyze their prospects for social responsibility using the same frameworks that guide their core business choices, they would discover that CSR can be much more than a cost, a constraint, or a charitable deed – it can be a source of opportunity, innovation and competitive advantage. (2006, p. 80)

The following criteria of programme selection are identified from a survey of corporations with successful CSR programmes that produce genuine social benefits and also serve corporate interests (Boatright, 2009).

- Manage the reputation risk by focusing on business activities that impact on ethically sensitive issues such as human rights, the environment and public activities. Such a focus enables the corporation to anticipate and address these issues in a timely manner. For example, Nike was slow to accept responsibility for the treatment of workers in its contract factories in South East Asia.
- Choose programmes and activities that are closely linked to the company's employment needs. For example, many companies in the computer industry have supported projects in computer literacy and science education among students throughout the world.
- Make use of the company's mission and core competencies. For example, United Parcel Services uses its core competency in shipping goods to transport relief supplies to disaster-stricken areas.
- Identify opportunities that fit with the company's strategy. For example, consistent with its strategy of promoting a family-friendly atmosphere in its restaurants, McDonald's supports Ronald McDonald House charities by providing accommodation for the families of seriously ill children undergoing treatment.
- Involve stakeholder engagement or dialogue. For example, Coca-Cola is a partner with other organizations in Africa to fight AIDS. By doing so, it understands the needs and outlook of others and engages them in the pursuit of mutual benefit.

Vision statement

After selecting the right social responsibility programme appropriate to the company's core business choices, an idealized vision should be formulated and articulated. The vision is the future goals to be achieved through the corporate social responsibility programme.

As discussed in the chapter on leadership, the more idealized the future goal advocated by the leader, the more discrepant it becomes in relation to the status quo. The greater the discrepancy from the status quo, the more likely the followers' attribution that the leader has extraordinary vision, not just an ordinary goal. Also, a discrepant and idealized goal provides followers with a sense of challenge and a motivating force for change. The attitude change literature suggests that a maximum discrepant position within the latitude of acceptance puts the greatest amount of pressure on followers to change their attitudes.

The idealized goal, despite its extreme discrepancy, should be within the latitude of acceptance when it is articulated to represent a perspective shared by the followers, and promise to meet their hopes and aspirations. Followers attribute charisma to leaders when their vision represents an embodiment of a perspective shared by them in an idealized form. The vision also reinforces the followers' sense of collective identity which facilitates their placing the interests of the organization over their own interests – even at personal cost (Shamir et al., 1993).

Code of ethics

There is an increasing realization today that organizational leaders need to be more sensitive to their moral obligations to the larger society, which includes all their stakeholders such as consumers, employees, suppliers, governments, and local communities. It is the recognition of these obligations that has led several large corporations to formulate **codes of ethics**, set up ethics committees, communication systems for employees to report abuses or seek guidance, ethics training programmes, ethics officers and disciplinary processes (Weaver et al., 1999). Experience suggests that unethical business practices are seldom due to a lone rogue employee but usually result from factors in the organization (Boatright, 2009), hence ethical programmes are designed to create an organization that fosters ethical conduct.

The corporate ethics programme communicates the values and vision of the organization, seeks to build relations of trust with all stakeholder groups and emphasizes the responsibility of each employee for ethical conduct. An integrative approach in implementing the programme aligns the standards of employees with those of the organization and enables them to act ethically. It seeks to create conditions that foster right action instead of relying on deterrence and detection. It also attempts to motivate employees by appealing to their values and ideals rather than relying solely on material incentives. It is an important reminder that individuals, not the organization, engage in ethical or unethical practices. It serves 'to map a high road to economic and ethical performance – and to mount guard-rails to keep corporate wayfarers on track' (Andrews, 1989, p. 99).

However, such ethical codes and structures need to be more than mere 'window dressing'. A survey of 10,000 randomly selected employees from all levels of six large US corporations that had a formal code of ethics found that

> specific characteristics of the formal ethics or compliance programme matter less than broader perceptions of the programme's orientation toward values and ethical aspirations. What helps the most are consistency between policies and actions as well as dimensions of the organization's ethical culture such as ethical leadership. (Treviño et al., 1999, p. 131, emphasis added)

The self-transformation needed for ethical leadership revolves principally around character development, yet a survey of the codes of conduct of more than 200 companies found that 'the most ignored item was personal character – it seemed not to matter' (Walton, 1988, p. 170). In view of the critical importance of character formation, we discussed it at some length in the section on personalism above.

Reporting and accountability

The commitment to CSR is considerably enhanced when the social benefits that are claimed can be measured. Boatright (2009) has identified the following sources of impetus for the measurement of social performance:

- Companies seek to evaluate the benefits of their CSR programmes to demonstrate their value to shareholders and the public.
- The social performance of companies is ranked by several influential rating organizations such as the Dow Jones Sustainability Index; these indexes are followed by investment managers and also the public.
- Socially responsible investment (SRIs) funds apply their own measures to company performance.
- Substantial academic research is engaged in the study of the company's social performance relative to its financial performance.

The Global Reporting Institute (GRI) and the Institute of Social and Ethical Accountability (ISEA) have developed complex and specific guidelines for measuring social and environmental performance; ISEA also offers a certification – AA1000.

> Even if social or ethical reporting cannot be fully comparable to financial reporting, the recent interest by companies and the public in gathering information about CSR and publishing the results is ... likely to encourage greater corporate social performance and also increase the transparency of CSR activities. (Boatright, 2009, p. 369)

Role of Leadership in the Development of a Moral Environment

The effective and enduring implementation of corporate social responsibility is critically dependent on the organization's moral environment. When asked about his primary job, the chairman of Matushita Electric said: 'To model love. I am the *soul* of this company. It is through me that our organization's values pass' (Blanchard and Peale, 1988, p. 89). Indeed, the leader creates the organization's moral environment, but it cannot be created by the fiat of the leader. As discussed in personalism, the 'personal virtue and moral wisdom of the leader provide the checks and balances upon power and self-aggrandizement ... The heart of the moral enterprise is the development of good character, which is defined by commitment to virtue in all circumstances' (Bass and Steidlmeier, 2004, p. 188).

As Aristotle said: 'We are what we repeatedly do. Excellence then is not an act, but a habit.' Truly, the leader is the *soul* of the organization. For example, one manufacturer continued to produce a product known to cause illness and death, while another (e.g., Johnson and Johnson) immediately withdrew a product from the market on the basis of a suspicion and at enormous cost, even though the product was proven to be completely safe (Lank, 1988). The actions of these CEOs sent clear, unambiguous messages about the ethical standards expected from their employees.

As discussed in the chapter on leadership, leadership effectiveness is greater and more enduring when leaders adopt the transformational influence process mode. The means used for this purpose – empowerment and related strategies – reflect their altruistic value and orientation. These strategies, by their very nature, involve a concern for 'others before oneself' which must be manifested at every stage of the charismatic leadership process – from the assessment of the environment, formulation and articulation of the vision, to the means to achieve the vision. It is therefore not surprising that the study of the business leaders in the 100 largest companies in India, cited earlier, found that their practices were consistent with the transformational influence process: 'inspirational motivation, idealized influence, intellectual stimulation and individual consideration' (Cappelli et al., 2010, p. 13).

The leader should also create opportunities for employees to exchange ideas and experiences in the implementation of the code of conduct, as well as the difficulties they might encounter in acting ethically in certain situations – especially if ethical dilemmas are involved. Some organizations hold periodical retreats or discussion forums which provide employees with the intellectual, emotional and moral support necessary to maintain the high ethical standards expected of them.

Codes of conduct, related policies and procedures and support structures are undoubtedly essential to the development of the organization's moral environment. However, in the final analysis, it is the leader's personal conduct that determines their effectiveness. Just as Mother Teresa's work for the 'poorest of the poor' is an external outpouring of her love for God, in much the same way the organization's moral environment is a natural overflow of the charismatic leader's commitment to ethical principles and values that is expressed not only in terms of intellectual assent but also in their daily struggle to live by them. A moral leader 'engenders virtue in self, others and society through example and virtuous conduct' (Bass and Steidlmeier, 2004, p. 188).

Cross-cultural Issues in Ethics and CSR

Capitalism has been successful enough in generating output and raising productivity. But the experiences of different countries are quite diverse. The recent experiences of Eastern Asian economics – most notably Japan – raise deep questions about the modeling of capitalism on traditional economic theory. Japan is often seen – rightly in a particular sense – as a great example of successful capitalism, but it is clear that the motivation patterns that dominate Japanese business have much more content than would be provided by pure profit maximization ... Indeed, there is some truth, oddly enough, even in the puzzling witty claim by *The Wall Street Journal* that Japan is 'the only communist nation that works'. It is as one would expect, mainly a remark about the non-profit motivations underlying many economic and business activities in Japan. We have to understand and interpret the peculiar fact that the most successful capitalist nation in the world flourishes economically with a motivation structure that departs firmly – and often explicitly – from the pursuit of self-interest, which is meant to be a bedrock of capitalism. (Amartya Sen, 1993, p. 32)

As discussed in previous sections, sustainability requires that CSR and ethics are at the top of global leaders' agenda. However, sustainability is not an issue that has the highest priority for all leaders of the world. As can be seen from Figure 10.2, CEOs' perception of the importance of sustainability for the future of their business success varies by region (Lacy et al., 2010, p. 18). In this section we will explore cross-cultural differences in the attitudes and practices concerning CSR and ethics.

Approximately 15 per cent of the world population live in so called **weak governance zones** with weak institutions that fail to protect property and intellectual rights, enforce rules and regulations and eliminate red tape (Huber-Grabenwarter and Boehm, 2009).

As a result, companies may be tempted to use bribery and other corrupt practices as a political risk insurance to protect investments. Similarly, they may be lured to manipulate rules in their favour, avoid enforcement of regulations, gain lucrative contracts or resource extraction permits, or simply to cut through red tape and administrative hold-ups. (Huber-Grabenwarter and Boehm, 2009, p. 47)

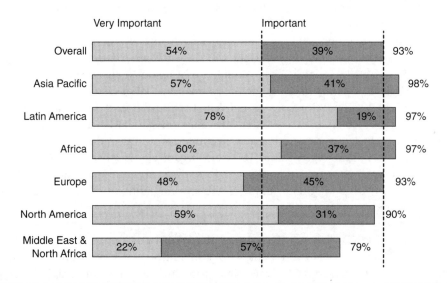

Figure 10.2 *Regional differences in the extent to which sustainability is important to the future success of businesses. (Lacy et al., 2010, p. 18)*

Conducting business in different cultural contexts that undermine the importance of ethics and CSR has become one of the key challenges in today's global environment: 'Ethical decision-making in the global context, sitting as it does at the top of the global competencies model, is increasingly the acid test applied by a multiplicity of stakeholders to judge global management competency' (McNett and Sondergaard, 2004, p. 167, emphasis added).

What is the evidence showing that ethics is on top of the global business agenda for cross-cultural managers?

- The number of companies in the Global 200 list that have business code of conduct increased dramatically over the years: from 2 per cent in 1997 to 85 per cent in 2007 (Kaptein, 2009).
- Some of the large global organizations now have a Chief Ethics Officer in their top management team.
- Increasing numbers of organizations (e.g., 77 per cent US, 55 per cent Asian Pacific, 32 per cent Western European) integrate 'whistleblower protection programmes' to fight fraud and corruption (Aldrighi, 2009).
- There is a growing body of academic research literature on ethics and CSR in cross-cultural context as evidenced by the level of debate in publications journals such as the *Journal of Business Ethics*.
- There are numerous non-profit organizations that guide cross-cultural managers to conduct business with high ethical standards, such as the International Business Ethics Institute (http://www.business-ethics.org/), Center for International Business Ethics (http://www.cibe.org.cn/en/) and European Business Ethics Network (http://www.eben.org/).
- There are international standards and codes to ensure ethical and responsible practices in global business, such as ISO 14000 (standards for environmental protection), ISO 26000 (standards for corporate social responsibility), SA8000 (standards for workplace practices to comply with international labor conventions and human rights), the UN Global Compact (principles of reponsible and sustainable corporate conduct), AA1000 Assurance Standard (evaluation standards used to evaluate the extent to which an organization is accountable to its multiple stakeholders), International Labour Organization (ILO) and Organization for Economic Cooperation and Development (OECD) guidelines for MNCs and the ETI (Ethical Trading Initiative; a UK-based code to improve the working conditions of people producing consumer goods).

The number of MNCs following these standards and guidelines is increasing over the years: ISO 14000 – 46 per cent; ILO convention – 35 per cent; UN Global Compact – 33 per cent; OECD Guidelines for Multinational Enterprises – 22 per cent; Ethical Trading Initiative – 17 per cent; SA 8000 – 17 per cent; AA1000 – 10 per cent (Knight, 2009, p. 100).

Cross-cultural managers face ethical dilemmas in a wide range of operations, including production, marketing, negotiations in bids, HRM practices and employee heatlh and well-being. Look at the examples in Thinking across cultures 10.1.

Thinking across cultures 10.1

Ethical Dilemmas in Cross-cultural Context

- In some countries laws prohibiting advertisements of cigarettes are less restrictive than others. Should cigarette-producing companies relax their rules in these countries and shrink the size of the warnings on the packages?
- In some countries there are no laws or regulations to prevent discrimination in hiring practices on the basis of gender, age, religion, ethnic and educational background. Should MNCs who are equal opportunity employers operating in these countries feel free to ask questions in the job application form that would be inappropriate at home but highly common in the local context ?
- Child labour is unfortunately still very common in the majority of less developed countries. In some countries children cannot attend school because of poverty. Children who do not go to work usually engage in criminal activities (e.g., theft) to provide for the family. As an organization completely against child labour, should you consider hiring children in such countries to keep them away from crime and let them contribute to family income?
- According to a new regulation production facilities can continue only if organizations go through a rigorous assessment conducted by government officials. It is known that the assessment takes a very long time (almost a year) and there is no guarantee that your company will pass it. It is also known that the process is shorter and easier if government officers are pleased to receive gifts as a token of appreciation for their time and care. Bribing government officials is strictly prohibited under the MNC's rules. However, not pleasing officials would risk production and hence the employment of 1200 workers who would live in extreme poverty if they lose their job. What would you do?

Sources: Francesco and Gold (2005); Lane, DiStefano, Maznevski (2006); Punnett, (2004)

- What would you do if you faced each of these dilemmas? (Please make sure that you write down your approach for each dilemma.)

(Continued)

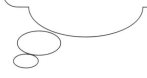

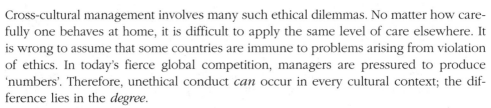

(Continued)

- Does your approach differ according to the dilemma you are facing or will you be consistent across cases? Explain why you prefer to be 'flexible' or 'consistent' in your approach.
- Compare your approach with one of your colleagues. What are the similarities and differences? Why do you think your approach was similar or different? Consider the role of age, gender, education, personality, cultural background, etc.

Cross-cultural management involves many such ethical dilemmas. No matter how carefully one behaves at home, it is difficult to apply the same level of care elsewhere. It is wrong to assume that some countries are immune to problems arising from violation of ethics. In today's fierce global competition, managers are pressured to produce 'numbers'. Therefore, unethical conduct *can* occur in every cultural context; the difference lies in the *degree*.

Table 10.1 shows the scores of selected countries on two indices: the Bribe Payers Index (BPI) which records the likelihood of firms from the world's industrialized countries

Table 10.1 Differences in perception of corruption and likelihood of engaging in bribing behaviour.

Country	Bribe Payers Index 2011	Corruption Perceptions Index 2010	Percentage of participants who paid bribe in the last 12 months for services*
Belgium	8.7	7.1	Data not available
Canada	8.5	8.9	4
Netherlands	8.8	8.8	2
Switzerland	8.8	8.7	2
Germany	8.6	7.9	2
United Kingdom	8.3	7.6	1
Japan	8.6	7.8	9
Australia	8.5	8.7	2
France	8.0	6.8	7
Singapore	8.3	9.3	9
United States	8.1	7.1	5
Spain	8.0	6.1	5
Hong Kong	7.6	8.4	5
South Africa	7.6	4.5	56
South Korea	7.9	5.4	2
Taiwan	7.5	5.8	7

Country	Bribe Payers Index 2011	Corruption Perceptions Index 2010	Percentage of participants who paid bribe in the last 12 months for services*
Italy	7.6	3.9	13
Brazil	7.7	3.7	4
India	7.5	3.3	54
Mexico	7.0	3.1	31
China	6.5	3.5	9
Russia	6.1	2.1	26

Notes.

Bribe Payers Index: Transparency International's Bribe Payers Index ranks the likelihood of companies from leading economies to win business abroad by paying bribes. A score of 10 denotes the lowest likelihood of companies from this country to engage in bribery when doing business abroad while a score of 0 denotes the highest likelihood of companies to engage in bribery when doing business abroad.

Corruption Perceptions Index: Transparency International's Corruption Perceptions Index measures the perceived level of public sector corruption in countries and territories around the world. In 2010, it scores 178 countries worldwide from 0 (highly corrupt) to 10 (highly clean).

*Data was taken from the Global Corruption Barometer 2010/2011. Transparency International's Global Corruption Barometer tracks worldwide public opinion on corruption. The 2010/11 Barometer reflects the responses of more than 100,000 people in 100 countries.

© Transparency International 2010, 2011. All Rights Reserved.

offering bribes abroad (http://www.transparency.org/news_room/in_focus/2008/bpi_2008) and the Corruption Perception Index (CPI) which records perceived levels of public sector corruption (http://www.transparency. org/policy_ research/surveys_ indices/cpi/2010). The last column in Table 10.1 also shows percentage of respondents who paid a bribe in the last 12 months in any form to institutions or organizations providing services in healthcare, education, justice, protection, trade customs and so on (Global Corruption Barometer, 2010 http://www.transparency.org/research /gcb/overview).

Unfortunately the scores in CPI and BPI are not 10, the so-called completely clean countries, for any of these countries. Countries differ in degree of cleanliness and we will explore the factors that can explain these differences in the next section.

National, Organizational, Individual and Cultural Correlates of Ethical and Socially Responsible Behaviour

CASE 10.1

Corruption in China – is it about Culture?

The 18th National Congress of the ruling Communist Party of China that was held in November 2012 again addressed the urgency and significance of fighting corruption. (*China Daily*, 2013, p. 7)

(Continued)

(Continued)

In a recent interview for *China Daily*, experts responded to the question as follows:.

Question: 'Some experts said that China's Confucian culture and deeply rooted family ties make officials prone to corruption compared to their foreign counterparts. Do you think there is any relationship between traditional Chinese culture and corruption?'

> In Western countries, people live by contracts – even if a father gives his son some property, there will be a contract. But in China, people trust family without a contract. Many corrupt officials buy apartments under the name of their children or their relatives, which is difficult for the anti-graft authorities to investigate. (Zhou Shuzhen, Professor of Politics at Renmin University of China)
> There are a large number of officials whose spouses, children and secretaries and drivers were found to be involved in corruption. That some officials' family members have become part of corruption has caused great harm to society. This also makes it difficult for supervision agencies to collect evidence. China has traditional ideas, such as being loyal and righteous, which to some extent informs the relationship between corrupt officials and their staff. (Jiang Ming'an, Professor of Law at Peking University)
> It is too simple to say some countries' cultures are good or bad and it is not right to define East Asian culture, or Confucianism, as easily corrupted. Confucianism indeed has some old ideas that may harm efforts to stamp out corruption, which needs to change. Cultures must be updated and develop with society. (He Zengke, Researcher at the Central Compilation and Translation Bureau)

I don't think there is any relationship between traditional Chinese culture and corruption and it is not necessary to put the two together. In the past, China had clean governance, so we cannot say corruption is caused or affected by a culture of Confucianism. If a country has good supervision system, corruption would be greatly curbed. (Ma Huaide, Professor of Law at China University of Political Science and Law)

I know someone said the so-called 'relation' and 'face' issues in East Asian cultures may lead to corruption, but we should take note that other areas with similar culture, including Hong Kong and Singapore, have made achievements towards stamping out corruption. We cannot lose confidence. (Ren Jianming, Director of Beihang University's Clean Governance Research and Education Center)

At the national level, unethical and socially irresponsible conduct is likely to occur in 'weak governance' zones. In such contexts, there are regulatory oversights, low levels of civil and criminal liabilities, inability of law enforcement and insufficient compliance and corporate governance systems (Huber-Grabenwarter and Boehm, 2009, p. 47). There is some evidence to link a high level of corruption to lower rates of economic growth, lower level of per capita income and smaller amounts of foreign direct investment (e.g., UNDP Report, 2001). There is also evidence to show that managers in wealthier countries are slightly more likely to take CSR issues into account in their decision-making compared to those in poor countries (McWilliams and Siegel, 2001).

At the organizational level, there is a positive association between CSR activities and firm size and resources. Large and financially secure organizations are found to be more inclined to engage in CSR activities (Sotorrio and Sanchez, 2008; Zu and Song, 2009). However, organizations that put high pressure on their managers to enhance the bottom line by increasing profits and reducing costs are more likely to engage in unethical behaviour (McNett and Sondergaard, 2004; Schneider and Barsoux, 2003).

Some scholars argue that in the organizational life cycle, organizations go through stages of moral development (Reidenbach and Robin, 1991). The first stage is the amoral stage where the organization believes that a conduct is ethical as long as it is not caught. In such organizations there is no code of conduct. Organizations at the second stage are legalistic and play with the legal rules. The code of ethics in such organizations is an internal document guiding people not to do anything to harm the organization. The responsive organization in the next stage acts not only on a legal basis, but also on a basis that would satisfy other corporate stakeholders. There is concern for economic output and a belief that 'ethics pays'. Organizations at the fourth stage have an emerging ethical orientation. They want to do the right thing but lack long-term strategic planning for that. At the most advanced stage, organizations are ethical. They develop strategic plans based on SWOT analyses – strenghts, weaknesses, opportunities, threats – that anticipate ethical problems and produce alternative outcomes accordingly. Organizational documents at all levels focus on ethical profile and reflect core values.

At the individual level, managers' values and cognitive moral development (the mental process of deciding what is right or wrong) are considered as factors associated with the likelihood of ethical and socially responsible behaviour. Some authors argue that managerial values are more important than organizational and national-level factors. For example, high integrity as a personal value and vision as a managerial trait are positively associated with ethical and socially responsible behaviour (e.g., Waldman et al., 2006). As aptly put by McNett and Sondergaard (2004, p. 166) ethical decision-making for global managers require '*traits* of integrity, humility, inquisitiveness and hardiness; the *attitudes and orientations* of cognitive complexity and cosmopolitanism; the *interpersonal skills* of mindful communication and creating and building trust; and the *systems skills* of boundary spanning and building community through change'.

At the cultural level, there is a growing body of literature associating ethics and social responsibility with cultural values.

- A recent excellent meta-analysis found that *individualism* and *uncertainty avoidance* are associated with high likelihood of avoiding unethical behaviour, whereas *power distance* and *masculinity* are associated with low likelihood of the same (Taras et al., 2010). That is, people avoid unethical behaviour to a greater extent in cultures that value individualism and certainty. People avoid unethical behaviour to a lesser extent in cultures that value hierarchical social order and achievement and affluence.

- Cultural *tightness-looseness*, defined as the strength of social norms and tolerance for deviant behaviour, is also associated with tolerance for immoral behaviour (Gelfand et al., 2011). Tight societies tend to adhere to moral conventions and rules and have criminal justice institutions with higher monitoring and more severe sanctioning. Gelfand and colleagues (2011) found that people in tight societies considered morally charged behaviour (e.g., cheating) less justifiable.

- In *particularistic* cultures, application of ethical rules depends on the person, situation, task, urgency and so on, whereas in *universalistic* cultures, application of ethical rules depends less on the circumstances. For example, in an experiment Chinese executives' level of ethical reasoning depended on the nature of the dilemma, while this was not the case for US executives (Fleming et al., 2010).

- *High-context* cultures prefer ethical rules to be stated explicitly (e.g., a book on codes of conduct, lists of principles posted on the company walls), while *low-context* cultures resent such explicit statements and consider them unnecessary or rude:

> I resent having notions of right or wrong boiled down to a checklist. I come from
> a nation whose ethical traditions date back hundreds of years. Its values have been

transmitted to me by my church and through my family. I don't need to be told by some American lawyer how I should conduct myself in my business activity. (Schneider and Barsoux, 2003, p. 305)

- High *power-distance* is associated with less concern for CSR, whereas high *institutional collectivism* is associated with more concern for CSR (Waldman et al., 2006). Managers in cultures valuing collectivism at the institutional level tolerate delaying of gratification (e.g., profits) for the well-being of the society. Managers in cultures valuing high power-distance seem to focus on self-promotion and satisfaction for shareholders, but lack concern for multiple stakeholders including the larger society.

Cultural relativism

Earlier in this chapter we discussed three theoretical approaches to ethics: utilitarianism, the Kantian imperative and personalism. In this section, we present a fourth approach – cultural relativism. **Cultural relativism** in ethics implies that interpretation of a behaviour as ethical or unethical depends on the cultural context. Therefore, the theory suggests that child labour, discrimination against women, or nepotism in hiring practices cannot necessarily be interpreted as unethical if a given cultural context endorses these practices (e.g., Thomas, 2002).

Cultural relativism poses challenges for international managers. Just like some legal practices can be unethical (e.g., marketing infant formula in developing countries where the product will be harmful if prepared in non-hygienic conditions; Lane et al., 2006), some culturally different practices can also be unethical. Such practices resemble the lyric of a popular song 'it's not right, but it's OK'. These situations pose the following challenges:

- How can international managers differentiate practices that are culturally different and ethical in the local context vs. culturally different but unethical in the local context? An example for the first case in a collectivistic culture is to hire family members, whereas an example for the second case in a collectivistic culture is to produce excuses to delay the delivery of a product to the customer so that 'face' is not lost, knowing that this will risk losing the business of the customer.
- Should the international manager accept practices that are culturally different and ethical in the host country (e.g., hiring family members), even though it is not ethical in the home country or according to the organization's code of conduct?
- What could be some local practices that are easier to accept even though they are not completely ethical according to the home-country standards?

- Is it ethical to impose one's own ethical standards in cross-cultural situations involving ethical dilemmas? 'To what extent should personal values, parent company, or host-country values apply? Head-office to insist on ethical practices or to install ethics programmes in foreign subsidiaries may be taken as another sign of cultural imperialism. These efforts may even be disparaged as moral hypocrisy.' (Schneider and Barsoux, 2003, p. 309)

We will present some guidelines to address these challenges in the next section.

Cross-cultural considerations for managers

Hamilton and Knouse's (2001) decision parameters in Thinking across cultures 10.2 provide answers to the above challenging questions.

The challenge of differentiating culturally different from unethical is addressed by their first question. The recommendation is to follow MNC or home-country standards if the questionable practice is not necessarily unethical but culturally different. If the practice is culturally different but not ethical, the recommendation is to assess whether or not the practice is a *major* or *minor* violation of ethics.

This addresses our second challenge. The recommendation is to follow MNC or home-country standards if the violation is major. When the violation is major, the MNC can follow its own standards if it has power in the host country and if the host country has the potential and willingness to learn from the MNC. These recommendations answer our last two challenging questions.

Thinking across cultures 10.2

MNCs should follow its own ethical practices rather than host country's (e.g., Russia) questionable practices (QPs) if:

- Decision rule 1: Questionable practices are less ethical (rather than different)

  o If QPs are not less ethical but simply different, the MNC can follow their own or host-country standards. If QPs are less ethical, the MNC must consider the next three decision rules.
  o Examples: Bribes and corruption are less ethical; nepotism in hiring may only be different if justified by the host country's background institutions.

- o Strengths: Prevents cultural imperialism by requiring an examination of the relationship of the questionable business practice to the legal, economic and social institutions.
- o Weaknesses: Requires reference to traditional ethical theories to determine whether practices are less ethical or different, so could challenge capacities of MNE manager or require an ethics consultant's expertise.

- Decision rule 2: Questionable practices violate ethical minimums

  - o If QPs violate ethical minimums, the MNC should not engage in these practices; if not, consult decision rules 3 and 4.
  - o Examples: Murdering competitors and dumping toxic waste are below ethical minimums; nepotism in hiring and paying bribes in some circumstances may not be below minimums for some corporations.
  - o Strengths: Makes an important distinction between activities which are never acceptable and acts which can be considered. Challenges businesses to examine what activities will likely raise ethical questions and design a corporate ethics code to address those activities.
  - o Weaknesses: Requires reference to traditional ethical theories to determine the ethical minimums. Could require ethics consultant's expertise.

- Decision rule 3: MNC had leverage in host country

  - o If MNC has leverage, it should follow its own standards if (1) host-country practices are less ethical and (2) host country has prospects for improvement.
  - o Examples: MNC can refuse to follow host practices because it has access to needed hard currency, home-country legal requirements or ability to either not enter or to exit the market.
  - o Strengths: Points out obligation of MNC to stakeholders in host country to contribute to improving the situation in their society, with the hopes of bettering the return for MNC employees and stockholders. Does not impose obligations on those without the power to act on them.
  - o Weaknesses: Requires analysis of a number of economic, legal, political and social forces. Could require consultations with a variety of disciplines. Risk of special pleading in weighing exit and opportunity costs.

- Decision rule 4: Host country has prospects for improving

  - o If the host country's practices have prospects for improving and the MNC has leverage, then the MNC should operate in such a way as to contribute to that improvement.

(Continued)

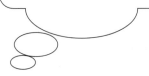

(Continued)

- o Examples: If McDonald's can improve the business climate in Russia (or perhaps only in Moscow) by refusing to pay bribes, then they should do so.
- o Strengths: Emphasizes that obligation is contingent on possibility.
- o Weaknesses: Requires analysis of a number of economic, legal, political and social forces. Requires weighing the welfare of other stakeholder obligations against the obligations to improve conditions for stakeholders in the host country and against possibilities for future benefits for employee and stockholder stakeholders if conditions in the host country do improve.

Source: Hamilton and Knouse (2001, p. 81)

The last decision rule in the Hamilton and Knouse model is particularly important and can be summarized as follows: if a MNC has the power to change certain unethical practices in the host country and if the host country is able and willing to change these practices under the leadership of MNCs as role models, then it is advisable to implement MNC rules.

Consider these two powerful opinions (cited in Schneider and Barsoux, 2003, pp. 310–11):

> Corporations are not formed to effect change but to sell goods. It can be pressured into treating employees more equitably. But it cannot be expected to challenge the laws of society. Those who insist otherwise are trying to get a business to do the job of a diplomat or a soldier. (Journalist Roger Williams)

> The private sector may not be able to answer the social problems of the world – but it can stop being part of these problems. (Alan Christie, Director of Community Affairs, Levi-Strauss Europe)

With this general understanding, let us move on to more specific suggestions for MNC and expatriate managers:

- Have a written code of ethical conduct especially for international business activities. The code should include commonly experienced problems and proposed solutions in accordance with corporate rules.
- Have a reward and recognition system to promote ethical behaviour in international business.

- Build strong and trusting relationships with business partners to assess the necessity and risk of engaging in unethical behaviour, to explain the reasons why you should not violate ethical rules and to produce legitimate alternatives.
- Avoid false dichotomies such as 'you either bribe or get out of business'. Think out of the box and consider all other alternatives. Don't let anybody to make you feel trapped.
- Avoid creating solutions that may be 'efficient' but equally problematic. For example, it may be an efficient solution to hire a local headhunter who is able to ask questions that it is not possible to ask to job applicants under company ethical rules. Letting others do the dirty work may save the day but keep your hands equally dirty.
- Make training on cross-cultural management dilemmas on ethics part of your annual training and development activity. The training should be applied with lots of examples of dilemmas and in-depth discussion.
- Never lose sight of the big picture: 'treat everybody with respect and dignity', 'do not harm anybody', 'protect the environment for future generations'.
- Partner with organizations that have certification of ISO 14000, ISO 26000, SA8000, who sign agreements such as UN Global Compact, or abide by ILO and OECD rules.
- Keep listening, keep learning: 'Ethical thinking is the result of organizational learning created from the interaction of diverse stakeholders and produces heightened sensitivity to ethical issues' (Francesco and Gold, 2005, p. 63).
- Take role models who lead with values and high ethical standards.

Chapter Summary

We are living in a world with shrinking resources. The organizations that will survive are those that stop wasting and start optimizing environmental and human resources. We start the chapter by discussing whether or not corporate social responsibility (CSR) and ethics are fad or reality (see Video 10.1). Clearly, they are the reality of today, without which sustainability cannot be achieved. Two seemingly contradictory viewpoints on CSR are presented. In shareholder theory organizations are defined as entities whose only responsibility to society is the maximization of profit for shareholders, whereas in stakeholder theory they are defined as entities whose responsibility is to maximize the benefits of multiple stakeholders, including customers, suppliers, employees and local and global communities. Common to both perspectives is the importance of ethical business conduct (see Video 10.2). The chapter presents three frameworks concerning the criteria used in ethical decision-making: utilitarianism, the Kantian categorical imperative and personalism. We discussed that in all situations concerning ethical dilemmas, leaders must adopt the key virtues including prudence, justice, fortitude and temperance. Managerial implications of these discussions are outlined in a section presenting specific guidelines for successful CSR initiatives and for decision-making in situations posing ethical dilemmas. The last section concerns cross-cultural differences in approaches to CSR and ethics. We emphasize that no country is completely 'clean' and that no country should be labelled as 'inherently unethical'. The differences are in degree and they should be attributed to variations in national, organizational, leadership and cultural characteristics of countries. In facing ethical dilemmas in cross-cultural contexts, the key is to differentiate whether or not the questionable practice is perceived to be unethical just because it is culturally different. We presented such dilemmas and guidelines for cross-cultural managers (see Video 10.3).

Key Terms and Definitions

Corporate social responsibility (CSR). Selection and evaluation of corporate goals and outcomes based not only on profitability, but also on positive impact on environment, employees, local and global communities and other key stakeholders.

Shareholder value theory. An approach suggesting that a socially responsible business is one that fulfils its responsibilities towards its shareholders by maximizing profits through legal and ethical conduct.

Stakeholder theory. An approach suggesting that organizations must fulfil responsibilities to multiple stakeholders (e.g., environment, customers, suppliers, employees, owners, local communities) and maintain survival by maximizing their benefits.

Utilitarianism. The moral doctrine prescribing decision-making made to maximize goodness for the greatest possible number of people.

Kantian categorical imperative. Doctrine suggesting that an act should be judged morally right if all rational beings engage in it and in a consistent way.

Personalism. The philosophical approach portraying individuals as responsible beings, who have the free will to act with others to achieve a fulfilling life and growth.

Cardinal virtues in ethical leadership. Four virtues recognized and promoted in ancient philosophical and religious texts, including prudence (foresight, wisdom), justice (fairness), temperance (self-control) and fortitude (courage).

Code of ethics. Guidelines assisting organizations' members in differentiating between ethical and unethical courses of actions in accordance with the legal, social and organizational norms.

Weak governance zones. Countries or regions of the world where institutions fail to protect property and intellectual rights, enforce rules and regulations and eliminate red tape.

Cultural relativism. The approach to decision-making which recommends that organizations and individuals should follow the local and cultural norms in their actions.

End of Chapter Reflection Questions

1. Some organizations complain that there is an unnecessarily strong emphasis on ethics and CSR and that it is a fad distracting attention from the organization's core business. To what extent do you agree with these concerns?
2. How should organizations handle the stakeholder and shareholder interests if they are in conflict? Explain with specific examples.
3. What are the pros and cons of respecting local practices (e.g., child labour) which may be 'functional' in one context but 'unethical' in another?

Further Reading

Adler, N.J. and Hansen, H. (2012) 'Daring to care: Scholarship that supports the courage of our convictions', *Journal of Management Inquiry*, 21 (2): 128–39.

Christensen, L.J., Peirce, E., Hartman, L.P., Hoffman, W.M. and Carrier, J. (2007) 'Ethics, CSR and sustainability education in the *Financial Times* Top 50 Global Business Schools', *Journal of Business Ethics*, 73: 347–68.

De Tienne, K.B. and Lewis, L.W. (2005) 'The pragmatic and ethical barriers to corporate social responsibility disclosure: The Nike case', *Journal of Business Ethics*, 60 (4): 359–76.

Maignan, I. and Ralston, D.A. (2002) 'Corporate social responsibility in Europe and the U.S.: Insights from businesses' self-presentations', *Journal of International Business Studies*, 33 (3): 497–514.

Ferrell, O.C., Fraedrich, J. and Ferrell, L. (2012) *Business Ethics: Ethical Decision Making and Cases*. Mason, OH: South Western Cengage Learning.

Husted, B.W. and Allen, D.B. (2006) 'Corporate social responsibility in the multinational enterprise: Strategic and institutional approaches', *Journal of International Business Studies*, 37 (6): 838–49.

Reade, C., Todd, A.M., Osland, A. and Osland, J. (2008) 'Poverty and the multiple stakeholder challenge for global leaders', *Journal of Management Education*, 32: 820–40.

Rischard, J.F. (2002) *High Noon: 20 Global Problems. 20 Years to Solve Them*. New York: Perseus Books.

Savitz, A.W. and Weber, K. (2006) *The Triple Bottom Line: How Today's Best-run Companies are Achieving Economic, Social and Environmental Success – and How You Can Too*. New York: Wiley.

Cases, Videos and Web Sources

Cases

The following cases present how organizations face and resolve ethical dilemmas while trying to keep competitiveness in global market.

Bartlett, C.A., Dessain, V. and Sjoman, A. (2006) *IKEA's Global Sourcing Challenge: Indian Rugs and Child Labor (A)*. Harvard Business School Case No: 906414-PDF-ENG.

Branzei, O. (2010) *Tata: Leadership with Trust*. IVEY Case No: 9B10M025.

Brett, J. and Grogan, C.D. (2006) *Google and the Government of China: A Case Study in Cross-cultural Negotiations*. Kellogg Business School Case No: 5-406-752.

Pless, N.M. and Maak, T. (2012) 'Levi Strauss and Co.: Addressing child labour in Bangladesh', in M.E. Mendenhall, G.R. Oddou and G.K. Stahl (eds), *Readings and Cases in International Human Resource Management and Organizational Behavior*. London and New York: Routledge.

Videos

Video 10.1 Anita Roddick: *Corporate Social Responsibility?* (2009) www.youtube.com/watch?v=k44WifxDSX4 – the legendary founder of Body Shop offers a critical view of CSR.

Video 10.2. Peter Eigen: *How to Expose the Corrupt* (2010) www.ted.com/talks/peter_eigen_how_to_expose_the_corrupt.html.

Video 10.3 Auret van Heerden: *Making Global Labor Fair* (2010) www.ted.com/talks/auret_van_heerden_making_global_labor_fair.html.

Web sources

www.transparency.org – Transparency International website
www.csrassn.com/ – Corporate Social Responsibility Association
www.unglobalcompact.org/ – United Nations Global Compact
www.societyforbusinessethics.org/ – Society for Business Ethics

References

Aldrighi, D.M. (2009) 'Corruption inside the enterprise: corporate fraud and conflicts of interest', in D. Zinnbauer, R. Dobson and K. Despota (eds), *Global Corruption Report 2009: Corruption and the Private Sector*, pp. 13–19. Cambridge, UK: Cambridge University Press.

Andrews, K.R. (1989) 'Ethics in practice', *Harvard Business Review*, 89: 99–104.

Bass, B.M. and Steidlmeier, P. (2004) 'Ethics, character and authentic transformational leadership', in J.B. Ciulla (ed.), *Leadership, the Heart of Ethics*, 2nd edn, pp. 175–96. Westport, CT: Praeger.

Benedict XVI (2010) '2010 Address to the sixteenth plenary session of the pontifical academy of social sciences'. Retrieved from www.vatican.va/holy_father/benedict_xvi/speeches/2010/april/documents/hf_ben-xvi_spe_20100430_scienze-sociali_en.html.

Blair, M.M. (1995) *Ownership and Control: Rethinking Corporate Governance for the Twenty-first Century*. Washington, DC: The Brookings Institution.

Blanchard, K. and Peale, N.V. (1988) *The Power of Ethical Management*. New York: William Morrow and Company, Inc.

Boatright, J.R. (2009) *Ethics and the Conduct of Business*. Upper Saddle River, NJ: Pearson Prentice Hall.

Cappelli, P., Singh, H., Singh, J. and Useem, M. (2010) *The India Way: How India's Top Business Leaders are Revolutionizing Management*. Boston, MA: Harvard Business Press.

China Daily (2013) 'Expert views on anti-corruption efforts', January 8, p.7.

Clarkson, M.B.E. (1995) 'A stakeholder framework for analyzing and evaluating corporate social performance', *Academy of Management Review*, 20: 65–91.

Evan, W.M. and Freeman, R.E. (1988) 'A stakeholder theory of the modern corporation: Kantian capitalism', in T. Beauchamp and N. Bowie (eds), *Ethical Theory and Business*, pp. 75–93. Englewood Cliffs, NJ: Prentice Hall.

Fleming, D., Chow, C. and Su, W. (2010) 'An exploratory study of Chinese accounting students' and auditors' audit-specific ethical reasoning', *Journal of Business Ethics*, 94: 353–69.

Francesco, A.M. and Gold, B.A. (2005) *International Organizational Behavior*. Upper Saddle River, NJ: Pearson.

Frederick, W.C. (1994) 'From CSR1 to CSR2', *Business and Society*, 3: 150–66.

Freeman, R.E., Wicks, A.C. and Parmar, B. (2004) 'Stakeholder theory and "the corporate objective revisited"', *Organization Science*, 15: 364–9.

Friedman, M. (1963) *Inflation: Causes and Consequences*. New York: Asia Publishing House.

Friedman, M. (1970) 'The social responsibility of business is to increase its profits', *New York Times Magazine*, 13 September: 32–3, 122, 126.

Galbraith, J.K. (1967) *The New Industrial State*. Princeton, NJ: Princeton University Press.

Gelfand, M.J., Raver, J.L., Nishii, L., Leslie, L.M., Lun, J., Lim, B.C., Duan, L., Almaliach, A., Ang, S., Arnadottir, J., Aycan, Z., Boehnke, K., Boski, P., Cabecinhas, R., Chan, D., Chhokar, J., D'Amato, A., Ferrer, M., Fischlmayr, I., Fischer, R., Fulop, M., Georgas, J., Kashima, E.S., Kashima, Y., Kim, K., Lempereur, A., Marquez, P., Othman, R., Overlaet, B., Panagiotopoulou, P., Peltzer, K., Perez-Florizno, L.R., Petrovna, L., Realo, A., Schei, V., Schmitt, M., Smith, P.B., Soomro, N., Szabo, E., Taveesin, E., Toyama, M., Van de Vliert, E., Vohra, N., Ward, C., Yamaguchi, S. (2011). Differences between tight and loose cultures: A 33-Nation Study. Science, May, 332, 1100–1104.

Hamilton, J.B. and Knouse, S.B. (2001) 'Multinational enterprise decision principles for dealing with cross cultural ethical conflicts', *Journal of Business Ethics*, 31: 77–94.

Handy, C. (2002) 'What's a business for?', *Harvard Business Review*, 80: 49–55.

Huber-Grabenwarter, G. and Boehm, F. (2009) 'Laying the foundations for sound and sustainable development: Strengthening corporate integrity in weak governance zones', in D. Zinnbauer, R. Dobson and K. Despota (eds), *Global Corruption Report 2009: Corruption and the Private Sector*, pp. 46–54. Cambridge, UK: Cambridge University Press.

Hummels, H. (1998) 'Organizing ethics: A stakeholder debate', *Journal of Business Ethics*, 17: 1403–19.

Kaptein, M. (2009) 'Ethics programs and ethical culture: A next step in unraveling their multi-faceted relationship', *Journal of Business Ethics*, 89: 261–81.

Karnani, A. (2010) 'The case against corporate social responsibility', *Wall Street Journal*, August 23.

Knight, A. (2009) 'From voluntary commitments to responsible conduct: making codes and standards effective and credible', in D. Zinnbauer, R. Dobson and K. Despota (eds), *Global Corruption Report 2009: Corruption and the Private Sector*, pp. 99–105. Cambridge, UK: Cambridge University Press.

Kupczak, J. (2000) *Destined for Liberty: The Human Person in the Philosophy of Karol Wojtyla/John Paul II*. Washington, DC: The Catholic University of America Press.

Kurucz, E.C., Colbert, B.A. and Wheeler, D. (2008) 'The business case for corporate social responsibility', in A. Crane, A. McWilliams, D. Matten, J. Moon and D. Seigel (eds) *The Oxford Handbook on Corporate Social Responsibility* (pp. 83–112). Oxford: Oxford University Press.

Lacy, P., Cooper, T., Hayward, R. and Neuberger, L. (2010) *A new era of sustainability: UN global compact-accenture CEO study 2010*. London, UK: UN Global Compact, Accenture. Retrieved from http://www.unglobalcompact.org/docs /news_events/8.1/UNGC_Accenture_CEO_Study_2010.pdf.

Lane, H.W., DiStefano, J.J. and Maznevski, M.L. (2006) *International Management Behavior: Text, Readings and Cases*. Malden, MA: Blackwell.

Lank, A.G. (1988) 'The ethical criterion in business decision-making: Optional or imperative', in T. Ross (ed.), *Ethics in American Business: A Special Report* (p. 47). New York: Touche Ross.

Leavitt, H.J. (1986) *Corporate Pathfinders: Building Vision and Values into Organizations*. Homewood, IL: Dow Jones-Irwin.

McNett, J. and Sondergaard, M. (2004) 'Making ethical decisions', in H.W. Lane, M. L. Mazneveski, M.E. Mendenhall and J. McNett (eds), *The Blackwell Handbook of Global Management: A Guide to Managing Complexity*, pp. 152–70. Malden, MA: Blackwell.

McWilliams, A. and Siegel, D. (2001) 'Corporate social responsibility: A theory of the firm perspective', *Academy of Management Review*, 26: 117–27.

Mele, D. (2008) 'Integrating ethics into management', *Journal of Business Ethics*, 78: 291–7.

Porter, M.E. and Kramer, M.R. (2006) 'Strategy and society: The link between competitive advantage and corporate social responsibility', *Harvard Business Review*, 84 (December): 78–92. River, NJ: Prentice Hall.

Punnett, B.J. (2004) *International Perspectives on Organizational Behavior and Human Resource Management*. London: M. E. Sharpe.

Reidenbach, R.E. and Robin, D.P. (1991) 'A conceptual model of corporate moral development', *Journal of Business Ethics*, 10: 273–84.

Schneider, S.C. and Barsoux, J.L. (2003) *Managing Across Cultures*. London: Prentice Hall.

Sen, A. (1993) 'Capability and well-being', in M.C. Nussbaum and A.K. Sen (eds), *The Quality of Life*, pp. 30–53. Oxford: Clarendon Press.

Sen, A. (2008) 'Does business ethics make economic sense?' in F. Allhoff and A.J. Vaidya (eds), *Business in Ethical Focus*, pp. 20–29. Peterborough, ON: Broadview Press.

Shamir, B., House, R.J. and Arthur, M.B. (1993) 'Motivational effects of transformational leadership: A self-concept based theory', *Organization Science*, 4: 577–94.

Sotorrio, L.L. and Sanchez, J.L.F. (2008) 'Corporate social responsibility of the most highly reputed European and North American firms', *Journal of Business Ethics*, 82: 379–90.

Taras, V., Kirkman, B.L. and Steel, P. (2010) 'Examining the impact of culture's consequences: A three-decade, multi-level, meta-analytic review of Hofstede's cultural value dimensions', *Journal of Applied Psychology*, 95: 405–39.

Thomas, H. (2002) 'Ethics and PR', *Journal of Communication Management*, 6: 308–10.

Treviño, L.K., Weaver, G.R., Gibson, D.G. and Toffler, B.L. (1999) 'Managing ethics and legal compliance: What works and what hurts', *California Management Review*, 41: 131–51.

UNDP (2001) *Human Development Report*. Oxford, UK: Oxford University Press.

Waldman, D.A., Sully de Luque, M., Washburn, N., House, R.J., Adetoun, B., Barrasa, A., Bibina, M., Bodur, M., Chen, Y.-J., Debbarma, S., Dorfman, P., Dzuvichu, R.R., Evcimen, I., Fu, P. and Grachev, M. (2006) 'Cultural and leadership predictors of corporate social responsibility values of top management: A GLOBE study of 15 countries', *Journal of International Business Studies*, 37: 823–37.

Walton, C.C. (1988) *The Moral Manager*. New York: Ballinger Harper and Row.

Weaver, G.R., L.K. Trevino and Cochran, P.L. (1999) 'Integrated and decoupled corporate social performance: Management commitments, external pressures, and corporate ethics practices', *The Academy of Management Journal*, 42 (5): 539–52.

Weigel, G. (2001) *Witness to Hope: The Biography Of Pope John Paul II*. New York: Harper Collins.

Wojtyla, K. (1979) *The Acting Person*. Analecta Husserliana Vol. X. Dordrecht: D. Reidel.

Wood, D.J. (1991) 'Corporate social performance revisited', *Academy of Management Review*, 16: 691–718.

Zu, L. and Song, L. (2009) 'Determinants of managerial values on corporate social responsibility: Evidence from China', *Journal of Business Ethics*, 88: 105–17.

Want to learn more? Visit the companion website at www.sagepub.co.uk/kanungo to gain access to videos from the end of each chapter, weblinks and flash cards of key terms.

Index

N.B. page numbers in bold indicate tables; page numbers in italics indicate figures.